CHASING THE
CRAIC

I0079171

CHASING THE
CRAIC

Itchy Irish feet through
smiling Irish eyes

NIALLALLSOP

LA
SCOGLIO

Published by Lo Scoglio

Text © Niall Allsop 2018 and 2025

All rights reserved.

No part of this book may be reproduced in any form or by any means, electronic or mechanical, including information storage and retrieval systems without prior permission in writing from the author.

The only exception being a reviewer who may quote extracts in a review.

ISBN 13: 978-1-9996116-0-6
ISBN 10: 1999611608

Cover and book design by Niall Allsop; niallsop@mac.com
Body text in Times New Roman and Gill Sans
Cover text in Gill Sans.

**For the extraordinary
Pat Douglas**

Thank you for inadvertently introducing
your northern cousin to the craic

ACKNOWLEDGEMENTS

I would like to thank all the fellow travellers, named and nameless, who allowed me into their world, sometimes as a fleeting encounter, ofttimes as a lifelong friend.

The only place all our paths cross is in this book.

I would also like to thank those who generously gave of their time to check my memory of events in which they too participated: Graham Allsop, Caroline & Mick Butler, Dan Chebac, Pat Douglas, Paddy & Yvonne Fay, Barry & Catherine Flood, Victoria Kelly, Charles Lister, Deane & Mary Logan and Denise Milone.

I am also indebted to the four natives of County Clare, Eoin Shanahan, Willie Thompson, Aidan Sweeney and Cora Gunter for their advice and support in respect of the first edition of *Chasing the Craic* which was launched in Ireland.

CONTENTS

THE CRAIC

The Craic is essentially an Irish word for describing the laughter and singing, typically accompanied by drinking and/or music, associated with a social, interactive setting.

It's not a word you'd associate with the 'fun' of attending a book presentation with friends or a healthy group-walk in the woods.

It conveys an absence of distrust and a sense of connection and interaction between a group of people who, in that moment, set aside the 'outside' world to simply enjoy each other's company.

It implies laughter, banter, bonhomie and a sense of camaraderie. It can be experienced anywhere in the world but is endemic to Ireland and the Irish.

THE CRAIC-OMETER

This is my purely subjective and non-existent, creative invention which, on a handful of occasions, is my handy 'measure' of the level of craic emanating from particular individuals. This is normally a negative reading.

PROLOGUE

It seemed like a good idea at the time.

In the summer of 1965, thumbing, hitch-hiking, our way round Ireland, Belfast to Belfast, really did seem like a good way for two 20-year-old students to get away from families; and on the cheap too.

Elsewhere, the 60s might have been a-swinging, but in most corners of Northern Ireland generally things swung more sluggishly. They used to say that, when an aircraft was approaching Belfast Airport, the pilot would come on the intercom and advise passengers to turn their watches back 50 years.

Alex, my partner in this misadventure, was my girlfriend of a year or more and at the time it seemed likely that we would end up married. First love and all that.

That said, our relationship was still at the fumbling and hard stirrings phase, policed officially by Alex's mother and unofficially by the keen ear of her father.

My fervent hope was that this, our first unchaperoned trip together, might give that hard stirring more legroom; the downside was that we would be staying at youth hostels that generally did not encourage the sort of thing I had in mind. Oddly, it never occurred to me at the time that this might not have been something on Alex's checklist too ... but that is another story.

———

The hardest part was escaping Northern Ireland. Nobody seemed to want to give us a lift and it was well into the afternoon before we crossed the border near Newry. Once in the Republic things went much better and we were soon in Dublin, our first overnight stop.

I was right about the sleeping arrangements and, even without Alex's father's hi-tech, glass-on-the-wall surveillance system, our collective virginities remained intact.

And thus we progressed ... Wicklow, Waterford, Cork, Limerick ... if there was a youth hostel on the map, we graced it with our virginal presence before sharpening our thumbs for the next phase of the journey.

We didn't have a sight-seeing agenda; getting to the youth hostel before dark was the daily objective, as was an early start the following morning. Nor did we encounter any strange, eccentric or sinister people behind the wheel, except perhaps the guy in the Land Rover pulling a trailer who confessed that he'd only picked us up so that we would talk to him and stop him from falling asleep. As it happened, it didn't work, our inane chatterings about life as a student in Belfast didn't do the trick and he pulled over by a crossroads and gave us the choice of watching him sleep or trying to get another lift. We opted for the latter.

And absolutely everyone who had to drop us off short of our destination, including our sleepy friend, did so with a version of the same apologetic optimism:

"Ah, sure, you'll get a lift from here, no problem at all. A grand place for getting picked up, is this so."

And they were always right; well, nearly always.

I had a motive for wanting to stop off at Limerick but when I saw the size of the place *and* the number of O'Briens in the phone-book, I soon kicked that idea into touch. The Limerick lad I shared a room with in Germany four years earlier might be in there somewhere but that particular quest was not for now. In any case, it was easy to convince myself that Liam might not even have returned to his native Limerick. As was his stated plan when I last saw him, he might well have moved on to Holland and met and married that rich ex-princess from eastern Europe.

With the idea of hunting down Liam O'Brien shelved and time on our hands, we decided to spend some of it in Limerick and, if we got to Galway quickly, we could do the same there. It was an unusually, gloriously sunny day when, thumbs rested and ready, we set off north towards Galway.

We soon got a lift out of Limerick and were deposited on what turned out to be a minor road somewhere north of Ennis. Nevertheless, as the sun seemed to turn itself up a notch, we remained confident we would soon be under way again ere long.

"Ah, sure, you'll get a lift from here, no problem at all. A grand place for getting picked up, is this so."

Famous last, well-intentioned words. It was, in fact, a shite place to get a lift; much as you would expect the middle-of-nowhere to be. The hotter it got, the fewer cars passed by. And they *all* passed by, scarcely an apologetic wave as hot and sticky people were intent on getting home to their shady nooks.

We waited so long at Shiteplace that we even considered crossing the road and taking any lift, in any direction; after all the nearest civilisation was where we'd been a couple of hours earlier though it felt like a lifetime ago.

My colouring dictated that I would feel the heat more than Alex; the hat that Alex had wisely brought with her was not for sharing for it was becoming increasingly obvious that the paucity of cars hereabouts was my fault. If I had been more dedicated to finding Liam, we may have stayed longer in Limerick, maybe even another day; a notion that only made sense to me if drivers in County Clare only gave lifts on alternate days.

Finally, when we heard a car coming from the wrong direction, I crossed the road and take pot luck; the time had come to abandon Shiteplace and return to Limerick or anywhere else for that matter.

Unfortunately I never made it to the other side; the energy I expended taking those first few steps was too much for my overheated, under-hydrated body and I slowly slithered to the ground. What Alex and the on-coming driver saw was my dying-swan impersonation in the middle of the road. Alex sprang into nurse-mode and the car stopped.

As Alex was struggling to get me to my feet, the driver of the car leapt out to lend a hand. No, it wasn't a ploy, I was really disorientated; that said, the sight of a stationary car did have a restorative effect and I was soon reasonably *compos mentis* again and eager to take advantage of the lift offered.

The next thing I recall is being bundled into the back of the car next to Alex and, after a short, uncomfortable drive, drawing up outside a red-brick building. Alex, still unsure whether or not I had faked the whole thing just to get a lift, brought me up to speed with the events I may have missed.

The lone driver, a local dentist and part-time Good Samaritan, seeing my graceful descent to the ground, and unquestioning of my motives, stopped to help. He then offered us a lift but only as far as the hospital in nearby Ennis. The red-brick building was Ennis County Hospital.

Within minutes I had been examined and there followed a huddle of medical staff which I can only describe as mutterings with a discernible undertone of incredulity. It was all more than a little disconcerting; perhaps I had some rare condition, some rare *incurable* condition, that only those who spend hours and hours at Shiteplace succumb to.

And, worse still, Alex might never lose her virginity.

I was already in a private room and tucked up comfortably in bed when I was told the awful truth … I had been diagnosed with sunstroke, possibly the first such case in Ireland, and was to stay in Ennis County Hospital overnight. Looking on the bright side, it was the first comfortable bed I had been in since leaving Belfast.

Alex got a good night's sleep too for the helpful dentist took her home where she stayed overnight with him and his family.

The following morning I was deemed fit to travel but before being shown the door, I had to fill out a pile of forms, the most important of which was the name and address of who was going to pay for the services of the nurses and doctors who had looked after me. This was pre-European Union Ireland and the concept of neighbouring countries helping out each other's citizens, even those on the same bloody island, with their medical issues was a long way down the line. If my face could have got any redder, I would have blushed with the embarrassment of forgetting that there was no National Health Service in Ireland.

I gave my father's details and then called my mother to confirm that he would indeed pay the ransom and, assuming he did so, I might be back home a bit sooner than expected.

When Alex was dropped off at the hospital she found me in a wheelchair and was not at all amused at my suggestion that she might have to push me back to Belfast. To our mutual relief we were directed to a waiting ambulance and taken, alas without sirens, to the local railway station where we were given one-way tickets to Dublin.

Another form I had to complete before being shown the door was to furnish details of someone who would lay claim to my body in Ireland; luckily my favourite cousin lived in Dun Laoghaire, just south of Dublin. A call to Pat ensured that her husband, Don, would be there to meet us at Dublin's Kingsbridge (now Heuston) Station, that fed the west of Ireland, and take us to Amiens Street (now Connolly) that pointed north to Belfast.

Don, the funniest man I ever knew, relentlessly milked the situation and was particularly taken with the redness of my face which he cunningly linked to my politics. For me that short journey across Dublin was excruciatingly painful as I tried so hard to stop myself from laughing. Alex, who had never met Don before, was both enjoying his craic and my pain.

Safely, straight-faced aboard the Enterprise, the express train to Belfast that I knew so well, I was resigning myself to the fact that Don was not going to be the only person to see the funny side of what had happened.

But there was one who didn't. My father was not overjoyed when he got the bill for over £80, which included the cost of the train tickets. As he had helped subsidise the trip in the first place, he was definitely less than amused. Even the fact that, like the Good Samaritan of Ennis, he too was a dentist didn't cut any ironic ice.

s

It is nearly 52 years later and, on an unusually warm spring day, I am standing outside that same red-brick building in Ennis. I am not expecting anyone to recognise me as my face is now as white as my hair.

I enter and explain to the woman at reception that I have come for my 50-year check up and apologise for being over a year late. I respond to her perplexed look by telling her an abridged version of my misadventure at Shiteplace—though I omitted to mention it by name—and here at the renamed Mid-Western Regional Hospital, half a century earlier.

She laughs out loud, alas not at my wit but at the very idea of someone going down with sunstroke in the south-west of Ireland.

I ask her if it's likely that there is still a record of my overnight stay here and she makes a call to a colleague upstairs. But before giving me directions to Sheila's office, she makes a list of dentists she believes were practising in the area in the 1960s; she puts a tick beside the name of the only one still living … she thinks.

Upstairs, Sheila too finds the story amusing and promises to try and locate my notes, assuming they still exist. As this could take several weeks, months even, she asks for contact details and assumes that I am staying with friends when I rattle off an Irish phone number and an Ennis address.

I respond to the question in her eyes …

"Ah yes, I forgot to say, I now live in Ennis … moved here two weeks ago from southern Italy."

"I don't know which is more surprising," she said, "… that you've moved *to* Ennis or that you moved *from* Italy."

I am almost out the door when I realise I've forgotten to tell her something that could prove crucial to her search.

"I should have told you that, back in the 60s, I wasn't a Niall, I was a Nigel. Now, be honest, do I look like a 'Nigel'? Do I sound like a 'Nigel'? I never was and never will be a 'Nigel'."

Without thinking, I stick a finger under my nose and push my head up to indicate my view of all those poor blokes saddled with being called 'Nigel'.

"And, anyway", I continue, "Niall is the Irish name for 'Nigel'".

As I withdraw my finger from mu nose, I immediately think better of my mimicry and ask, almost apologetically:

"Your husband's not called 'Nigel', is he?"

"No," she says trying to stifle a snigger, "he's got a good Irish name."

"Thank goodness ... I made that mistake once before during an interview and her husband was indeed a very large, rugby-playing 'Nigel'. Mind you, I think she agreed with me for I still got the job."

Lest she forget the point of this diversion, I remind her of my sordid past, my skeleton in the cupboard, just one last time ...

"So it's Nigel Allsop's records you'll be searching for."

For the record, there weren't any.

WONDERING WHAT TO WRITE NEXT, CALABRIA 2025.

INTRODUCTION

I conceived and wrote this book when I was living in Ireland, in Ennis to be precise. Seven years on, and living once again in Calabria, I decided to re-edit it and add some chapters, a dozen in total.

In doing so I have broadened the books original theme of travel, to include more of a biographical element. For example, the two chapters of my time as a Headteacher in rural Wiltshire, *The champion of the world* and *Tales out of school*, are more on the autobiographical side of the spectrum but are not lacking in craic.

As I described in *Under a Calabrian Sky*, turning off the motorway in pursuit of the road-sign to Ennis in February 2017 was a spontaneous decision. I had no idea what to expect, only that I felt impelled to take a look for the first time in over half a century. Six weeks later, I was Ennis' newest resident.

The road that brought me here began with a solo trip I made to Galway the previous October from our then home in Calabria, the toe of Italy.

My travels were inspired by the television series, *Jack Taylor*, which was set in Galway and, apart from the murders and mayhem that maverick gumshoe Jack Taylor had to deal with, it seemed an interesting and compelling place. It was also the place that eluded me back in the 60s and, with Kay visiting family in England, I took the opportunity to see what I had missed.

I booked four nights at the Airbnb home of Caroline and Mick, a short walk from the city centre. It turned out to be a life-changing experience.

It started with the craic.

For those of a non-Irish background, the online *Urban Dictionary* defines the 'craic' as follows:

"Irish word for fun/enjoyment that has been brought into the English language. usu. when mixed with alcohol and/or music."

The Galway version that Caroline, Mick and I indulged in and seamlessly perfected did not involve music—though arguably Caroline's voice was music enough—but fun, enjoyment and alcohol were definitely on the agenda as we sat round the kitchen table, glasses in hand, putting the world to rights and talking as if we'd known each other a lifetime. Mind you, Caroline and I did have something in common other than our good looks: we were both escapees from Northern Ireland or 'Norn Iron' as we called it.

On my third night there a new dimension infiltrated proceedings when Caroline suggested that I might return to house-sit for two months in January and February when she and Mick planned to visit their son and grandchildren in Australia. They said I could bring Kay too.

Naturally I assumed this unexpected invitation was just part of the craic and that, in the absence of that alcoholic haze, it would soon be forgotten. And indeed at first that appeared to be the case, for there was no further mention of it until the morning I left.

Locked in the embrace of Caroline's farewell, she said:

"Keep in touch … don't forget, we're expecting you in January."

I realise it might seem a tad odd that Caroline and Mick were prepared to leave their home in the hands of someone they'd met only a few days earlier and somebody else they'd never met. When I returned to Calabria, Kay said as much and rushed to the obvious conclusion that it was probably alcohol-related; probably on both sides. It was only when I reminded her of her English and Welsh background, and that the craic generated round an ordinary Irish kitchen table had no real equivalent outside Ireland, that she got it.

Furthermore, she was not unaware that our travelling experiences had frequently thrown up some unusual, some might say off-the-wall, episodes; more so in my case perhaps. We had even discussed it a number of times in the context of an 'affliction' and wondered what, if anything, we could do about it.

Surprisingly, Caroline and Mick didn't have second thoughts and in late November we exchanged emails to confirm the details.

Kay and I arrived in Galway at the beginning of January and spent one final craic-filled evening with Caroline and Mick before they headed for the Antipodes leaving, not only their home, but also their car in the hands of one complete stranger and one virtual stranger.

Kay already knew how much I liked Galway and she soon felt the same way and it was here that the idea of a move to Ireland was first mooted.

For some time Kay had been keen to return to England; now a grandmother she felt obliged to be closer to her children and grand-children. Also she never had been at home in Santa Severina in the same way I had. She knew I did not want to return to England—I had already served my time by living there for over 40 years—and in so many ways felt more at home in Santa Severina than anywhere else.

A move to Ireland was a possible compromise between these two positions, and eventually one that we were both prepared to consider. Sadly, despite our affection for Galway, we soon realised that we could not afford to live there. Then where else?

Wexford on the south-east coast was our first choice: its good communications with Dublin Airport and the moderate cost of renting were the main considerations and we did visit a couple of times to view properties. We also visited the small inland town of Roscrea and it was on the way back from here that, purely by chance, we turned off the motorway and followed the signs to Ennis.

Ennis was a name I recognised from my past and I was keen to see if being back there might jog a memory or two. It didn't. Nor, as far as I could see, was there any wall-mounted plaque in memory of my brief, but medically-significant, visit.

———

Reflecting on the catalyst for this unplanned and unexpected turn of events after eight-and-a-half years in Calabria—my solo Galway visit in October 2016 and the craic I endured there—caused me to look again at how, when I don my travelling persona, there is the distinct possibility that something out of the ordinary will happen.

To travel to Galway for four days and to end up house-sitting for my hosts two months later is on the unusual side of the spectrum. But to then decide to move to Ireland, to find a new home within six weeks and to make the move there less than a month later, is closer to super-hero powers.

Although, as I have said, a part of Kay was at first sceptical about whether or not Caroline and Mick had *really* asked us to house-sit for two months, she also knew it wasn't as far-fetched as it sounded. She was used to my travelling encounters; she might even say 'mishaps'.

The events that brought us to Ennis themselves were a catalyst for this book for, without knowing the full story, family and friends saw it as an extraordinary sequence of events. It was indeed a busy, life-changing four months but not altogether unique. Nothing two senior citizens and copious amounts of red wine couldn't cope with. For one it was undoubtedly harder than for the other, something the red wine helped with too.

Nevertheless, it set me thinking about some of those other travelling experiences that seem to have become the norm for me; often alone, sometimes accompanied, seldom straightforward; frequently off-the-wall, occasionally thought-provoking.

———

Travelling is about exploring and experiencing different places, cultures and people. For me the most important of these is the people. Neither the churches nor the castles do it for me.

There are those who travel to exotic parts and never meet, talk or otherwise engage with anyone who was actually born there; their travelling experience is restricted to sharing space with other people, frequently from their own culture, doing the same thing and they rarely, if ever, explore what lies beyond the boundaries of their hotel, apartment or villa. That would bore the pants off me.

For my sins, I have a propensity to the other extreme, to engage with people, both while travelling to my destination and when I get there. If there's a bit of local craic on offer, I often end up participating in it. Sometimes I have even been known to initiate it.

I realise that from time to time I get myself into situations that I might end up regretting but, generally, I survive my indiscretions, potential and actual.

Travelling is also about experiencing people and places no matter what the original impulse or intention may have been; pleasure *per se* is not the only motive for taking to the road. On a few occasions I have found myself in what are popular travel destinations for reasons other than holiday leisure.

I have always considered myself a traveller rather than a tourist. The difference, it seems to me, is that the traveller has experiences and encounters that are his or hers alone; the tourist generally only meets and interacts with people, invariably like-minded tourists, in an environment chosen and promoted by others.

Arguably to travel is to have a mind of your own, to be a tourist is to do what you're told. As you will observe, I have never had the inclination to do as I was told.

―――

I was no more than six when I first demonstrated a dubious capacity for wandering off by myself and have therefore given some of these childhood memories of 'travelling' their first airing here. It could be argued that such travels are more arbitrary than substantive but they do illustrate journeys that became important to me both in reality and in crossing the uncharted waters from childhood to adulthood, from reliance to independence, from reading between the lines to understanding the craic. And, if nothing else, they provide the reader with some biographical information.

As my independence streak matured, I shed the do-as-you're-told mentality of the Northerner for, unusually and from an early age, I was travelling to and from the south of Ireland, to Dublin and beyond, with not an adult in sight.

Such experiences were, for me, significant and relevant for many of my views on life have been formed by travelling, others reinforced by it. I therefore make no apology for when, on occasion, I am direct with my opinions of certain institutions or modes of behaviour or social and political stances.

I am fortunate in having a reliable memory of events right back to my childhood and generally recall the detail of times, places and feelings with clarity. That said, I sometimes have a blind spot with names. As far as possible, people's names in this book are their real names; I have had to invent some because I don't recall them while others I have changed for reasons apparent from the nature of the text.

And from time to time too, *à la* DH Lawrence and in the absence of a name, I give people nicknames which seem appropriate to a characteristic or trait they display or simply who or what they remind me of.

Above all else, *Chasing the Craic* is a travelogue. Sometimes literally so, sometimes figuratively, occasionally tenuously. Its stories, episodes and sketches are about exploring, about observing, about participating, about off-the-wall reactions and about taking risks. It is *not* about places, neither is it a guide to the locations where I found myself, whether by accident or design. Of course these locations do have a part to play but generally it is the people and the occasion that are the stars; settings are the backdrop, little more than co-stars and extras.

Chasing the Craic's chronological format inevitably adds a biographical element, occasionally peppered with tangents where the travel element hangs on by a thread. It is a memoir of a life defined by tales and anecdotes, adventures and misadventures, encounters and reflections, chaos and design, a journey where I always tried to communicate with others by sharing a bit of the craic with them.

A few chapters in the second half of the book include stories or parts of stories that have been published elsewhere in other books.

That said, none of these is reproduced verbatim. There are additions and deletions, changes in style and in perspectives will, I trust, bring something new to those who may have read those books.

There are also a small number of chapters that have a consecutive connection, separate parts of an on-going story. At the same time, all have a stand-alone quality too.

Very occasionally the chronological element alluded to earlier has been temporarily dispensed with to facilitate the bringing together of related stories from different locations or times that have an obvious and crucial connection and relate to a previous chapter, In this respect the main interloper is entitled *Mostly Dolly*.

And to liven up what would otherwise be a blank left-hand page, I have included some self-portraits which more or less correspond to how I looked around the time of the chapter before or the chapter that follows. The related captions are just a bit of fun.

Finally, as I have already mooted, I must remind any readers of a nervous disposition that I am prone to saying what I think. I have opinions about what I see and experience and feel duty bound to share these in writing.

THE BOY WHO LOST A BEST FRIEND, C.1954.

CHILD ON THE RUN

Sometimes adults embellish and distort the memories of events involving their children that they think are funny or off-the-wall. That said, I have no recollection of my parents ever having done so in what follows and, besides, for them it would have been a reminder of an incident best forgotten. In addition, I do actually recall those parts of the story where no adult was present.

The only problem I have with repeating it is that I'm not entirely sure whether it qualifies for inclusion in this book; it does however demonstrate a burgeoning degree of independence which may or may not throw light on some of the other things that have happened when I abandoned the safety of family and home.

I was at infant school. It was a time when children began their formal education when they were five; play-groups and nursery schools for the masses had not yet been invented.

The nearest school to my father's dental surgery was about 100 yards away, literally just round the corner at the bottom of an adjacent side-street, Euston Street. But that school was where all the working class children went, the issue of my father's patients, so I was carted off to another school, Harding Memorial, about a half-a-mile further along the main road out of town, just beyond where Belfast's working-class Woodstock Road morphed into the more middle-class Cregagh Road.

This being the late 40s, fear of being abducted on the way to school hadn't been invented yet and, by my second year as an infant, I was clearly old enough to get there under my own steam, by foot or on the trolley-bus that stopped right outside the door. Therefore, when I decided that I positively hated my new class teacher, Miss White, as an independent traveller I was in a position to do something about it. I just didn't go to school.

I did, of course, go through the motions. I would set off for school each morning, wave goodbye to my mother—my father was already pulling and filling—and stride off school-wards. Once out of sight, I would take a detour down some back alleys—we called them 'entrys'—that linked the side streets until I ended up halfway along another street at right angles to the main road. Here, on my first day of freedom, I chanced upon a younger boy who had not yet started school and had time to play. He became my new best friend that day and every day until I was found out.

From this street I could see the back of the other school, the one nearer home. This was a bonus for, as I normally went home for lunch, I was able to get the time right on my truanting days too by observing when the kids from that school were let out for lunch. I just went home when they did.

A combination of a call from the school I wasn't attending and the curiosity of my new best friend's mother led inevitably to my downfall in a matter of days.

The next day my mother frogmarched me back to school where I was to be returned to the malevolent custody of Miss White. Or that was the plan, the natural outcome as perceived by all the adults involved.

But they hadn't reckoned on me being a stubborn little git and even the headmaster, the genial Mr Taylor, could not persuade me to return to the evil clutches of the villainous Miss White. I can still see myself, arms folded, scowling, trying hard not to soil my neat grey shorts but defiant beyond my years. Little wonder I went on to read and enjoy all of Richmal Crompton's *William* books. Or perhaps I had already started?

Surprisingly my stand bore fruit and it was agreed that I was to be transferred to another class where I settled in without any problems.

But, unknown to me at the time, the class I was moved to was the next one up, where everyone was a year older.

Nobody told me about the age difference; indeed nobody ever told me about it. I worked it out myself many, many years later when I was a teacher myself and still recall the moment when, out of the blue, a penny dropped and suddenly so many other things fell into place … like always being the smallest in the class.

I am retelling this story to illustrate that, even at six, somehow, somewhere, I had acquired an independent, some might say defiant, streak. My ability to travel alone, both on foot or by public transport, was perhaps not so unusual at the time.

Now, my father used to tell a story about a boy on a bus—it may have been himself, it may have been me, it may have been neither—and, true or not, it was possibly my first encounter with a bit of the craic.

The boy was sitting next to a woman when he began to search the floor around his feet. The woman asked him if he'd lost something.

"Yes," he said, "I've dropped my little green ball."

The woman joined him in his search for the green ball and before long almost everyone on the bus was looking around and under their feet for the missing ball.

It was time for the woman to get off and she gave the boy a thrupenny bit (a 12-sided, pre-decimal coin worth three pence for those not old enough to remember) to buy himself another ball.

"It's okay, "he said, sticking his finger up his nose, "I'll just roll myself another one."

This story may have scarred me for life for, thereafter, I couldn't resist watching what people—children and adults alike—did after they withdrew their finger and its bounty from their nose. I never saw anyone make a little green ball; some flicked it away, most looked to see if anyone else was watching and then just ate it.

When I was seven we moved to a new home on the outskirts of the city and I continued to attend the same school; my father's place of work (also my mother's as she was his part-time receptionist) hadn't changed and each morning I had a lift as far as the surgery. After school I would play locally with school friends until my mother was ready to leave and we would go home together via two public transport buses.

Still at primary school, and as I got older, I started to make my own way home on the same buses straight after school to be with my new friends closer to home. Although I was the only pupil making such a daily trek across Belfast, it never occurred to me that this was anything but normal.

As I worked my way up through primary school, John McVeigh became my best friend. I didn't know he was a year older than me; nor was he aware that I was a year younger. I assume that my comparative juvenility went unnoticed because I was a September child, and therefore, three weeks into the new academic year, would be the same age as the rest of the class.

Although birthdays had been invented, chaotic, indulgent, extravagant, gratuitous child birthday parties were still a decade or three down the line. Birthdays came and went with little or no pomp or ceremony; as a present perhaps no more than something from the latest film merchandising like Robin Hood's emerald-green tunic and accessories or a fake-fur-tailed Davy Crockett hat or a look-alike Winchester '73 rifle. And, as a treat, a colourful Battenburg cake in its scrumptious, yellow marzipan wrapping which I always peeled off and kept for last.

Such occasions were always a low-key family affair that neither involved friends, aunts and uncles nor grandparents. In the case of the latter it was also because I didn't actually have any; only one survived my birth and he, my father's father, was gone before I could focus on either form or features.

Neither John McVeigh nor I had reason to be suspicious about the age difference; even when we had to line up in height order and I was always at one extreme with John closer to the other. Apart from the statistical differences, known and unknown, John and I were also from different social classes, initially something that we were not directly aware of though possibly sensed.

As fear of children being allowed to do things independent of adults had also not yet been invented, John and I became intrepid travellers. Together we would walk to the cinema, to the Saturday Club 'flicks', to watch Roy Rogers and Trigger or Hopalong Cassidy and Topper accomplish all manner of heroic deeds in a sanitised, bloodless Wild West. Or we'd laugh till we ached at the madcap misadventures of the Bowery Boys and Old Mother Riley. We'd venture up Daddy Winker's Lane and soak up the intoxicating aroma of the speedway track. And once we travelled further afield and took the number 33 trolley-bus into the centre of Belfast.

And all of this without an accompanying adult or older sibling. Indiana Jones had nothing on us.

Sadly, our first and last excursion into the city was to be the most significant journey of my young life, one which continued to have ramifications for both John and I throughout our lives and one which we never shared for another half century.

The 33 dropped us off by the side of the City Hall and we headed for Woolworths in High Street where, without any planning, we both decided, independently, to liberate a few pocketfuls of sweets from Woolworths' famous Pick 'n' Mix sweet counter.

The combination of the buzz we were experiencing (adrenalin hadn't been invented yet) and the fact that we were not experts at furtively slipping contraband into our pockets, soon alerted the store detective to our poorly planned heist and we were duly collared.

Indeed we were literally collared; I can still feel the store detective's grip at the back of my neck as we were unceremoniously half dragged, half frog-marched to an insignificant little back-room out of sight from other innocent, law-abiding shoppers where she quizzed us before calling the police and our parents.

As the large police constable took notes I was unaware that what was unfolding was my first political experience

For a start, I had never before seen one of these larger-than-life custodians of the status quo up close and personal. His bulk, his green-black uniform and his truncheon were bad enough but I was fixated on the other item in his armoury: his gun. I had never been in such close proximity to a 'peeler' before, never been that close to a gun. His armoury and his stature all seemed more than a little out of place in this corner of Woolworths.

The fall-out was in itself undramatic; no wielding of the truncheon, no shots fired, no handcuffs clicked into place, no ride in the back of a peeler's car. Nevertheless what happened next has always stayed with me in the form of its social and political implications rather than any criminal ones. I'm sure this was a defining moment in my young life, a moment that helped mould much of my subsequent outlook on almost everything.

My father was a mason, an ex-king of his lodge and its honorary secretary, the latter a role which involved me and my older brother in folding letters and stuffing envelopes once every couple of months to summon the faithful to their secret little love-in and dressing-up party.

Several—if not most—of Belfast's senior police officers were also masons and therefore buddies of my father though of course, as all masons, and members of similar elitist groups, will avidly corroborate, there is absolutely not so much as a whiff of nepotism among the fraternity: it's all about helping others.

I have no way of knowing to what extent, if any, this had an impact on what happened next in that back-room but the upshot was that John and I were both given a verbal slap on the wrists, told to reform or end up in Borstal and not let down our families.

All of which does not sound an unreasonable outcome but there was another rider to it: we were also told that our friendship was at an end and that we were no longer to have anything to do with one another. And this came directly and forcefully from my side of the family divide for clearly it had been decided that the innocent little middle-class boy (me) had been led astray by the offspring (John) of a more-prone-to-criminal-behaviour, working-class family. It was manifestly important that the order of things should not be challenged lest it herald the collapse of the class structure.

It felt almost as if I hadn't actually been there. The blame for what we had done was shamefully shifted from both of us to John. After all, given our respective backgrounds, wasn't it more likely that he had been the mastermind, the Mr Big, the Don Corleone behind the whole episode?

This outcome not only made me feel guilty about having been born into such a background, but also inevitably forced me to look at how these things worked. I was not stupid, I knew exactly what had taken place and understood how my family, for what they saw as the best of reasons, had directly and indirectly manipulated the situation. It was a lesson I never forgot.

Neither our independent bus journey nor our minor crime spree had a ringleader. It was not planned. Neither of us knew what the other was doing, we were acting independently and spontaneously. I was to blame for what I did and John was to blame for what he did. Neither of us pointed a finger at the other simply because it was not relevant.

John and I continued to be classmates but kept our distance; I assumed he knew he had been shafted while I was left wondering whether he would think that I had somehow betrayed him. We never spoke to each other again; it was our final term at primary school and a short time later we went our separate ways to different schools.

We never saw each other again. Ever.

My parents never mentioned the incident again. Ever.

To finish the story I will toss chronology aside and jump 50 years to when, from his home in South Africa, John McVeigh shared with me the same story from his perspective.

It was both refreshing and uncanny how our recollections matched in every detail. John told me how his father explained to him the reality of what had happened and how the social order of the time had triumphed and determined that I, the son of a respected dentist, should come out on top, irrespective of the truth. It left a bitter taste.

It was clear that this seemingly minor event had also stayed with John and, like me, thereafter he challenged the status quo and the accepted or preconceived order of things. And, also like me, John came to understand how the Northern Ireland cup overflowed with things worthy of challenging.

For me, questioning the accepted social structure, as represented by the political establishment, was to become an important focus; for John it was also the religious establishment. Unusually—some would say bravely—John went against the accepted mores of the time drummed into most Protestant lads and fell in love with and later married Trudy, a Catholic girl. Thereafter he felt life was going to be better away from the land of his birth and, as I too did, left Northern Ireland for good.

Though we never met again, John McVeigh and I travelled on remarkably similar journeys down the years and throughout our separate lives.

Coincidentally, we both joined the Civil Service and at the same time. For John it was a career choice whereas, for me, it had always a stop-gap between school and College though at the time my employers were not aware of this. Had I found it stimulating, I might well have stayed on.

In 2016, in South Africa, John died of an illness that I survived. I wish we had found each other again sooner. It is only right that John should have the last word on our misadventure at Woolworths, a journey that in many ways defined our adult lives.

"Over the years, and probably because of Woolworths, I have thought of you often. It is strange as we only had a year or two together.

"One of the reasons is that the incident coloured my thinking for some years afterwards in that I recall with great clarity after we were caught the shop-woman asking what our fathers did. You said 'dentist' and she had such a look on her face of 'my god what a good background'; and then patronizing me with 'Yes that is also a good job—docker'.

"This stuck in my mind for years and I foolishly worried about peoples' status in life until I had some success in my own right.

"It really was a silly incident which did not mark us out as future criminals."

In a later chapter, *Leaving Belfast*, I will return to another aspect of this story and how, ultimately, and in different ways and for different reasons, John and I both left Northern Ireland, never to return. For me it was the catalyst for the most significant travel decision I ever made.

But first, I will press forward into my teens where my urge to travel outside my comfort zone showed no signs of abating.

———

In the mid-1950s there was a new kid on the cycling block. It was a modern, must-have bicycle that surpassed all others in style and sexiness. It had Sturmey-Archer three-speed gears, a Dynohub for charging its lights and, like the movies, it reflected the burgeoning, post-war world of colour. Even the names of the only two colours available had an exotic ring: Flamboyant Royal Carmine (red) and Electric Blue. It was called the Triumph Palm Beach and, more importantly, it was just about affordable. Mine was blue.

I had left primary school, but nevertheless wanted to cycle to other side of town, to my father's surgery on my electric blue Palm Beach. I didn't see it as anything but a relatively straightforward two-and-a-half mile cycle, no more than half-an-hour for my pre-teen legs. But I was not encouraged in thus venture and for a for a short time I kept to the rules.

At the time, if someone had asked me if I had a hobby I would probably have said "fiddling with bikes". What I would have been alluding to was that, in the pre-Palm Beach era, I was for ever taking bikes apart, customising them, amalgamating them, adding this, taking off that, creating an 'engine-like' sound with a clothes-peg and a bit of cardboard that hit the wheel spokes. But with my new Palm Beach, everything was already boringly in place, I didn't want to change a thing … well, not for a month or two anyway.

First I turned the handlebars upside down so that the grips had the appearance of being racier. Then I replaced them altogether with dropped handlebars like a racing bike; of course I changed the saddle too, in keeping with my new 'racing' image, even if it was less comfortable than the original.

With my friends I started to cycle further afield but was always more adventurous than they were. We would cycle to Bangor, a dozen miles down the coast, but I always wanted to go further, to Donaghadee, to Millisle. Few had the same wanderlust.

Like my friends, at first I always cycled with my swimming trunks and a towel in my saddlebag; unlike my friends, I did not have the same need to charge into the nearest bit of water, be it the sea or a swimming pool. Given the choice, and despite the more obvious dangers for a non-swimmer, my preference would have been for the former.

The reason was an incident at Bangor's Pickie Pool, a weekend magnet for boys and girls of all ages. My friends and I had cycled there and, as per usual, they were soon frolicking in and out of the water having the time of their lives. The nearest I got to getting my face wet was from their spray as they jumped into the pool, time and time again. Bored with watching them, I moved down to the deeper end where there were several diving boards and stood by the edge of the pool watching, with the merest hint of jealousy, the antics of those leaping into the water from a greater height.

Lost in wonderment, I did not see who pushed me in; friend or foe, I had no idea who was responsible. Now I'd heard, probably an old wives tale with no substance in fact, that when you are drowning you rise and fall three times. I was counting and had just got to three when someone took hold of me and helped bring me over to the side of the pool from where I was half pushed, half dragged, onto *terra firma*.

I was frightened, relieved and exhausted and can still see all those faces staring down at my embarrassed body. All I wanted to do was get dressed, get on my bike and cycle home. Which is what I did. I never returned to Pickie Pool; I never told my brothers or my parents what had happened. Thereafter, I avoided swimming pools, the smell of the chlorine would give me a headache; if I was ever to learn to swim, I knew it would be in the sea.

Despite this minor mishap, I retained my passion for cycling, it was just that, while Bangor was generally at the top of everyone else's list, it didn't figure on mine. Perhaps I became more adventurous with my choice of destination, just to avoid Bangor.

I recall once, on a lone excursion down the Ards peninsula, miles away from Bangor, I was heading home and, approaching Newtownards, realised it was getting dark sooner that I expected and I knew my lights were not working. Those were the days when nobody ventured out without working lights and a bell. Nor did anyone cycle on the pavement or in the opposite direction to other traffic.

All was not lost for I remembered that my uncle Walter, my mother's brother, lived on the outskirts of Newtownards; I wasn't sure exactly but I knew he was famous locally for his prize-winning chrysanthemums so when I asked a few locals it wasn't long before I turned up at their door in search of a bed for the night. Also I needed to phone home.

I explained my predicament regarding the sudden onset of dusk and uncle Walter, sitting in his favourite chair by the fire, came straight to the point with the dry wit he was known for.

"Do you think the sunglasses could be the problem?" he queried as he waved his finger in the direction of my head.

He was, of course, right. When I took them off I returned to a brighter world where, had I not wasted 40 minutes trying to find the house, I could easily have made it home. As it was, now it was definitely too late for me to cycle to Belfast and I had to stay the night. Thereafter, it was a story that Walter revelled in repeating—and embellishing—every time our paths crossed.

I even conceived a plan to cycle to Dublin, over 100 miles away, but there were no takers. For most of my friends the very thought of travelling to Dublin without an adult was as far-fetched as flying to the moon and it was not even considered as a serious proposition. Nobody was impressed with the fact that I had it all worked out: what time we'd have to set off, where we'd stop for a break every couple of hours, what time we'd arrive in Dublin and where we'd stay overnight .

At the time I assumed that my friends' reticence was to do with the distance (I always omitted to mention that it was another ten miles, less than an hour, to my cousin's house in Dun Laoghaire, my anticipated overnight pit-stop) but I came to realise that I was the only one who knew Dublin; the only one who regularly went there by himself.

They were, of course, right about the distance; with the advantage of almost 60 years of hindsight, I realise it was probably a venture too far without an overnight break en route.

Nevertheless, most of my peers saw Dublin as no more than the capital of another country, a place where 'southerners' practised their un-northern ways. That I didn't see it like that was, of itself, unusual as I was from a Protestant background where many were in the habit of accentuating the negative rather than the positive when it came to the 'republican' world south of the border where, they mistakenly convinced themselves, the likes of them were not welcome.

The evidence of personal experience was, as it often still is, not on everyone's radar.

The reason that I wasn't tainted with such tunnel-vision was that I had my cousin Pat …

SUN, SAND AND CONTRABAND

After my mother, the woman I respected and loved the most was my cousin, Pat Douglas.

Pat lived in Dun Laoghaire, south of Dublin. She and her older sister Betty, who lived in nearby Dalkey, were the daughters of my father's brother Harry, a very reluctant southerner. Pat and Betty had it routinely drummed into them by their loving aunt, their father's sister in Belfast, that the North had its 'guns pointing at them'.

Pat was the cornerstone of what was, it seemed to me at the time, almost an idyllic family unit. Pat's husband Don was, as I have said, a very funny man; their two children, Jean and Gordon, were my best friends even though they were quite a few years younger than me. I got to know them all so well because I would travel to and from Dun Laoghaire at the beginning of every summer holiday and spend up to ten weeks with them.

This routine started when our side of the family visited its 'southern' branch one summer. Pat and Don and the kids were preparing to go and spend a few weeks in their 'caravan' at Brittas Bay, between Wicklow and Arklow. They foolishly offered to take me as well so my family returned to Belfast, minus one. At the end of the summer I travelled back to Belfast on the fast 'Enterprise' train from Dublin … alone.

I was almost twelve.

Thus began what, in retrospect, was an idyllic summer ritual. Every June, as soon as school finished, I packed my case and headed south to spend the holidays in and around Dun Laoghaire, Dalkey and

Brittas Bay. Soon this became twice a year as I did the same every Hallowe'en.

I would catch the Enterprise at Belfast's Great Victoria Street Station and travel to Amiens Street (now Connolly) in Dublin; I would walk up Talbot Street and Earl Street and turn right onto O'Connell Street as far as the stop for the 7a bus to Sallynoggin; I would get off the 7a on Glenageary Hill, Dun Laoghaire, and walk back about 20 yards and turn into the driveway of Pat's house called St Quentin.

For me it was the most exciting journey in the world and at no time did I ever feel vulnerable. The worst bit was waiting for the 7a in O'Connell Street where, if I'd just missed a bus, I could stand impatiently for half an hour. The best bit was pressing the bell at St Quentin and listening for Pat's footsteps as she rushed to open the most welcoming door in the world.

These days it is almost inconceivable that any twelve-year-old might make this same journey alone. That I was invariably carrying some sort of contraband just made it more exciting.

At the time there were things that some southerners craved, like potato bread, that you could only buy in the north. There were things that northerners craved, like Hafner's sausages which you could only buy in the south. There were also items like watches and cigarette lighters which were much cheaper south of the border. Thus my regular trips between Belfast and Dublin helped satisfy everyone. Nobody suspected that the little boy with the suitcase might just be a seasoned smuggler with half a dozen watches strapped on his arm. Perhaps I am exaggerating, maybe there were only three or four.

I recall once sitting opposite a priest on the train to Dublin. Only now, with the knowledge of hindsight and recent events in most corners of the celibate-priest world, do I realise that I might have been in greater danger on that trip than any other, before or after. He seemed innocent enough, though—never once did he indulge in any I'm-a-trusty-priest knee-patting—and I recall thinking that, not only does he not know that he's talking to a non-Catholic heathen but that this particular heathen has a suitcase full of fireworks which you could not buy in the Republic of Ireland then or now.

Nor could he have known why I was fiddling in my trouser pocket as we passed through the depressing, northern outskirts of Dublin, nor why I deliberately and quickly 'lost' him on leaving the train. What he was blissfully unaware of was that his innocent young travelling companion had developed his own *modus operandi* for the circumventing the customs check in Dublin.

The Enterprise would pull in slowly to Amiens Street, passing, as it edged along the platform, a long line of trestle tables. Standing behind these were the stern-faced customs officers, no doubt subconsciously rubbing their hands with glee at the prospect of confiscating some contraband.

On disembarking—and before leaving the station—passengers' luggage was checked at these tables; on exiting the platform there was one more hurdle, the sharp-eyed ticket inspectors would check all bags for a chalk cross which 'proved' that it had been inspected.

The platform customs check was always a bit of a scrum with people pushing and shoving to get to the tables and then turning to drive their bodies and bags against the flow to get out of the station.

I, on the other hand, never had that problem for I was in a hurry, I had a bus to catch, I just didn't have time to hang around waiting my turn at the table, I had a fireworks party to go to. How fortunate therefore that, in my right-hand trouser pocket, I always carried a piece of chalk.

This first time I did it, I was very nervous. If there had been security cameras at the time, those watching would definitely have picked me out as suspicious, possibly a drug mule. After my first successful DIY white cross I became both confident and cocky: suitcase in left hand; right hand in pocket; small stick of chalk between finger and thumb; walk towards the trestles; partially enter the melee; hand with chalk out of pocket; quick cross on side of case; chalk back in pocket; nifty about-turn; head for the barrier. Worked every time.

And every Hallowe'en the residents and friends of St Quentin were the only ones with a back-garden firework display. Probably the only other person who could have got away with it was my friend, the priest; his dog-collar would have given him the same absolution as my chalk.

———

While I loved Hallowe'en in Dun Laoghaire, the long summers, especially at Brittas Bay, where, as I recall, the sun always shone, were magic.

Part of that magic was 'the box', so-called because it had more of the characteristics of a large box than the caravan it was supposed to be. From the outside it seemed impossible that it could sleep five and often up to eight when Betty's kids tagged along. Inside it became the prototype for Dr Who's Tardis and somehow we all managed to eat and sleep there in harmony.

After breakfast we'd tear along the sandy, dune-protected path towards the sea, pass left or right of the lone caravan tucked away in the fork where its gaggle of kids would pour out to swell our number. Seconds later we were custodians of miles of golden sand with its fringe of dunes and their swaying grasses. I've often wondered how it was that I never learned to swim in this idyllic place?

Instead, at 13, I learnt to drive; perched up on cushions and with the seat pushed well forward Don would take me round and round the field edged with caravans, proper caravans, in NIK 90, his black Austin A55.

When the box blew over one time too many, it was replaced by a more conventional caravan which, though it didn't have the charm of the box, was clearly better at accommodating growing children. It was also more stable.

It was at this point that I was going to indulge in a bit of name-dropping but I thought it prudent to first check out the person in question's autobiography *Is This It?*.

Not a word. I was pretty sure he, a frequent summer visitor to his uncle's caravan, tucked away in that fork in the dunes, would have remembered the slightly older, strangely handsome northerner with whom he and all the rest of the Geldof clan played throughout those warm Brittas summers. Never mind, I'll not mention him either.

As I got older I began to outgrow Brittas Bay and didn't go there as often; I still headed south but opted instead to stay in and around Dun Laoghaire and Dalkey. I always had the option of staying with cousin Betty in Dalkey.

In the summer of 1959, cycling on a borrowed bike along the Metals, the path that runs alongside the railway south of Dublin, a sudden downpour saw me scurrying for the shelter of a covered walkway crossing the tracks. It was here that I bumped into John Collins and together we watched the rain and began a friendship.

For me, John was—and still is—the personification of the craic: larger-than-life, witty, extravagant, outlandish and, above all else, erudite. John went on to become an acclaimed defence barrister in three countries.

In the late 50s he led a more sheltered life in the sense that his family background was quite regimented and strait-laced; some might say austere. John's burgeoning wit, belied such origins. I, on the other hand, was over a hundred miles from home which in itself indicated that I was used to a more open and relaxed life-style.

From that chance encounter there blossomed a friendship that eventually embraced my cousin Pat and her family. Apart from our age, we seemed to have nothing in common except an unspoken curiosity about what made the other tick—much as you might regard an alien—and a mutual propensity for sharing a bit of the craic.

Years later John told me that I had introduced him to what he called the 'Unionist World', a world 'totally alien' to him. He assumed that I, being a northerner and not from a Catholic background, was a Unionist (a supporter of Northern Ireland's Union' with great Great Britain and not a Republican in favour of a united Ireland). Had we talked about it at the time, I would have explained that being from a Unionist background in terms of family, does not make you a Unionist. That said, it does work that way for 99% of people, John had no way of knowing he had just befriended the exception.

———

Looking back, it's no exaggeration to say that by my late teens I had done more independent travelling than many do in a lifetime. I also had experience of two cultures and of being equally independent in both.

Unlike most of my peers, I had friends on both sides of the border who were Protestant, Catholic, undecided or indifferent.

I was equally at home in Belfast's Smithfield Market as I was in Dublin's Moore Street. Later I became almost as well known for my drinking prowess in Walter's Bar in Dun Laoghaire as I was in Belfast's Washington Bar.

Few, if any, of my peers had ever travelled outside their immediate family circle unaccompanied. Most had never seen a Fiat or a Renault or a Simca or a Volkswagen or any of the other European cars commonplace in Dublin, almost unknown in Belfast.

Nor did they experience the ambience, the more relaxed way of life, the craic that, it seemed to me, was the natural way of things as soon as you crossed the border. Every time I journeyed south I felt I was abandoning gloom and doom to embrace a culture where it didn't matter who or what I was.

KEEPING UPRIGHT

I was shite at German until 'Kit' Carson became my teacher. In three years I went from being bottom of the class to being top. Literally.

I was therefore eager to go on the school trip to Germany and Austria. School trips were not a new venture for the all-boy Royal Belfast Academical Institution (Inst for short) but a school trip shared with the all-girl Bangor Grammar was an innovation and in due course became a revelation.

Apart from holding hands with an actual girl, there are two things that stand out about that trip.

At the small Rhine-side town of Königswinter I somehow got into conversation with a group of German lads from nearby Bad Honnef and did an address swap with one. Why and how I'd broken away from the main party, I don't recall—it's possible I'd seen someone pick their nose and wanted to see what Germans did with it or I was just taking the opportunity to speak German to Germans who were not serving coffee or selling postcards.

The second experience of note was that on our way home our party got caught up in the 1960 seaman's strike. We had already crossed the English Channel before the strike started and were in mainland Britain when we discovered there were no ferries crossing from Liverpool to Belfast. We were potentially stranded and by the time the news filtered down to us we were all looking forward to an extension to our holiday, albeit in England.

But all was not lost for our leader, the fastidious Mr Fitzsimmons, had everything under control as he had insured the party against such an eventuality. After a flurry of stops and phone-calls, 'Fitz' announced that we would be reunited with our families after all and that we were en route to Blackpool Airport from where we would be flying home. He didn't mention that the plane would resemble a toothpaste tube with wings.

For everyone, including, I suspect, the teachers, it was a first; an exciting, unprecedented experience borne out of necessity. Perhaps this is where I picked up my complete lack of fear about flying.

By the following spring I had exchanged several letters with Konrad in Bad Honnef which led to an invitation—which I had cunningly orchestrated—to come and stay with his family for a week in the summer.

Organising such a trip these days would be easy, half an hour on the internet would sort everything out. In 1961 it was a tad more complicated, especially as, in my case, I was going to be doing it on a shoestring. Also, and unknown to Konrad, my plan was to stay in Germany for all ten weeks of the school holiday and to do so I knew I would have to find gainful employment in or near Bad Honnef and perhaps independent accommodation.

Assuming I didn't get cold feet, this was to be the first summer for as long as I could remember when I had not spent at least some of the time with Pat and Don south of the border.

At the time I was a keen badminton player and played to a fairly high level for several local clubs including one in Dalkey during the summer. In one of these I sometimes partnered Michael, a man 25 years my senior who worked for Kelly's Coal, a local company that shipped coal from Liverpool to Belfast and other coastal towns. Michael told me about the berths available on the coal boats for Kelly's staff and how, on most trips, these were left unoccupied; he said that if I ever needed to get to England, then all I had to do was give him a call.

The idea of taking a coal boat to and from England fitted perfectly with my budget and became the first, and last, piece of the do-it-yourself jigsaw that was my planned itinerary for getting to Bad Honnef and back. It went something like this:

Catch Kelly's coal boat in Belfast.

Arrive Garston, near Liverpool.

Somehow get to Liverpool Pier Head.

Pick up Crosville coach to London Victoria.

Catch train to Dover.

Take cross-Channel ferry to Ostende in Belgium

Catch train to Cologne

Change trains for Bad Honnef

Find Konrad's house.

Indeed apart from one slight hiccup at Cologne, it went exactly to plan; but the devil is in the detail.

———

Michael was as good as his word and it was a very excited but apprehensive 16 year-old who turned up as instructed at Kelly's yard at the appointed hour. The boy who didn't get cold feet and who nervously climbed the gangplank in June was not the same person who walked down a similar gangplank in September.

Michael accompanied me on board the Bally-something-or-other (the Kellys' boats were all called Bally-this or Bally-that) and handed me over to the benevolent custody of Captain Hood who in turn passed me on to one of his crew who showed me to my cabin, situated just below the bridge. It was basic: two bunk beds, a table, a sink, a toilet and a window. But it was free and that was what mattered at the time.

Within minutes we were under way and I returned to the deck to watch our slow progress up Belfast Lough. I recognised Carrickfergus Castle on the left as we approached Bangor on the opposite side. I recognised the blue sea wall of Bangor's infamous Pickie Pool and gave a shudder as, momentarily, I recalled the time I had almost drowned there.

This wasn't the first time I had crossed the Irish Sea but nothing prepared me for what happened next. As we passed Bangor, which I still considered to be a place protected by the shelter afforded by Belfast Lough, the boat began to rise and fall, pitch and roll, in a most dramatic fashion. Thinking of the Pickie Pool incident reminded me that still I couldn't swim; common sense and the survival instinct dictated that I head indoors where I foolishly accepted an offer of lunch in the galley.

I was the only one there and, ominously, the table was already sectioned off into neat compartments that kept plates and cutlery more or less to hand rather than sliding all over the place. Now this of itself should have been a warning sign, but no, I immediately accepted the offer of the lunchtime equivalent of a full Irish breakfast, cased in a mountain of grease.

I didn't finish it and apologised to the cook as I made a hasty exit and returned to my cabin in the forlorn hope that lying down might take my mind off things and in particular the lingering smell of fat and oil.

The ten-hour crossing that I was expecting took 16 hours; I scarcely slept and lost count of the number of times I braved being thrown around like a cork as I clutched at walls and furniture for temporary support en route to the toilet bowl; I tried crawling on the floor but that was worse. In between these debilitating, vomiting visits—a fearful and watchful eye ever on the sea pounding angrily outside, as if furious that there was no way in through that small window—I fought off taunting visions of Brittas Bay

When we finally entered the calming waters of the Mersey Estuary, it felt like the first moment of the rest of my life. Dark was becoming dawn as I stood on the wet deck and watched the diffused lights of Liverpool at sleep come and go—a couple of miles away John, Paul, George and Ringo were still tucked up in bed.

Almost unheard, we continued upriver drawn to the only concentration of lights: the small port of Garston, awake and working, awaited our late arrival.

Before disembarking Captain Hood beckoned me up to the bridge and told me three things which I guess were meant to make me feel better.

First of all he explained how coal boats are like corks in a whirlpool when they flit from Belfast to Liverpool because they are empty; on the other hand, on the return journey, being laden with tons of coal, they are very stable. If that was intended to make me feel better about my return journey, it didn't work.

He then showed me a chart to explain how, on this particular crossing, the winds were so fierce that the boat was blown to the south of the Isle of Man, instead of passing on the northern side as intended. That explained the extra six hours I'd had to endure.

Finally, he showed me his log in which he had written that, in 40 years of crossing the Irish Sea, this was the worst voyage he had ever experienced. That did make me feel moderately better; at least he had suffered too.

Weary, weakened and very hungry, I left Garston's coal-grim, albeit well-lit, dockland and disappeared into the gradual dawning of a new day in search of a bus into Liverpool city centre; I knew there was a coach leaving the Pier Head at eight for London.

My day-long journey to London was uneventful; I drifted in and out of sleep most of the time and, once at Victoria, made the switch from coach to rail.

On the train I chatted with a man in his mid-20s who was also heading for the Ostende ferry but at Dover we got separated in the melee of people moving from train to ferry.

Once on the ferry I found a safe place for my luggage and settled down for the crossing, secure in the belief that it couldn't be any worse than what I'd experienced 24 hours earlier. In one sense it certainly wasn't, in another it was almost catastrophic.

Despite being very tired, there was too much going on around me for me to settle; I had (and have) always found it difficult to sleep anywhere but in a bed. There was no way I was going to catch any sleep crunched up in a corner of the deck of an overcrowded ferry with a lovey-dovey couple puffing and panting next to me.

I checked that my bags were still where I'd left them and started to wander round the boat observing how people set free from the routines of their day-to-day lives become a new frenetic race of travellers. I passed the window of one of the lounge-bars and glimpsed my Dover-train companion, glass in hand, propping up the bar.

I was not a drinker, though while in Germany the previous year on the school trip, I had downed a glass or two of Pils and didn't really like it all that much. Nevertheless I decided to join my friend and, if nothing else, rekindle our tenuous friendship to while away the time. Maybe we'd enjoy a bit of craic.

Well, that was as much of a plan as I had and it still seemed to be working as I drank my first glass of beer. After the second I needed to empty my bladder and, on my return, number three was awaiting my pleasure. With number three nearly finished it was his turn to point Percy at the porcelain and when he returned I had already bought number four.

At some point there was probably a split second when I realised that this was not part of the plan but it happened so fast that I missed it completely and was carrying on regardless with plan B.

Plan B dictated that our drinking should continue in this vein until I literally sank into oblivion. And I still didn't know his name.

Until I woke up several hours later reeking of vomit and booze, alone in a carriage, on a corridor train, somewhere in Germany, I have always had but two recollections.

The first of these was of a uniformed man, tall with an uncompromising, lugubrious visage framed below his officious looking military-style cap. He was standing over me, his long lugubriousness almost touching my face; and initially he had only one word in his vocabulary.

"Passport!" It wasn't a question, it was an order.

Another extraneous hand appeared which seemed to be trying to help me locate my passport but it was aggressively brushed aside.

"Passport!," he repeated, "You must show me passport. No passport, no train."

As one part of what remained of my conscious mind was preoccupied with my lack of luggage, I somehow managed to retrieve my passport of my own volition and Uniformed, Uncompromising, Lugubrious Man straightened up momentarily to examine it. Apparently satisfied that I was a very drunk version of who I was supposed to be, I was allowed to enter Belgium. I can only assume that's where I was for, to get to Germany, I clearly traversed Belgium but, other than those few moments, I have no memory of it.

My second fleeting recollection is of being on the train and being forced by another man in uniform, a guard I imagined, to clean up my vomit—at least I assume it was mine—from the corridor floor. He had kindly supplied a bucket and some rags. I suppose I can count myself lucky he didn't want to see my passport too.

So there I am, still alone in a train compartment somewhere in Germany and having missed Belgium. The train stopping has momentarily roused me from my slumbers and I survey my kingdom.

I see that miraculously my luggage has accompanied me through my misadventures and assume that my erstwhile drinking companion was responsible for reuniting me with it. On realising how fortunate I am to be still in one piece after what transpired between Dover and somewhere in Germany, I promise myself that I will never let alcohol pass my lips again. Well, maybe not for a few days anyway.

I close my eyes again but my anticipated glide back into unconsciousness is interrupted.

The two middle-aged women who wake me as they slide open the compartment door are just looking for somewhere quiet to sit. I open a curious eye just as the drift and the whiff of vomit and stale alcohol accosts them. For reasons unknown they change their minds about sharing this space with me, slide the door to and seek out fresh, vomit-free pastures.

I fall asleep again and wake up as the train is passing through the outskirts of Cologne. I have just enough time to find the toilet and try to eradicate some of the nauseous odours emanating from my person.

———

I was standing on the platform at Cologne station adjusting my clothing and organising my luggage when I felt a tap on the shoulder.

"Didn't know you were coming to Germany too."

It was Duncan Stewart, a fellow pupil from Inst. I didn't know him too well; his father I did know for he was a teacher at the same school. We went for a cup of coffee and discovered that our onward journeys were in different directions; Duncan was intending to stay overnight in Cologne and though I had been planning to head down to Bad Honnef at the earliest opportunity, I was clearly in no state to do any more travelling that day. We decided therefore to find some overnight 'digs' together and share the cost.

The woman at the accommodation kiosk was very helpful but everything she offered us was way too expensive. The more we shook our heads, the further out of town we would have to go. It seemed almost as a last resort that we were told about a place some distance out of town that was within our price range; we jumped at it. The helpful young woman seemed sceptical.

Frau Müller was the personification of the stereotypical landlady at the time;. A battle-axe of a woman, unhelpful verging on obnoxious. We were shown to our room at the top of a gloomy, somewhat sleazy, apartment block and that was it. She took cash in advance, told us the house rules—no guests, no smoking, no drinking, no eating, no noise and out by nine in the morning—I seem to remember that breathing was permitted, but only quietly.

I didn't really care, I was exhausted and all I wanted to do was sleep, I was pretty sure the worst was over. I had Duncan by my side, a calming influence, the sort of person that wasn't going to be much trouble then or at any time in the future. From Frau Müller's point of view she could be confident that her current guests would come and go like the proverbial church mice.

Later, before I went into an alcohol-induced coma, I took the precaution of taking all my money from my jacket and hiding it somewhere safe. A wise decision I thought at the time but, when I woke the next morning, I had totally forgotten where that safe place was. Hastily I started turning the room upside down to make sure we were not still on the premises at nine.

With the second hand racing towards one minute past nine, Frau Müller arrived at the open door and demanded to know why we hadn't left. Although Duncan's German was not as good as mine, he was quicker off the mark and offered what he thought was a plausible explanation.

"He can't find his money," he said.

"I put it somewhere safe last night but I have forgotten where," I added, trying to shift the blame directly to me.

But the damage was done. From being demonstratively annoyed Frau Müller went into berserk-mode.

She decided that she was being accused of stealing the money in the night and no amount of reasonable argument to the contrary was going to alter what she thought she knew. Eventually she stomped off, still shouting and gesticulating; the last word I caught was "Polizei".

Our search for my money continued feverishly—we just wanted to be out of there—and the very moment I found it (inside my pillowcase) was the same moment that two large German policemen appeared in the doorway.

The whole way up the stairs they had been subjected to Frau Müller's version of events and her unshakeable belief that these two troublesome foreigners were accusing her of theft.

With the Müller going on and on from behind the policemen, I explained about our long journey (I omitted all of the more incriminating personal details) and how tired we had been and how I had hidden my money and that we were definitely not accusing the Müller of stealing it, just trying to remember where it was hidden; and now we had just found as we always knew we would.

And still Frau Müller went on and on.

While one of the policemen was checking our documents, the other, unseen by the Müller, gave me a friendly, almost apologetic, glance before rolling his eyes upwards while tilting his head backwards in the direction of the Müller. I interpreted this as his unspoken way of saying he was on our side, that we shouldn't worry and that the woman behind him was an evil, ranting nutcase.

On reflection, he probably just meant 'nutcase', the 'evil, ranting' bit was my exaggerated perception of her. On the other hand, by communicating with us surreptitiously he was clearly demonstrating a lack of enthusiasm for confronting the mad Müller.

The same policeman suggested we get our things together and get on our way as soon as possible and that they would walk out with us. He didn't mention the word 'protect' but I think that's what he meant. We didn't argue and, sandwiched between two policemen, we left the premises with the voice and venom of the mad Müller still following us down the stairs and out into the street.

As we headed back to the city centre and the station I wondered if Duncan was still trying to fathom out how it was that I couldn't remember where I'd hidden that money … perhaps if I'd told him more about my journey thus far, he might have understood. I resisted the temptation for it was obvious that the craic was no more in his experience than the word was in his vocabulary.

At Cologne station I had just missed a train to Bad Honnef while Duncan's timing was perfect. As we parted company I wondered if, or how, he might explain his sojourn in Cologne to his irascible father and whether, on my return to school, Mr Stewart would be a master to avoid.

To kill some time, and to give future impoverished visitors to Cologne a fighting chance, I returned to the accommodation kiosk and suggested to the woman on duty that she cross Frau Müller off the list. I also explained why.

———

On the train to Bad Honnef, I reflected on events since I stepped onto the Bally-something-or-other in Belfast less than three days earlier.

I had been violently sick, terribly drunk and verbally abused but despite everything I felt pretty good about finally arriving at my destination and getting to know my German hosts.

I was also looking forward to seeing whether or not the Germans were as humourless as people thought. Maybe I could unearth some hitherto untapped German craic.

THE BOY WHO HELD HANDS WITH A GIRL. C.1959.

FINDING MY FEET

There were five in the Braun family: Herr and Frau Braun and their three children, Konrad, Günther and Ingrid.

Frau Braun, Günther and Ingrid were wonderful hosts. Initially Herr Braun, who had fought in the war, seemed a little reticent about sharing his home with a foreigner, particularly one who had recently been the 'enemy' but, after a day or two, he became more relaxed.

At least he was not like his son, Konrad, my pen-pal, who was a sociopath. Having just landed in Bad Honnef, I knew pretty quickly that I would have to find alternative accommodation, sooner rather than later.

Out and about with Konrad I met some of his friends, a few of whom I remembered meeting the previous year. He was showing me off and I got on well with them but it was clear that even they were wary of Konrad. It seemed to me that most just tolerated him while, from some, there was downright antipathy towards him which he did not seem to pick up on. He had a permanent smile, almost a leer, which did not help his cause.

How come, I wondered, given that all his friends seemed relatively normal, how come I'd ended up with Konrad as a pen-pal? Maybe it was while nursing that thought that I felt drawn to rying another glass or two of Pils. So much for the promise I'd made to myself on the train.

My wariness of Konrad morphed into undisguised repugnance a day or two later when he took me down the garden to show me the rabbits the family kept there. Günther was with us and he was as horrified as I was when his brother proceeded to demonstrate how he could choke rabbits until their eyes almost popped out and then, at the last moment, reprieve them from further distress. Konrad thought it was incredibly funny and was repeating the exercise with another rabbit when Günther and I headed back up to the house.

If I hadn't already decided to curtail my stay here, that would have convinced me.

Over the next ten days I focussed on my exit strategy; first a job and then somewhere to live. From some of the other young Germans I'd met I discovered that the local jam and preserves factory, Dienel und Jakob Konservenfabrik, took on German students during the summer. I went to the factory and got work starting almost immediately; the main group of students would start the following week .

I was already working at Dienel und Jakob when I heard about the youth hostel just out of town so went up there one evening to suss it out as possible alternative accommodation. It was here that I met Liam O'Brien from Limerick.

Liam was three years older than me and had left Ireland having failed his Leaving Certificate. He was, in his own words "wandering round Europe". Somehow he ended up working in the Bad Honnef youth hostel where he seemed to do all the work for no recompense other that his food and board. When I met him for the first time he was broke and more than a little fed up with his lot.

Together we conceived an exit strategy for both of us. It seemed simple enough, and it was. I spoke to the guy who'd hired me at Dienel und Jakob about taking on Liam and he agreed; the summer fruit harvests were a busy time. As Liam couldn't leave his work at the youth hostel until he had somewhere else to live, the obvious answer to both out predicaments was to find somewhere to live together, preferably with two single beds. This is how we did it and, modestly, I have to take all the credit for the idea.

At random, we chose a house in a street we liked the look of— the only other criterion being that it was nowhere near the Braun family home—and knocked the door.

I did the talking as Liam's German was as good as my Mandarin.

"I've been told that you have a room to rent … ?"

Woman scratches head.

"No, not here … but why don't you try Frau Schmidt, number 13, just round the corner."

At number 13, just round the corner.

"Frau Schmidt? The woman at number 42 just round the corner said she thought you might have a room to rent … ?"

"No, I used to have … let me think … have you tried Frau Goertz two streets up the road on this side, I think she's the third house on the left?"

Two streets up, same side, third house on left.

"Frau Goertz? Frau Schmidt said that you may have a room to rent … ?"

"Yes, I do. Been empty for just over a week … would you like to take a look? It's got two single beds …"

It was as simple as that and a couple of days later we moved in together. Curiously, bearing in mind Bad Honnef is quite a small town, at the time around 18,000 people, I never saw Konrad again, nor any other member of his family.

―――

Life in Bad Honnef for Liam and me soon evolved into routine and ritual.

Liam was a likeable bloke, as a double act he would have been the straight guy feeding me the lines; he was also a lazy bugger. Mind you, arguably, he worked harder than I did as, being over 18, his lunch-hour was half-an-hour shorter than mine.

I got up before him every morning made breakfast for both (a bread roll with cream cheese and jam), ate mine and left his, set off towards work, bought the bread for later that evening and the next morning en route, clocked myself in and, if Liam wasn't already in sight, clocked him in too.

At first lunch was the same fare except that we'd put the cheese on top of the jam for a bit of variety. It all changed the day we were standing on the footbridge that crossed the adjacent railway line; on one side of the tracks was Dienel und Jakob and on the other a massive steel and engineering works.

From the bridge you could see that the engineering works had a large canteen at the side where workers would queue up with their trays. But, and this was the important thing, when they were given their 'soup of the day' no money seemed to change hands. A free lunch appeared to be one of the perks of working across the tracks.

The next day we took a walk over to have a closer look, mingling, as we did, with some of the workers from the factory who'd come out to stretch their legs, have a smoke and watch the trains. Out of their overalls, they looked just like us; nor did they give any indication that they'd noticed the two cuckoos in the nest.

The next day we gave it a go. We crossed the railway, did a bit of mingling, wandered casually into the canteen, picked up a tray, joined the queue and took what was on offer, a bowl of soup and a bread roll. Then all we had to do was choose our cutlery, seek out an empty table and eat.

Thereafter we did this every day and only got away with it for three reasons.

At the time German workers came to work in normal, everyday clothes but almost everyone carried a briefcase. In the briefcase they had their working overalls and, when they went to lunch, they popped their working clothes back in the briefcase. We two outsiders looked the part.

In addition, some students were also given casual work during the summer and, once again, we fitted in. Not being recognised by the hundreds of regular workers was not an issue.

And, most important of all, from the moment we set foot in the canteen we never spoke a word to anyone else, or to each other.

Our silent ritual over, we would discard our trays, mutely mingle a bit outside the canteen, recross the tracks and reclaim our Dienel und Jakob identities. If high fives had been invented then we would probably have indulged, such was the buzz of getting away with this.

Nobody ever challenged us.

Other routines included hanging round the youth hostel in the hope that some foreign girl might fancy us; it never happened. They never knew what they were missing.

Once a week we would take the train to Königswinter, at the time quite a popular Rhineland destination for British coach parties. We used to listen out for and stalk English-speakers who would invariably buy us a drink.

Twice a week, Saturday and Sunday, we would eat a proper, albeit basic, meal in a small, local restaurant.

At work I was befriended by Otto an elderly man with a shock of white hair and a matching moustache who was originally from what had become East Germany, the Deutsches Demokratische Republik. Otto had worked at Dienel und Jakob as long as anyone could remember and continued working long after he should have retired. He was a Dienel und Jakob institution and even had his own large shed on the site, Ottoland, his own little kingdom which only he entered.

After two or three weeks when I had done most of the menial tasks around the factory, I was told to help Otto shift some discarded cherry stones. Otto was so captivated with my charm and dedication to the task at hand that he decided that I was to be his permanent assistant. Nobody argued with Otto.

Day in, day out, while everyone else was working on the bottling and tinning of the good quality fruit, Otto and I were working the machine that broke down the poorer quality stuff which would eventually be made into jam in the winter months. Indeed at that time we were the only two involved in the jam-making process.

When we had filled a barrel with, for example, the mashed up strawberries which had been first soaked in acid to kill off any nasties, we would trundle it to a large wooden door in the floor, the gateway to the underground storage vats. Otto would pull back the doors to reveal the sticky, red pre-jam goo liberally topped with the remains of dead bees who thought they had found a nirvana that was worth dying for.

Otto, his hygiene gene kicking in, would reach for a long pole with a metal cup on the end and would start to scoop up the bees; the only problem was that for every one he scooped up, he pushed several others further down under the surface with the back of the cup.

At that moment one of life's great mysteries was revealed to me for, finally I knew what the crunchy bits in the jam were.

When the supply chain couldn't keep up with us, Otto and I would slope off to his shed where he would light up his pipe and show me all the things he made from wood, all the tools he used; he had a story for every single one.

Otto and I became inseparable; everywhere he went, I was but a few paces behind, like a doting groupie, and only I was allowed into the inner sanctum of Ottoland. If one of the foremen needed me to do something else, Otto would argue with him and usually he would have his way. Sometimes I went off and did other things of my own volition but Otto would always find me when he needed me.

On one such occasion I wanted to catch up with two Italian lads who started working there the same week as I did. Before Liam came on the scene we three foreigners had developed a unique alliance but since I'd become Otto's slave I hadn't seen as much of them. Liam had also got to know them and I was curious to see for myself if what he said was going on in the tin-labelling department was true. Liam was convinced these two Italians were on a secret mission to sabotage the post-war recovery and rebuilding of German industry.

Liam was not exaggerating. I can still see the two of them

standing idly, innocently, expectantly, in the corner of the tin-labelling room as, arms folded, they watched the fruits of their nefarious tweaks to the system rattle through the machinery and exit as dozens of tins without a label followed by one or two with dozens of labels shooting off in all directions. The tall, wiry foreman, his slate-blue overall flailing behind as he twisted and turned like a headless chicken, his black-rimmed glasses bobbing up and down on his nose, as he screamed *"Halt! Halt!"*.

Thursday was pay day and we were always skint by then. Saving anything was simply not an option. I had money put aside for getting home but I didn't dare touch that. We lived on bread rolls with cheese and jam, the latter from rejected or damaged jars or tins from work; from time to time we had to help a few tins to become damaged. Once, the evening before pay-day, we were down to our last Mark and bought a tin of meat from a vending machine and very tasty is was too until I noticed the picture of the dog on the label. Despite not reading the dog-food label properly, my German was improving leaps and bounds; had I not been around Liam it probably would have been even better. I remember the day when I realised I was thinking in German and how good it felt. I was shaving and looking at my reflection in the mirror and everything I thought and did, I did in German. I could cut myself in German and then swear in German too. I wondered would I lose my virginity in German?

Liam was a dreamer. He had this vision of a life wandering round Europe until he bumped in to that illusory European princess who was also wandering around Europe in search of an Irish Prince Charming … but prepared to make do with Liam instead.

Apart from the princess part, the idea was beginning to sound appealing to me, the more so as, having had a taste of independence in another culture, the thought of returning to school in Belfast was becoming increasingly unappealing.

I gave it a lot of thought before writing a letter to my parents with the good news: I'd decided not to return home in the immediate future but instead to join a Limerick lad on his European adventure. Next stop Holland.

This was mid-August, a time when I should have been planning my return trip. Ten days later Frau Goertz called for me to come downstairs where she handed me the phone's handset. She didn't need to say who it was, I knew it was my mother.

I had a sense of foreboding as I put it to my ear. I was anticipating a 'come-back-son-all-is-forgiven' conversation. But it wasn't like that.

My mother obviously expressed her disappointment that I had decided not to return and finish my education but there was no attempt at persuasion or pleading, just concern that I was sure this is what I wanted to do and that I was going to be alright in Holland. Basically she pushed all the right buttons and none of the wrong ones; she was either one smart cookie or already thinking of the benefits of having one less mouth to feed.

It was a week later that I told Liam that I'd changed my mind, that I'd decided to return to Belfast and go back to school; he could have all the unspoken-for European princesses to himself. He was dutifully disappointed but not surprised. We both knew he had survived before I was around to hold his hand so we assumed he could do it again and perhaps find a prettier hand to hold. I was never made to feel that I was letting him down or that I should feel guilty. While I was preparing to leave, Liam was still talking about heading for Holland after I'd gone.

It was difficult to leave Bad Honnef. Otto was distraught, he even went to the management and arranged for me to be taken on permanently with a proper wage and not as a student. But it was too late, I'd already been in contact with Kelly's in Liverpool and arranged when I was going to show up there for my coal boat crossing to Belfast.

I omitted to tell my parents that I was coming home.

Compared with my journey to Bad Honnef, my journey home was generally uneventful.

On the train to Ostende I found myself in a compartment with a returning school party from Britain, a mixed group of teenagers about the same age as me. For several reasons they came to the conclusion that I was German. My colouring suggested that I might be; my clothes *were* German and quite different in cut and colour to anything British at the time; and I spoke German. Even their teacher spoke to me in German.

They didn't realise that I understood everything they said, including what they said about me. I continued with my subterfuge throughout the journey but was nearly caught out once. There was a passport check when we crossed into Belgium and of course I had a British passport—at the time I didn't realise I ticked all the right boxes to hold an Irish passport. When the officer entered the compartment, I made an excuse and explained that mine was in another compartment with a friend. Out in the corridor I 'remembered' I had it after all and showed it to him unseen by prying eyes.

Passing from train to ferry, one of my two recollections from my outward journey came flooding back in the form of Uniformed, Uncompromising, Lugubrious Man. He was still there, still on duty, still checking tickets and passports, his long, disproportionate visage looked every bit as unsympathetic and ominous as it had when I was trying to find my passport and not vomit at the same time. Just in case he had a photographic memory, I turned my face away from him and crossed to a different queue and a different officer.

On the ferry to Dover I found myself once again in the company of the same school group and finally could not resist telling them that was in fact English-speaking and not German at all. The reason I think they were not best pleased was that they couldn't be sure what, if anything, they'd said about me while on the train. Clearly they knew nothing about the craic.

One later told me that some of her friends had challenged their teacher about how he had not realised I wasn't German. I don't know what he said, but the answer was simple, at the time my German was probably better than his; I also spoke a form of *plattdeutsch*, which had its own non-standard pronunciation and of course made me sound more like a native German-speaker. In addition, I had another secret weapon in that the northern Irish accent has a guttural quality that, for me at least, endowed me with a more natural German accent.

As Captain Hood had predicted, the crossing from Liverpool to Belfast in a fully-laden coal boat was like crossing a mill pond and I arrived in Belfast before seven in the morning, walked into town and caught the bus home.

My mother answered the door in her dressing gown, not at all surprised to see me even though she couldn't have known I was coming home.

After breakfast she confessed that she gone to my school (which had already started a week earlier) and 'secured' my place; she had told them I'd been delayed in Germany and would be back shortly.

It was clearly the time for confessions for my younger brother later admitted that he had had to reschedule his plans for laying claim to my bedroom; he had to wait another six years.

Duncan Stewart and I were not the only Inst scholars in Germany that summer, not the only ones to share our adventures and misadventures with our peers. My experiences were outdone only by Dave Saunders and his stories of living in Hamburg with a middle-aged, one-legged homosexual.

I wrote to Liam once and never received a reply; to this day I have no idea what befell him ... though it's possible he uses the name of the Dutch royal family these days.

66

LEAVING BELFAST

Apart from on-going visits to Dun :Laoghaire, my Bad Honnef adventure, a failed attempt to get summer work in North Wales and the Ennis episode, my propensity for travel over the next few years was confined to Northern Ireland. That said, by the time I had finished my Teacher Training, I was ready to leave Belfast.

The social and political repercussions of the Woolworths' incident were, in Northern Irish terms profound. I will not dwell too long on the minutiae of this, save to note that my day-to-day life was different from my peers in that I had friends in both the Protestant/ Unionist and Catholic/Republicans communities and often visited and socialised in parts of the city that few from a Protestant background would venture into.

The following examples, the third of which did not involve me directly but had major repercussions within Northern Ireland, impacted my decision. I will assume you understand how working-class Belfast was divided into areas generally based on religion. However, being Protestant did not always mean you were Unionist in political outlook; similarly being Catholic did not mean you were a Republican so I use these terms only as a shorthand.

Having left school abruptly in January 1963 partly because the system botched my curriculum and partly because my experiences in Germany had left me restless. I already had a place at Teacher Training College in September and, in the meantime. applied for and got a job in the Civil Service, specifically in the National Assistance

Board, the department tasked with assessing and supporting those in need. I was led to believe that I would soon be climbing, rung by rung, up the ladder to Civil Service nirvana. I never even got on a rung, I was holding the ladder. I opened the post and did other menial fetching and carrying jobs. It was as if they knew I intended to leave.

My overseer in this exacting position was a nasty piece of work. Everything about her said she was a mean-minded, petty, back-stabbing bitch … and that was on a good day.

She was, like most of the office, of Protestant stock and, within seconds of meeting me she made certain she knew whether or not I was of the same persuasion.

"I assume you're one of us?" she spat from her tight little mouth.

Spinster Madge Craig knew everything that went on and would lean over towards me every so often to bring me up to speed with who was doing what, to whom, and why.

She would focus her attention on the few non-Protestants in the office and hadn't a good word to say about any of them, especially Aileen and Martin, a young couple who were knee-deep in the innocence of first love. Madge, of course thought it was disgusting.

"And before you know it, they'll be breeding like rabbits," she predicted with no hint of compassion.

On the other hand she did turn a blind eye to some other practices that a number of her co-religionists were up to for it was obvious that some officers, whose job it was to access people's claims for benefit, were favouring non-Catholic claimants.

In Belfast it was generally easy to tell whether a person was 'one of us' by their address. There were some blurred localities but people normally resided in Catholic areas or Protestant areas. And I watched as officers took a file from the top of their pending tray, noted the address and either started work on it or put it to the bottom of the pile. Not all officers were like this, but many were.

Whatever Madge thought Aileen and Martin were up to she would have been apoplectic had she known what was going on in another office in a nearby building where John and Trudy worked.

———

Unknown to me at the time, John McVeigh also worked for Northern Ireland Civil Service (see also *Child on the run)*. Here he met Trudy, a colleague from a Catholic background, and was soon approached by his female boss with the rank of Junior Staff Officer and told to immediately stop fraternising with 'that Catholic girl'.

Of course this warning had the opposite effect and it was not long before he was summoned to the Office of the Deputy Principal who was. in Civil Service terms, the equivalent of God to an 18-year-old.

John was told he had a great career ahead of him which he could ruin by continuing to liaise with a Catholic. In his innocence he retorted that he didn't see what this had to do with anything.

John, recalls how the Deputy Principal lectured him as follows: "Catholics comprise about half of all Civil Servants. The ranks are Clerk, Senior Clerk, Junior Staff Officer, Staff Officer, Deputy Principal, Principal Officer and Private Secretary. The highest rank ever attained by a Catholic (and only once) was Staff Officer. Mixed marriages precluded the Protestant from any rank above JSO."

Not unnaturally, John got on his high horse and said he would report their conversation to the *Belfast Telegraph*. The DP just laughed at his naivety.

Soon afterwards, in an effort to keep John and Trudy apart, John was promoted and transferred 40 miles away to Dungannon. It didn't work. John and Trudy continued with their relationship, got married and moved to South Africa.

Ironically, when I worked for the Civil Service, the 'Catholic' Staff Officer referred to above was my boss and loathed by Madge Craig.

———

As a student I worked every Christmas in the Post Office, the first two years as a sorter. It was here that I came across yet another nasty, little quirk in the psyche of my co-religionist co-workers.

Now I don't wish to tar all my then colleagues with the same brush but what I am about to describe was not an isolated occurrence. It goes without saying that most postal workers were of Protestant stock.

As at the National Assistance Board, it was easy for the sorters to pick out letters destined for Catholic localities. Most, of course, got through but not all did so unscathed. The practice I observed related to Catholic organisations, like Churches, Convents and Charities, that had a clear role, symbolic or actual, within the Catholic Church.

When such a letter was spotted by particular unsavoury sorters it would be dropped to the floor and then the sorter would grind his shoe onto it, twisting it this way and that until it became dirty and defaced. Then it was thrown into the right compartment for delivery.

A local working practice that I found particularly offensive.

———

I had a friend, a bus conductor called Eddie Spence. One week in four Eddie's shift included the number 76 bus, to Gilnahirk which was my bus home from my city centre school. This was how we met.

Eddie was from Protestant stock but was generally not welcome in the streets where he was brought up because he had married a Catholic girl with whom he had two children. Eddie and his family lived in a working-class community off the Grosvenor Road, a Catholic/Republican area.

I was eating at Eddie's house the evening in 1966 when his brother, Gusty, participated in the murder of an innocent Catholic barman. Gusty was a member of an extreme Protestant/Unionist organisation while his brother Eddie was doing his bit to foster the normality of relationships between religions and their political aspirations.

This is the background within which I was a mere cog, albeit, as I described most recently in *Calabrian Tales*, a curious, questioning, skeptical cog already wrestling with what I'd learnt at Woolworths, my experiences south of the border and in Germany.

The story of what befell Eddie and his extended family was only the last straw, in that it reinforced a decision I had already made. The endemic sectarian spite, particularly from the Protestant/Unionist side, essentially from the community of which I was a part, told me I should leave Belfast. I had visited Eddie that evening to tell him of my decision. I was aware that we might never meet again.

During my college years, the only travelling of note I did was the aforementioned brief trip to North Wales and to Ennis County Hospital and back.

As my final year approached I knew that, if I wanted to make use of my training as a teacher, I would have to leave home permanently, most probably to England. I was open to considering emigrating further afield—Canada, Australia, New Zealand—but for my then fiancée, Alex, England was as far away as she'd venture.

This was, in a sense, a self-inflicted exile. I have already touched on some of the brutal realities and absurdities, as I saw them, of specific aspects of the Northern Irish mentality. But this was not confined to working-class communities for, in the mid-60s, polite society too, even at the level of higher education, was not immune.

The college I went to was one of two in Belfast that specialised in teacher training; basically there was one Catholic and one non-Catholic. Non-Catholic generally meant anyone who considered him- or herself to be one of the numerous Protestant denominations. Unwittingly the non-Catholic college also gave asylum to people like me: the nondenominational, the non-religious, the heathens.

In my year-group there were three lads who were brought up as Catholic but who, recognising the same absurdities as I had, were moved to break down these historical, nonsensical and divisive categorisations. Religious Education was one of the subjects that everyone had to study for, this being Northern Ireland, it was impossible to teach in a 'Protestant' school if you weren't a declared Protestant or a declared 'pretend' Protestant; similarly it was not possible to teach in a Catholic school without being Catholic and having trained at a Catholic college.

When I say 'everyone' studied RE, I do of course mean everyone except me; like the Catholic-Three I was doing my bit to change the system. That said, it appeared that I was the only one from a 'Protestant' background prepared to do so. Ignoring absurdities and social and political irregularities in the interests of a quieter life is perhaps another characteristic of many of my fellow countrymen.

In our final year all four of us realised that, even if we wanted to, it would be impossible for us to teach in the six counties of our birth. I wouldn't get a job because I would have no qualification in religious indoctrination, in any case, it was something I couldn't bring myself to do. The Catholic-Three couldn't get a job in a Catholic school because they had not trained at the Catholic college; and they would not get a job at a Protestant school because they were Catholic.

The Catholic-Three pursued one other option which seemed a logical way out of their Catch 22 situation and, at the beginning of their final year, tried to change colleges. Their application to the Catholic college was rejected because they had chosen not to go to that college in the first place. I believe it's called Christian charity.

Christian charity evolved into downright hypocrisy when, coincidentally, another student in the same year-group from England— where he had been brought up as Church of England—somehow managed to get himself converted to Catholicism around the same time. As a convert, he was welcomed with open arms and successfully changed to the Catholic college at the beginning of that same final year.

Assuming we still wanted to become teachers, the Catholic-Three and I had no other choice but to apply for teaching posts in other parts of the UK. In my case, I got a job in the London Borough of Haringey. Unlike the others, I had no axe to grind, I chose this path rather than compromise my humanist principles.

This self-inflicted exile, at the time my first experience of emigration and at exporting the craic overseas, lasted some 42 years

Unknown to me at the time, in another part of the city, my childhood friend, John McVeigh, was packing his bags too.

FIRST CARS

As I alluded to in an earlier chapter my frequent independent travels between Belfast and Dublin were eye-openers at so many levels. It was like swapping a monochrome world for one in colour and one of the manifestations of this was the variety of cars *and* their colours south of the border.

I alone among my peers had first-hand experience of 'foreign' cars and could tell a Fiat from a Renault, a Simca from a Volkswagen or an Opel from a Citroën. I alone knew that cars didn't have to be black or dark green or muted tones of grey and beige.

'Foreign' meant 'European' and something different, more stylish and literally more colourful than the British cars I was accustomed to. For a young teenager interested in such things, Dublin streets were a revelation. It seemed to me that even the European Ford range was more stylish and somehow brighter than its British counterpart.

It was not until the end of the 50s that British car manufacturers joined the party and a spate of new, more flamboyant and innovative cars was introduced: the Austin A40 Farina, the Triumph Herald, the Ford Anglia and the Mini. Nor was it any accident that two of these were designed by Italians.

By the late 60s and living in London, I was in the market for my first car and, with Alex back in Belfast for the week, I found myself drawn to a local garage to see if they had anything to offer within my modest price-range.

There were only two that I could afford and I faced a car

enthusiast's dilemma ... a new-style Austin A40 or a much older, but eminently collectable, Riley. I was aware that, in five years time, the latter would inevitably have increased in value while the former would have gone in the opposite direction.

Nevertheless, not wanting to appear to be an old fuddy-duddy, I opted for the red Austin A40 and the innovative Italian design and flare, or so it seemed at the time, of Battista Farina.

Of course I had bought a crock but knowing it might be a crock didn't stop me extolling its virtues to Alex on her return and pointing out all the positive ways our lives would change now we were car owners.

I omitted to mention that we might also cause traffic chaos in Bristol by coming to an abrupt halt on a roundabout with the brakes locked on; or that we might not make it to the top of a particularly steep Devon hill without the clutch giving up the ghost; or the delightful bonus of being able to drive between London and Bristol three times in the same day.

Alex's sister, Andie, and her husband Terry, lived in Bristol. Terry had his rituals which I first became aware of while we were at College where, rain or shine, he always carried an umbrella with a theatrical flair as if it were a fixed extension of his arm. Later I noticed too how he always spread a very thin layer of jam on his toast with the attention to detail of a tool-maker. At the time, the fact that he was also English appeared to explain such idiosyncrasies and the low reading on the craic-ometer.

Another of Terry's rituals, that I was not initially aware of, was that it was almost impossible for him to negotiate the Christmas break without watching the *Morecombe & Wise Christmas Special* on television. And it was this latter foible that led to the 'three times in the same day' London-to-Bristol episode.

To show off our 'new' car, we had arranged to drive to Bristol for Christmas. I pulled up outside Andie and Terry's Bristol flat and started to unpack the car. Naturally Andie and Terry lent a hand but

I soon became aware that Terry was becoming more than a little agitated. Finally he came out with it ...

"Where's the telly?" he asked in an incredulous tone, verging on distress.

The penny dropped. Not only did we have a car, we also owned a television set and, as Andie and Terry did not, Terry had assumed that we would have brought ours with us. Of course we would have done so if either he or Andie had asked but it just never occurred to us.

You have to remember that this was not only light years before streaming, but also decades before video-recording and that, if you missed the *Morecombe & Wise Christmas Special*, you missed it for ever or until someone invented video. Also, televisions in the late '60s were big and bulky. Not at all easy to manhandle in and out of a car.

I still don't know how he managed to persuade me but, half an hour later, and after a quick snack, Terry and I were back on the road and heading for London. Today that 115-mile journey would take two and a quarter hours. Back then the distance was about the same but there was no motorway, no M4, and, time-wise, it was at least half as long again from door to door.

It was only as we approached Bristol on that return journey that I had a sudden thought and asked Terry what should have been my first question before we left Bristol.

"Terry," I said, "does you flat have a television aerial?"

I suspect you can guess his response ...

Nevertheless, our little A40 did well that day, close to 350 miles trouble-free though, as if in protest, it did have a hiccup a few days later when it stopped dead on a roundabout, its brakes locked on.

When the clutch eventually ceased to function, I decided that I could replace it myself and bought the appropriate Haynes Manual with its step-by-step guide to every procedure. It being the summer, Alex sat in a deck chair and read out the instructions to me as, slowly and not without many setbacks, I managed to complete the job in two days.

Nobody was more surprised than I when the car started and ran normally afterwards.

Apart from the aforementioned episodes, our A40 had taken us all over the south of England and instilled in me a love of driving which I have never lost. Nevertheless it was beginning to look sorry for itself and, still on a high from replacing the clutch, I decided to give it one last chance. So I took it apart.

The doors, the bonnet and the boot-door were inside the house in various states of repair in preparation for their face-lift. All traces of rust had been eradicated, visually at least, and the few holes here and there repaired with filler, sanded smooth and primed.

When everything was ready, I began the paint job, by hand. After two coats, the erstwhile faded and jaded red had become a vibrant, pillar-box red, albeit not one from the normal A40 colour range.

Dry and reassembled, I put an advert in the local paper extolling the distinctive charm of this hand-painted A40 Farina with its new clutch and functioning brakes. Within 24 hours it was sold; a young, excited, discerning youth, recognising a bargain when he saw one, snapped it up and drove off into the sunset.

We were happy for him. Our first car was now his first car and we looked forward to seeing it's distinctive redness flash by in the days to come from the comparative luxury of our new, but old, Hillman Minx.

The next day, his less excited alter ego was back on the doorstep—he'd forgotten to ask for a receipt and, this being our first such transaction, we had not thought to furnish him with one.

As I hastily provided him with proof of ownership, he explained the urgency. He needed it for insurance purposes for, on his way home in his new, hand-painted, rust-free, first car, he'd had an accident and it was a write-off.

Only then did we feel its loss.

NOTHING VENTURED, NOTHING GAINED

In the late 60s there was a London-based travel company called Vista Tours which ran a service called Hop-on-a-Bus where they sold unreserved seats on scheduled coach tours going to all parts of Europe. This was at a time when most package holidays were coach-based though, increasingly, some tour companies were using air travel.

Alex and I, now newly-weds and living in west London, booked ourselves on a coach travelling from London to Rijeka in Yugoslavia. I sent Vista Tours a cheque in the post.

Yugoslavia was our destination of choice for several reasons. Alex, a physical education teacher, had studied the traditional dance of Yugoslavia as part of a final project at college and felt an affinity with the country. I had that same affinity as I had worked on her project too but for me the main draw was Yugoslavia's position as a satellite of the Eastern Bloc at the time and its apparent openness to different influences. Its ruler, Marshall Tito, appeared to be a benevolent dictator and I was keen to see how his brand of communism worked on the ground.

Two weeks before our scheduled departure, I was getting a tad concerned that we had not yet received any tickets or confirmation. In the end I called Vista Tours.

That conversation didn't quite go as anticipated:

"I'm calling you about a Hop-on-a-Bus trip I booked over a month ago. We haven't received our tickets yet and it's only a couple of weeks till we travel from London for Rijeka …"

"We don't have any London to Rijeka service."

"But I booked it. It was advertised several months ago in *The Observer* and I booked it …"

"We don't run that route any more."

"But I've paid for it. I sent you a cheque and I'm still waiting for my tickets."

"Ah, I understand … you're the one who's paid?"

Her 'the one' was not encouraging, it felt unnerving to the point of being ominous.

"Yes, paid, booked all my accommodation in Yugoslavia … just waiting for my tickets …"

"Just a moment …"

I had a few minutes to reflect on my little white lie … we had nothing booked in Yugoslavia. My assertion to the contrary was a sort of insurance policy against being fobbed off with some alternative destination.

The voice returned.

"Okay, I've checked your booking and because you have paid we will get you to Rijeka though, as I said, we no longer have a coach service to Rijeka. What we can offer you is …"

I was becoming agitated and, in my best, 'don't-mess-with-me' voice, persevered with my little white lie.

"Everything is booked in Rijeka and other places and …"

"Don't worry, we'll get you to Rijeka but just not by coach. We can fly you with Britannia Airways from Luton to Milan and you'll travel from Milan to Rijeka by coach. There will be no extra charge and the dates will remain the same. Are you happy with that?"

Of course we were happy. There was no contest when you came to compare a few hours in the air to Milan as opposed to a day or more in a hot and sticky coach full of hot and sticky people.

Nevertheless it was unsettling to think that Vista Tours had been aware of our booking yet had failed to tell us that they no longer operated the service to Rijeka. Did they, I wonder, think that we'd just forget that we'd booked and paid for a holiday? Did they plan to tell us or did they hope that we'd just not bother to enquire further?

These were questions that I planned to follow up on when we returned but, in the end, other events became more of a priority.

—

We arrived in Milan and transferred to a coach for the onward journey to Rijeka. It was dark when we reached Lido di Jesolo on the Italian coast just north of Venice, though at the time neither of us had any idea where we were. Here we had an extended food and watering break before continuing through the night to Trieste and into Yugoslavia, the part now known as Slovenia, and on to Rijeka, now part of Croatia.

We arrived in Rijeka early in the morning and, not being part of the official party, were deposited in the town centre while our fellow passengers continued on to their hotel. They were the tourists, we were the travellers; we would make our own craic.

We spent the day hiding from Rijeka's sun before catching the afternoon ferry to our final destination, the island of Rab, where we intended to spend the next month.

We landed on Rab at the island's main port, also called Rab, around nine in the evening and began looking for hotel accommodation for that first night. The place was buzzing; even in the evening it was wonderfully hot and all the bars seemed to be overflowing with visitors.

The receptionist at the first hotel we tried, just shook her head, shrugged her shoulders and showered us with pessimism:

"We have nothing, and I don't think you'll find anything for tonight, anywhere in Rab."

We spoke in German as it was clear that German travellers had long since discovered that Yugoslavia was a good place to holiday, not least because it was a short overland journey and cheap. All signs and notices directed at visitors were in Serbo-Croat and German, sometimes Italian too. Few spoke or understood any English. The notion that English was to be everybody's second language may have been *de rigueur* in some countries but it had not yet reached Yugoslavia in the late '60s.

We continued to haul our bags round every hotel in the town and in every one we heard the same mantra: there was not a bed to be had that night in Rab.

It was gone eleven and we were back where we started, standing outside the first hotel we had tried. I glanced in and noticed that the receptionist had changed since our first visit; nothing ventured, nothing gained, I decided to try again.

A man in his mid-40s was now in charge of the front desk but, predictably, he shook his head, much as his predecessor had done though in a more charitable way; there was still no room at the inn, nor likely to be. As we turned to walk out and search for the nearest bench, he too went for the 'nothing ventured, nothing gained' option and, almost apologetically, flew a kite …

"You could stay at my house out of town, I've a room you can rent."

The good news was quickly followed by the bad news.

"But I can't take you there until tomorrow morning, I'm on duty here all night and can't leave."

The relief that momentarily had lightened our load, changed once more to despair for, while this was a promising offer and what we were looking for in the long term, it didn't solve our immediate problem. I asked him what time he finished his shift and then came up with my second 'nothing ventured, nothing gained' suggestion of the evening. Time, I thought, for a bit of blackmail.

"Okay … we'll come home with you tomorrow morning as long as tonight we can sleep here in the lounge on those couches," I said pointing to the large vacant space behind me.

He hesitated but became visibly more enthusiastic and deferential when I added that we were planning on staying on in Rab for at least four weeks, maybe longer. He was clearly warming to my proposal but insisted that, before we could commandeer a couple of the couches, he hid our bags in a storeroom so that we looked less like the homeless and more like a couple of guests who had over-indulged and fallen asleep before getting back to their room.

It's hard to sleep discretely; it's hard to look as though you're not sleeping when that's really all you want to do. Still, it cost nothing and we did have a roof over our heads; the latter particularly fortuitous as there was a heavy thunderstorm in the wee small hours.

Just after seven in the morning, with the smell of fresh rain still in the air, we left the hotel with Mirko to follow him home. Once clear of the town, we started to climb gently along a narrow, well-worn track past the occasional farmstead and through a canopy of olive trees until we reached Mirko's family home, a modest, white, two-storey farmhouse surrounded by land actively worked to supply the family with food.

It was only then that Mirko broke the news to his wife, Vesna, and their three children that, for the next month or so, they might be sharing this paradise with two *engleski*. While we sampled our first ever cup of *turska* (Turkish coffee that you could almost walk across), Vesna disappeared for a few moments—I suspected she was evicting one or two of the children out of what became 'our' room— then called us upstairs. The room was not large, but adequate, but best of all it led out onto a covered veranda as large as the room itself.

The view across the trees towards the town and the sea beyond was stunning, as was the price we agreed, the equivalent of £1 a night which included breakfast.

I am not a beach person; at least not these days anyway. I find all that sitting in the sun boring to the point of tediousness, nor am I all that keen on getting sand in every orifice. Also, given what had happened to me a few years before at Shiteplace, I didn't fancy my chances of surviving too much in the wall-to-wall, unrelenting Rab sun.

Or maybe, in the modern parlance, County Clare had the wrong kind of sun back then.

The nearest I have ever come to enjoying such a scenario was on Rab. It was a 20-minute walk to the nearest sea, to a cove where the beach was pebbly rather than sandy and where the sea itself was a deep azure. I almost learnt to swim here.

Despite two years of lessons in two different schools, I never learned to swim in the conventional sense; I did eventually learn to move in the water and invented my own version of the breast stroke as I crawled through the water like an italicised slash ($/$), at roughly an angle of 45°.

Alex taught me this in the Adriatic at Rab where the salt content helped keep me more buoyant. Perhaps I milked these lessons for I found her supportive, cupped hand on my groin made the learning experience more pleasurable than it might otherwise have been. Without that cupped hand, and in a life-and-death situation in anywhere other than the Adriatic, I suspect that my 'swimming' would not be of much use.

Nor have I ever been able to float; as soon as my legs come up towards the horizontal, my head goes down in the opposite direction. If I could have perfected this I might have been good at synchronised swimming as long as I could have gone round and round like a Ferris wheel all the time. There was a time when I thought I was just panicking but have since discovered that there are metabolic reasons why some people are unable to float.

It's always satisfying to find a rare medical complication to explain why you are unable to do something that everyone else can.

Apart from the swimming lessons and trying to find a comfortable way to sit or lie on a pebbly beach, we would go for walks into the mountains that ran along Rab's spine and dropped away dramatically to the sea on the uninhabited side of the island that looked towards the mainland. Mirko and Vesna's oldest son, Davor, was usually our guide; on the many times we felt completely lost and disorientated, 13-year-old Davor would always know the way home.

Every morning we were woken by the light of the rising sun and had breakfast on the veranda, usually *turska*, bread and a boiled egg wrapped tightly in a paper napkin, the top third left uncovered. This was Vesna's answer to the egg-cup, a device not yet a recognised kitchen utensil on Rab nor, as I later discovered, in many parts of southern Europe.

The kitchen of Mirko and Vesna's home where, increasingly, we would eat with the family, was a strange amalgam of the old and the

CHASING THE CRAIC

new. It was traditional in terms of its utensils and work surfaces but there was also a place for the latest gadget. These were all piled up, one on top of the other, with dodgy cables and wires hanging all over the place: there was a toaster on top of a television, on top of a fridge and another, smaller fridge supporting a radio on which there was a mixer and an iron.

The meal of the day was often *cevapcici*, a round sausage-like mix of ground pork, beef, lamb, garlic and herbs; but when Mirko and Vesna really wanted to impress friends and family, out came the bacon. Alex hated this and pretended to eat it while in reality she slipped it to me. It wasn't that she didn't like bacon, it was just that she didn't like *raw* bacon. Actually I wasn't a great fan myself but didn't want to offend.

All good things come to an end, except that ours reached that point a few days sooner than planned as we were running out of money. We knew that the Vista Tours flights flew to and from Milan only twice a week so we let them know that we'd be catching an earlier coach from Rijeka and an earlier flight from Milan.

That was the easy bit, the hard part was saying our goodbyes to our adopted Yugoslavian family. The large open-air gathering in our honour was both touching and inebriating; the climax of which was when, to almost everybody's approbation, they brought out the bacon.

We promised we'd return … and we did.

Crossing back to Rijeka and catching the coach there was straightforward but the tour company's representative was not at all happy that we had turned up three days early. She cheered us up further by suggesting that we might not be able to fly back to Luton except on the Tuesday flight, the one we were scheduled to fly on.

What happened thereafter at Milan Airport has always puzzled me.

The Vista Tours representative had been right—at the check-in desk we were told we couldn't fly. We watched as all those with whom we'd shared body odours and toilet breaks on the coach from

Rijeka checked in and filed through into the departure area. I tried again, and again, to get us on the flight but the guy behind the desk would have none of it.

When I noticed there was a different member of staff now manning the check-in desk, reprising my 'nothing ventured, nothing gained' shenanigans at the hotel in Rab seemed like a good idea. But this woman was not for turning and she sent me away with a flea in my ear. I suspect her colleague had already warned her about the persistent Irishman and his smooth-tongued ways.

I started accosting anyone and everyone who looked as though they might have some official standing at the airport. Finally, I gave up and instead directed my energies to trying to work out how we might survive in Milan from Saturday to Tuesday completely broke.

We were sitting, tired and despondent, in a near empty airport lounge when he approached us.

He was not anyone I had already spoken to with our sob story, nor anyone I'd ever seen before.

He was wearing a uniform which I took to be that of a pilot or first officer. Definitely neither cabin crew nor police.

He established that we were the couple who wanted to return to Luton.

He told us to remove all the labels from our baggage that indicated we were part of the Vista Tours party.

He asked us to follow him but not to talk to anyone, or respond to anyone except him.

Unquestioning, though bewildered, we followed the letter of his law and, three hours later, landed at Luton.

Whoever he was, I was eternally grateful to him for, the next day, I unexpectedly found myself on another flight. I was returning to Belfast to tell my dying father about our adventures in Yugoslavia.

He died the following Tuesday, the same day as we were scheduled to return.

Neither fate nor divine intervention, just the way things turned out.

GIVE US A BRAKE

The next spring we bought an old, three-geared, column-change, Bedford CA van with windows down each side. Four of us bought it, two couples and I converted it into a space where we could eat and where two could sleep. We also bought a tent for whichever couple wasn't sleeping in the van.

Jennie worked with Alex; Simon was her boyfriend. We were going to drive to Yugoslavia. The lure of the bacon was just too much for Alex.

Being Physical Education teachers, Alex and Jennie had occasional weekend access to their school's swimming pool and it is here that I decided it would be prudent to hone my swimming skills before returning to Yugoslavia.

I reckoned I could maybe swim a length in the unique style I'd perfected in Rab and set off from the middle of the shallow end. Big mistake.

By the time I had 'swum' two-thirds of a length I was flagging and wasn't sure if I could make it to the wall at the far end. It was then that I realised that, being in the middle of the pool, I was equidistant from three sides: left, right and straight ahead; Nor had it escaped me that I was now in the deep end, somewhere I'd never been before.

Alex told me later that she could see that I had suddenly understood the error of my ways and was already preparing to put her life-saving course to practical use. With great difficulty I struggled on, every stroke propelling me forward less that the one before. Finally I hauled myself onto *terra firma* utterly exhausted and very relieved.

Super-swimmer Simon asked me if I was okay; he said he thought he'd seen a look of panic on my face. I reassured him I was fine and that it was a long time since I'd last swum a length. The reality was that I had never swum a length; it was not only the first time but also the last.

I just hoped he wasn't the sort who'd want to frolic in the Adriatic doing boy-man things like snorkelling or diving off rocks or, worse still, splashing. That was most definitely my idea of hell. Walking in the shallows twixt land and breaking wave was—and would continue to be—good enough for me.

———

The van was ready; the last act was buying the breakdown insurance for Europe.

In late July, three demob-happy teachers, and super-swimmer Simon, set off on their adventure of a lifetime. It was an adventure of sorts; just not quite as planned.

We took it in turns to drive and generally we kept to a strict rota. The van behaved itself and attracted many strange looks when on the move and even closer scrutiny when parked; this particular, snub-nosed model was not a common sight in mainland Europe.

We crossed the Alps, passed through the north-east corner of Italy, entered Yugoslavia and drove south to Rijeka.

We caught the ferry to Rab and fulfilled our promise to Mirko, Vesna and family and had a wonderful reunion evening with them all. Alex and I had omitted to tell Jennie and Simon about the highlight of the local cuisine … the raw bacon.

We spent a couple of days on Rab before recrossing to the mainland, to the much closer port of Jablanac, to head further south. We knew we would not get as far as Dubrovnik. Split was our more modest goal. But we never got there.

We had spent the afternoon in Zadar and were continuing south down the Adriatic Highway to a campsite near Vodice. I was driving and, when we pulled into the campsite, I noticed that the brakes had become very spongy; I just about managed to stop at the camp office and again at our allocated pitch.

We did all the usual things like kick the tyres and check the brake fluid; the latter we topped up before heading into Vodice to eat. The brakes seemed a little better but, when we were on our way down to the seafront from the coast road, to where the road ended at a line of parked cars right at the edge of the sea, the brakes failed completely. It was all I could do, using the hand-brake and the gears, to bring the van to a stop before we hit the low sea wall.

Later we returned to the campsite, slowly but safely, and the next morning we called in at a mechanic's workshop we'd spotted the night before. The diagnosis was as quick as it was straightforward; all the master cylinders inside the brake drums needed replacing, the seals had stopped sealing. That was the good news, the bad news was that there was no chance that these would be available for this vehicle in Yugoslavia.

Nevertheless, he did try unsuccessfully to fit seals from other vehicles. When he'd given up, he put everything back together, topped up the brake fluid and said if we could find the master cylinders he would fit them.

It was while this was going on that a battered Morris Minor pulled in with brake problems too. Its occupants, two French girls, knew all they needed was brake fluid.

I overheard their conversation with the mechanic and later checked with them that I'd heard right. I had.

When their brakes went a bit spongy and they realised the brake fluid level was low, they did what any self-respecting French mademoiselle would have done and topped it up with red wine.

"It was the same colour … and look, we are here," they giggled, "so it must work. Only more expensive that the right stuff, I think."

For years I carried a bottle of Rioja in the boot … just in case.

We returned to the campsite to consider our options over a glass or two of brake fluid.

It took several days to source the master cylinders through our UK breakdown cover but eventually the good news was that they were en route from Amsterdam to Zagreb and then on to Zadar, our nearest airport. We had to make phone contact regularly to track progress until finally we were told they would arrive the following day at Zadar. If nothing else, I was perfecting the now-defunct art of shouting down public phone-lines while manipulating a handful of coins.

The next morning we crawled north again, hoping that we were nearing the beginning of the end of the brake saga. We were in fact at the beginning of the beginning.

When we checked at Zadar Airport, the bad news was that we had been misinformed and that our package was still in Zagreb, the good news was that it would arrive the following morning. Vodice, and our tent, were 40 miles away, 40 very slow miles away and, for me—the only one prepared to drive without the aid of brakes—an exhausting hour and a half of trying not to get into situations where I might have to stop quickly.

We therefore decided not to return to Vodice that night but to find bed & breakfast accommodation somewhere close to Zadar. Earlier in the day there seemed to be no shortage of kids standing by the roadside with their makeshift signs which always emblazoned with a single word *Zimmer*, German for 'room'. At the time it was assumed that all those travelling this route would be Germans which was, of course, generally true.

On a straight bit of road we passed two boys holding their sign, only problem was that when we eventually stopped it was 100 yards beyond them. Nevertheless they guessed we were potential customers and legged it along after us, waving and shouting frantically lest we drive away.

In unison they nodded excitedly to confirm that they had two rooms. The younger one was about nine and, clearly unaware of the niceties of sibling hierarchy, was already climbing on board when he got a slap on the head from his older brother and, still protesting, was despatched to run across the fields and tell the family there would be hosting four *engleski* that night. I always suspected that the younger one had another mission, to make sure that there were indeed *two* rooms available by the time we arrived there. It was more than likely that at least two of us would be sleeping where the boys normally slept.

The older brother, almost bursting with excitement, jumped into the front passenger seat, touched and tapped everything like he would a new toy, and told us to drive straight ahead and take the first right towards the sea. Before doing his bidding, I dragged some more detailed directions out of him in case I had to make any sudden turns that might normally involve using the brakes. But most importantly, I tried to get a handle on whether or not their house was on a hill.

We four were the first *engleski* that the family had ever met. Now, it seemed, was not the right time to be pedantic and explain to them that not everyone who speaks English, *is* English.

That said, being '*engleski*' was definitely an advantage, it was almost as if the Beatles had dropped in to say hello. It was party time.

We were going to eat *alfresco* on the large veranda adjoining the house. All attempts at lending a hand with the preparations were shunned, the guests of honour were not allowed to lift a finger. I was expecting a small family gathering, just the eight of us enjoying the warmth of the evening and trying to make sense of communicating in Serbo-Croat, German and possibly some English.

But it was not to be as simple as that; the first clue was the way in which the table just got longer and longer. In the end there was seating for over 20 people though not enough chairs; no problem, word had got out and some people brought their own.

Those who weren't actually on the official invitation list, began to gather on the road outside the house, presumably to confirm our relative normality and to be able to tell their friends that they had actually seen us even if they weren't able to work out which one was Ringo.

The family, friends and neighbours who were invited got to rub shoulders with us and share a table with the *engleski*, a table where the food was as varied as it was endless, the wine was limitless, the liqueurs were exquisite and the spirits literally breathtaking. And the bacon was, well, raw.

We were the undisputed centre of attention and anyone who had even a few words of English would try and engage us in verb-less conversation just to demonstrate their linguistic prowess. One young man insisted on calling out just one word like 'pencil' and then wait for one of us to verify that it was indeed an English word; he would then clap himself and bask in the delight and approbation of others. The game went on and on until he ran out of words. When he started to repeat himself and a few looks from others signalled the end of this particular interlude.

It was an evening of almost unimaginable generosity, bonhomie and laughter; an evening to savour, to relish and to recognise the essential humanity in others.

It was gone midnight when, sated and exhausted, we dropped into our respective bedrooms either side of the front door. I didn't sleep for a little while as my mind relived the events of the evening; it was an experience I never forgot.

It seemed that I had been asleep for only minutes when the cockerel started proclaiming the dawning of a new day from just outside the shuttered window. It went on, and on and on until, one by one, we all got up and joined it outside while shielding our hangovers from the early morning sun. All evidence of the previous evening's banquet had gone. All that remained was the original, normal-sized table and a scattering of chairs awaiting our pleasure. Breakfast was a coffee liqueur, the local equivalent of 'hair of the dog'.

We had time to kill before the Zagreb flight landed at Zadar so I drove up to the main road, pulled over and eventually stopped; time for another doze in a cockerel-free zone.

$$\Sigma$$

At Zadar, after having confirmed that our package had arrived, we were ushered into a small office where there were two uniformed customs officials—one male sitting, one female standing—and on the desk for all to see was our consignment of master cylinders, still neatly packaged and festooned with labels that told of its unique journey across Europe

The male officer was in charge and scrutinised the paperwork several times before speaking. He made no concessions to our lack of Serbo-Croat and his apparent lack of German and so his female colleague was delegated to act as interpreter. He was asking if I had brought the old cylinders with me and quickly got the gist of my reply when I shook my head and answered with a single word from my extensive Serbo-Croat repertoire, "*Ne*". He said that he could only release the package when he had seen and examined the original cylinders.

As I was the only one who understood what was happening, I had to translate for Alex, Jennie and Simon which also served to clarify the expletives that had somehow slipped out of my mouth.

I then explained to the officer how ludicrous this was. I spelt it out in words of one syllable: we had just driven here in the vehicle which had the defective cylinders so how, I wondered, would we be able to give him the old ones? As far as I could tell, his translator did not translate my sarcasm.

He shrugged his shoulders adamantly; he would not release the package without having the old cylinders in their stead. After all, we could be international smugglers, couldn't we? I never quite understood how his warped mind saw brake cylinders for an ageing Bedford van as potential contraband. He could have opened the package and had a look himself to make sure there were no drugs in them.

There then followed an animated argument between the two officers. You didn't have to understand Serbo-Croat to know that the woman saw the logic of our position and was speaking on our behalf; I heard her use the word *pedantan* but being called 'pedantic' didn't shift her colleague's position one inch. He was determined to stick to his rules. This was a man with a negative-reading on my craic-ometer

To emphasise the point he pulled the package towards him like a child claiming his toys while continuing to argue the finer points with his more reasonable colleague. Their collective raised voices came to an abrupt halt when I put my hand in my pocket, took out my passport and threw it on the desk.

"So?" he said, probably assuming I was playing the 'but I'm British' card.

In German, I spelt it out slowly and deliberately and with more than a touch of disdain. I also mimed what I was saying in the hope that his sight was better than his hearing.

"I give you my passport; you give me the package. I go and get the cylinders changed. I return with the old ones. You give me my passport. We go home. Okay?"

For the first time it was clear that he understood more German that he had previously let on and was about to bluster further until he was stopped in his tracks by his colleague who had clearly had enough of his officious antics and decided to accept the deal on his behalf.

All the paperwork completed, we left Zadar Airport with three passports and a box of brake cylinders.

We had already decided not to return to the mechanic at Vodice and on our way into Zadar earlier that day had booked in with a repair shop on the outskirts of the town.

—

Being curious by nature about how things are done—lest I should have to do them myself one day—I invited myself behind the scenes and into the workshop to watch the procedure. I wasn't snooping on the mechanic because he was clearly an apprentice, I was genuinely curious and it was important that I kept an eye on what happened to the old cylinders.

He had no problem with the front cylinders and had everything replaced quite quickly but, even though I had already told him that we needed to keep the old cylinders, I still had to retrieve them from the trash which gave me the opportunity to add some discarded oil and grease to them for my friend back at the airport.

The back brake-drums proved more problematic; he couldn't get the brake-shoes to bed in properly. He tried everything, even took a hammer to them before he decided they were just too large. But he knew exactly how to remedy that.

With me as his constant shadow, he walked to a corner of the workshop where there was a vice, put the first shoe in the vice and rummaged around till he found a hacksaw. It was when I realised he was going to cut a bit off the shoe that I stepped in with a single word … but lots of them.

"*Ne, ne, ne, ne, ne, ne, ne* …"

I didn't know what the problem was but I did know that the brake-shoe in question had been an integral part of the van's braking system for many years and had always functioned normally; lopping a bit off it was clearly not the answer.

Pointedly I intervened and rescued the shoe from the jaws of the vice and the blade of the saw and was returning it to the van when I had a flash of inspiration, something I'd seen the mechanic in Vodice do. I opened the passenger door and pointed to the hand-brake and then pointed underneath the vehicle in a questioning manner. The gist of my charades-inspired question to the mechanic was "Is the hand-brake off and its cable disconnected?"

It wasn't; and when he did release it and disconnect its cable, all the remaining shoes dropped into place perfectly. The job done he smiled at me, shook my hand and was clearly proud of his handiwork.

Soon we were on the road back to Zadar Airport to formally dump a box of dirty, oily, used brake master cylinders on the desk of a pedantic, unaccommodating customs official ... and to reclaim my passport. The transaction was completed in almost total silence though I did manage to throw in an unseen wink at his fellow officer. Unseen by Alex, that is.

Starting and stopping with confidence, we made it back to Britain, having once again crossed the Alps without incident. Back home, we sold our converted Bedford van and its 'as new' master cylinders as had always been the plan.

A SCHOOL TRIP

It was the Easter holidays and Alex and I were en route to Holyhead in Anglesey by car to catch the ferry to Dun Laoghaire. Apart from wanting to spend some time with my cousin Pat, there were two other motives behind the trip.

I was the Deputy Headteacher at a primary school near leafy Ascot in Berkshire and a month earlier had had the audacity to call out the school's Headteacher for corruption and conspiracy involving two children and recent tests that would decide which school they would move on to. In other words I was under a lot of pressure and needed a break. (The full story of these events can be found in *Heads will Roll: corruption, conspiracy and confrontation in an English Primary School*.)

Also, at the end of May Alex and I would be bringing a party of 30 boys and girls (my class) on a school trip to nearby Bray in County Wicklow. This would be their first great adventure without parental scrutiny and we had come here to prepare ourselves for and rehearse how we would share with them this part of Ireland that I knew so well. Unknown to the tour company which oversaw the organisation of such trips with 'set-piece' outings and excursions, I had plans to change some of their traditional itineraries.

Seven weeks later, and a few days after I'd decided to liven things up at school by tendering not only my resignation, but also of all the staff, parents and children were assembling in the car park. The air was buzzing with excitement as 30 children bound for Ireland climbed aboard their coach.

Two children stood out. There was Brenda, beaming from ear to ear, who wouldn't have been there at all had it not been for the generosity and initiative of her classmates. Her parents hadn't been able to keep up with the weekly payments and had withdrawn Brenda from the trip at the last moment. Step forward two of her friends, Jane and Susan, who put a simple proposition to me. They offered to organise a sponsored swim in the school pool to raise the money required to make sure that Brenda would not be left behind. These two organised everything and raised enough money to make sure that their friend joined them on their Irish adventure.

Then there was Chris who was in tears before the coach left the car-park. He wanted his mum. I spent the first five minutes of our journey to the Welsh coast consoling him and reassuring him that he'd see his mum in a week and that in the meantime he'd have the time of his life. Thanks to the many kindnesses his classmates showed him, Chris did have a wonderful time and only started to cry again when the coach turned back into the village a week later.

In April I had bought 30 postcards and stamps and the week *before* we left Ascot everyone wrote a secret postcard home saying that they had arrived safely and were having a great time. I knew they would be too excited to write home when they did actually arrive in Ireland, so the first thing I did on setting foot on Irish soil was to post all 30 cards.

We stayed in a small hotel in Bray owned by a local bookmaker and had three days when we had a coach at our disposal. Each day when the driver turned up all set to head off on a routine jaunt round a selection of the more boring sightseeing delights of the area, boring for children that is, I presented him with an alternative itinerary. Luckily we a had a driver who was amenable to doing something new.

Brenda, Chris and their classmates spent an unforgettable day at Brittas Bay. As we all ate out packed lunches I told them of *my* childhood in this place, how I learned to drive, how I never learned to swim and how I watched the hotel on the distant cliff burn down.

On another day we headed for the Sugar Loaf mountain and

climbed it, just as Alex and I had done in April to check the route and whether it was a feasible climb for 30 boys and girls. It was.

On another day we walked along the East Pier at Dun Laoghaire, had an ice-cream at Teddy's and caught the local train, the Dart, to Glenageary Station from where we walked to Pat's house and spent the afternoon drinking orange juice and snacking in her back garden.

Yes, I knew I was on a trip down Memory Lane but I wanted this group of kids, the best class I ever taught, to understand some of the people and places that were important to me. I knew I had had unique childhood experiences in all these places and I relished the opportunity to share some of experience and knowledge.

Of course at the time they didn't know how I was embroiled in a fight for the future and integrity of their school, a fight, incidentally, which, even though there were many dark, frustrating days ahead, my colleagues and I went on to win (see *Heads will roll*).

I saved the best for last as I persuaded our driver to cut back on the trip around an adult's idea of the sights of Dublin and make time instead for a visit to St Michan's Church to shake hands with the mummified remains of a long-dead crusader. A bit of medieval craic.

The children knew what to expect for I had explained everything to them at school. They knew there was nothing to be frightened of and they knew the science of how the rarefied atmosphere of the vaults had preserved the bodies. They knew there was nothing 'spooky' in the sense that anything was going to happen to them down there. Nothing or nobody was going to jump out of a cupboard. And there was the bonus of shaking an old, leathery hand.

Everyone was both excited and a little apprehensive as the guide took us through it all once again and reinforced what they already knew—that the bodies were dead, stone dead, and that their skin hadn't decayed as you would normally expect.

Only two children weren't sure they wanted to descend into the St Michan's vault: Brenda and Archie.

Archie was the son of a local millionaire who flaunted his father's new wealth as if it gave him rights over and above those of his classmates. Archie was already on the lower rungs of becoming a stereotypical bully and his circle of friends was already dwindling.

Thus far nothing had gone right for poor Archie in Ireland. First of all there was the bed-making issue. Everyone, even the adults, was expected to make their own beds but only Archie saw it as an onerous task. His reasoning was straightforward—he had a maid at home who made his bed and so it was outside his experience. Sooner than he could ever have anticipated, and despite some initial reticence, Archie learnt how to make his own bed.

And then there was the pocket money saga. Each child was allowed a fixed amount of pocket money which was doled out every morning; it was an exercise in managing money and worked for everyone except Archie. Someone in Archie's family had packed sock-loads of additional cash and, as it was not for sharing, word soon got around and it was confiscated. Archie wasn't best pleased.

And here we all were at St Michan's poised to descend into the unknown. Brenda was unsure but otherwise was having a wonderful time and her friends soon cajoled her into accompanying them down into the vaults to shake hands with the stone cold, dead crusader.

The only one who could not be persuaded was Archie and any respect his classmates had for him dissipated that day. And Archie knew it. By exposing himself as fearful of the dead crusaders *and* the fact that all the girls had gone down, Archie had put paid to any potential career he might have aspired to as a fully-fledged bully.

I have no way of knowing if my self-indulgent trip to Ireland had any lasting memories for my charges. All I hoped for was that they would have been touched by the allure of new horizons and of travelling outside their comfort zones and without their parents.

Later when I tried to ascertain what memory they cherished most, it was the wild, empty expanse of Brittas Bay than won hands down, at the time it was over three miles of golden sand that only locals and travellers knew about. Years later it was discovered by tourists.

THE CHAMPION OF THE WORLD

I first read Roald Dahl's collection of short stories, *Kiss Kiss*, in the 1960s. I recall being particularly drawn to one story, *Genesis and catastrophe: A true story*, set in late 19th-century Austria. I won't elaborate on the story, if you have read it, you will understand why. Another story from the same collection that intrigued me was *The champion of the world*.

It was as a young teacher that I first came across Dahl's children's books and frequently read the likes of *Charlie and the Chocolate Factory* and *Fantastic Mr Fox* to my classes. For those who don't know Dahl's writing, he was, for three decades or more, the most prestigious, respected and prolific writer of books for children. He is the only writer to have four titles included in the top 100 in Britain and America. Nevertheless that did not exclude him from becoming a target of the pernicious promoters of Cancel Culture in recent years.

The publication of *Danny the champion of the world* coincided with my first couple of years as Headteacher of a small, two-teacher school in rural Wiltshire.

As I was reading *Danny*, before I re-read it to my class, I realised that I was the Headteacher of the sort of school, both in its size and its location, as the school and community featured in the book. There was even a petrol station round the corner from my school. The only major difference, and here I must defer to an element of bias, was that the Head of Danny's school, Mr Snoddy, was an amiable drunk.

The gist of the story has local beer magnate and landowner,

Victor Hazell and his disdain for locals on one side and Danny and his garage-owning father and occasional poacher on the other. Danny and his father plan to scupper Hazell's upcoming pheasant shoot by surreptitiously and humanely 'capturing' the pheasants before the fateful day. With this goal in mind, Danny and his father come up with three different methods of temporarily incapacitating the local pheasant population: the horse-hair stopper, the sticky hat and the sleeping beauty.

The focus of the book is on which one of these they choose and what happened next.

What Roald Dahl did not know, until I first made contact with him, was that the fictional community which he had created in *Danny*, had its likeness in the real world. Of course this likeness did not apply to every aspect of life in and around my school— apart from the fact that the Head was not an 'amiable drunk', for example, the local landowner was definitely neither a bully nor a scoundrel—but there were, I surmised, enough similarities to rouse Dahl's curiosity.

I knew that Dahl was scheduled to talk at a Bristol venue because I was attending the event. I also knew that he lived in Great Missenden in Buckinghamshire, north-west of London. As getting from Great Missenden to Bristol by public transport would not be easy, I guessed he would probably drive. One of the two possible routes he might take, albeit the less likely, would literally pass the the front of the school. Perhaps I could persuade him to return home via the scenic route and to drop in as he passed by?

My letter to Roald Dahl said all of the above and more. I mentioned that pheasant poaching was not unknown locally and that those in my class who kept chickens, had tried, as Danny had done, all the methods detailed in the book to subdue an unsuspecting pheasant. I deliberately didn't elaborate on the outcome of these experiments.

I told him how, every few weeks, we held a whist drive at the school to raise money and how, the evening before the event, I would always find a brace of pheasants hanging in the porch of the

School House. This regular donation, as one of the whist drive prizes, was both popular and anonymous. Although I asked no questions, I did have my suspicions as to their origin,.

I told him how *Danny the champion of the World* was the school's favourite book and how the children had turned their classroom into what was essentially a shrine to *Danny* and every aspect of the story. It touched a nerve in that they recognised so many elements of their own lives and the small community into which they were born.

I received a reply from Roald Dahl in which he said he would be pleased to visit the school, suggested I send him directions from Bristol and that we should have a chat to finalise details at the end of his talk there.

His talk over, I joined the queue of book-clutching teachers to have their copy signed. I kept having to let latecomers (probably those who rushed out to buy a book) 'jump' the queue as I needed to be the last in line. As my hands were book-free I got some very strange looks, as if I had somehow joined the wrong queue and was expecting a bowl of soup when I reached the end. Clearly I didn't need him to sign a book, I would have him all to myself the next day.

Supping our soup, Roald Dahl and I finalised details and agreed that he would arrive mid-morning and stay as long he wanted. He was as good as his word.

Dahl's BMW swung into the school's driveway at around 10:30. Two people got out and, although I knew that, at the time, he was married to American actress Patrica Neal, I could tell that his companion was more than just the 'secretary' he introduced her as. Less than a decade later she was to become his second wife, Felicity Dahl.

Before he even came in contact with the children, he was clearly taken with, and marvelled at, all the displays and artwork which his book had generated. He didn't give them a chance to be in awe of his presence as he began by praising them for everything they had created and then just started talking to them, not in a 'teacherly' way but rather in a friendly and unassuming manner, about Danny and his exploits.

He asked them about the three methods that Danny and his father had come up with for confusing the pheasants into surrender.

There was the 'horse hair stopper' which relied on them eating a raisin which had a short piece of horse hair pushed through the middle with the aim of 'tickling' the pheasant into submission.

Number two was the 'sticky hat' which was an upended cone of paper with a raisin at the bottom and glue on the sides which would disorientate the birds when they couldn't shake it off.

And finally, the one that did the trick, the 'sleeping beauty' which was a soaked raisin with some of Danny's father painkiller medicine sealed inside.

Roald Dahl conceded that all three were inventions and wouldn't work, something that the children already knew from their backyard experiments with the family chickens.

He told them that how, if you were driving and hit a pheasant and killed it, it was against the law to take it home for the pot. But it was legal for any car-owner who came across a bird already dead on the roadside to take it home.

He went on to given them some advice by explaining that, if their dad killed a pheasant on the road and was just about to put it into the car's boot when a policeman arrived, then he should point up ahead and explain that it was the car in front that killed the bird.

Ethically dubious but probably something all the local adults already knew. Even if I didn't.

He had the knack of extracting what might have been otherwise seen as personal information from the children about the various things their families got up to in pursuit of the humble pheasant.

Freddie explained that his much older brother, who now lived away, sometimes brought a pheasant home for his girlfriend. Dahl, picturing the blissful domestic scene, innocently asked if the two of them enjoyed their meal.

"Three," was the reply nobody was expecting, particularly the school caretaker, the fount of all local knowledge, who was also in the room.

"Three," he continued, "there's also the baby, Jimmy. He likes pheasant too."

The intake of breath from the caretaker was audible as I exchanged a glance with Felicity. It was clear that, until that moment, nobody knew anything about this family's little secret. Only Roald Dahl never batted an eyelid.

Another hand shot up, another story shared.

"My brother … he catches pheasants in the woods," was Paul's contribution as he pointed to the woods just across the road.

"And which method does he use? Does he use … raisins?" Dahl asked tentatively.

"No, he just stands behind a tree and bonks them over the head when they walk past," was the honest, if slightly disturbing, reply.

Eager to find out more about the local cuisine, Dahl continued.

"And how does he cook them?" he asked.

"He don't cook them," Paul replied, "he just cuts them up and feeds them to his ferrets." And, as if in anticipation of Dahl's next question, he continued.

"He keeps the ferrets to catch rabbits. We prefer rabbit to pheasant." was Paul's matter-of-fact response, almost as if it should have been obvious that you fed pheasant to your ferrets in order to eat rabbit.

In some circles pheasant is the delicacy, in others clearly it is the rabbit at the top of the culinary food chain.

Actually, come to think of it, I think I prefer rabbit to pheasant.

Dahl was clearly enjoying himself, particularly when he asked the children whether their Head was like Mr Snoddy in the book and was rewarded with a resounding 'no'… and a lone 'yes'. Little bugger, I thought as I focussed my gaze on the class prankster.

With all questions and answers exhausted, he spent the rest of his time signing all the children's copies of all his books which, in some cases, was more than an armful.

Before he left he had one more surprise for everyone as he shared with us the title and first few words of his next book. The book would be called *The enormous crocodile* and was to begin with the enormous crocodile thinking about what to have for his next meal.

"For my lunch today, what I'd like is a nice juicy little child."

Roald Dahl may not have known the word 'craic' but he certainly knew how to partake.

I stayed in touch with Roald Dahl over the next few months and he sent me a very special book, the American edition of *James and the giant peach*. It was special because it was more colourful and accessible than the then British edition. I read it to my class.

In his accompanying letter, he also said how much he enjoyed his time at my school and then brought a lump to my throat by adding:

"I wish my children had gone to your school."

Danny the champion of the world was the last Dahl book I ever read. It was as if I wanted to encapsulate the experience that day in its own little cocoon, as if nothing could ever surpass that experience, both for me, my school and its community.

Later I was to realise something else about *Danny the champion of the world* for it is the only one of Roald Dahl's children's novels that is not a fantasy, in the sense that it revolves around real people in a plausible, if sometimes unlikely, scenario.

There are no magic worlds, strangely-named people or talking animals with which I had become jaded and bored and these days never read or watch. As soon as any character appears on screen from another dimension, has phoney (clearly) psychic powers or met Moses when he was a boy, I reach for the remote.

After all, you rarely see characters from other dimensions, time-travellers and people with blue faces enjoying a bit of the craic.

Not down my way, anyway. Only real people do that.

TALES OUT OF SCHOOL

I never strayed far from my school while I was the Headteacher of the local, two-teacher school for my home was the School House. Home and school were linked by a short corridor, an arrangement not uncommon in rural schools, My daily walk to work took no more than 10 seconds.

And, with three young children with less than 27 months between them, we rarely ventured far from home.

Until I became a Headteacher, I had no idea that all schools had a Log Book wherein Heads were obliged to enter anything of note that occurred in the school, a bit like *Star Trek*'s Captain Kirk.

Down the years, the sort of event deemed noteworthy, generally related to punishments, almost all of which were inflicted on boys, and a mix of pupils excluded by the school nurse for having nits. I noted how one boy in particular seemed to spend more time at home having his hair treated than he did at school.

Earlier in the century when the local Church of England vicar visited the school he would made an entry in the Log Book to confirm his visit and that all was well. He would then sign his name.

It was easy to trace his demise by observing how his handwriting became increasingly erratic and, eventually, almost unreadable. The news of his death followed his last signature as it trailed at an acute angle off the page.

I became particularly interested in how some of the local septuagenarians, with whom I shared a pint at the local pub, behaved themselves as youngsters and discovered that some of them featured in the records of punishments. In those days, invariably the punishment meted out would be a caning across the hand.

Charlie, for example, was given the cane for being late for school and when I mentioned this heinous crime to him, he recalled, as if it were yesterday, exactly why he was late that day.

"I left home on time as usual but at the bottom of the hill I noticed that the walnuts on the tree there were ripe for picking so I stopped, found a log stick and collected a few. That's why I was late."

Others too could remember the detail of their misdemeanours.

Then there was the mystery of the stuck-together pages in the Log Book which seemed to coincide with some health issue at the school, specifically relating to the local water, and the departure of the Headmistress. I managed to prise the pages apart and found that the unhappy Head had asked for a salary increase and was summarily dismissed. Clearly she had tried to cover up her departure by recording the events in the Log as was required, but then stuck the pages together so that nobody could read about it … until I came along, that is.

I asked my septuagenarian friends if they could remember anything about these events and was initially met with a mixture of furtive and guilty looks as they collectively pondered whether or not they should come clean. As usual, it was Charlie, the king of craic, who was the first to weaken.

"You have to understand that Miss Sykes was a bit of an old dragon. She treated us like skivvies sometimes and then she asked us to fetch her water for her from the village pump. That's a fair old walk and it's uphill all the way back to school, not so easy carrying buckets of water."

The knowing looks were now trying to cover up smiles and clearly laughter was just a few sentences away.

"You see, one day we'd had enough of fetching and carrying for her. Let's just say that, when we got back to school with them buckets, there was more than water in them," he said with a wink.

They could stop themselves no longer. They all burst out laughing as the memory of peeing into the buckets flew back across the years.

This was a misdemeanour that had gone undetected and unpunished and explained the complaints Miss Sykes had made about the condition of the local water supply.

On another occasion I encountered exactly the same look from my mischievous friends when I accidentally unearthed another story relating to their extra-curricular activities, albeit now as adults.

There was a bungalow at the edge of the school grounds occupied my an amiable elderly couple, Jack and Doris. Jack was known locally for the weather statistics relating to the village which were published in the local weekly newspaper. He also wrote local-interest articles in the defunct Wiltshire dialect as a way of keeping it alive.

Jack was ailing and it wasn't long before I found myself at the door of their bungalow offering my condolences to Doris. When I mentioned his work for the local paper, Doris insisted on showing me his weather station at the back of the bungalow. It was impressive and I said so.

On the evening of Jack's funeral I was in the local pub chatting to the usual suspects and happened to mention Jack's dedication to sharing his weather statistics with the world when I saw that look again. Charlie was, as ever, the first to break.

"Weather statistics, my arse," was his thoughtful contribution.

He quickly responded to the expression on my face which indicated that I wanted to hear more ...

"Well," said Charlie,"there was many a night when we'd had a skinful here, when we'd walk up to old Jack's bungalow, sneak round the back ... and top up his rain-gauge.

"Nobody noticed that the village seemed to have higher-than-normal rainfall some weeks," he continued.

"And yellow rain, too," added one of Charlie's mates, laughing.

Out of the blue one evening Charlie asked me if I knew the story about the plane crash. When I told him I didn't, he admitted that he didn't know all the details but that I should speak to one of the local farmers, Jeff Barnes, for it all happened on his grandfather's land, maybe 60 years back.

Following a morning at Jeff's farm, I came away with the most extraordinary story. A tale of new technologies and inventions sharing the same space with unforeseen consequences.

Less than two miles west of the farm, near Upavon, was Britain's first military flight training school which opened in 1912. It was here that the British pilots were trained before participating in dog-fights with the likes of Germany's notorious 'Red Baron', Mannfred von Richthofen. DH Lawrence *aficionados* will recognise the surname as being the same as that of Frieda, Lawrence's wife, for they were indeed distant cousins.

Jeff's grandfather was all for progress and was happy for his land to be used to try out a new mechanical method of ploughing that used horse-power instead of horses. Two steam engines with a horizontal rotating pulley at either side of a field were used to pull a plough, fixed to a steel hawser, back and forth across the field. The connecting hawser was, of course under pressure so that it remained taut. As each row was ploughed the steam engines would move forward slightly and repeat the process.

Ploughing was already under way as a plane took off from Upavon and headed east, low over the fields. As it crossed the land being ploughed using the steam engines, the connecting hawser snapped and one end shot up into the air and hit the plane. The plane dropped into the field, killing the pilot.

On that day, in a remote part of Wiltshire, two new technologies collided with tragic results. The aircraft technology survived and blossomed, while the steam engines and their connecting plough were abandoned in favour of the embryonic tractor.

When I'd finished telling this story to my class, a hand shot up and Stephen told me the end of the story, the part Jeff Barnes certainly didn't know.

"My grandad was there," he said, "he saw the dead pilot and took home his seat. My gran still sits in it every night and watches telly."

My curiosity got the better of me and I agreed to visit his gran one evening to watch her watch telly sitting in the dead pilot's seat. Now, in the absence of a provenance certificate, I couldn't swear this was the actual seat, but it looked sufficiently different to every other seat I'd ever seen, that I'd say it was most likely the real thing.

Not long before I moved on to another school, I had arranged a school outing and was waiting outside for the coach to arrive. When it did, I got on board to check with the driver that he knew about the itinerary change. He had a curious expression on his face as he stared at the school before telling me that he had come here as a kid.

When he told me his name, almost instinctively my eyes shot to what was left of his hair. I would be sharing the rest of the day on a coach with the boy, now a man, who had been regularly excluded from school because of his nit problem.

As I involuntarily scratched my head, I decided not to probe any further.

A DEPUTY HEADTEACHER ON THE CUSP OF A FIRST HEADSHIP. 1971.

TROUBLED TIMES

With the arrival of three children, including twins, in just over 26 months, travelling was to become generally confined to visiting family in and around Belfast.

Before the firstborn made himself known, there was one moment of madness when, despite some ignoble disasters in the field, I still felt the need to have two wheels in my life.

In the late-60s bicycles with small wheels were all the rage and I saw this fashionable innovation as a way of enticing Alex onto two wheels ... and then suggested we go to Belfast on them. Not the whole way, you understand, but as far as the railway station in London, then from the train to the Heysham ferry, and from the ferry terminal in Belfast to Alex's family home.

Despite feeling slightly self-conscious about the lack of drop-down, racing handlebars, I enjoyed it; Alex did not.

Apart from having to cycle through London and through Belfast, Alex never forgot—nor forgave me for—the incident on the train when I got off to buy a snack on Preston platform and, from her perspective, forgot to get back on before the train pulled away from the station.

Sitting there alone on the moving train, Alex had conflicting images of herself trying to manoeuvre two bicycles between the train and ferry at Heysham and signing the divorce papers. I had in fact managed to swing myself through the moving door of the last carriage and was working my way up the train while Alex was visualising her fate at Heysham and mine should we ever meet up again. When I eventually found her and acted as if nothing had happened which, from my point of view, was indeed true. Well, shall we say she was not best pleased.

That said, she saw no conflict of interest when she tucked into the bag of crisps I'd bought her.

When we returned to England our four small wheels were sold. Other than a brief, and disastrous, flirtation with a unicycle in a friend's kitchen, a line was finally drawn under my interest in any moving vehicle with fewer than four wheels.

———

Our continuing search for the perfect four-wheeled mode of transport now had to take into account that we had one small addition to the family. Ironically, despite our camper-van experience in Yugoslavia, we decided to buy a ready-made one with functioning brakes. Like the small-wheeled bicycles, it seemed like a good idea at the time; a way of having some sort of holiday with our son and being able to go to and from Belfast while carrying all the infant paraphernalia in a miniature version of home.

In the motor-caravan conversion business in the mid-70s there was a new kid on the block to compete with Volkswagen. Toyota had introduced their HiAce and a number of companies were rushing to convert them into the perfect motor-caravan.

Just to be different, we bought one and the following week drove to Belfast in it.

It was at the height of the so-called 'Troubles', when the consensus was that it was not the best time to be driving in and around Belfast, particularly after dark … which is precisely what Alex and I found ourselves doing one evening with a small group of friends. Lest you think we had abandoned our firstborn, he was with his grandparents.

Returning from a popular eatery on the coast, we were heading for the university area, to the apartment of one of these friends. Also with us in the HiAce was Alex's young nephew, Paul, who had just arrived from America via Paris that afternoon, his mother's last words of advice ringing in his ears:

"Now don't get into any trouble over there."

Crossing the city, I was aware that I might have, in movie parlance, picked up a tail. It was just too much of a coincidence that the vehicle behind always made the same turns as I did. I couldn't make out what or who it was but I knew we'd soon find out for we were close to our destination. I saw a parking place on the left and started to pull in. Nothing prepared me for what happened next.

With the nose of the HiAce almost by the kerb, the vehicle behind shot past and hemmed us in at the front. Another—which I had not realised was behind the first—blocked us in at the back. Out of each jumped four or five heavily armed British squaddies, all but one of whom threw themselves on the ground enclosing us in a circle; half had guns pointing towards us, the other half pointed theirs outwards, towards anyone who might be daft enough to want to 'rescue' us or otherwise interfere. The one in charge, Top Squaddie, ordered us to step out. At the time no one thought of asking him to show his ID or, if they did, any such thoughts were quickly dispelled.

Top Squaddie wanted to know who owned the vehicle. I owned up to that. He wanted to check my driving licence and asked me to repeat the vehicle's registration. I did so very slowly, trying to picture it in my mind's eye; and, just in case I got it wrong, added:

"That's it ... I think ... I only bought it last week ..."

Another squaddie appeared from the vehicle at the back with a telephone handset to his ear ... I assumed he was going to check that I was who I said I was and was indeed the owner.

Top Squaddie asked where we were going; I pointed to the building outside which I was almost parked and Alex's friend Ian raised his shaking hand up to confirm that he lived there.

Squaddie Two must have had positive information about me and ownership of the vehicle for, after going into a huddle with

Squaddie One, the mood lightened. The Lesser Squaddies on the ground relaxed their grip on the asphalt as Top Squaddie started to engage me in near-normal conversation about the HiAce.

Standing at the front: "Don't think I've never seen one of these before. How big is the engine? How many miles to the gallon do you get?"

Looking in the opened side door: "How many does it sleep?"

Standing by the open back doors: "Did you do the conversion yourself? Could you fit an elevating roof?"

It felt as if we'd been pulled over, not because we looked in any way suspicious, but because Top Squaddie, clearly a motor-caravan enthusiast, wanted to bring himself up to speed with the latest developments. To be able to do so while working must have been a bonus.

With Top Squaddie's curiosity sated, he removed his trigger-finger from his weapon for the first time and shook my hand. A nod of his head was all it took for the heavily-armed, subordinate Lesser Squaddies to jump back into their armoured vehicles and speed off into the Belfast night, no doubt in search of an unsuspecting Volkswagen camper-van with which to make a quick comparison.

I completed my parking manoeuvre and followed the others into the apartment. Jet-lagged, young Paul disappeared into the bathroom and didn't reemerge for over half an hour.

He looked very pale; this was not the sort of craic he was expecting when he left America. When he finally felt able to communicate again, he made it clear to everyone that this was an incident his mother did not ever need to know about.

Still staying close to home and still driving the HiAce, and with another two simultaneous additions to the family to consider, we went on our first and last camping trip with all three.

Top Squaddie would have been proud of me for I had indeed fitted an elevating roof by myself which involved cutting a huge hole in the HiAce's roof. I had also installed a gas fridge—a curious omission in the original conversion—and there were now two appliances running off separate gas bottles, the fridge and the cooker.

We were staying at a campsite near Swanage in Dorset when our mini-holiday came to an abrupt end.

The kids all safely strapped into their seats, we left the tented annex at the campsite and drove into town to have a walk alongside the sea and to change the cooker's empty gas bottle. We picked up the replacement bottle on our way into town before parking up along the seafront. As Alex started the process of unstrapping the children, I went to the back of the van to attach the new gas bottle to its hose via the regulator. Some of what happened next I pieced together later.

While screwing the regulator into the valve of the new bottle, I crossed the threads just as the valve opened a little and, for a few seconds I could neither tighten it further nor release it, both of which would have closed the valve and stopped any gas escaping. But gas *was* escaping, I could hear it and feel it.

I was working frantically to unscrew the regulator to close the valve and only managed to do so nanoseconds before the ball of flame hit me. The force threw me backwards and I ended up sprawled across the bonnet of the car behind, my hair, eyebrows and beard singed to stubble and my burnt face stinging like hell.

I can still see the look of utter shock and disbelief on the faces of the elderly couple sitting in the other car as, carefully sliding myself off their unblemished bonnet, I turned round to apologise for both being there and for my appearance which, at that moment, I could feel rather than see.

Alex had finished extricating all three boys super-fast and she and they were standing in a protective huddle on the pavement wondering what the hell had happened and who the guy with the red face was and why he had been sprawled across the bonnet of the car behind. The only other casualty, apart from some parts of the

HiAce and my face, was our eldest son's favourite teddy bear.

I was taken to hospital and later discharged with superficial burns to my face. Ironically the hospital staff initially thought I was just another case of sunburn, of which there had been many that morning. It was as if they had already requisitioned and received a copy of my notes from Ennis. I think it was the burnt beard stubble that got the sun off the hook on this occasion.

What had happened was simple and when I installed the fridge I should have been aware of such a scenario; I had all the facts, I just hadn't joined up the dots.

Being gas-powered, the fridge had a pilot light, essentially a naked flame, which was situated at its lowest point near to the floor, to where heavier-than-air butane gas would naturally gravitate. The gas that escaped when I crossed the threads did just that and, when it drifted into the pilot light, ignited. Had I not managed to separate the gas bottle and the regulator when I did, then the bottle, with its valve still open, would almost certainly have exploded.

In almost complete silence we returned to the campsite and packed up. Two hours later we were back home, our eldest son still clutching what he thought was his favourite teddy; it was in fact its un-singed identical twin we bought in a petrol station as we exited Swanage.

For a while, until it was sold, the HiAce became like an everyday car; it was never again used for what it was intended … a home from home.

A few years later Alex and I divorced and she returned to live near Belfast. In the papers that I signed there was no mention of being a liability away from home; nor of my propensity for acquiring a red face.

GOOD MORNING, VIETNAM ...

These days news is instant. Within minutes a mass shooting in the United States, a botched air-raid in Syria or the downfall of an international politician are front-page headlines.

The 'page' too has changed. Fewer people read the printed word but choose instead the visual world of television, computers, tablets and smart phones.

Six years before I bought the bus, in March 1968, when Esther and Abi Ofarim's *Cinderella Rockefella* was topping the UK charts and moviegoers were rushing to see *Planet of the Apes*, it was very different. At the time, nobody was aware that, on the other side of the world, the most terrible atrocity of the Vietnam War, the My Lai Massacre, was taking place.

It was another 20 months before the world's press became aware of what had occurred and even then the accounts were patchy and, at first, downplayed.

Eventually a name came to the fore and Lieutenant William Calley Junior was universally denounced for orchestrating the events that resulted in the slaughter of nearly everyone in two hamlets of So'n My village.

The estimated death toll was somewhere between 350 and 500, all unarmed civilians, men, women, children, infants even.

Twenty-six US soldiers were charged with criminal offences but it was not until March 1971 that platoon leader, Lieutenant William Calley, was convicted and found guilty of killing 22 villagers.

Calley was the only one to be convicted and he was originally given a life sentence. He served only three and a half years under house arrest before being pardoned by Richard Nixon.

Thus, for a short time in the early 70s, William Calley became almost a household name; less so the three US servicemen who had tried to stop the massacre and rescue the hiding civilians instead. To varying degrees, all three were ostracised and even called traitors by a mindless few.

———

While Lieutenant Calley was engaged in defending his actions, I was first appointed as a Headteacher at the tender age of 27 and was told by my employer that, at the time, I was Britain's youngest Headteacher. In less than a month I was a year older but remained 'Britain's youngest Headteacher'.

My second Headship, four years later, coincided with the legal wrangles surrounding Calley's sentence, his house arrest and his unexpected rehabilitation into polite society. It also took me further west towards Bath where I took over a school that was based on two sites, half a mile apart, with children from five to eleven being taught on both sites.

Within a year I had managed to amalgamate the school onto one of the sites, a beautiful open, rural setting. It was unusual too in that, because it had been built during the War to serve adjacent, prefabricated housing which had since been demolished, the nearest pupil attending the school now lived more than half a mile away.

Parents without cars, as well as those children deemed incapable of walking that sort of distance twice a day, relied on a bus service operated by the local bus company to get them to and from school. As the occasionally unreliable service was on the cusp of becoming a 'frequently' unreliable service, I invited one of the company's Inspectors to the school in the hope that together we might pinpoint the problem and avoid any in the future.

On the day, two Inspectors turned up with the intention of putting this young Irish upstart in his place. After all, wasn't it just a trifle unrealistic to expect a dedicated bus service to arrive on time *and* turn up every day, rain, hail or snow?

Both Inspectors wore long, black, all-weather, body-hugging overcoats. Their matching black, peaked caps added little to their overall drabness. Neither seemed happy with his lot and, for one, things were going to get worse, thanks to my random predisposition to speak before engaging my brain, to indulge in a bit of craic.

The lead Inspector proffered a feeble hand and introduced himself.

"Inspector Calley," he said confidently.

I thought I would be breaking the black ice by responding with a touch of black humour.

"No relation to Lieutenant Calley, I suppose?" I quipped.

I was not expecting what followed next. In seconds Inspector Calley's previously pallid complexion morphed to an unmistakable red. He looked decidedly uncomfortable before replying.

"He's my cousin," he said, almost apologetically.

"I never knew that," was the immediate response of his wide-eyed colleague as he swung round his head.

With seven words I had inadvertently and innocently undone Inspector Calley's darkest secret and, worse still, had done so in front of a colleague whose demeanour suggested that this was a piece of gossip worthy of sharing with others before the day was done. These days it would have been on social media in seconds.

"We're eh, we're not a very close family." was Inspector Calley's last ditch attempt to rein in some of the damage.

I did my guilt-ridden best to bail him out by quickly changing the subject and to focus instead on the reliability of the school's bus service. That said, I could see he did not appreciate the Irish craic.

Even so, my mind could not help but wander back to a Vietnamese landscape where so many lives had come to a truly awful and pointless end. And how, I wondered, had this Bristol bus inspector processed all the negative media attention his cousin had received? And how was it that no-one, apart from me, had ever made the connection?

Inspector Calley's attempt at getting his buses to run on time and assure me that an inch of snow was not going result in a cancelled service, didn't succeed. It did cross my mind that my exposé of his family history may have somehow contributed to the ongoing decline in relations.

Nevertheless, the realisation that the service was never going to function smoothly had unforeseen consequences which dovetailed neatly with another issue that I was eager to solve.

On its new site, the school now had football and netball teams that played in after-school leagues against other local schools, with parents helping to ferry children to and from matches.

Some other schools had managed to buy a minibus which carried no more than 15 children and adults but this only facilitated the transport of one team which meant schools still had to rely on parents or make two minibus journeys when playing 'away'.

In other words, it seemed to me, that to invest in a minibus was not a helpful solution and, besides, it was useless as a means of taking children on an impromptu school visit as most classes had around 30 children.

It was Duncan, my Deputy, who came up with an innovative solution and, one Friday afternoon, we caught a train to London and, specifically, London Transport's Chiswick Garage, the last resting place for their decommissioned buses.

We took it in turns to drive our newly-purchased, semi-automatic London Transport red, single-decker bus, seating capacity 41, back to school. We paid less for our bus than we would have for a minibus.

Although our normal Driving Licences covered us for driving what was technically a 'Heavy Motor Vehicle', I thought it was incumbent on both of us to take, and pass, a Public Service Vehicle (PSV) licence before we carried any children. And this we did and, later, the school's caretaker also passed his test as a back-up in case neither I nor Duncan was available to drive.

Not long after we passed our tests we took a party of 30 children on a week-long visit to the Isle of Wight … and we didn't pay for a single coach excursion.

———

With the bus service to and from the school continuing on its downward spiral, it was but a short mental leap to the idea of running our own bus service which, even though we already had the bus, was not as easy as it sounded.

In the real world it was fraught with regulations, the main issue being how we could fund such a venture as the Office of the Traffic Commissioner, which oversaw all local bus services, would not allow us to take fares.

It was while brainstorming all the options that we came up with the idea of running our own version of a lottery, essentially a 'draw' rather than a lottery, which focussed on the parents whose children used the bus though, in theory, anyone could participate, otherwise it became a fare. And, of course, the parents of children who used the bus didn't *have to* buy a ticket for the monthly 'draw' and there were indeed a minority who didn't.

At the end of each month there would be three winners of cash prizes which, for them, covered the cost of the non-existent 'fare' and the remainder of the 'draw' money paid for the fuel and maintenance of the bus. It was not only clever but also legal and it actually worked.

That said, on one occasion when I was taking the younger children home, I realised I was being followed and guessed it had to be some sort of officialdom in relation to the bus. When I returned to pick up the older children, I asked Duncan to take over while I returned to my office to make sure my bus paperwork was up to date and hastily signed up a parent-friend, who didn't use the bus service, to the 'draw'. This was to make it doubly clear that it wasn't a 'fare', anyone could participate.

It was indeed the Commissioners who were on our tail that day and not only were they satisfied that we were not breaking any rules but congratulated us on our ingenuity.

Thus, there is a dubious and debatable thread from the events in Vietnam involving Lieutenant William Calley down the years, and through the British arm of the Calley family, to the inception of an innovative bus service operating in an English primary school.

Arguably, had the My Lai Massacre not occurred, then nobody would have heard of William Calley and I certainly would have had no reason to accidentally discredit his cousin, Inspector Calley, in front of his colleague. And an un-discredited Inspector Calley might well have left the school that day determined to upgrade and improve the school bus service for his new best friend.

And I wouldn't have been forced into running a bus service which, I might add, got me into trouble with another local Head who accused me of 'poaching' his pupils with my bus. As if?

Before his death in 2024 it had been reported that William Calley, at the time a retired jeweller living in Atlanta, Georgia, demanded at least $25,000 for an interview. Had he lived another four years he could have expected to make a killing, pun intended, in 2028, the 60th anniversary of those other killings in Vietnam.

The three US servicemen—Hugh Thompson, Glenn Andreotta and Lawrence Colburn—who had tried to stop the My Lai Massacre were eventually honoured for their actions; for Hugh Thompson this recognition was posthumous.

It took retired Lieutenant William Calley Junior over 40 years to issue an apology, in which he also restated his oft-repeated defence that he was only obeying orders ... presumably the same orders that Thompson, Andreotta and Colburn saw fit to challenge.

DID HE OR DIDN'T HE?

A few years later, when Nigel became Niall, I had left teaching and was living in Yorkshire with my partner Kay in the house of a friend. We knew we could only remain there for a few months.

It was while walking beside the Leeds & Liverpool Canal at Skipton in Yorkshire that the idea of living on a narrowboat germinated. This was April 1982 and three months later we were the nervous owners of the narrowboat *Dolly*, a 54ft steel boat converted into a home by Jimmy Perry, the co-writer of, among other things, *Dad's Army*.

For several years we lived on Britain's network of waterways, its natural rivers and its man-made canals, and almost every day there was a story to tell. However, the stories involving Gus Waters have several threads which encapsulate what it was like to be a living-on-a-boat pioneer and to have the unique ability to be on the move at any time and, like a snail, take your slow-moving home with you.

We were part of a sub-culture that few land-based people—even those who lived a few dozen yards from a canal—knew existed. To have the option of waking up each morning to look out on a different garden, a different wood, different wildlife, even a different pub, is truly an unparalleled and sentient experience.

Dolly's erstwhile home had been on the Thames near Staines and it took us four days to move her on to the canal network and on to Braunston on the Grand Union Canal.

We chose Braunston for all the wrong reasons. We wanted a base where we could work on the boat and at the same time be close to the motorway and to East Midlands Airport so that my children could come and visit. On a road map Braunston ticked all the right boxes but in waterways terms, and unknown to us at the time, it was the very heart of the canal world. Braunston was not only an important canal junction, it was also a place where the old and the new met.

Dolly was tied up along the towpath about 200 yards from a lock; it was right by a wider part of the canal where boats could turn, or 'wind' in boating parlance. We were such novices that, initially, we didn't know whether it was pronounced as the wind that comes after eating lots of beans or what you do to a watch; it's the former.

So we were in pole position to learn how to turn a boat and lots of other things that those who wore a checkered necktie, a boatman's cap, smoked roll-ups and carried their windlass (the steel key for opening and closing lock paddles) in their belt could do without thinking.

In a matter of weeks we had absorbed so much about boating just by being at Braunston. I was even sporting a brown 'John Lennon' cap, the modern version of the boatman's cap.

———

One morning I was working outside *Dolly*, sandpapering some of the old paintwork in readiness for my first attempt at painting traditional 'roses and castles' and rewriting the name either side of the bow. A man walked past, said "Morning" and continued on up the towpath; he stopped momentarily to scrutinise the boat moored next to us. Then he turned, walked back and stopped behind me.

"This your boat then?"

"It is." I replied

"Do you live on it?"

Now this was a question that those living on their boats never answered directly for, strange as it may seem, in those days you could own a boat such as *Dolly*, go out on it every day, but you were not supposed to live on it.

The secret to getting away with living on a boat was to do so unobtrusively, to try not to get noticed, to blend in, to become an acceptable, even welcomed, part of the community where your home was tied up. There were those who gave 'living on a boat' a bad name by their attitude: perhaps their boat was an unpainted eyesore, festooned with bits of wood, car tyres, crates, redundant bicycles or mattress springs, that nobody wanted to be living next to.

Perhaps too it was the way some people colonised and cluttered the towpath as if it was their private garden through which walkers and cyclists had to pick their way; perhaps it was their livestock, everything from dogs and cats to chickens and even horses. Keeping a low profile and demonstrating a lack of respect for your neighbours and their environment, don't go hand in hand.

There were, supposedly, such people as the Waterways Police who could move people on and discourage them from their nomadic lifestyle though I always wondered if they were a myth for, in all the boating I did, I neither met one nor knew anyone else who had. There were of course apocryphal stories that suggested the contrary.

Even so, we and others always had to have a ready answer to the question, "Do you live on it?" just in case the one asking was not as innocent as he or she looked. We considered several options:

"I'm looking after it for a friend."

"It belongs to my father."

"Just doing a bit of spring cleaning."

"I'm the butler, she's the maid and his lordship is out for the day."

The man on the towpath, interrupting my work, is still there, waiting patiently for a reply; he doesn't realise I have gone off at a tangent because he asked about living on *Dolly*.

"We spend a lot of time on it," was my noncommittal reply.

"I'm going to buy a boat. Was having a look at that one back there, it's for sale, but I don't like the look of her. Not been looked after," he said as he paused to kneel down to take a closer look at what I was doing.

"Saw one advertised for sale on the Thames about the same length as this, *Dolly*, I think it's called. Heading there next to take a look."

"I wouldn't bother," I said with the slightest hint of anticipation.

"You looked at it, then? he surmised.

"Yep, looked at it, liked it and bought it. This is *Dolly*."

So began a friendship with Gus Waters, a short, effervescent man with a tidy goatee beard, already sporting the boatman's cap, never quite straight, and with a story for every occasion. With no need now to head south to see *Dolly*, he stayed on her that night and for another week or so before returning, empty-handed, to his home on the Isle of Wight.

Our unofficial tenancy arrangement was simple. We provided bed and breakfast—and lunch when he hadn't wandered off boat-hunting—and he paid for the evening meal at the *Old Plough* in Braunston village; we shared the cost of the drinks though Gus only ever drank orange juice.

When Gus left us, we still weren't sure whether we had imagined him or not. Somehow we had adopted—or been adopted by—this stranger who appeared out of nowhere and then just vanished again, leaving us no way of tracing him or keeping in touch.

He enthralled us with his wit and his stories of working in Africa helping small, isolated communities find water on behalf of the United Nations. One story I recall above all others.

Apparently Gus had successfully helped a Mandingo community in West Africa to locate and pump water, for which the local chieftain was extremely grateful and, as a way of demonstrating this gratitude, offered Gus a special gift … his daughter. Not for ever, but on nightly loan for as long as Gus remained in the village.

Gus had now got to the part of the story where he either had to admit to declining the 'gift' or welcoming her with open arms. It was at this point that he realised he'd inadvertently tossed himself instead into the arms of a dilemma.

In starting the story, his intention was to tell us something about himself, about either Gus the Horny or Gus the Righteous, but he couldn't be sure which we might find the more acceptable or whether we might think more or less of him depending on how the story ended. In truth all we wanted to know was whether he did or he didn't and whichever it was would have made no difference to our opinion of Gus the Gus. Of course, whatever the ending, I admit we might have teased him a bit, feigned offence or wanted the nitty-gritty details, but then all three of us already did that sort of thing to each other, day in, day out.

He never did tell us and, even when he knew us better, he kept his secret about the Mandingo girl. Every so often I would try to catch him unawares and say, "Come on Gus, did you or didn't you?" Gus would just smile, tap his nose and change the conversation.

Gus also got away with calling Kay 'baby'. Nobody else would have dared, still less lived to tell the tale, but there was something about this stranger that we both found endearing, compelling even. Was it his impish grin, the angle of his cap, the way he rolled his triangular cigarettes, even his name? Whatever it was, it gave Gus, and only Gus, licence to call Kay 'baby'.

Gus had now retired. He had given up finding water for others and wanted to find and live on his own stretch of water instead. It was not only us that saw the irony of the coincidences in Gus's life: his name, his job and his goal … he even lived on a small island, surrounded, of course, by water.

Every morning he would set off on his boat-hunting quest and return empty-handed. On one occasion when I asked him about his day, he complained bitterly that there was something wrong with his cap as he flung it onto the bed.

"All day it's been falling over my eyes, either it's got bigger or my head has shrunk."

"Or you've been wearing mine all day," I offered as a more likely scenario, "I thought you normally slept in yours?" I added.

"I do. but I usually take it off for a few minutes in the morning to give my head an airing. Must have put on yours by mistake."

Every evening he would call his wife from the *Old Plough* and give her a progress report which was always a variant of the same story: there was no progress. The problem was that Gus was comparing every boat he saw to *Dolly* and nothing he saw ever came anywhere close.

We shared with Gus a goal of our own, an adventure we were planning for the autumn. For lots of reasons we wanted to take *Dolly* to Bristol and eventually to Bath and on to the Kennet & Avon Canal; at the time the entrance to the canal on the river Avon at Bath was closed but we had hopes that it might reopen the following spring.

Bristol was the waterways gateway to Bath and the only way to reach Bristol was to approach it from the sea. This was technically possible but potentially dangerous by narrowboat as such craft are flat-bottomed and top heavy and, if challenged by rough water, would probably float better upside down. Nevertheless that was our plan.

Gus returned to the Isle of Wight at the end of July but before he left he reminded us that he wanted to be on *Dolly* "when she rounded the Horn", his way of equating our planned journey to those pioneering mariners who rounded the ferocious seas off Cape Horn. We promised him we would.

Gus's departure temporarily left a void in our lives; it was while reminiscing about him that evening in the *Old Plough*, that we realised he'd left us no way of contacting him.

———

The summer drifted into autumn and our plans were nearing fruition. We knew it would be hard to leave Braunston where we had not only become accepted by the boating fraternity, old and new, but also respected by it: we could not only wind or turn *Dolly* like the best of them but we could pronounce it too.

When we finally set the date for leaving Braunston, we turned our attention to finding the elusive Gus, from whom we had heard not a word since he left two months earlier. It wasn't too difficult for, although there were several 'G. Waters' in the phone book but only one 'G. & J. Waters'; his wife's name was Judith, that much we knew.

We called and spoke to Judith for the first time. We explained who we were and asked her to pass on our departure date to the absent Gus. After that we heard nothing.

I realise I am talking about a time pre-mobile phones but within the boating subculture there were ways of getting messages through to people; the name of their boat and a general location was normally enough. In our case we invariably made use of the *Poste Restante* service available at most post offices and Gus knew this.

It was early October and our last full day at Braunston. It felt like the cusp of winter. All day we'd stayed close to *Dolly*, always on the look-out for Gus.

Our imaginary traveller had left the Isle of Wight hours ago and caught the train from Southampton to London Waterloo; he'd then crossed London to Euston Station to catch the train to Daventry, whence to Braunston by bus or taxi.

Our imaginary traveller should have arrived by now; clearly Gus wasn't going to make it.

We couldn't wait any longer for we had one final chore here at Braunston: we had to take *Dolly* down to the chandlery at Bottom Lock to collect a black, wood-burning stove that I planned to fit on our journey.

Disappointed and in low spirits, we started the engine, cast off, winded and made our way slowly to the chandlery. It was dusk and many of our fellow boaters stopped what they were doing to wish us well as we slipped past their moorings.

With the stove on board, and dark overtaking dusk, we returned to our mooring one last time. It was an emotional experience as more people appeared on their boats and on the towpath and bridges to shout messages of good luck and to wave goodbye. Many thought we were mad and on our way to a watery grave. We both struggled to hold back tears as we bade farewell to an extraordinary community that had been our home for over three months.

Still touched by such displays of friendship and goodwill, we approached our mooring in reflective mood and glided slowly past the boat which had been, for a few weeks, our neighbour. As we did so, a shutter shot open, a capped head poked out of the window and the stillness of the evening was forever shattered by two words directed at Kay:

"Hi-ya baby!"

Our imaginary traveller had made it into real time after all.

A last supper at the *Old Plough* beckoned.

Narrowboats travel at a maximum of four miles an hour on canals and six on rivers though, in reality, it is rarely possible to maintain such average speeds.

From Braunston to Sharpness—the gateway to the Severn Estuary and the sea—is approximately 67 miles as the crow flies but it's 113 miles were the crow to go by canal and river, and includes 110 locks. We had allowed ourselves two weeks to get to Sharpness though it would have been possible, barring hold-ups and not having to fit a wood-burning stove and chimney, to do it in about ten days.

In boating terms our route from Braunston to the sea at Sharpness was straightforward:

From Braunston to Lapworth on the Grand Union Canal.

From Lapworth to King's Norton on the North Stratford Canal.

From King's Norton to Diglis Basin at Worcester on the Worcester & Birmingham Canal.

From Diglis Basin to Gloucester Docks on the river Severn.

From Gloucester Dock to Sharpness Dock on the Gloucester & Sharpness Canal.

Getting to Sharpness was the easy part; thereafter it was more complicated. We had to exit the sea-lock at Sharpness on a high tide before heading down the Severn Estuary to Avonmouth's Prince Edward Dock. Here we would spend a night before going up the river Avon on the morning tide, under Brunel's stunning Clifton Suspension Bridge and into Bristol's Floating Harbour.

In early 1983, the national waterways magazine, *Canal & Riverboat*, published my first ever waterways-related article. It was the story of our unique journey 'round the Horn' from Sharpness to Bristol in a narrowboat, with Gus, in late October.

Gus remained with us in Bristol for a few days before returning to the Isle of Wight with his stories of derring-do on the high seas, despite the fact that he watched it all from *inside* the boat.

We made Bristol's Floating Harbour our winter-quarters home but also made regular trips upriver to Bath.

The following spring, the Kennet & Avon Canal was once again accessible and we joined the flotilla of boats in the inaugural cruise up through the six Bath locks. The calmer waters of the canal now became our home and it was here, at our mooring near the closed Dundas Aqueduct—and at the time the new limit of navigation— that we were joined once again by Gus.

———

This time Gus was determined to find a boat. He had no option for he had sold his home on the Isle of Wight which he and Judith had to vacate by a certain date. He was never specific about the date; the only thing we knew for sure was that, with every day that passed, it was getting closer.

The more of our boating adventures and misadventures in and around Bristol and Bath we shared with Gus, the more determined he became to join us in our nomadic lifestyle. Not literally, of course, for we knew that he would never reprise our 'round the Horn' trip. Once was enough.

Gus had come armed with a long list of potential floating homes. As this list was going to take him, and us, all over the country, he hired a car and named me as his preferred driver. As he'd done at Braunston, every night he would call Judith and bring her up to date with his viewing plans or explain why this or that boat was not what they were looking for. As ever Gus was just pleased to be on *Dolly*, the benchmark for his future home.

All that had really changed since Braunston was the name of the pub. It was now at *The Viaduct* that Gus paid for the evening meal in exchange for bed, breakfast, lunch, board and driving. It was from *The Viaduct* that he relayed all his 'hard-luck' stories to the ever-patient Judith. Although we were never privy to her side of the conversation, when he repeatedly said "I know, I know …" we suspected that Judith was reminding him of their deadline and the spectre of homelessness.

There remained a couple of boats in the north-west that we still hadn't seen and, having discounted everything closer, we headed north, aware that we might have to stay overnight at a bed & breakfast, preferably one that doubled as a canal-side pub.

The first was not what Gus was looking for and so we pressed on further north to a house near Ellesmere Port and the Shropshire Union Canal.

Unusually, the boat that Gus had arranged to see was not actually in the canal but in the owner's driveway alongside his house; he wanted prospective buyers to see it was in good condition above and below the waterline. We left Gus to look it over by himself, we knew if he found something he liked, he'd want us to take a look too.

This was the first time we were invited to voice an opinion and the first time we'd climbed on to a boat by ascending a ladder; a boat with no name. Finally Gus had found his *Dolly* and in minutes negotiated a price, shook hands on the deal, got the owner's bank details and asked if he could call Judith.

Within moments Judith—the only one with a phone that didn't need constant feeding—was custodian of all the information she needed to conclude the transaction and arrange for their new home to be dropped into the Shropshire Union Canal when they were ready to move in.

Gus returned to *Dolly* with us and life, for him, went on as before for the next ten days or so. Mission Control was on the Isle of Wight where Judith managed and organised everything. It appeared that Gus' only contribution was to find the boat, to offer advice and to keep out of her way. Every evening, from the safety of *The Viaduct*

Gus would call Judith to evaluate progress and to pass on his latest thoughts about what to bring and what to get rid of or leave behind.

Sitting in *The Viaduct* listening to these one-sided conversations was hilarious and Gus, though he must have known we were listening, never once explained some of the more bizarre exchanges. And we knew better than to ask him:

"Yes, bring the washing machine … yes, I know, but we'll find a way round that … no, we won't have room for the dryer …"

"The table, the oak table … yes, I know it'll be too wide but just bring the legs, leave the top, just the legs … well, get someone to help you, it's not a difficult job …"

"No, don't give away the lawn mower, bring it with you … no, I'm not going to cut the grass on the towpath … yes, I know I do … nevertheless just bring the lawn-mower, it's important you bring it."

"No, I'll meet you there … no need for me to come back to the Isle of Wight when I'm already over here … just tell me when the van is going to arrive and I'll make sure I get there around the same time … Niall will drive me … have you remembered to arrange for someone to paint the name on when we get there …?

"I wrote it down for you … it's by the phone … look inside the little drawer … just read it back to me … yes, that's right, like the dog …"

When we asked him what he was going to call his boat, Gus would just tap his nose and say, "You'll see."

As we never heard him tell Judith the name, we assumed they had already chosen it before finding the boat.

It was early May when we pulled into the car park of a small boat-yard on the Shropshire Union Canal near Chester with Gus and his few possessions. The remainder of his worldly goods had already arrived and Judith was overseeing their removal from the van and soon the canal-side was littered with an array of bags, boxes, table legs, various household appliances and a lawn mower. Judith was scrutinising her new home for the first time but had waited for Gus to arrive before stepping on board for the guided tour.

Kay and I hovered in the background. We were never sure what

Judith was expecting, all we knew was that this woman had the patience of Job and that she'd soon sort it, and Gus, out.

Judith's inaugural inspection over, we helped carry things on board until there was only one thing remaining on the towpath ... the lawn-mower, from which Gus quickly removed some bits and pieces he deemed recyclable. Then he had a few words with the boat-yard owner who disappeared momentarily and returned with a sledgehammer. We all watched, open-mouthed, at one final act of retribution as Gus, sledgehammer poised, approached the lawn-mower and, with calculated relish, beat it to a mangled mess, uttering a string of expletives at it as he did so.

Although Gus' fervour, as he landed blow after blow, was a side of him we'd never seen before, in no way was Judith fazed. She just rolled her eyes and explained.

"That thing, and having to use it regularly, has been the bane of his life. He'd complain every time he had to cut the grass. He'd get irritated and angry just knowing that it was growing again seconds after he'd cut it and that soon he'd have to cut it all again. It's one of the reasons he wants to live on a boat ... so that he'll never have to cut the grass, ever again."

Before we left Gus and Judith to sort out their new home and the rest of their lives, I asked Gus what he was going to call his new home. He did, as I knew he would, his nose-tapping thing again and just said, "You'll see."

We played along and didn't tell him we already knew; Judith had told us.

I was tempted to ask Judith the "did he or didn't he?" question but thought better of it just in case Gus had omitted to mention to her about being given such a choice in the first place.

Back in Bath and on *Dolly,* we were, for a while, unsettled as, for the third time, we found ourselves coping with the inexplicable void left by the irrepressible Gus and the craic he always brought with him.

UP, UP AND AWAY

Dolly was generally moored on the Kennet & Avon Canal, close to the limit of navigation at the time, Dundas Aqueduct. In the early 80s, restoration work to reestablish through navigation from the Thames at Reading was continuing at a snail's pace.

At Dundas there is a wide basin and wharf where the canal turns sharp left to cross the river Avon on a stunning aqueduct and, next to the basin, is an original lock-keeper's cottage where the Somersetshire Coal Canal joined the Kennet & Avon via a single lock. This was the fiefdom of Tim and Wendy Wheeldon who lived in the renovated lock-keeper's cottage.

Tim had commissioned a wide-beam boat to ply the canal as a trip boat offering outings for groups in the day and up-market dinner cruises in the evening. The *John Rennie* was launched in Bristol's Floating Harbour and I brought it upriver to Bath and onto the canal; subsequently I became the boat's first skipper and Kay worked in the galley with Wendy.

Over a decade later we had our wedding party on the *John Rennie*, our first time on it as guests.

In normal circumstances we would never have happened upon the Wheeldons as the four of us were unlikely bedfellows. Yet Tim and I forged a unique bond, a sort of waterways-inspired camaraderie fuelled by some of the off-the-wall situations in which we frequently found ourselves. I would have called it the craic but such a word was not in Tim' vocabulary, even when he was indulging in it with the reckless relish of a native Irishman; albeit without the alcohol and the music.

The most memorable bit of craic we shared was the April Fool hoax I conceived for *Canal & Riverboat* magazine about the miraculous re-opening of the long-derelict canal, the Somersetshire Coal Canal, the original channel of which ran under his rose garden. The article never referred to the date, just the day, Good Friday, which also happened to be 1 April.

Nationally and locally many were taken in by the story, as were the local police in the form of PC Peach who, unknown to us at the time, was a waterways enthusiast and a *Canal & Riverboat* subscriber. The stir it caused in the Bath area and north-east Somerset affected Tim more than others as the contact number at the end of the article 'for further information' was his, though I had of course asked his permission first.

Tim became masterful at letting people down gently, of steering them towards Good Friday being 1 April without making them feel embarrassed. How he resisted shouting 'April Fool' down the phone, I'll never know.

Nearly four decades on, Tim still has a copy of the article and laughs every time he reads it and reflects on the many laughter-filled days we shared because of that little white lie. Above all, he recalls the dressing down one woman gave him on the phone. For her it had been a wasted hour at the wheel to drive to Paulton in Somerset to witness the arrival of the flotilla of colourful craft on the inaugural cruise along the restored canal. She was not best pleased when all she found was a waterless and overgrown hollow in the ground, the erstwhile canal basin still in dank, derelict mode after half a century of inactivity. On this occasion, Tim's conciliatory tone didn't assuage her annoyance.

———

For me there are two unrelated stories that are typical of our atypical relationship. The first relates to my time as the skipper of the *John Rennie*.

Tim always did a commentary on the *John Rennie*'s daytime group cruises, informing our passengers about the various historical and physical features of the canal as we went along. I steered, he talked, we worked well together. The boat's wheelhouse was wired up for a mike and I was keen to do the commentary too, but it was not to be. Perhaps he suspected I might have a propensity for going off-script. As if?

Then, out of the blue, everything changed. Tim asked me if I would mind being skipper *and* man-with-the-mike. I was over the moon … finally I was allowed to pass on my knowledge of our scenic route and its history.

As I pulled away from the bank to cross to the nearby wharf to pick up our passengers, a smiling Tim called to me from the safety of dry land with some additional information about the group.

"Sorry, Ni … meant to say … this is a Royal National Institute for the Blind outing. Good luck!"

He smiled a knowing smile as he threw me the stern rope and waved us on our way, leaving me to do the commentary for a group of people who couldn't see what I was describing.

I should have seen that coming.

—

For me, the most memorable Tim-related story was when he was sent to Coventry; a journey we did together.

As well as being a canal enthusiast, Tim was also an ex-navy helicopter pilot and, in the early 1980s, alongside his canal enterprises and pursuits, was still flying helicopters regularly to check the south-west's underground gas pipelines to make sure that nobody was contemplating digging a big hole where it might be rather dangerous to do so. Clearly not all of the farming community seemed to understand the significance of the white post topped with an orange angled 'roof' strategically sited on their land. Tim had many horror stories of having to land quickly to stop just such an eventuality.

Dolly was moored 100 yards from Dundas Wharf when our sleepy Sunday morning was interrupted by a knock on the roof. It was Tim with an offer I couldn't refuse.

He explained that he had to work the following week checking the pipelines but that, to do so, he had to drive to Coventry to pick up a helicopter and fly it back to Bath … and would I like to come with him?

"Is the Pope Catholic?" Was my standard reply to questions with such an obvious affirmative answer. Before I'd finished nodding my head, he was running back to the cottage, turning only to briefly to call out:

"Don't forget your cameras. See you by the car in a quarter of an hour."

Our *modus operandi* evolved as we drove to Coventry. It was quite simple: rather than the direct route, we'd fly the more scenic route above the canals.

I'd never been in a helicopter before and even found our pre-flight manoeuvre, a mere two or three feet above ground, to bring the helicopter out of its hanger and onto the tarmac, quite thrilling.

Underway, Tim took out a battered OS map—one of many I later discovered he had in his bag—and unfolded it across his knees to work out our route; for some inexplicable reason, conventional flight charts didn't feature canals. He seemed to know what he was doing but somehow I guessed this wasn't normal procedure on a helicopter flight deck for, clearly, scrutinising a map did not sit comfortably with the concentration needed to keep an eye on what else might be in the air at the time. That's where I, and my extensive experience in such matters, came in. Tim explained my role as his recently-conscripted co-pilot.

"If you see anything else in the air, let me know, particularly if it's coming in our direction," he said in all seriousness, before adding, "I won't be offended."

And that was our strategy for getting ourselves safely back to Bath:

Tim with a map on his knee, the rest of him on automatic as he flew the helicopter, both of us keeping a lookout for canals … and any low-flying craft.

When we found ourselves above an interesting part of a canal, we'd check that there was nothing else around, then hover above it for a while and I'd take photos. To make this easier, I would check that my seat-belt was securely fastened, then open my side window while Tim tilted the helicopter slightly my way so that I would have an uninterrupted view of what was below. Between us we became quite good at locating our 'target', taking a few photos before shooting off somewhere else.

We were having a ball up there. We were like two teenagers let loose with a Ferrari for a couple of hours. At no point did it feel as if we were doing anything remotely dangerous or unusual, the only thing I felt was exhilaration. On the other hand, for my co-pilot Tim, it was all in a day's work.

Finally above home turf, we made a pass over where *Dolly* had been earlier that morning only to find that Kay had moved her up to the wharf to await our arrival. Not that it made any difference for I'd already run out of film so there would be no photos of *Dolly* from the air as I'd hoped.

We were approaching Tim's garden and I could see Kay and Wendy with Tim's two sons, Matthew and David, looking up at us as we did a couple of laps of honour of the basin and the aqueduct.

"Can you see Matthew?" Tim asked.

"Yes." I replied.

"Right, as I start to bring us down, I want you to tell me everything Matthew does. Okay?"

Tim positioned us above his garden so that I had an uninterrupted view of Matthew who was standing by a flower-bed with his arms wide apart.

My first instinct was to carry on with the craic we'd shared on our inaugural flight together and say something ridiculous, like 'he's taking off all his clothes' or 'he's peeing against a tree' but I thought better of it and, uncharacteristically, decided to take things more seriously.

"Matthew's got his arms outstretched … still outstretched … he's moving them closer … they're about four feet apart … still four feet … the same … the same …"

When Matthew put his hands by his side, I realised he was not, as I initially thought, telling Tim how far above the ground we were as we had not yet landed.

We touched down and while we waited for the blades to stop rotating, I asked Tim about Matthew's role …

"I've never actually landed here before," Tim replied matter-of-factly, "Matt was just telling me how far away I was from the trees. Didn't really want to clip them, did I?"

Even as we touched down I knew that, before long, landing here would not be possible. The rose garden that grew atop the original canal lock, the junction of the two canals, was destined to go. Tim's plan was to excavate the lock and the basin that lay beyond and reopen this short length of the Somersetshire Coal Canal as a waterways amenity: private moorings, a hire-boat base and a dry dock.

What I didn't know initially was that, on our flight that day, Tim spotted, near Reading, a redundant lift-bridge, the perfect answer to a potential problem with his project … allowing boats to pass through the excavated lock while safeguarding the towpath for walkers and cyclists across it.

Tim's plan, our plan, was that *Dolly* should be the first boat to pass through the restored lock, finally back in water for the first time in almost a century; but before Tim's pipe-dream came to fruition *Dolly* was once again on the move.

———

The restoration of the Kennet & Avon Canal was still a work-in-progress when Kay and I returned to the main canal network the following summer which meant we had to take *Dolly* back up the

Severn Estuary and into the calmer waters beyond Sharpness Lock. Our destination was Nottingham where we were going to work on *Canal & Riverboat* magazine.

We were approaching Tardebigge Tunnel heading north-east on the Worcester & Birmingham Canal when I could see the headlight of a boat inside the tunnel, slowly coming towards us. I slowed down as its bow gradually reemerged into sunlight. Out of habit, we began to spell the name ... *M-a-n-d* ...

Aboard the approaching boat, the man on the tiller, puffing away on his triangular cigarette, his boatman's cap at a slight angle, was doing exactly the same ... *D-o-l* ...

Dolly and *Mandingo* had finally met.

———

Two years later, as we had all anticipated, *Dolly* was indeed the first boat to leave the Kennet & Avon Canal and turn right to pass under the raised lift-bridge, the same one that Tim had spied on our helicopter trip. Slowly she passed through the reclaimed stone walls of the now gate-less lock chamber—atop which Tim had once landed a helicopter—and into the adjoining basin of the only part of the old Somersetshire Coal Canal, finally in water and navigable for a couple of hundred yards.

Tim, Wendy, Simon and Matthew Wheeldon were a proud family.

Sadly, both Kay and I heard this story separately and second-hand for neither of us was aboard *Dolly* that day; a year earlier we had finally succumbed to the lure of being mere landlubbers once again.

Dolly had passed on to our friend Tony Jackson who brought her down the Severn Estuary yet again and back onto the Kennet & Avon Canal; against all the odds *Dolly* had, in the words of Gus, proud owner of *Mandingo*, 'rounded the Horn' three times.

A PHOTO-JOURNALIST AT PLAY.. 1983.

LEAPS OF FAITH

Living on the water was a leap of faith for Kay and me. One day we were novices, the next seasoned boaters on Britain's waterway network. Few others who lived on a narrowboat ever made the journey we had made by sea to reach the stretch of canal that we now called home.

But there were others who felt the need to live by the water and this is the story of how our three very different lives intertwined on the same stretch of water. In our different ways we were all seasoned travellers.

Vic lived *near* water because he had to. John lived *beside* the water because it was in his blood. We lived *on* the water because it was our home and a new challenge

Vic was a traveller, a hobo, a wanderer. He lived in his small encampment in the woods between the canal above and the river below. To keep himself clean and to drink, Vic always needed to be near a source of water. Just as we did, Vic was savvy enough to make sure he lived below the radar, that his presence did not upset anyone in the local community who might see him as a visual threat to their neighbourhood or their sensibilities.

John was a Baronet, a Knight of the Realm with the title 'Sir'. In John's case it was an inherited title that he would pass on to his oldest son. John lived by the water because, after he left the Navy, he became a working boatman and, in the 1950s, was the last carrier of goods on this waterway before much of it became derelict and unnavigable.

Kay and I owned our narrowboat home, *Dolly*, and had lived on the water for a year or more. Our lives were an on-going journey.

Vic's imaginary leap, saw him leaving his life in the woods to live a different itinerant life on the water.

John's ambitious leap was to the day when his beloved canal would be open once again to navigation, and that the water outside the front door of his canal-side cottage could once again carry him to Bath in one direction and to Reading and London in the other. As it was, his cottage was only a few miles from the then limit of navigation and half a mile from the nearest road in the opposite direction.

We had already made that leap from a predictable life to something more uncertain. To survive would be enough, to have the capacity to make a living on the water, skippering and working on trip boats and perhaps writing about it would be a bonus.

Dolly was generally moored between Vic's encampment and John's cottage. We were near neighbours. Our shared passion was the same stretch of water which we called home.

The wife of Howard-on-the-Hill didn't like having an itinerant for a near neighbour. Well, not exactly a neighbour, all she could see from her lofty window, a 300-yard leap across the valley and its river, was the occasional plume of winter smoke from Vic's camp-fire. The wife of Howard-on-the-Hill had never heard of the craic.

Because we often did share a bit of craic with Vic, Kay and I were the only people ever to visit Vic's camp-site and knew it was organised, discreet, clean and very difficult to find. Vic was not unaware that some people might be hostile to his lifestyle and it was important that he keep a low profile. I suspect he'd been moved on more than a few times in his life but he never spoke of such things. His optimism knew no bounds.

When a benefactor offered Vic an old 12-foot cabin cruiser in need of love and attention, Vic spent hours cleaning, patching, repairing and painting it in readiness for that special leap into the unknown. Finally he was going to live on the water.

The canal we all lived by or on was, at the time, land-locked, which meant that you could only access it from the sea beyond Bristol, which is how *Dolly* came to be there. Parts of the channel eastwards were still being restored and would eventually provide access again to and from the Thames. But Vic couldn't wait that long.

Vic's plan was to have his new, sparkling blue and white home taken to the main canal network at Sharpness from where he would begin that new life travelling northwards into the heart of England.

Uncharacteristically, or so I thought, Howard-on-the-Hill stepped forward to lend a hand and soon Vic had packed all his belongings into bags and was watching excitedly as, with the help of our mutual friend Tim, his new home was winched onto Howard's trailer. I could imagine the wife of Howard-on-the-Hill watching from her window, a satisfied smile on her face.

It was several hours later that I got a message via Tim, whose number Vic had for emergencies. Vic was in trouble. Howard-on-the-Hill had literally just dropped the boat into the water and driven off. Vic's boat was taking on water. His home was sinking.

We sped north to see if we could help but it was soon clear that Vic's boat was not going to be his home for a while. I spoke to a local lock-keeper on the Sharpness Canal who agreed to keep an eye on it until he could get a friend to take a look. I told him Vic's story and, in a leap of faith, he assured me that he and his friend would sort it out over the next few weeks. I gave him a number and Vic returned with us to the camp-site he'd vacated that same morning.

Vic slept on *Dally* that night and the next day the wife of Howard-on-the-Hill, once again saw that tell-tale plume of smoke she thought had gone for good. Or perhaps she thought a new Pope had just been chosen?

John's title meant that many touched their forelock, both

metaphorically and even literally, when they met him and called him 'Sir John'. But neither John, nor his wife 'Lady' Martin, cared about such things. Their titles, a quirk of birth, meant nothing to them, nor to us.

They lived in a canal-side cottage in what a mutual friend described as 'discreet squalor'. We knew their home well and ate there many times and 'squalor' was unfair, more a bit chaotic and a little eccentric, perhaps not what a forelock-toucher might expect. I recall how, the first time we ate there, Martin, with a mischievous smile, blew the dust off her beautiful crystal glasses before pouring the wine.

Over dinner one evening John mentioned he was going to a Royal Navy reunion in London the next morning and I offered to drive him to Bath railway station as I knew the weather forecast was not good.

I called on him around eight and together we walked along the wet and mucky towpath for half a mile to the car.

Like me, John was wearing wellington boots but, unlike me, he was wearing a dark blue suit and carrying a plastic bag with a packed lunch and the black shoes he was going to change into when we reached the car.

Just before we arrived at the car, John showed me a part of the hedge, adjoining a nearby garden, that opened into a small, out-of-sight clearing literally in the heart of the hedge. This is where, John explained, I was to leave the bag with his wellies. On his return from London that evening he would pick them up and change out of his shoes for the walk home.

Clearly this was something John did on a regular basis.

When we reached the car, John sat on the passenger seat, feet outside, to change into his shoes.

"Oh, bugger," he said calmly, seemingly not at all concerned, "... only one bloody shoe. Must have left the other in the bedroom."

"Don't worry," I said, "we've got plenty of time, I'll run back to the cottage and get it."

After Martin got over the shock of an out-of-breath me turning up on the doorstep, I quickly explained the problem. She was clearly enjoying John's predicament as she rummaged around in search of the elusive shoe.

"No, can't find it ... no idea what he's done with it," she said with a hint of exasperation and a note of finality.

"Has he another pair I could take?"

"He has ... but they're brown. He won't like that. Brown shoes and a navy-blue suit? That's against Navy tradition." I could tell that Martin was enjoying this.

"I'll take them," I said.

I ran back to the car to find John already tucking into his packed lunch. He saw the question in my face:

"Was feeling a bit peckish, no breakfast. I'll get something else on the train, " he offered without being asked.

"These were all Martin could find," I explained as John delved into the bag and, without batting an eyelid, started to put on his pair of gleaming, brown shoes.

I couldn't stop myself.

Tongue firmly in cheek, I thought I'd pretend to be Martin and be a little mischievous.

"John," I said in a voice that suggested I knew what I was talking about, "brown shoes with a navy-blue suit ... em, isn't that against Navy tradition?"

John, his mind as sharp as a razor, was having none of it and gently rebuked such a notion.

"Lord Mountbatten always wore brown shoes with a navy-blue suit," he replied almost as if that had always been his intention.

—————

Vic finally made that leap into the unknown and neither Kay nor I, nor John, nor the wife of Howard-on-the-Hill ever saw his again.

John's long-overdue ambition came to fruition and he was a guest-of-honour at the re-opening of the canal he loved so much.

Sadly, his wife, and my dear friend, Martin, didn't make it. It goes without saying that the photo-journalist who wrote all four editions of the then definitive guide to the canal, but who had also previously written about the ineptitude and lacklustre strategy from those entrusted with this project, was not invited.

For Kay and me, living on *Dolly* had become a way of life and a means of earning a living and, with yet another leap of faith in *Dolly*'s ability to defy the sea, we followed in Vic's wake and once again took *Dolly* 'round the Horn' to work for a Nottingham-based waterways magazine, *Canal & Riverboat*.

Our journey took us past the place where Vic's boat almost sank and, several days into our journey north, we passed under a bridge and spotted a message scrawled amid the graffiti: "Niall and Kay. Bridge 47, Vic."

Later that day, we passed under Bridge 47.

Sadly there was no small, blue and white boat in sight. Like us, Vic had moved on.

THE HIGH LIFE

Working on *Canal & Riverboat* also meant that I had to have an input into its sister magazine, *Popular Motor Cruiser*, which in turn necessitated taking part in the annual International Boat Show at Southampton. All of which I hated but, on one occasion, I was able to get something positive out of it.

By chance, at the Boat Show, Kay and I got into the same lift as two men who spoke just like me; one was familiar to me, one wasn't. The stranger turned out to be the Chief Executive of the Northern Ireland Tourist Board (NITB), at the Boat Show to promote Northern Ireland as a boating haven. The two men were on their way to a special press lunch, the second was the guest of honour, someone I did recognise as well-known comedian Frank Carson.

We got talking and, thanks to my accent, and the fact that I worked for a boating magazine, they insisted that we join them for a bit of craic. When it came to our sense of humour, Frank and I talked the same language. It's even possible that he got some new material as a result of our shared lunch for which, of course, I take full credit.

As a result of this encounter, I was invited to come to Northern Ireland,, at NITB's expense, to cruise on Lough Erne. Naturally this was on condition that I wrote about my experiences in terms that might attract others to do the same.

Kay and I took my three children on the cruise and a couple of months later the article was published detailing our experience and the delights of pleasure boating on Lough Erne. I had no need to exaggerate.

There were, however, at least two stories from that trip that never made it into print. The time has come to remedy that.

———

It was the evening before we had to return the boat to its hire base on the mainland before returning to Belfast and then England. As usual, we moored up at one of the hundreds of islands, sprinkled like confetti on both Upper and Lower Loughs Erne.

Like many of the islands there was a small jetty for hire craft and no sooner were we tied up than the children went off to explore. One found some mushrooms and so, not to be outdone, the other two joined him on a mushroom hunt.

They returned to the boat with enough mushrooms for three but not five, so Kay and I decided we'd cook them just for the children, as a reward for having found them.

It was not until we returned the boat the following morning that we fully understood the events of the previous evening. Making conversation, the hire base owner, Harry, asked where we'd moored the previous evening and we pointed to the island just visible from the base.

"That's a popular little place," he said, "particularly with the students. Sometimes they just hire a boat for the day."

Preempting my question, he continued.

"It's the shrooms, that's what brings them."

Now, even though I'd never tasted a 'shroom', I knew he was talking about so-called 'magic' mushrooms and their hallucinogenic properties. It was now clear that, by insisting that the children should enjoy the fruits of their own labours, we had unwittingly fed them magic mushrooms which in turn explained their behaviour later that evening.

They just wouldn't, couldn't, go to sleep. It was three in the morning before they finally passed out after hours of laughing, giggling and jumping around. We thought it was no more than all the fresh air and the excitement of a holiday coming to an end. That evening we too were partaking of our drug of choice—a bottle of red wine—so eventually all five of us were on the same planet.

We convinced ourselves that they hadn't really eaten all that many and, besides, there didn't seem to be any noticeable after-effects. Nevertheless, best not to mention it to their mother.

———

Harry told us he'd had a call from the Tourist Board and, as our driver back to Belfast was running late, he suggested that we take a run up to his brother-in-law's house, about a mile away, from where there were not only superb views over the lough, but also lots of animals that would be an interesting diversion for the kids. Despite picking up from him that there might be an ulterior motive, we agreed. We couldn't quite be sure whether or not what looked like a wink and a nod was no more than a nervous tic.

While his sister took the children under her wing in the adjacent stables and barns, Harry ushered us into the house to meet brother-in-law Stuart, a local magistrate.

Stuart, the good host that he was, offered us a drink in a way that suggested we had already been primed about his extensive collection ... and perhaps we might have been, had the children not been around. His cabinet was indeed impressive; it went from wall to wall and was full of an assortment of unusually shaped bottles each containing delicately coloured liquids, mostly pinks and yellows of various intensities, though mostly subtle hues rather than strong colours.

"Any flavour you particularly like? There's raspberry and strawberry ... that darker one is plum ...? Some of my collection is over 20 years old ... this 1972 strawberry is particularly fine, you don't feel its strength at first."

Frank cut in:

"Stuart is an expert at flavouring it. Some can be quite rough, you know, but with just the right amount of flavouring, the potency is still there without that rawness ..."

Slowly, ever so slowly, I was beginning to understand. The 'it' we were being invited to sample was moonshine, *poitín* (poteen in English), at the time an illegal Irish spirit made from the humble potato. My impression was that Stuart had acquired his collection of fine Irish *poitín*, not through his own labours but through his role as a local magistrate.

But who were we to judge? We were just there to taste and it would have been impolite not to have given the 1972 strawberry due recognition … and the 1981 with a hint of elderflower … and a …

Stuart talked us through each variation with the passion of a sommelier eulogising about a favourite bottle of wine; he described the 'bite' of each, talked about how the water source was important, even the potatoes.

He was right about the strawberry … exquisite.

These days you can buy *poitín* off the supermarket shelf for there are a few Irish distilleries with licenses to produce it. But there remains a trade in illegally-distilled moonshine which is stronger than the sanitised supermarket versions and maintains the traditional sourcing technique of a nod and a wink as opposed to queueing at the check-out.

Like most Irish who enjoy a wee nip now and then, At the time of writing, I have a bottle of 'made in Connemara' *poitín* in my drinks cabinet. Despite being in a 500ml plastic bottle, it took pride of place next to the Bushmills whiskey less than week after we moved to Ireland … and cost no more than a nod and a wink and a bit of the craic.

CONFESSIONS

I was not one for travelling in Spain prior to 1975, the year of the death of its fascist dictator General Franco. Even after Franco's death it was still not a place that excited me, the more so because of what I knew some, mainly British, holidaymakers had done to many of its coastal communities. It was more than a decade post-Franco before I was ready to test the waters and visit Spain.

I was living in the Midlands where I had two friends, a mother and daughter, who owned a small apartment at Carvajal, west of Benalmàdena on the Costa del Sol line between Malaga and Fuengirola. Maria and Maggie invited me join them for a short break.

Benalmàdena was, I was pretty sure, a place that encompassed all the things I hated about holidaying en masse with British tourists. I didn't travel abroad to eat fish and chips, drink Watney's Red Barrel and talk about English football.

Nevertheless, I accepted my friends' invitation in the hope that it would take my mind off other things or that I might find something to write about. Perhaps I would find a way of earning some money that could allow me to stay there for months rather than the two weeks envisaged when I bought my return ticket.

Most people who arrive at Malaga Airport head straight for their sun-trap of choice and never return to Malaga except to catch the flight home. I had other plans and, having settled in at Carvajal, and before checking on the delights of the local hot-spots like Benalmàdena, I headed back to Malaga itself to explore the old town and to look for the offices of an English-language magazine I'd heard about. I was job-hunting.

I liked Old Town Malaga, a reminder that the south of Spain had not all been decimated by a particular breed of foreign tourist.

The magazine's offices were not easy to find. They were deftly camouflaged in an area where the street name and number don't seem to exist unless you are *au fait* with the local idiosyncrasies. When I did eventually find the top-floor garret, I was already losing the will to live; it was not the slick operation I was expecting.

Nevertheless, had they been in employee-seeking mode, I would have gone for it, but they weren't. It was soon apparent that, despite my recent writing credentials, including having been Features Editor of two national magazines, it cut no ice. My services were not required in Malaga; perhaps I was too pale. Their loss. I coped with mine by reminding myself I would never have to climb all those stairs again.

I was now faced with having to entertain myself for a further ten days in a place which was geared to people who wanted to sit in the sun all day and drink cold beer. This was Maria and Maggie's idea of holiday heaven and I felt no remorse about leaving them to it and tried to do my own thing.

———

In Carvajal there was not a lot besides the station so I began to explore Benalmàdena, two stops away, and soon found a bar that was not on any tourist trail and did not sell Watney's Red Barrel. The owner was French but most of his clientele were either Dutch or German which gave me the opportunity to see if I could still hack it in German after 20-plus years.

There was a woman who had also found Antoine's;. Her lack of a tan suggested traveller rather than tourist. She was tall, elegant, a few years my senior but ageing well, contemplative more than gregarious, and always by herself.

For a few evenings we sat at opposite ends of the L-shaped bar and she will have noticed me for, like me, she did a lot of people watching, often using the long mirror behind Antoine as a convenient cover. She talked mostly with Antoine but occasionally exchanged pleasantries with the regulars, in much the same way as I did, from which I gleaned she was German. It was inevitable that we would eventually end up in each other's company.

Magda was a contemporary artist based in Heidelberg. As I suspected, neither of us did beach or pool-side holidays and, like me, she wondered how on earth she had ended up in the Costa del Sol. Our ideas of hell were remarkably similar. Her excuse was much the same as mine; she was staying at the apartment of a friend though, unlike my hosts, her friend was still back in Germany.

We spoke in both English and German although, like most educated Europeans, her English was better than my German. She talked little about her art for at the time Magda was preoccupied with her daughter and whether or not to interfere in her relationship with an older man. Her instinct told her to keep her counsel and not to get involved but, according to Magda, this particular 'older man' was a well-known film director who had a public and controversial past regarding relationships. He was also nearly 30 years older than her daughter.

My own local difficulty to which this trip was also a kind of antidote, paled into insignificance when compared to Magda's story. I was on the cusp of a potentially complicated relationship with a squash-playing friend who was also the wife of my dentist. I think it was the thought of him finding out that triggered my recurring dream involving a particular scene from *Marathon Man*. Disappearing for a while seemed like a good idea.

Magda found my story funny whereas, because I correctly guessed the name of the director involved with her daughter, I could see how it paled into insignificance given the possibility that she could so easily become the focus of media attention and their penchant for exaggeration and misrepresentation.

So there we were, two reluctant visitors to the Costa del Sol, barflies who, while sharing some woes, found compensation in looking

---

forward to having a drink or three together each evening. Gloom and doom was not in either of our natures and in each other's company we had found the perfect antidote to being stuck in Benalmàdena with our problems, real and imagined.

We discovered too that we both had an indecorous bent; Italians would call it *cattivo*, naughty but not necessarily in a bad way. This became clear when I told Magda about my time in Bad Honnef and in particular about crossing the tracks every day to have a free lunch in the adjacent engineering plant. Magda's equivalent story was about being caught out in a heavy rainstorm in Brussels and gate-crashing the nearest up-market hotel where she went into a bedroom being cleaned and used towels and a hair-dryer.

Magda confessed that she did what she did through desperate need at the time but felt a twinge of guilt afterwards; telling me was the first time she had shared her transgression with anyone. I reassured her it was unlikely that Interpol were still on her case.

We agreed that in both our stories we got away with our indiscretions because we looked the part: I looked like a German student in Bad Honnef; her elegance marked her as a client of that particular Brussels hotel. Here in Benalmàdena neither of us looked the part; nobody could ever mistake us for being anything other than out of place. We felt like two travellers who had got on the wrong train and had ended up in an enormous open-air amusement arcade.

It was from such musings that the idea germinated. I can't recall who was the first to put it into words, only that the mix of alcohol, friendship and daytime boredom coaxed it out of us. Despite not looking the part, could we get away with doing the same here? Could we wander into one of those larger impersonal hotels and have breakfast with the other guests? Could we go up to the rooftop swimming pool and sit on the loungers or take a dip? Could we?

We decided we probably could and it would be a bit of craic to find out. After all, what would happen if we were caught? Prison was unlikely, deportation we might view as a positive result; a rap on the knuckles, a shaming lecture or paying up were more likely.

The following morning was the first time either had seen the other in daylight. We met outside the park and set off towards the sea in search of a hotel which seemed large enough to be impersonal. In this respect we were spoilt for choice and perhaps not being able to make up our minds initially was a symptom of our nervousness.

Our indecision succumbed to pangs of hunger and we entered a large white monstrosity, trying to look as if we actually knew where to go for breakfast. That wasn't difficult, we just tagged along with the flow of bronzed guests doing the same. Before committing ourselves, we made sure that the path to tray and food was uninterrupted, that there were no obvious checks or anything else to suggest that our cover might be blown.

Magda was a natural whereas, for me, that first breakfast was an edgy affair. Sitting among happy, holidaying families made me feel conspicuous. I sensed that every eye in the room was directed at our table which was illuminated by a bright theatre spotlight. Of course people had better things to do than watch a couple of middle-aged oddities eat. Wolfing down their own breakfast before heading for the beach was their priority. If anyone was going to notice the two cuckoos in the nest, it was more likely to be hotel staff and, from what I could see, the two on duty that morning appeared to have eyes only for each other.

Flushed with success, we joined everyone for breakfast again the following day, only this time we helped ourselves to some of the fruit for lunch and Magda actually made herself a sandwich for later. She was braver than I was, I was still in edgy mode.

We planned one more such breakfast rendezvous only this time Magda wanted to go for a pre-breakfast swim in the hotel's rooftop pool. This was definitely her idea; there is zero chance that a swim of any kind would ever be on my agenda.

This meant getting to 'our' hotel a little earlier and taking the elevator to the roof, all of which we accomplished without a hitch. I sat on a pool-side lounger while Magda had her swim; my excuse for not being in the water was that I had forgotten my costume and, besides, we needed a lookout. Magda dried off, changed and we went downstairs for breakfast as normal.

That was our last breakfast there for I reckoned I saw one of the staff look at us suspiciously; I couldn't be sure, and perhaps I was just being over-sensitive, over cautious. We'd had a good run and it was time to move on and, anyway, Magda was returning to Germany the following evening.

We met that evening at Antoine's and again the following morning after breakfast to say our goodbyes. We had coffee in a bar next to a large hotel which had a pool for guests outside at street level but in a fenced-off compound. Its resemblance to a prison yard—albeit one with lots of screaming kids—amused us both from which the idea of breaking in was but a short mental leap.

With the swagger of confident grifters, we entered the hotel through the front door and exited the side door and into the compound and its enclosed pool and surrounding loungers and chairs. I wondered to what extent Magda had planned this for, under her dress, she was wearing her swimsuit and within minutes was cooling off in the water while I kept watch.

Magda was drying off when I saw him. He had all the build and charisma of a night-club bouncer and one of the hotel's uniformed flunkies was pointing us out to him. As he was lumbering his way round loungers, tables and undisciplined bodies, we had just enough time to gather everything together and make for a side gate that only opened from the inside. By the time Lumbering Man reached the gate we were well on our way to a stiff drink; I could even have downed a Watney's Red Barrel.

Magda flew home that evening, still unenthusiastic about where her daughter might be going in her relationship and no more certain about how to deal with it. I never heard from her again.

Like Gus, I often wondered whether she was a figment of my imagination until, that is, I rummage around at the back of a drawer to check that I still have the scarf she left at Antoine's.

THE CHOSEN ONE

For a while, life was generally unstable and I didn't have the wherewithal to travel far. Nevertheless it didn't stop me getting across to Ireland every once in a while.

I had penned a few books about canals, mainly guides and histories, and had some copies with me to give to my cousin Pat in Dun Laoghaire. It was the first time in well over a decade that I had crossed the Irish Sea by ferry as opposed to 30,000 feet above it. My plan was to surprise Pat and have a few days chewing over old times and share a bit of craic. At the time I needed such a diversion.

Living in England the 'Troubles' had not generally impacted on me; I was, of course, aware of them when I went back home but in the Republic, although there had been a few high-profile incidents, day-to-day life was generally more normal. It never occurred to me, for example, that someone of suspicious pedigree who wanted to travel from, say, London to Belfast, could avoid some of the more rigorous scrutiny by travelling overland and by sea via the Republic of Ireland; travellers by train and ferry are more difficult to police.

Nor did it occur to me that sitting innocently sharing a bit of craic with a fellow-passenger on the train to Holyhead in north Wales, while still sporting what was clearly a northern Irish accent, might have alerted the antenna of a member of the security forces within earshot.

When I first noticed that there were plain-clothes Special Branch officers patrolling and policing the train, I assumed they were looking for those on their 'wanted' list or anyone wearing a balaclava or with I-R-A tattooed on their knuckles or the butt of a pistol sticking out of their belt. I had not thought this might include anyone who talked funny and I was therefore a mite surprised when I got a grilling from one such agent of the Crown who had clearly picked up on my accent and wondered why I was heading south and not north.

"Excuse me, sir, what is the purpose of your visit to Ireland?"

"To visit my cousin."

"Where are you travelling to after the boat docks in Dun Laoghaire?"

"Just up the hill."

"Sorry?"

"Up the hill … to my cousin's … she lives in Dun Laoghaire."

I knew I was being obtuse and, although I was enjoying it, perhaps it wasn't the best policy.

"You're from Northern Ireland?"

Full marks on accent identification, I thought. I knew that 20-plus years in England had softened my accent but I never lost it.

"I was born in the north, yes."

I deliberately called where I come from 'the north' as opposed to 'Northern Ireland'. This is a political preference, as I consider my home city to be in the north of Ireland as opposed to being in Northern Ireland; though of course, for some, it is both. Also, by saying 'the north', I was aware that I was flagging up something about me in the eyes of my interrogator.

"Are you going to Northern Ireland?"

"No, I'm visiting my cousin in …"

"Where do you live?"

"England."

"Where in England?"

"Bristol."

"Are you intending to travel to Northern Ireland?"

His transparent attempt at catching me out with the same question using different words didn't work.

"No, I'm visiting …

Even if I had been going up north, I would have still have replied in the same vein.

Unimpressed, he went about his business, leaving me in that philosophical no man's land between realising he was only doing his job—and one which I suppose he thought was important—and feeling irritated by his intrusion.

I had already seen the same super-sleuth pass along the train several times; he—and his colleagues—stood out so much that they might as well have had a sign around their necks saying 'Special Branch'. Now, if I had been an aspiring terrorist, the last thing I would have done within earshot of any of them, would have been to speak. And, if I'd been a Special Branch agent, I would have been looking out for all those who stopped talking as I approached. But, then, what do I know, I didn't go to Special Branch school?

I was not asked for identification, about which I was quite relieved for I didn't have any. I didn't bring my passport as, at the time, it was not obligatory and I had left my driving licence at home as I was not driving. I only thought of my potential oversight after my 'interrogation'.

Disembarking at Dun Laoghaire I was surprised to see that there were customs tables similar to the Amiens Street Station set-up I had experienced as a teenager light years earlier. Unlike Amiens Street, not everyone had to stop and open their bags; people were extracted from the masses by the summoning wave of a customs official's hand.

When I saw my nemesis, the persistent super-sleuth from the train, and watched as he approached one of the customs officers and whispered in his ear, I was not entirely surprised when I became the chosen one and was given that summoning wave.

The officer, a bespectacled man perhaps five years my junior, was the personification of politeness, almost apologetic at having to impose on me. He rummaged through my bags as he asked me where I was going and how long I was staying in Ireland. He then asked to see my identification in a very matter-of-fact way; he just assumed I would have some.

"You don't have any ID?" The disbelief in his voice was almost tangible when I confessed to having nothing to prove who I was, or wasn't.

"No," I said. "it never occurred to me. In all the times I've come here, I don't think I've ever been asked for it ... only when driving."

"You have absolutely nothing on you that can identify you ...?" Still not quite grasping that it was possible.

I thought for a moment ...

"Just a minute ..." I rummaged in my bag and found the book I was looking for, *Towpath Trails*. I showed him the book's front cover where there was a photograph of a canal footbridge. Atop the bridge there was a couple, the woman carrying a child on her back and the man apparently pointing out something to her.

"I wrote this book ... look, there's my name." I said, jabbing the cover.

He looked impressed, despite the fact that I actually co-wrote it; but at least my name was first though, in reality, he had no way of knowing it was indeed my name.

"And that ..." I said, still jabbing, "... that man on the bridge, the man pointing, that's me. I know you can't see my face clearly ... but look at the sweater ... it's the one I've got on now. I'm still wearing it." I said almost triumphantly, at the same time pulling at the sweater as if to emphasise the point.

He looked at the book, at my sweater, at the book again. He was convinced. There was no doubt about it, I was the guy in the photo, surely no one else could have a sweater like that? To consolidate my identity crisis, I took out another book with an even bolder version of my name—and only my name—on the front cover but, alas, no photo. As identification went, it was not orthodox, but it was good enough for this open-minded customs official.

He wasn't quite finished with me for he went on to talk about his wife and how she was a writer, unpublished at the moment but very talented, he said. Long after my bag was zipped up, we were still chatting like two old friends who'd just bumped into each other and were sharing a few drinks and talking about old times.

As we parted, I assured him that in future I would always travel with some kind of more official identification, while he assured me that he'd get his wife to buy one of my books.

Before exiting the customs area, I cast a last glance around in the hope that I might espy my super-sleuth friend lurking in the shadows. He was nowhere to be seen; reluctantly I put the index finger I'd prepared for him back in my pocket.

MANCHESTER MAGAZINES MAN C1990.

AND GOD CREATED MANCHESTER

In the late 1980s I was in the doldrums and only applied for the job in Manchester because it wasn't in Bristol where I then lived.

The small publishing company were looking for a typesetter for their design and production department and, although I wasn't a typesetter (I couldn't, still can't, touch-type), I knew the basics of what was required. My experience of designing and producing magazines in the boating industry would be, I knew, better than most applicants. I had also written several related books and had worked closely with the publishers in the design of each.

In retrospect I probably got the job because the then head of production was planning a move and was thinking ahead by looking for someone who had most of the skills to run the production department as and when he moved on.

The company was a co-operative and everyone received the same wage. There were three distinct departments: the staff, editorial and advertising, who worked on a fortnightly regional listings magazine, the staff who worked on a monthly national gay magazine and the design and production staff who produced both magazines.

There was some crossover in that, although I later became the head of the production department, I sometimes wrote articles for the listings magazine and also the occasional restaurant review for the gay magazine. When needed, I also took photographs for both.

The first feature I wrote took me to Spain. Not literally of course bur to a supplier of modern kitchens owned by the infamous Spanish matador known as El Inglés who, outside the bullfighting season, based himself at his store in nearby Salford. He was better known locally by the less romantic name of Frank Evans.

When the editorial staff of both magazines discovered I could write as well, they threw me the occasional crumb, usually something that nobody else wanted to do. When they discovered I could also focus a camera, I would turn up at, for example, a pub opening, in an official capacity, as both journalist and photographer.

Another crumb that landed at my feet was an interview with one of Manchester's biggest names in music and media: co-founder of both Factory Records and the Haçienda nightclub and late-night television host, Tony Wilson, also known as Anthony H Wilson. It was at the Haçienda that a young American singer made her UK debut in January 1984. Her name was Madonna Louise Ciccone, stage-name Madonna. And, despite indisputable video evidence to the contrary, she claims not to remember having performed *Holiday* in such a red-brick venue in a post-industrial city.

We met at Wilson's iconic *Dry Bar* on Oldham Street one lunchtime. My interviewee was both late, clearly preoccupied and close to irascible. For me the interview did not go well and, much to Wilson's relief, I brought proceedings to a premature and unsatisfactory close. As I headed back to the office, I caught a glimpse of the early edition of the local evening newspaper. The bill-boarded headline was all about Tony Wilson and the breaking news about his impending divorce. It was then I then realised I'd done quite well.

Gradually a pattern emerged to my editorial contributions: the crumbs thrown by the listing magazine were normally writing assignments whereas, with the gay magazine, they were generally photographic ones. When I was out and about with members of the gay magazine's editorial or advertising staff, I was normally introduced as their 'token Hettie', their token heterosexual colleague. When I was on my own, I was on my own.

The assignment seemed straightforward. Our local pub, which we had nicknamed *The Tarpaulin* as it had been shrouded for weeks in a blue tarpaulin that hid on-going renovation works, was re-opening as a gay bar and somebody had to record the evening's activities.

Apart from the festive atmosphere, the highlight of the evening was to be a male stripper. And so it turned out to be. But, in the meantime, I was having a drink at the bar and got talking to a heavily made-up, attractive, young woman. It took me at least ten minutes to realise that I was actually enjoying the company of a heavily made-up, attractive, young man.

I remember how he registered the moment when I realised that he was male, as he gently thumped me on the shoulder and told me I was not the first to have made the same mistake. Having explained that I was here to record the evening for a gay magazine, I took several photos of him and told him that, thus far, he was the highlight of the evening.

The stripper emerged and I reverted to work mode as, camera clicking, I watched him gyrate between two rows of baying punters, mostly women and mostly straight, as he shed his clothes with gay abandon. Down to his skimpy undies, his gyrating became more suggestive as he stopped with a bottle of oil in front of a middle-aged woman, fag in mouth, on the front row.

By this time I had already been given permission to stand on a bar-towel atop the bar counter itself from where I got a bird's-eye view of what happened next.

Still gyrating, he took the cigarette from the woman's mouth and poured some oil into one of her hands while indicating that she should rub it into his groin area. She did so with relish. What she did not see, but what I and everyone on the other side of the central aisle could see, was that he had inserted her cigarette between his buttocks. Not actually in any nearby orifice but close enough to give the impression of that being its temporary location. Smoke curled discretely upwards.

Gyrating and massage concluded, and before skipping out of view to wild applause, he gave her a kiss, retrieved her still-smoking cigarette, placed it in her dry hand and watched as she immediately put it back in her mouth, taking long, deep, satisfying drags.

It goes without saying that everyone who knew where her cigarette had been in the interim, burst into hysterical laughter. It also goes without saying that not all the photos I took that evening appeared in the magazine.

———

A second memorable assignment, started innocently enough with a query about whether or not I might be available to take a few photos the following Saturday. I said I was and was told there was a 'Leather-Fest' at a gay club in its basement area known as the Mineshaft and a photographer was needed. Was there, I wondered, an over-emphasis on that last syllable?

What I did not discover until much later was that all the other gay photographers on the magazine's books had declined the gig.

I was initially accompanied by two gay members of the editorial staff, one male, one female. We drank for a time at one of the club's several themed 'gay' bars but, when it was time for me to descend to the Mineshaft, my male colleague had someone else to hook up with while my female colleague was off to the adjacent women-only bar. On my own, I innocently descended into the multi-levelled cavernous basement of the Mineshaft.

It took me only seconds to realised that I had not cottoned on to the dress code. Everybody, except me, was wearing leather, some were barely wearing anything but, from jackboots to skimpy, leather was the only attire. My favourite pink denim jacket and the camera singled me out as a person of interest.

I ignored the mix of querulous stares and questions that suggested I might have taken a wrong turning on my way down the stairs and got to work. In those days, my style of photography for such people-centric occasions sometimes involved lying on the floor, camera pointing upwards to get an unusual perspective. I saw no reason to alter my technique.

As I worked my way round the various levels and clusters of leather-clad men, people gradually started to ignore the pink cuckoo in their black and skin nest. As word of my reason for being their slowly drifted among the clientele, so too did their inclination to ignore me or to start posing, individually or in like-clad groups, From military-style to skimpy-style, from boyish good looks to seasoned hairy chests with contrasting medallions.

During the couple of hours that I wandered round trying to get that award-winning, original photo, I became aware how one leather-clad individual was frequently in my photos. This was pre-digital days, so there was no way of checking, it was just a sense that I had seen his face and his leather attire more than a few times, often in the background. That said, as everyone was wearing leather, it was not easy to discern who was who.

I did not feel intimidated by the experience, it was no different from being the only one on a beach who is fully dressed in a sea of bikinis and speedos.

The magazine had access to a fast turn round on developing and processing photos so, come Monday morning, we were already choosing which ones might appear in the next edition. As if on cue, the phone rang on a distant desk.

The person at the other end wanted to speak to Saturday night's Mineshaft photographer and I was duly summoned to said desk where I found myself speaking to the guy who had hustled his way into more photos than he should have.

In apologetic tones, he explained how we couldn't publish any photo that included him because he was the Branch Manager of a bank and Head Office, he surmised, might not approve. Apparently Head Office was not aware that their young Branch Manager was in the habit of parading himself around town dressed in leather. On the other hand he did offer to buy any of the photos that he had forbidden us to print.

——

It was in Manchester that I met more than a few interesting people, many of whom were in the public eye. I never saw their apparent status as setting them apart from me or from the general population but then that too seemed to be part of the Manchester culture at the time. You could literally end up rubbing shoulders with Mick Hucknell (*Simply Red*) at the supermarket vegetable counter or chatting to comedian Caroline Aherne (*Mrs Merton, The Royle Family*) at the bar. Music-wise it was on a par with Liverpool in the 1960s, as evidenced by Sarah Champion's brilliant book. *And God created Manchester.*

Britain's most enduring television soap, *Coronation Street*, was Salford-based (Salford is a part of Greater Manchester) and Manchester-made and sharing a pint or a coffee with one of the cast was neither unusual or noteworthy. In addition, many of the up-and-coming comedians in the early 1990s, such as Steve Coogan, had their roots in Manchester and were often to be found in the Cornerhouse bar.

All of this somehow became a natural part of my world, the more so when I became the in-house graphic designer at Cornerhouse, at the time Manchester's prestigious cinema and gallery complex, an arts centre with both a national and international reputation for its photographic books and projects. On several occasions this work took me to Frankfurt and its annual Book Fair where, for some inexplicable reason, we always seemed to eat in Italian restaurants.

It was also at Cornerhouse that *Reservoir Dogs* had its first UK screening and, not surprisingly, the director turned up and spent the day with us. It was, after all, Quentin Tarantino's first movie and, at the time, no UK distributer would touch it which is why it premiered at Cornerhouse. I recall how, at the post-screening Q&A session with Tarantino, someone asked him about the absence of either a reservoir or any dogs in the movie. Momentarily Tarantino was speechless.

In the early '90s, less exotic than my Frankfort trips, were my monthly commutes to and from London.

Cornerhouse had taken on the production of one of the UK's most prestigious and long-standing photographic magazines, *Creative*

Camera. In the wake of a complete redesign and a new editor, I was tasked with the interpretation of Pavel Büchler's innovative design and working with London-based editor, David Brittain.

Of all the work I did in Manchester, this was by far the most rewarding. Not only did I get the opportunity to travel out of town for a day, but I also had the satisfaction of being associated with a unique and respected project, established in 1968, that had a loyal national and international following.

Finally an off-the-wall Manchester encounter about which I had almost forgotten.

Somewhere between the listings and gay magazines, and working at Cornerhouse, I designed, produced and occasionally wrote for a Manchester-based magazine that focussed on Greater Manchester's many theatres and their various projects and productions. My colleague, the magazine's editor, was also the son of one of Britain's most respected furriers with an international clientele.

Once described by Orson Wells as 'the most exciting woman in the world', American singer-songwriter, Eartha Kitt, was also known for her acting, dancing … and her furs. But few knew that she sourced this part of her wardrobe in Manchester. I knew through my colleague and, through him, I also knew that she was back in Manchester to see her favourite furrier.

I was walking down a city centre street when I passed her walking in the opposite direction, ostensibly heavily disguised in extra-large sunglasses. I turned back and went up to her with the intention of talking about our mutual furrier friends. At first she thought I was an autograph hunter or a camera-less paparazzi and was inclined to shoo me away. But, when I mentioned the name of her furrier, she instantly mellowed and we stood in the street and talked about how I knew the family through their son and how we worked together on the same magazine, the same theatre magazine. And together we shared our affection for Manchester and all its furry friends.

I only ever told one person, my editorial colleague and her

furrier's son, of my brief happenstance encounter with Eartha Kitt in a Manchester street. I think he was a bit miffed.

Bumping into Eartha Kitt in this way was a surreal experience for me. She was the only so-called 'celebrity' that I ever felt in awe of when I met them. Although our brief conversation focussed on the mundane, I had been an admirer of her songs and music for over 40 years and was always glued to the television when I knew she was performing. And, no, at no point did I say, "I'm your biggest fan."

Of all the many well-known faces that I have encountered down the years, Eartha Kitt was the only one that I did not treat as anything other than an ordinary person. It was a deeply personal moment and I didn't share it with anyone because it was also tinged with a hint of regret for I always felt guilty about invading her private space when I had no right to do so.

That said, I like to think she forgave me my impetuous indiscretion. After all, she did give me a big smile when we parted.

———

I took me just six years to pass through Manchester at a time when, it seemed to me, it was the epicentre of British music and culture, a vibrant city with craic in abundance, a city I adored being a part of.

I had arrived as a 'fake' typesetter and left as a freelance graphic designer and, with Cornerhouse and *Creative Camera* in my portfolio, I knew I would never be short of work.

EYE-OPENERS

In the early 90s Kay and I formally brought an end to our time apart, our Interregnum as we called it, and, in so doing, inaugurated the veritable travelling spree which lasted more than 25 years.

Our first port of call was Portugal where we knew we had friends from our boating days; we just didn't know where they lived. Kay was sure I had the slip of paper they pressed into our hands as they fled; I was convinced she had.

We assumed that Frank and Pen had gone to live in the Algarve, a safe bet as it is to the Algarve that most British ex-pats seem to gravitate. And, it was to the very same Algarve that our dirt-cheap, last-minute break took us on our first—and last—package holiday.

A quick browse through the local phone-book soon located Frank and Pen and our friendship took up where it had left off, almost as if the intervening nine years had lasted no more than a fortnight. The reunion itself remains a blur, apart from the pig that ran across the road in front of the car.

We visited the Algarve and other parts of Portugal several times over the next few years and through our friends we had our first taste of the ex-pat lifestyle.

True, I did have some exposure in Benalmàdena but this was altogether different. For a start the sky-high, tightly-packed apartment blocks that pepper much of southern Spain never happened to the same extent in Portugal. In any case, what I observed in Benalmàdena was people on holiday, not people who had moved there; though of course most ex-pats started their journey of a lifetime by holidaying in or near their eventual home of choice.

In many parts of the Algarve there were English-speaking ghettos, mainly in towns but also in the countryside. It was clear that the British—and probably other nationalities too—liked to be in each other's company which was at odds with what I thought travelling was about. There seemed to be an unashamed mind-set which said everything British is good, everything non-British is flawed; except cheap wine and free sun, of course.

What I did not get—and still do not get—is why anyone would emigrate to another country and expect things to be the same as where they were accustomed to living. For me the clue is in the name: in this case the country is called Portugal, the language they speak is Portuguese, their Portuguese culture has evolved over thousands of years. Why would any emigre with a brain either want or expect things to be the same as they are back home? The only common factor they share is that the sun shines over both; just more often in places like Portugal.

But there can be something more insidious with this type of ex-pat mentality, this inclination to embrace the ghetto. It's not only that so many expect things to work in the same way as they do 'back home' but also there is the more scurrilous notion that how things are done 'back home' is intrinsically better, that there is right and wrong, and the way they have been used to back home is, and will always be, the right way. I repeat, if you would like everything to be the same as 'back home', then why would you emigrate?

That said, Frank and Pen were not like this but a surprising number of the ex-pats whom we encountered, most definitely were. I realise I am generalising but only because it's what I observed many times on our frequent visits to the Algarve. I realise too that not everyone can be tarred with the same brush but, those that can be, do the nationality they hold in such reverence and awe a great disservice.

An example ... one ex-pat who had lived in Portugal for many years, a man who had benefitted from the openness and generosity of the local people, somehow thought it was just a bit of craic to call these same people, his neighbours, 'Porkies' behind their back and belittled everything they did and everything they stood for. Equally reprehensible was that, when he spoke in such insulting language, nobody challenged him. Nor did I ... but I did get up and leave his company in what I hoped was a pointed way.

To be closer to Frank and Pen, we did consider a move to Portugal in the belief that we wouldn't have to be part of this, that we would develop our own circle of Portuguese friends ... you know, the people who were actually born there and grew up there. I'm sure there are people who have done this successfully but in parts of the Algarve it would not have been easy.

The notion of the ex-pat (the expatriate), a label I have used liberally, is of someone who has taken up residency in another country but it is, I believe, a term that places more emphasis on their country of origin and their past and not a word that expresses enthusiasm or affection for what lies ahead. I have used it only because it was how those I was referring to generally defined themselves.

Also, lest I appear to be singling out the British ex-pat, I realise too that there are those who emigrate to, say, Britain and Ireland from other European countries and never actually make a friend who is a native of their adopted country. Such people choose to live instead in a bubble where there is only room for their own national language, culture and food. Sadly, I knew someone from Calabria who never managed to have a single indigenous friend when he lived abroad. So, yes, it does work both ways.

A decade later, when Kay and I went to live in another country, at no time did we ever see ourselves as ex-pats; on the contrary, in the country we chose to live in, Italy, we saw ourselves as its two newest citizens. We lived in a town where, for eight and a half years, we were the only English-speaking people and, truth be told, had we inadvertently set a trend and become the catalysts for an ex-pat community, we might have decided it was time to move on. I hasten to add that when we did move on it was not for such a motive and, at the time of writing, there are now no English-speaking residents in that town.

———

Like most tourists and ex-pats, we flew to Faro when we went to Portugal but, unlike most, we got to know the town itself and not just its airport. It became one of our favourite places and it was here we met Spike.

We were sitting on a wall by the sea, only occasionally did a train on the line in-between block our view. A man approached from the town and sat close to us; he was in his 70s, wore a white tee-shirt and crumpled, almost matching shorts, a floppy hat and shoulder-bag to match; also white.

He didn't look Portuguese but then he didn't look British either. I had plumped for German but, when he spoke, it was clear he was English and most probably gay.

"Found Faro, then?"

It was obvious that Spike himself had 'found' Faro a long time ago for he told us that he had been coming here before it was fashionable, before the ex-pat community spoilt the Algarve. His words not mine.

Now here was an 'ex-pat' who did not typecast himself as such but rather as someone who liked Faro and its people and respected them as well. He talked about the town with affection, almost as if he'd lived there all his life. He wanted to share his experience with others and, because we'd 'found' Faro, he surmised we might be of like mind, travellers rather than tourists. And he was right.

We took him up on his offer to show us round the town, after which we ended up in what he described as Faro's most authentic bar, a place that had scarcely changed in all the years he had been coming here. He said that with little optimism, as if he already knew there was a developer with a bulldozer waiting around the corner.

Spike didn't join us for a drink which puzzled us initially but, on reflection, I suspect he didn't want us to think we should feel obliged to pay for him. He had befriended us because he thought we might like to share a corner of his beloved Faro and not for any sort of reward or recompense.

Though we sought him out on subsequent visits to Faro we never bumped into Spike again and, the last time we were there, the bar he introduced us to was still hanging on. However, a recent Google search for it would suggest that Spike was right in his prediction.

We travelled in other parts of Portugal, including Lisbon. And it was near Lisbon that we had the sort of experience that every traveller dreads.

We had been in Lisbon's stunning Praça do Comércio (Commercial Square) trying to make sense of an installation of large red-brown figures, animals and humanoid. One caught my eye and I had my photo taken with my head between Sumo-man's huge feet. I remember thinking at the time that some day I'll use that photo on the cover of a book and maybe I'll superimpose my head on it; I'll use the one from the 80s when my beard and long hair were a similar red-brown. I have just described the original cover of this book.

On the outskirts of the city, I espied a pedestrian crossing where an elderly woman was standing on the kerb-side longing for a break in the traffic or some benefactor. It has been my experience that, in southern Europe, the latter is a rarity, drivers generally do not stop to allow someone to cross the road, even at a designated crossing.

I, on the other hand, being from northern Europe, am a product of the 'stopping' culture and, aware that she could have been standing there for a quarter of an hour, did stop, as a result of which two things happened in quick succession. A car ran into the back of our hire car and a helmeted, erstwhile motor-cyclist, shot across the roof of the car that had hit us and banged into our rear window before rolling onto the ground.

Naturally everyone's immediate concern was for the motor-cyclist who was clearly shaken but otherwise unhurt and more concerned about his mangled bike than his injured body.

The sequence of events was simple: I stopped to let the old lady cross the road; the car behind me braked too late and hit me; the motor-cyclist behind him also braked too late and hit him, propelling said motor-cyclist across the roof of one car like a human cannonball and into the back of another; ours.

Now, we all know that, in such incidents it is the person behind who is at fault but that doesn't always stop that person trying to wriggle his or her way out of taking responsibility, particularly if they realise that the driver of the car in front is a foreigner and doesn't speak their language. How much more of a disadvantage could you be in?

This was my immediate, albeit uncharitable, thought. Already I was picturing a similar incident happening in the UK and could see my imaginary foreigner being well and truly taken to the cleaners by my imaginary British driver-from-behind.

I was thus expecting to get shafted once the other car driver became aware that I was not Portuguese. In fact the opposite happened and he tried as best he could to take me through, in English, the forms that had to be completed.

True, he did question why I had stopped when clearly I did not have to and didn't seem to appreciate the logic behind all those black and white stripes straddling the road. Also, my explanation was somewhat neutered by the fact that my alibi, the elderly woman, having seen the chaos she'd inadvertently initiated, decided she didn't really need to cross the road after all and was now nowhere to be seen.

Maybe, I thought, this was Granny's hobby, a bit of craic in her older, greyer world. Maybe she came and stood at this very crossing every day just to see what chaos she could create? Perhaps at this very moment she was sitting back home in her rocking chair chuckling to herself and marking a '3' on her calendar.

Despite his reservations about why I had stopped and the disappearance of my star witness, the driver-from-behind did not question his own culpability, nor did the motor-cyclist behind him. One or other had already called the police or, on reflection, maybe this too was party of Granny's eccentric pastime?

Moments later the long arm of the law pulled up alongside us and within a quarter of an hour everyone had been breathalysed and the insurance accident forms duly completed and signed. Ultimately everyone was satisfied with the outcome and we all shook hands in a business-like way and continued our journeys. Two driving, alas one pushing.

Five minutes later I was at the hotel bar enjoying the stiff drink I was glad I hadn't had an hour earlier.

Later, when we returned the car at the airport, we had to forfeit €100 for the damage but this was repaid within a month when the paperwork found its way through the system to confirm that I was not at fault.

Clearly the ex-pat-speak that I'd frequently heard about the slow-moving cogs of Portuguese bureaucracy did not seem to apply when it came to incidents such as this.

On reflection, visiting the Lisbon area a couple of times had sounded the death knell for the Algarve. Being neither inclined to sit on a beach nor by a pool, increasingly there didn't seem much point in heading for the coast. In the end the only attraction was the price of the air fare and the few friends we had there.

This was brought home to me when I had a surprise message from my younger brother. He had just booked an apartment on the Algarve and it had a spare bedroom. A few days later he picked me up at Faro Airport. Kay was involved in a college reunion so I alone was my brother's designated guide to the Algarve.

Apart from Frank and Pen and a few of their friends I realised that there wasn't much else that drew me to the Algarve and, if anything, the ex-pat scene had the opposite effect. As I mentioned above, there was a time when we considered a move there but by then we had already had our first taste of Italy which led us to look at the Algarve and Portugal in a new light (see chapter *Just following directions* on page 195).

Sharing the delights of the Algarve with my brother, including Frank and Pen, was the last time I visited the Algarve.

Some years later, while living in Italy, we discovered that the only way to get to Galicia in north-west Spain for a family wedding was to fly to Aporto in Portugal and then drive north. It was only then that I realised there was another side to Portugal that we had missed by being fixated on the Algarve.

HAPPY BIRTHDAY TO ME …

It was our first time in North America where we were planning to spend two weeks in the America's Pacific North-West and south-west Canada. On the advice of an American friend we had deviated from our original itinerary to benefit from the financial rewards of shopping in 'no-state-taxes' Oregon.

We arrived in Portland late but planned to spend all the next day there. It was also my birthday.

The same American friend—clearly in the pay of a local tourist agency—also told us that upriver on the Colombia, in the shadow of Mount Hood, you could take trips on a sternwheeler, a river steamer theoretically propelled by a large paddle wheel at the rear.

His sales pitch knew no bounds for he threw in what he thought was an additional incentive by telling us that this particular sternwheeler was the one featured in the most recent *Maverick* movie. Little did he realise that, for me, such information was more likely to be a disincentive, until I discovered that it was complete baloney.

Nevertheless, and despite the hype, I was drawn to the idea of a trip on a paddle steamer out on the mighty Columbia.

It was truly a magnificent beast in its red, blue and white livery, the centrepiece, albeit at the stern, the huge red paddle wheel which gave it its name. Once under way, the rotating paddle churned up the Columbia into a foaming froth. What a job, skippering this wonderful craft.

As we cast off, my mind flitted back 20 years to my own boating days, to the time when we lived on Britain's inland waterways on our narrowboat *Dolly*; to the time when, to make a living, I had obtained a Boatman's Licence, a sort of driving licence for skippering trip boats on Britain's rivers and canals. For a time, I skippered three such craft, *John Rennie, Viceroy* and *Claverton,* in and around Bristol and Bath. My Boatman's Licence had long since expired, nevertheless it was a unique qualification and one which, I reasoned, might prove useful here on the Columbia.

More in hope than expectation, I had a word with one of the sternwheeler's crew and plied him with two arguments that he might put to the captain to solicit an invitation to visit the bridge. The first was my afore-mentioned Boatman's Licence which gave me the right to skipper trip boats though perhaps I was unclear about the size and scope of these craft in relation to a sternwheeler. The second was the indisputable fact that it was my birthday.

What self-respecting captain of a sternwheeler would have had the heart to refuse?

Certainly not this one for it did the trick; and a few moments later Kay and I were escorted along a maze of corridors and up a narrow flight of stairs onto the bridge where we were introduced to Captain Miller.

From the land, even from the deck, the boat looked like a traditional river paddle steamer but it was all a modern façade; likewise the bridge was almost as sophisticated as an aircraft's flight deck with its hi-tech, state-of-the-art, push-button consoles and levers. Captain Miller seemed delighted to show off his domain and explain how everything worked and how the stern wheel itself was only for show for it was the two engines, one either side, that did all the work. He showed me how, when he powered one up but not the other, the boat would start to turn.

At first I didn't imagine that this was anything other than just idle, albeit informative, chatter between like-minded mariners until, that is, the penny dropped and I realised he was taking my Boatman's Licence credentials seriously and was coaching me on how to handle his boat. It was as if I'd been used to flying the old Vickers Viscount and now I was going to take Concorde for a spin and needed a modicum of instruction to upgrade me.

By using my Boatman's Licence to spark his interest, he had assumed I wanted to have a go myself; perhaps I had overstated my credentials a little. Clearly he had never seen a photograph of a British canal or a top speed of four miles an hour for the well-heeled of Bath.

Then there was the rudimentary nature of the test I did up and down the calm waters of Bristol's Floating Harbour where I obtained my Licence. It was conducted by a retired Merchant Navy skipper who had experience only of sea-going ships and for some obscure reason, asked me what I'd do if I had a boat-load of passengers and the boat's propeller fell off. That sort of experience and being on the bridge of this sternwheeler were not on the same page, not even in the same book.

When I tried to explain to the good Captain the reality of what my Licence entailed, he clearly thought I was being modest. To demonstrate his confidence in me, he took off his Captain's hat, plonked it on my head, vacated his seat and left me in control of his sternwheeler with several hundred passengers on board. Satisfied that I knew what I was doing, he adjourned to the back of the bridge to chat to Kay and left me at the helm.

Kay, aware that the largest boat I had ever skippered held 40 and plied a canal about the same width as this sternwheeler's bridge, was the only one showing any sign of anxiety.

It took me a good five minutes to feel I really was in control. By that time I had stopped wiping my sweaty palms on my trousers and had become attuned to the sensitivity of the two joy sticks I was manipulating to keep us going roughly in the right direction.

Captain Miller was sufficiently impressed that he asked me if I would like to bring it alongside a jetty on the other side of the river—in the state of Washington—where they sometimes dropped or picked up passengers. He pointed to what looked to me to be a very flimsy structure protruding from the far bank and I realised how easy it would be to totally demolish the jetty with this beast of a boat. Nevertheless, egotistically it was tempting, and I even took a closer look through his binoculars, but then I remembered what I once did to a similar jetty on the river Thames with a hired cruiser, long before we lived on *Dolly*. Reluctantly I declined and gave him back his cap and his chair and watched in awe as he slid gracefully up alongside the jetty to pick up a single passenger.

As we left the bridge, I thanked Captain Miller for his generosity and his faith. It was evident that he too had enjoyed the experience; after all, it was not every day a highly-qualified Irish skipper dropped by on his birthday.

Back in among the other passengers, I looked up at the bridge and could scarcely believe that I'd been at the helm of this amazing craft. Even more remarkable was the fact that we had all survived the experience and there had been no cause to use the lifeboats.

Best birthday ever.

Still on a high from the boating experience of a lifetime, we returned to Portland, left the car at the motel, and went into town on public transport to find somewhere to eat, somewhere to wind down, relax and reflect on being in charge of a sternwheeler on the mighty Columbia river.

An Irish restaurant next door to an Irish bar seemed just the ticket and, when we had eaten our fill, we forsook the former for the latter.

I was enjoying my second pint of Murphys when my craic-o-meter picked up the guttural intonation of a Belfast accent from a nearby table. The voice in question just happened to be that of the manager who ran both the pub and restaurant for his father.

I was not in grovelling mode when I told him that of all the Irish stouts, Murphys, a Cork drink, was my favourite, and that the best Murphys I'd ever tasted was sitting on the table in front of me. As I said, I was not in grovelling mode, I meant it for it truly was the best and I've told many people the same since. It's a pity it's such a long way to go for a good pint ...

Sadly my stomach has limited capacity for long drinks like Murphys so I changed tack and began working my way through the Irish whiskey menu when my new best friend, having been told it was my birthday, offered me something different. It was, he said, the best bourbon I would ever taste; he even told me its name.

He was right about the bourbon; I recall telling Kay how exquisite it was just before I passed out from a craic overdose and was bundled into a taxi. Alas, I forgot the name of the bourbon.

Best birthday ever.

For ten years I tried to recall the name of that nectar and every time I saw a list of bourbons, I scoured it hoping that something would reactivate those brain cells that ceased to function in an Irish bar in Portland Oregon. Eventually I got it, the name, the label and the taste came flooding back across the mists of time ... but that's a story for a few chapters down the line.

ON THE WATER. 1996.

MOSTLY *DOLLY*

That day near Portland, Oregon when I took temporary charge of a sternwheeler on the Columbia river was the last time I stood at the helm of a boat, a ship, a cruiser, anything that floated.

.Given that I was a non-swimmer, as detailed in related anecdotes in earlier chapters, it would not be unreasonable to wonder how it was that, for a significant part of my life, I lived on a boat and made a living from Britain's waterway network. Everything about canals, rivers, and even the sea, was to become second nature to me.

I could probably have brought that sternwheeler into moor at the jetty on the Washington side of the river but I did not know enough about the Columbia river and its currents. Also I did not want to botch my first time in America, I might not get invited back.

In a short window of time over a decade earlier. I had learnt about how water in the wild worked, its idiosyncrasies, its capricious nature, its immutable power. I learnt to respect it, how to manage it and when to be fearful.

The boating stories in this book thus far are essentially about my experiences with others who were involved in similar pursuits, living or working on Britain's waterways network of canals and rivers.

What follows are the other stories, the ones that speak of near misses and narrow escapes. and maybe a touch of recklessness. While their chronology predates the Columbia river trip by more than a decade, their place here draws a line under my passion for water.

When *Dolly* first arrived in Braunston her crew of two were no more that boating virgins. All the experience we had under our belts was the time it took us to navigate from the river Thames near Egham to Braunston, in less than ten days.

Yet three months later we had garnered all the know-how and experience to take on the 'round the Horn' voyage that few of our seasoned boating friends, despite their years of experience, would ever have considered, particularly in October. As we cruised slowly past their boats the evening before we left Braunston (see *Did he or didn't he?*), their emotional farewells were genuine, in quiet salute grown men doffed caps that had never before left their head in daylight. Others offered a gentle salute; a few clapped.

It is not surprising, therefore, that there were a couple of incidents relating to that journey that I omitted from the earlier chapter. It's time to rectify that and add a few other narrow escapes which might throw light on why I declined Captain Miller's invitation to slide his huge, passenger-laden sternwheeler alongside that wooden jetty.

The canal part of the journey from Braunston to Sharpness went smoothly and we descended the 30 Tardebigge locks and the next six at Stoke Ptior to Diglis Basin in the heart of Worcester expecting to join the river Severn there.

Although there is little flow on canal water and the channel itself is usually no more that four to five feet deep, each lock is a potential hazard when filling or emptying the chamber, to climb or descend. Falling into a lock or above a lock during this process will inevitably draw a body toward the underwater channel or sluice through which the water is automatically and forcefully drawn to fill or empty the lock. Should this happen there is really no escape.

I respect locks and have never fallen into one and this despite my then reputation for leaping on, up, around and off their black and white-gated architecture like a sure-footed, whirling dervish.

The river lock at Diglis was closed. Following torrential rain in the Welsh hills, the Severn was in flood, running so fast that no craft was permitted to pass through onto the river. When the lock was eventually reopened the next afternoon, *Dolly* was the first boat onto what was still a veritable torrent. Narrowboats are not permitted to cruise at more than 4mph on a canal and 6mph on a river. With the flow behind us, *Dolly* managed 9mph on our one and a half hour dash to Upton-upon-Severn where we planned to spend the night.

For the uninitiated, it's worth pointing out that a narrowboat, like all other craft, large and small, has no brake. Stopping is all a matter of engaging reverse at the right moment and with the right amount of power.

At Upton the river was at least twice as wide as normal and there was just enough headroom at the bridge to duck under it. The moorings by the pub were mostly under water. There was another narrowboat tied up which had basically sunk, its stern was under water while its bow was on dry land, a lone rope stopped it from sliding into the river. It was a hire-boat so a holiday had been ruined and there was a representative of the hire-company trying to pump out the water. He did not inspire confidence as he had the pump in the underwater part of the boat and was basically trying to pump the Severn dry. The water pumped out went back into the river and back into the boat.

We managed to tie up against a mostly underwater and barely discernible jetty but, for the rest of the evening and night, had to check the river level and adjust the length or our mooring ropes to allow for any change. The secret was to have the adjustable end of the rope back on *Dolly* and not on land.

The river did drop overnight and in the morning we were still tied up to the jetty, most of which we could now walk on. Meanwhile our friend next door was still trying to pump the Severn dry. Surely there must have come a point when he realised that the level inside the boas was not dropping?

Although not life-threatening, the events at Upton had the potential to be, at the very least, dangerous. Had we not adjusted the mooring ropes during the night, *Dolly* could have ended up partially on dry land, depending on how fast the river level dropped. Having Gus on board meant that we had an expert to hand on how water 'worked'. Much of the credit for keeping *Dolly* safe in that difficult, and potentially hazardous, situation, must go to our learned stowaway.

Our next stop was Gloucester Docks and, out of sequence, I will jump to events that happened here on another occasion when, over 18 months later, we were doing the same journey in reverse and entered the basin around dusk on a very windy evening.

———

I circled the basin searching for a mooring space that would accommodate 54ft of steel. There was only one spot and it was barely 60ft long and between two white 'plastic' cruisers. Such cruisers and narrowboats do not mix for, if the steel hull of a boat such as *Dolly* hits a cruiser, it will do considerable damage.

I knew that, in normal circumstances, I could squeeze Dolly into that space and touch nothing except the side of the Dock but I was worried about the gusting wind. I knew too that I could also use the wind to help push Dolly into the space.

The owner of the boat that I was gliding past was already on deck making sure that I did not hit his pride and joy. We both knew about 'staving off' which meant that, in my case. I would use one foot to keep the two boats apart, one foot on Dolly and one foot ready to push against the other boat to make sure we didn't touch. Kay was up front ready to jump off and tie up a rope.

All was going well. With one hand on the tiller, one foot on Dolly and by this time, one foot hovering close to the cruiser, we were nearly there when the wind suddenly dropped. I no longer needed to be staving off as the gap between the two boats suddenly began to widen but, at that precise moment, I now had one foot firmly on each boat. Lest I split down the middle, the only thing I could do was close my legs and drop into the water.

In describing what happened next I am relying on the accounts of others as well as my own experience of trying to survive being in the water with the possibility of either drowning or being crushed between two boats. Clearly neither of those things happened.

Kay immediately made it known to the cruiser owner that I was a non-swimmer and he quickly and expertly dropped me a lifebelt which fell neatly over my head. Flailing about before the arrival of the lifebelt, I was aware that the wind must have picked up again, which I later confirmed, for I could feel *Dolly* drifting back in towards me and was aware that I could easily become the main ingredient of a boat sandwich. It was at that point that the lifebelt dropped over my head and I had something to cling on to.

With the bow rope tied up, Kay came to the stern and threw a rope a bystander watching as events unfolded and *Dolly* was pulled into the space without touching anything or anyone. Not even me. With the help of others I was hauled out of the water onto the stern deck of *Dolly*. I returned the lifebelt to its owner and thanked him.

There was no-one at fault. Yes, it was a tricky manoeuvre and, had the wind not dropped at the precise moment I had one foot firmly planted on each boat, there would have been no drama. Fortunately the outcome was more or less as anticipated, *Dolly* was safely tied up between the two cruisers. What was not part of the plan was that I needed a change of clothes and a shower before heading into town in search of the nearest pub.

———

Back to the original journey and still heading for Sharpness. where we had two priorities.

First of all we had to book a registered Pilot, someone who knew the waters of the Severn Estuary and who could get us to Avonmouth's Prince Edward Dock which was our overnight destination. But, in case we couldn't make the Dock before the tide turned, we needed to buy an anchor so that could we ride our a tide at sea near Portishead where there was some shelter. Because we knew that *Dolly* had an engine which was more powerful than necessary for the length of boat, we were confident that we'd make Avonmouth in time.

Because the weather had been unpredictable for a couple of days, we only had about half an hour's warning to get to the Sea Lock at Sharpness where we would take our Pilot on board.

Once out onto the Estuary the Pilot confessed that this was the first time he'd even been on a narrowboat and that, when he was given this particular assignment, some colleagues asked what flowers he'd like at the funeral. He, on the other hand saw it a challenge.

He was, as I expected, surprised at *Dolly*'s power and was confident that we'd not be riding out the tide at Portishead. He didn't seem to be too worried that his hand-held, two-way radio was on the blink and of no use whatsoever. At first the water was calm.

All was well until after we passed under the Severn Bridge when the Pilot suddenly said that we should get everything off the roof immediately and tie everything down that might move. He checked that my motorbike, fixed to the side rail, was stable. Moments before I had taken a photograph of it and the bridge above as I imagined it was the first motorbike to pass *under* the then M4 motorway bridge.

At the time it seemed to me that nothing had changed as the sea still seemed reasonably calm, but his experience was telling him something different and, after all, that's what we paid him for.

Within minutes *Dolly* was battling against more than just a choppy sea as water broke over the bow as she rose and fell with a slapping sound and rolled from side to side. From inside Gus reported that water was splashing against the side windows too.

Although this was not the place for a flat-bottomed boat, *Dolly* ploughed on and gradually we could feel we were over the worst. Ahead, we could see another, much larger boat, the *Matthew*, approaching the Entrance Lock to the Prince Edward Dock but it held back and waited for us to swing to port and enter first.

As the Pilot climbed up the ladder out of the lock, he thanked us for the experience and said that what *Dolly* went through out there was as much as she could take. She was, he added, a fine boat with a brute of an engine. The *Matthew*, a survey ship, tied up behind us and the skipper admitted that they'd been watching us for a while and had hung back in case we got into trouble and they were needed as part of a rescue mission. They also knew the Pilot had no working radio.

In early summer over 18 months later, *Dolly* and I, minus the motorbike and without a Pilot, made this same journey in reverse. On board was a group friends who just wanted the craic. Gus was off on his own adventure and Kay was waiting for us at Sharpness.

Dolly had a permanent base in Bristol Floating Harbour but every few weeks he headed upstream on the river Avon to Bath. At that time the limit of navigation was Bath itself, the flight of six canal locks that ran up from the river were not yet open bur there was hope that they might reopen by Easter.

We were heading back to Bristol on a river in flood and had already found several locks almost inoperable as the water level on both sides was nearly the same. As we approached the last lock, Hanham, we could see that it was completely under water with only the white tips of the beams that supported the gates visible. The lock-keeper was gesticulating and shouting at us to turn back which, given that the river was in flood, was not going to be as easy task. I felt we had only one option and that was to turn down the weir channel, also in flood, and by-pass the lock by shooting over the top of the weir where, in normal conditions, we would have run aground.

I could not be certain we wouldn't touch the top of the weir but was more concerned about damaging the rudder than scraping the bottom. At the same time I had quickly made a calculation about the depth of water under us and the fact that the lock was overflowing and was not surprised when we heard no grinding noises from down below and, with the lock-keeper still shaking his fists, made it safely into the channel that led to Bristol's Floating Harbour where the water level was regulated.

At the time we did not know that our next trip up to Bath would be our last.

Once again we were battling against a river in flood and the journey to Bath took almost twice as long as usual. We should have turned back but we had arranged to meet up with Kay's daughters in Bath and they would stay overnight on *Dolly*.

We tied up as usual, facing upstream as was always safer, where the grounds of the Sports Centre sloped down to a riverside path complete with a waterside railing. Unusually the water was lapping the foot of the railing and, we realised, was visibly rising. We saw the potential danger for, if the river continued to rise and went above the top of the railing then it was possible that *Dolly* would cross over the top and find herself on dry land when the water dropped.

The river was running so fast now that there was nowhere for us to go. Our only option was to increase the height of the railing to stop us crossing over and above 'dry' land. We would also need to attach ropes to the railings which could be adjusted from *Dolly* as the waters rose and later fell. We had two long poles on *Dolly* and, on our way upriver, had picked up a long tree branch with the aim of feeding into out wood-burning stove. By lashing these to the railing we increased its height by almost five feet. If these three extensions held they would prevent us from crossing over the top of the railing. We knew we were in for a sleepless night.

Whole trees were now shooting past us as the river collected and carried all the detritus from upriver. Sometime things, probably large branches, crashed into Dolly above and below the waterline. We spent the night checking the ropes and loosening them out a little more as the waters rose and we got dangerously close to the top of one of our makeshift railing extensions which was shorter than the other two. We knew the higher we rose, the weaker would be those extensions, and the more likely they were to break under the power of the river and the weight of *Dolly*'s steel hull.

As dawn approached we became aware that we were no longer the target for water-borne debris and that our recent rope-adjusting expeditions had not been necessary. The river was still very high but, it seemed, was not going to get any higher. Because of the sloped ground down to the pathway by the railing, it was impossible to get off *Dolly*. Real dry land was about 15ft away.

With *Dolly* still intact and on the right side of the railing we were surveying the day when a policeman arrived and from 12ft away across the water, asked if all was well. I said I would like to make a call from the Sports Centre to alert friends to our predicament and suggested he find someone with a long ladder. Someone always had to be on board *Dolly* for, with the water falling, the ropes still needed to be adjusted so that *Dolly* was not left hanging from the railing.

It took the policemen half an hour to find a painter with a long ladder, an irascible painter who spent the whole time protesting that the longer this took, the more money he would lose. I crossed the ladder, made my call and returned to *Dolly*. The painter grabbed his ladder and scarpered, closely followed by the policeman, his good deed done for the day, An hour later our friends arrived with provisions which they threw to us, still marooned on *Dolly*.

When the waters dropped enough for us to remove our makeshift pole extensions, we discovered that one of the poles had been worn through by continually rubbing against the edge of the railing to within a centimetre of snapping.

It was not until the next morning that we could safely leave *Dolly* but first we decided to vacate our mooring and turn round in the still fast-flowing river. Moving downstream we passed our goal, the entrance to the still-closed Kennet & Avon Canal. With difficulty, we turned again to face upstream and tied up by the entrance to the canal in the hope that it would indeed open at Easter.

And, until it did, this would be our permanent mooring. We'd had enough of the river Avon and its flash-flooding ways.

The canal did indeed reopen as scheduled and, though we happened to be first in line to enter, we were not members of the Kennet & Avon Canal Trust and had to wait our turn. Such inanities didn't bother us, we were just glad to finally be on water that didn't have the propensity to suddenly become a raging torrent.

———

There were a few other, less dramatic incidents that had the potential for being causes for concern. The time I fell into Bristol Floating Harbour while jumping onto a boat that was drifting away could have been the most life-threatening. I realised my mistake and tried to turn in mid-air and, in doing so, managed to grab hold of the decking from which I had launched myself. I knew that here in the Harbour, the problem with entering the water was not drowning but dying from Weil's Disease caused by rat urine in the water. I had only ever fallen in twice, Gloucester and Bristol, the two deepest parts of the waterways network.

Then there was the time when, reviewing a narrowboat holiday for a magazine, the river Wey flooded and pulled one of our mooring pins from the saturated bank. All this happened while we were asleep and the next day we had to contend with a boat swinging about on a river that we did not know well and which had visually changed overnight so that we were no longer sure where the correct channel was. We survived but lost a mooring pin in the process.

And finally, another incident at Hanham Lock. While coming upstream with the river in flood, *Dolly* was emerging slowly from the entrance to the lock channel when the huge force of the river tried to force her down the channel to the weir. As this was the first river lock beyond Bristol, I had underestimated the strength of the flow and was emerging too sedately. Eventually I managed to turn *Dolly* away from the weir but, for a time, it was touch and go. This was not the first time I was glad that Dolly's engine was more powerful than it needed to be for navigating canals. Nor would it be the last.

———

It is no coincidence that most of these potential mishaps took place on rivers. Many narrowboats could not have coped with the off-canal trials we unwittingly put *Dolly* through. We were glad to have passed her on to our friend Tony Jackson who brought her back to Bath from the Midlands and, like us, lived on her.

Later, after Tony sold her, she became what seemed like an abandoned and unloved eyesore on the Kennet & Avon Canal near Bathampton. That was the mid-'90s and I suspect locals complained, about her condition and the owner was asked to move her on. *Dolly* deserved better. She was, in the words of our 'round the Horn' Pilot, 'a fine boat with a brute of an engine'

I'd would like to think she still is.

REACH FOR THE SKY

The above title has a serious meaning, The phrase, and title of a war-time film, is about having a specific aim and then having the ability, opportunity and wherewithal to achieve it. For many years my ambition was to learn to fly.

There was a time when I seriously investigated the American Flying Schools, mostly in Florida, where you could go for a month's intensive training and return home with a Pilot's Licence. At a cost of course. When I had the money, the timing was not right; when I had the opportunity, I did not have the money. It never happened.

When, two chapters back, I described my sternwheeler experience on the Columbia river as the 'best birthday ever', that was not the full story for I had another present yet to redeem, a 'ticket' for a flying lesson at Bristol Airport.

It was the spring of the following year, almost six months later, that I drove to the Flying School round the corner from the Airport itself for my lesson. I was accompanied by Kay and her daughter, Mara.

When we met the Pilot in the School's lounge, he asked if anyone would like to accompany us. The very idea would be, I knew, Kay's worst nightmare but, even had she been mulling it over, it was too late for Mara's hand had already shot up. *Me me, me*, was the unspoken gist of the gesture.

Now it's possible that Mara's enthusiasm was borne of a deep need to remain close to me, or perhaps an equally deep yearning to experience flying an a small aircraft, or it could have been the fact that the Australian pilot was ruggedly handsome and only a few years older than she, or it could have been that she wanted to refine her coquettish skills My money was on one of the last two. Maybe a combination.

It was equally clear that our Australian friend was having thoughts along some of the same lines which is probably why, observing this, I immediately forgot his name and mentally renamed him 'Biggles'. Those of a certain age will appreciate the reference, others will have to resort to the internet.

The 'training' Cessna 152 is technically a two-seater with dual controls but there is another seat behind the two front seats, a bit rough and ready but serviceable. With Mara safely belted-in behind and, with Biggles in command at the right-hand controls, we headed for the runway. Clearly he was not going to let me take off … I tried not to make my disappointment show.

To my surprise, accompanied by all the usual chit-chat with the Control Tower, we took off from Bristol airport's main runway, the same runway that that I had taken off from on normal commercial flights. That, in itself, would have been enough to make my day.

Once we were in the air, Biggles having already confirmed that I wanted to fly to and over Bath, where I lived, and to return via the Severn Estuary, pointed the plane in the right direction and explained the nuts and bolts of the left-hand controls I would use to get us there. He also emphasised the importance of keeping the horizon indicator level, and then more or less left me to it. He had other, more important, matters to think about.

Now that the plane was in my safe hands, Biggles abandoned his controls, turned round in his seat and, apart from eventually landing the plane, spent the rest of the hour chatting to Mara. For me, this was a first for, beside and behind me two others were sharing a bit if craic and I was not involved.

For the first five to ten minutes my level of concentration was intense. I was focussed on keeping the horizon indicator where it was supposed to be and the slightest deviation brought renewed correctional pressures to my mind and body. I could feel my hands sweating on the control yoke (the steering wheel) as I make adjustments and several times I was forced to take one hand at a time off the yoke to wipe it on my trousers. Mara and Biggles were, of course, oblivious to my sweat trauma as, gradually, I got the hang of it and was even able to take an occasional glimpse at the landscape out the side-window.

This was a landscape I knew well both from driving its roads and navigating the river Avon and I knew when and where we crossed over the city proper. For those who know Bath on the ground, it's not a gigantic leap to appreciate how its stunning features are equally stunning from above. I asked Mara if she could see the city but she wasn't in sightseeing mode. I knew she wasn't really interested in Biggles, just that he was interested in her.

Biggles indicated that it was time to head back towards Bristol and told me to turn the yoke gradually to the left to make the turn and to straighten up once I saw the Severn Estuary dead ahead.

It was a nail-biting sensation to see the wing on my left dip. I assumed, the opposite was happening on the other side but was disinclined to even look as I was mesmerised by a different, angled view of the world below. When I saw the estuary dead ahead, and as instructed, I levelled off and rediscovered my horizon.

I was to head for the part of the Estuary close to where it became open sea. I tried to inspire confidence by telling Biggles I knew the terrain well as, without further assistance, I headed for the flatness of the water in the distance.

It was as we approached Bristol that Biggles began to take more interest in the information he was picking up about other possible aircraft in the vicinity of a busy airport. There was also another airfield on the northern edge of the city at Filton where the supersonic Concorde was built and Airbus had a base and where there was occasional flight activity.

As Biggles told me to make another turn south away from the water but parallel to it, I could just see the span of the Severn Bridge out of the window. This was the same bridge I'd swept *under* on *Dolly* over a decade earlier. As it was to the north of where I made my turn any notion of flying *over* it too was clearly beyond reach.

It goes without saying that, as we approached the airport, Biggles' interest in Mara abated somewhat as his survival-gene kicked in and he took over the controls to make a safe landing back at Bristol Airport where an easyJet flight was waiting to take off.

It is hard to explain how I felt as I stepped back onto the tarmac. I had experienced something that had always been at the top of my 'to do' list. Better still, and thanks to the irrepressible hormones of the young, I had had more independent control of that little Cessna than others might have had. And, although I had felt intense pressure early on, this slowly but surely became intense pleasure.

Despite what I told myself, I did realise that I was not really flying solo up there. I had a competent pilot by my side and, though he gave the impression of being distracted, he would have been aware if I'd done anything untoward. In reality he was the one in control but he unwittingly gave me the opportunity to feel that I was the captain. And that felt good.

Nevertheless, I had fulfilled part of an ambition and knew that I would talk of little else for the rest of the day. Thereafter, all new experiences would have to be rated against that hour in the sky.

Best actual birthday ever on the Columbia river; best birthday present, an hour flying from Bristol to Bath and back.

JUST FOLLOWING DIRECTIONS

For a number of years Kay and I had travelled a lot in Portugal but the time was right for a change on the European front. Early one evening, we stopped off at our favourite Italian restaurant in Bath, Capetti's, with an idea and a map. We ate, spread the map out on the table and started to plan our next jaunt; it was a map of northern Spain.

I can't recall why we chose northern Spain, but all thoughts of touring the Basque country and visiting Barcelona were soon dispelled when Vic Capetti, friend and co-owner with his brother Ivano, saw our map. He was clearly not best pleased with our intended destination and rolled his eyes in genuine disgust before unhooking a lopsided map of Italy from the wall and plonking it on the table.

His jabbing finger said, "This is where you should go. This is where the craic is."

We did as we were told and, a few months later, had booked to stay in an old *casa colonica* (farmhouse) near the village of Monterchi on the eastern edge of Tuscany, only a few hundred yards from the border with Umbria. The building was being restored and renovated by a London couple whose plan it was to eventually settle there. In the meantime, while the work continued on the top floor, the rest was available to rent.

The transaction had been completed by post and we received the key—not a Yale, you understand, but a proper key, the sort you might imagine hanging from a monk's belt—and the directions from Pisa Airport, eastwards towards and around Florence to and through Arezzo and then on to Monterchi itself.

When we reached the town it was already dark but we had our detailed directions, although these omitted to mention that our arrival might possibly coincide with the local Polenta Festival.

Naive we undoubtedly were. I mean, now we know that almost every weekend from late spring to early autumn, in every small town in Italy there is a *festa* or *sacra*, a festival, an excuse for a party and, more often than not, one that involves consuming a lot of one particular food washed down with the local wine.

While we never actually saw first-hand what this Polenta Festival entailed, we were aware that, on that evening, the thought of a bowlful of polenta plus trimmings seemed to lure hundreds of people to this small hilltop town and the resulting traffic chaos bordered on anarchy.

At the time I was, of course, a driving-in-Italy virgin and, this being our first encounter with the Italian driving psyche, we played it by our north-European rules and stopped to ask a mustachioed man in uniform for some guidance through the chaos. This Manuel from *Fawlty Towers* look-alike appeared to be in charge of directing traffic—possibly a policeman but in Italy not necessarily so as we later discovered—and we had high hopes that he would be able to point us in the right direction.

All we had was Manuel and our three pairs of hands for, unfortunately, none of us had the ability to converse in each other's language other than by gesticulating and attempting to pronounce names of places. Nor were there any pages in our phrase-book that remotely covered such a situation. The 'Asking Directions' sections in such books are generally confined to more manageable and mundane pedestrian situations, with time to practice, generally in daylight, and without the sound of honking of impatient horns.

What was clear was that all normal driving conventions had been abandoned for the evening, the challenge was being able to get from A to B without meeting another vehicle doing the same in the opposite direction or causing a diplomatic incident.

Manuel was thinking; he looked to the left and to the right and at the piece of paper we showed him with the address. It was clear he desperately wanted to help these two strangers who didn't speak his language, if only to keep the cars moving.

In the end it was his hands—as it so often is with Italians—that did all the work; he was talking as well but it was the hands that did the communicating and pointing, the sweeping to the left, the right, down and up, until finally he sent us on our way, down the hillside, out of the chaos that was Monterchi and back into the unlit countryside with a rough idea of where we were going.

Beyond the town and its on-going Polenta party, we turned right off the main road and up yet another winding hill towards the tiny hamlet of Fonaco. The directions from this point seemed clear enough and we thought that at last the end was in sight ... except, of course, that it was dark, very, very dark.

Following a brief difference of opinion, I conceded and we turned left off the road and approached the silhouette of a house, a house with an ageing Renault 4 lurking, perhaps abandoned, half in the bushes, half on the gravelled driveway. I had my doubts about this being our destination for I felt sure our hosts might have mentioned a notable landmark such as a car tucked in the bushes.

The barking of a distant dog broke the silence ... a closer, responding bark, added to our twitchiness. Were there any wolves in Tuscany, I wondered, making a mental note to google 'wolves' and 'Tuscany' when I got back home. If I got back home.

Of course this was the house, in daylight it probably would have fitted the description, well, more or less, and we were bloody tired and for the moment it was the only option staring us in the face. I still wasn't convinced but felt that, if all else failed, at least we could eliminate this from the list and try again further up, or down, the hill.

In case we were trespassing, we crept forward to the door, as silently as the gravel allowed, with Kay clutching the key in a nervous hand. She tried it in the lock, this way and that way; the grinding of metal on metal, seemingly amplified tenfold in the still of the evening, told us that this key was not meant for this lock. At least the house seemed empty, no lights went on, we hadn't disturbed anyone ... except the dogs, or the wolves.

The words 'I told you so' were on the tip of my tongue but I thought better of it at the time—perhaps later in a book would be more appropriate—and suggested instead that we read the directions once again just in case *we* had make some obvious mistake.

Up and down, down and up, that road we went until, weary and disorientated, we turned off to the left and parked outside what proved to be our goal, the beautiful Casa Fonaca, complete with *il pipistrello*, a welcoming Italian bat.

Of course at the time, we didn't know it was beautiful but, after a good night's sleep, our first ever in Italy, we were ready to explore and take in our environs.

And, yes, there are wolves in Tuscany.

———

Some time later we were caught out again on our first visit further south, to Apulia, the heel of the boot.

We had flown to Brindisi and were booked into the Hotel Torino close to the town centre. Armed with the definitive directions taken from the hotel's website we were confident that we'd soon be sampling the local red nectar at a nearby bar.

We turned off the *autostrada* and on to the Via Appia—the south-eastern extremity of the Appian Way that starts in Rome—and headed into town. The directions were all based on turning left or right at traffic lights and the first three turns went according to plan; the final direction was, 'turn left at the fourth set of lights and take the first right and you'll see the Hotel Torino in front of you'.

So far so good ... first set ... second set ... third set ... it's bound to be the next set ... but the next set never materialised. Unless our basic counting skills had let us down, there was definitely no fourth set of lights.

We carried on and almost before we realised it, we had turned into a wide, two-lane thoroughfare, an avenue lined with elegant shops and busy bars, which had clearly been pedestrianised for the evening. To complicate matters further, we were tailgating a police car which was, for some inexplicable reason, in the left-hand lane.

The people of Bríndisi were out walking in the balmy evening air, partaking in the *passeggiata*—a ritualistic evening stroll generally unimpeded by moving traffic which features in a later chapter *A walk on the wild side*—was in full summer swing. Apart from giving them a wide berth, nobody seemed particularly bothered about the slow-moving police car and its attendant hire car. Perhaps they thought we were on 'plain clothes' duty; perhaps even the *polizia* in front of us thought we were 'plain clothes' colleagues keeping our distance.

Our private, two-car convoy continued towards the sea which we could now see 100 metres or so ahead. As we approached the end of the avenue, the police car slowed to a snail's pace; we followed suit.

It stopped. Expecting the worst, we stopped about ten metres behind; for a few moments we sat silently transfixed, watching and waiting.

The passenger door of the police car opened. A uniformed officer stepped out, donned his cap and purposefully adjusted the crutch of his trousers, a sure sign that he meant business.

I suggested to Kay that we go into 'dumb tourist' mode and prepare to apologise profusely for being on the wrong side of this closed-off road. As the policeman was on her side of the car, I was expecting, and hoping, that she'd have to do the explaining.

The policeman glanced in our direction and then strode off to his right and embraced a friend in the middle of the road. They talked, they laughed, they waved their arms, they shrugged, they hugged, they shook hands. They completely ignored us.

Greetings, chit-chat and goodbyes concluded, the policeman returned to his car, got in and it drove off with not so much as a glance in our direction. Naturally, and there being no other option, we followed and both cars turned left along the seafront.

At the next left-hand turn they carried on ahead while we took the opportunity it offered to finally put as much distance between us and them as possible. I turned left and parked; alone at last we needed to calm down and to take stock. We had no idea where we were, nor could we understand where we'd gone wrong and what had happened to that fourth set of traffic lights.

It was time to switch on the satellite navigation, otherwise known as my sense of direction. I knew roughly where we should have been so started to head back 'inland' and, as far as possible, parallel to the main thoroughfare we'd just left. We stopped to ask directions and were given accurate and precise instructions which seemed to include going up a one-way street the wrong way. When I put this to our kerbside benefactor—by pointing to the nearby road sign—he just shrugged his shoulders and repeated that it was definitely the quickest way to the hotel while implying that the conventional, legal route was far too complicated to explain.

Who were we to argue? We did as instructed and he was right. A few minutes later we pulled up outside Hotel Torino.

When we'd signed in and got uncomplicated walking directions to the nearest bar, I asked about the traffic lights. The man on reception shrugged his shoulders in fluent Italian and explained that the fourth set of lights had been removed some three weeks earlier. Unfortunately the directions on the website had not yet been updated.

When I checked several years later, this still remained the case; unless, of course, it was no longer a problem and the fourth set had been reinstated.

RELATIVE STRANGERS

The new glasses my optician said would arrive before we left for Sardinia never materialised. The ones I was wearing were held together with fuse wire and were unlikely to last much longer. Just in case, I had an emergency roll of fuse-wire in my pocket as we stepped off the plane at Alghero.

When we arrived at our destination, the small, off-the-beaten-track town of Scano di Montiferro, it was, as arranged, about four in the afternoon. We parked up and started to look for our bed & breakfast, *La Meridiana del Sole*. After about ten fruitless minutes we found ourselves in a small piazza and stopped a local lad and, in my best Italian, I asked, "*Dov'è La Meridiana del Sole?*" He turned round and pointed behind me; we were standing with our backs to the door.

In vain, we knocked the door with varying degrees of brutality. An elderly woman, dressed in black, emerged from a house on the other side of the square and shuffled over to speak to us, making no allowances for the fact that we might not speak any Italian. But we got the gist of it. He (Angelo) had left and was in Cagliari working. Having delivered the good news, and unwilling to share any more of her craic, she shrugged her shoulders and slowly retraced her steps and closed the door on what happened next.

As one door shut, another opened. It was the door to the right of 'our' door, it was the door of the *Pro Loco*, a sort of tourist information centre, opening (a little late) for the post-siesta session. It was manned by two women (if that's possible), one of whom said "*Meridiana?*" with a definite question mark at the end. We nodded in broken Italian and she raised a restraining finger, said *"Un attimo"*, stuck her *telefonino* to her ear, made a call then looked at us and said *"Cinque minuti"* as she held up five fingers.

Five minutes later there was a screeching of rubber as a battered Fiat Uno shot round the corner, came to a halt and deposited a nervous young woman at our feet. Trying to regain her composure, while adjusting her glasses and re-arranging her dark curly hair, she introduced herself as Rina and in passable English explained the problem. Well, actually, she explained, now that she was here, there wasn't a problem.

Angelo, a painter of stage scenery (we think that's what she said but he could just as easily have been an airline pilot), had indeed taken up some last-minute work in Cagliari and, as we were booked in for bed & breakfast while he was away, he had found a much more attractive substitute in the only out-of-work English speaker in Scano.

Rina took us into the house and showed us round. There were three bedrooms so we had a choice; there was a living room, a dining room and a kitchen though the last was Rina's territory as she would be coming in each morning to make and serve us breakfast.

She was very eager to please and kept apologising for her poor English; if we spoke Italian as well as she spoke English we'd have considered ourselves fluent. While she was explaining something or other to Kay, I noticed something about Rina and got very excited. I reached for the phrase-book and the dictionary. I had to get this right. I practised it in my head. I waited for a break in the conversation …

"C'è un ottico a Scano?" I said, pointing first to Rina's glasses and then to my botched repair job.

"A Scano, no. A Cuglieri però … ottica Dory Perria a Cuglieri," she replied, clearly astounded at my Italian.

"È lontano?" I was on a roll.

"No, non è lontano, sei chilometri." I wondered whether these were six Italian kilometres which always seemed much longer.

"Aperto domani?" I had nearly used up all my Italian words.

"Si, alle nove e mezzo."

Rina went on to sing the praises of the local optician, Dory Perria, and assured me that she could sort me out. So, problem solved, all I had to do was turn up at Dory Perria's place in Cuglieri at 9:30 the following morning and, hey presto, I'd leave with a new pair of specs. I don't think so.

Next morning I woke and switched on the bedside lamp I'd 'borrowed' from one of the other bedrooms. Nothing, the bulb had gone. I got out of bed and switched on the main light. Nothing. Kay tried her lamp. Again nothing. Clearly there was no electricity.

Nevertheless, we could hear Rina downstairs preparing breakfast. Might not be any coffee, but we could cope. We took our time washing and dressing, giving Rina as much time as possible to solve the problem. We went down to the kitchen and got the feeling that, yes, now there was light. And there was.

I think Rina had requisitioned every candle in Scano and covered almost every available surface with them; there were thin ones, fat ones, coloured ones and scented ones and they were all lit. As the dining room was downstairs in a window-less basement there was little natural light except from the kitchen which did have an outside door and a window.

Rina explained how she'd arrived earlier and discovered the lack of electricity and, not wanting to spoil our first morning in Sardinia, she panicked and called Angelo in Cagliari who suggested a breakfast that didn't require electricity. Still in panic mode, the candlelit bit was Rina's idea … nevertheless it was much appreciated and we'll never forget our first breakfast in Sardinia. She'd even nipped home to bring us coffee in a flask.

After breakfast we set off for Cuglieri and Dory Perria, my glasses still flaunting their delicate fuse-wire bandage and perched precariously between nose and ear, I was fervently hoping that the legendary Dory Perria was going to perform some sort of miracle. I had a plan but knew that what I was going to ask of her was something that no UK optician would do.

Of course, not wishing to make a spectacle of myself, I swotted up and rehearsed all the words relating to being 'At the Opticians' and, the moment we stopped outside the premises of Ottica Dory Perria, I forgot the lot. It was just as well her shop was *chiuso*, closed.

We once met an American in Umbria who claimed, after years of dedicated research, that *chiuso* was the most common Italian word. He had probably suffered the scourge of the *siesta* but it is true that even outside the *siesta* shutdown, there are still many *chiuso* signs around, particularly when you're about to run out of petrol. I digress … back to Cuglieri.

It was time to regroup, find a bar, have a *caffè* and consult the phrase-book. Twenty minutes later we returned to the shop … it was open, but packed. We sat down and awaited our turn.

At last we had Dory Perria's undivided attention and I asked her if she spoke English. As she shook her head I took off my glasses and handed them to her. She guessed the fuse wire was an added extra and removed it, trying to hide a giggle as she did so. She told me they were beyond repair, *non si può ripararli*. That bit I think I already knew.

Deep breath … now for the rehearsed bit. I was trying to say that my glasses had three lenses when she looked at me, held the glasses up to the light, and summed it all up in a single word, *varifocali*. I couldn't have put it better myself, we were talking the same language after all, but not for long.

Between us, Kay and I managed to get across the next bit. We wanted Dory Perria to find a pair of frames into which she could put my lenses. Now this was more complicated than it sounds; I knew she would never find an exact match so she'd have to come up with something very slightly smaller and regrind the lens' edges to make them fit while making sure the centre point remained, well, in the centre.

She agreed and so together we started the search for suitable frames. We found some that would have worked but for the bridge being too wide or too narrow, but eventually we came up with the answer.

She took the frames and indicated that she'd have to go to her workshop at the back of the shop and suggested we return in an hour.

An hour or so later Dory Perria had indeed done the business. When I emerged from her shop I was sporting my new designer specs and carrying my free gift, a lens cleaner that resembled a pen. It had cost me €60 (£40 at the time). I couldn't wait to get back to Bath and wave them at the optician who hadn't managed to deliver my new pair on time.

I always take my special Dory Perria glasses with me when I travel … they are my emergency pair.

It was our second evening in Scano and, not keen on reprising the off-road experience of the night before, we were working our way round the town's six bars in search of food. We found four, all of which served only snacks.

Approaching the fifth, on a road heading out of town, we could just make out a sign hanging over the footpath. As we got closer we read the word *pizzeria* and began to get excited but when we actually got there we could see it was an old sign and that this was probably just another food-less bar. By this time we were thirsty so we decided to have a drink and, if all else failed, we could drive the six kilometres back to Cuglieri where we'd spotted a small restaurant earlier in the day.

The bar counter was to the left of the door but there was another room to the right with tables and chairs but no people and no indication that anyone was expected. We ordered two glasses of red wine and sat by the bar to await developments. Nothing happened so we asked if it was possible to eat. The barman said he'd check and disappeared only to reappear a few moments later to continue serving other customers at the bar.

Then she appeared. She stood, arms folded, framed in the entrance to the table-and-chairs room. I half expected that she would become enveloped in swirling smoke rising from the floor announcing the presence of a super-hero. She was tall, elegant and slender for her age, mid-50s I would have guessed, but she had that old-fashioned headmistress demeanour. She seemed capable of putting you across her knee at the drop of a hat. And yet ... perhaps we just caught sight of a twinkle in her eye.

She focused her gaze on us, perhaps she's admiring my new glasses, I thought. It was as if she was waiting for us to make the first move. Kay broke the silence and asked if we could eat. She looked us up and down as if assessing our character; finally she said, "*Si*", directed us to a table in the corner and introduced herself as Nunzia. Having checked that we were happy to eat pork, she disappeared into the kitchen to prepare our meal from scratch, with neither microwave nor packet; every vegetable we ate came from her garden, as did the fruit. We ate like royalty.

Nunzia, was a great cook and we booked in, same time, same place, the following evening and every evening thereafter though we knew we'd have to find an alternative on the Wednesday when, according to the notice on the door, the bar was closed all day. After each meal, she would tell us what she was going to prepare for us the following evening. She was on a roll and the meals increased in quality, quantity and variety as the days went by. But the best was still to come.

To thank Rina for her various kindnesses, and in particular the late-night guided tour of Scano's sub-culture she had taken us on, we asked her if she'd like to eat with us at Nunzia's some evening. She said she couldn't by which she did not mean that it was inconvenient, she meant that Nunzia's was somewhere she could not, would not, go.

What we didn't realise until then was that Nunzia and Rina were related. Nunzia was Rina's *zia*, her aunt. Pietro, the barman and Nunzia's husband, and Rina's father were brothers. And there was a family feud, *la vendetta*.

It was par for the course. The two people we knew best in Scano are at odds with each other over some family dispute though, that said, the 'problem' did appear to be one-way. Nunzia would have been happy to cook for and eat with Rina, but Rina wouldn't eat with Nunzia.

Σ

On the Tuesday we ate as usual at Nunzia's and later she joined us for a *liquore*, *grappa* for me and *limoncello* for Kay. As we were about to leave, and with the bar being shut on Wednesday, we confirmed we'd see her on the Thursday. But it was not to be, for Nunzia insisted that we eat there as we usually did. The doors to the bar might be closed but her plan was that we should come to eat, not as customers, but as guests of the family.

We weren't sure of the etiquette for such occasions but decided to take chocolates and the bottle of Irish whiskey that I'd already bought for myself.

We were slightly nervous when we arrived at the bar, closed to locals but open to us; it didn't seem quite right. The door opened to an altogether different Nunzia; this was the Nunzia at home, not the Nunzia at work.

Returning to her kitchen, she delegated Pietro to become our temporary host; he grabbed a torch and we followed him outside, down some steps and into his own private hide-away, a *cantina*, a place to make and sample his home-made wine. Until then, we hadn't realised that Pietro made the red wine we had been drinking. He made many others too and wanted to share them with us, an *aperitivo*, a couple of whites, a red or three.

Naturally we took the tasting very seriously—first of all we had a whiff of the bouquet, then made reassuring sounds of approval before swirling it round a little and then down it went. We decided not to do the spitting out bit as it might seem impolite and, besides, we were both brought up not to be wasteful.

Pietro also told us he made *grappa* and *limoncello* and showed us the still that he said was his brother's. Later Kay and I gave each other a knowing glance; we had both gone down the same mental track and wondered whether this still was somehow at the root of the brothers' feud?

Nunzia summoned us back upstairs where the *antipasto* was already on the table and we were joined by one of her sons, Ricardo, the other, Salvatore was working away. Nunzia had gone for the full monty: *antipasto*, *primo piatto*, *secondo piatto*, *dolce* and *liquore*, a real Italian feast.

Apart from the meat and fish, everything that Nunzia cooked for her extended family that evening was from her own garden: courgettes, broad beans, aubergines, tomatoes, onions, peppers, garlic, asparagus, herbs and olives and those that were in season, and not from the freezer, were gathered in fresh that day. And none of this was for our benefit, this was how the family ate day in and day out but, as ever with eating in Italy, they took their time, so it was well past ten before the last plates were cleared away.

But the alcohol continued to flow and, as it did, everyone's command of their various second and third languages (Italian, German, French, Portuguese and English) got better. I recall putting together one sentence that contained four different languages and then made matters worse by trying to explain what I'd just done. A few moments later I turned to Kay and said something in French ... she looked bemused and reminded me that I could actually speak to her in English.

With tongues loosening I couldn't resist taking this opportunity to remind Nunzia about our first evening here and asked her what she was thinking when we first asked to eat. She laughed and admitted that she was indeed eyeing us up, deciding whether or not she liked us enough to cook for us. She decided she did and the rest, as they say, is gastronomic history.

A memorable evening was coming to an end but, before we staggered back to base, Nunzia took us through to the back of the bar and opened the door into a bedroom.

"Next time you're in Scano, this is where you'll stay." Nunzia announced. And we did.

———

What a difference six months makes.

We arrived at Nunzia's at eight to the usual round of greetings. By now we were getting the hang of the double kiss and were looking less surprised when the second kiss sneaked up behind the first. Nunzia and Pietro were delighted to see us—as, indeed, we were them—and showed us to our room and told us to come through to the dining room when we were ready.

In the dining room, busier than usual, a less chirpy Nunzia was waiting for us at our usual table. Things had changed here, we could see that, and we could sense that Nunzia didn't embrace the changes. For a start there were menus on all the tables but they were not for Nunzia's creative cuisine, they were for pizzas; and, of course, Nunzia was on the customer side of the serving hatch and her son, Ricardo was in charge of the pizza-making.

It was clear that Nunzia did not embrace this turn of events but she realised that, as and when Ricardo was ready to take over the business, then he had to do things his way, the modern way and the young people of Scano clearly couldn't get enough of his pizzas. Nunzia was not one to fly in the face of progress, though there was no reason why she couldn't go along with things *and* grit her teeth at the same time.

Almost embarrassed she passed us the menu and asked us to choose our pizza … and, no, she didn't follow up with, "Hi, I'm Nunzia and I'll be your personal waitress this evening".

I have to say, give Ricardo his due, it was a really good pizza, and I'm not the world's biggest pizza fan.

So, while we were firmly focused on the Scano of six months earlier, things on the ground had moved on and, like it or not, take-away pizzas were literally the order of the day.

Yes, we were disappointed that things had changed but more for

Nunzia than for ourselves and, whether or not she picked up on this I can't be certain but, whatever the reason, Nunzia decided to rebel.

For the next three evenings she invented a loophole in the arrangement with Ricardo which stated that her paying guests would be fed by her and her alone or else there would be trouble. The Independent Republic of Nunzia was born and the *status quo* was restored—while all around us could be heard the chomping of pizzas, across an imaginary border in our corner of the dining room things were as they had always been.

The twinkle had returned to Nunzia's eye. We could expect another craic-filled evening, after al

RELATIONS IN REGGIO

As Kay was off to a reunion, I naturally headed straight for the Ryanair website and started to hunt for cheap flights to Italy. It was already Wednesday so the earliest I could fly out was the following day, back on the Monday.

At the time I had no destination in mind but eventually landed a bargain to a place called Lamezia Terme in Calabria. I had no idea where that was or what was there but what I did notice was that its proximity to the tip of Italy's toe meant it was only a stone's throw from Sicily.

Sicily is one of those places that conjures up all sorts of intriguing images, invariably linked to men in dark glasses, darker suits and the darkest of intent. Movies such as the *Godfather* trilogy and the more tongue-in-cheek *The Sopranos* series have ensured that the reputation of *la cosa nostra* (our thing), the mafia, is global.

Obviously I wasn't immune to these preconceptions but, being of rational mind, I guessed they were only part of the truth and, besides, there was no way I was going to be that close to this fascinating island and not take a peek. The only other thing I knew about Sicily was that it was home to the spectacular Mount Etna, an active volcano that would still be around long after the mafia had gone.

Before heading for the airport I had time to book a hire-car at Lamezia but had no time to arrange anywhere to stay—bed that night was to be a surprise. And, yes, it turned out to be exactly that.

At the time travelling alone had its benefits, particularly when flying with a budget airline that didn't allocate seats, an economy that clearly put a pressure on couples or families. The lack of such pressure can be strangely liberating, calming even, and the fact that I had no specific destination in mind for that evening didn't seem to matter. I was going with the flow.

The plane departed a little late and as soon as we were off the ground I unfolded my map of Sicily which was all the airport bookshop had on the island but, if nothing else, it served a purpose in that it helped initiate conversation with my sole companion in the window seat.

"Heading for Sicily, then?" he asked perceptively.

"I hope so … depends on how easy it is to get across," I replied.

"Shouldn't be a problem, there's plenty of ferries from Reggio and Villa San Giovanni, it only takes about half an hour."

"You going to Sicily too?" I enquired.

"I'm hoping to but I'm staying with a friend in Reggio for a couple of weeks first. I'll be in Italy for a month or so."

The ice broken, we went through the formalities of introductions, how we each made a living, where we lived, marital status … the usual sorts of things that seem to matter when you first meet someone. Jack, a London-based architect, was gay. He didn't mention the latter but, having several gay friends, I just knew.

We talked mainly about travelling, finding cheap flights on the internet. We played a round of the inevitable lets-see-who's-found-the-cheapest-flight game—I won, one penny plus taxes—and, as we both worked for ourselves from home, about our respective jobs.

As the flight progressed, our chit-chat was increasingly punctuated by Jack looking at his watch and the more he did so, the more agitated he seemed to become. When we eventually landed he explained that he had just missed his train to Reggio and that he wasn't sure if there was another that night.

Step forward Sir Galahad.

I had told Jack I'd be collecting a car at the airport and so, though I hadn't planned specifically to head for Reggio that evening, I was happy to do so and offered him a lift. I knew it was the sort of place where I'd easily find a hotel for the night.

Jack accepted my offer and, as we left the airport, made a call to his friend Paolo, a university lecturer in Reggio, to explain the change of plan—he'd now be arriving by car and there would be an extra mouth to feed and a bed to make ready. My accommodation in Reggio di Calabria had been sorted.

The welcome from Paolo and his friend Octavia was effusive and genuine; they were both delighted to see their friend from England and extended their welcome to me, his last-minute, straight companion and chauffeur.

I'd been in this position before. For some reason some gay men think that I might be gay or, more likely, they pick up that I am at ease with their sexual orientation. I have ways of telling them I'm straight and that's fine too so, all round, it's no problem, we all play by the same rules. .

On only one occasion, as I recall, did someone tried to bend my rules. It was when I lived in Manchester and was part of the design team that produced two magazines for the same company. One of the magazines was aimed at the gay community.

I was in a bar with the gay magazine's editorial and advertising team and friends. I was, in their parlance, their 'token hettie' (heterosexual).

When tanned medallion-man with his white, open-neck shirt came up to our table and asked me specifically if I wanted a drink, all my gay friends told him that he was wasting his time and that I was a 'hettie'. He took the hint and wandered off.

Later, bolstered by the confidence of another drink or two, Medallion-Man thought he'd give it another go. This time my friends were more persistent about my 'hettie' credentials and, to emphasise the point, and clearly picking up on Medallion-Man not being the sharpest pencil in the box, each in turn came up with the name of one of my alleged girlfriends. Apparently, among others, I'd been out with Maureen O'Hara, Lauren Bacall, Greta Garbo and

Bette Davis; one even threw in Truman Capote on the correct assumption that Medallion-Man wouldn't pick up on Capote's essential maleness.

Convinced I was an incorrigible and irremediable 'hettie', Medallion-Man reluctantly threw in the towel. It was no more than a bit of craic but it reminded me that I hadn't called Lauren in a while.

We ate and drank well in Reggio. Paolo and Octavia had prepared an exceptional welcoming feast with several courses served with exquisite wine, though for much of the time my over-active mind was trying to work out the relationships between all these people. Jack and Paolo were clearly 'warm brothers', of that I was certain; Octavia was married and was taking a break from Milan to where she was returning the following day; but there seemed more to her relationship with Paolo than met the eye. It was all too fascinating, not to mention speculative.

I was enjoying myself—eating, drinking and watching—and not at all phased when Agnella arrived to say farewell to Octavia. I was beginning to get the picture—albeit one that didn't quite fit in with my original alcohol-induced speculation— Agnella and Octavia were an 'item' just as Jack and Paolo were. Now I understood why Octavia's husband was still in Milan.

The laughing, drinking and general craic, without the music, continued as the clock swept past two in the morning and we decided to call it a day. But before we all hit the sack, it was agreed that after breakfast I would follow Paolo down to the ferry and that he'd see me on my way across to Messina in Sicily.

Breakfast came and went for five weary bodies—yet another of Paolo's culinary delights made all the more glorious by my first glimpse of Sicily, basking in the mid-morning sun in a limpid green sea. I was impatient to be on my way, I just wanted to get the goodbye hugs and kisses over with and get down to the ferry. But this was southern Italy and I realised I would have to adjust to the slower pace of Paolo and his friends.

As he cranked up his scooter, he gave me his number and insisted that I call him from Messina on my return so that we could all lunch together.

Three days later, having parked the car in the queue for the ferry to cross back to the mainland, I called Paolo as arranged and he and Jack met the ferry at Reggio and we drove to Paolo's apartment for lunch. It was like the reunion of three old friends and, once again, Paolo conjured up a veritable feast.

Sated, we drove a few miles north to the small coastal town of Scilla to join some friends for an afternoon *siesta* by the sea. In normal circumstances this would just not be my thing but I was both tired and excited about getting home.

It was with gratitude and sadness that I said my goodbyes and headed further north to Lamezia Terme and the flight back home.

Two weeks later I was back in Sicily with Kay.

———

I had rattled on so much about my time in Sicily, and in particular the astonishing Siracusa, where I'd stayed for all three nights, that Kay threw in the gauntlet and suggested we go there together.

Except for meeting up with Paolo and Jack en route to Sicily as I had done, we more or less reprised my earlier trip, but I intended to rectify this on the way home. Before leaving Siracusa, I called Paolo to ask him and Jack out to lunch, I was keen to repay their numerous kindnesses to me. He accepted and explained that Jack was now over in Sicily himself but that if I called again when we got to Messina he'd meet our ferry in Reggio.

True to his word, he was on the quayside waiting for us. I introduced him to Kay and he invited us up to his apartment to freshen up before we had lunch.

I suppose I should have smelt a rat but it never occurred to me that he had no intention of letting us take him out to lunch. Instead he was preparing another mega spread; yet again his hospitality knew no bounds. The least we could do was give him a hand.

While I was in and out of the kitchen, Kay had cleared the table in the dining room that looked out over the Straits of Messina. I had just started to bring in the food when Kay picked a piece of paper off the floor and was just about to replace it on Paolo's desk when she noticed it was written in English.

Now, what would you have done? Of course she read it and then forced me to read it too. It was from Jack to Paolo. It was the story of broken trust and hurt, of a long friendship and relationship, now ended; it was an angry and disappointed Jack saying his farewells to Paolo before leaving Reggio and heading for Sicily ... alone.

There you go, I leave these two on their own for a couple of weeks and can they get on? No, they cannot and now look what's happened?

We wondered whether or not we were meant to find Jack's note and, if we were, then how were we expected to react? It was all getting too complicated, too incestuous, so we decided to return the note to the floor, ignore it and speak about Jack as if nothing had happened.

As Paolo brought in the last embellishment to the table, a carafe of cold, white wine, he deftly scooped up Jack's note and placed it on his desk. Another nonpareil lunch passed off with only the occasional mention of Jack and all these were positive; whatever had happened here in those two weeks since my last visit was now water under the bridge. Paolo, at least, had got over it.

By mid-afternoon we were all heading for Scilla and another gathering of the faithful on the beach. With Calabrian guile, Paolo snatched up the last parking space in Scilla; we could find nothing, not even a half-space in which to park badly. We settled instead with double parking temporarily alongside Paolo to say our goodbyes to him and thank him for his presents; yes, lunch, sexual intrigue *and* presents.

Before we were told to move on by the approaching local policeman, we pulled away and headed for Lamezia and home.

THE OTHER SIDE OF SICILY

I let out an audible 'Yes!'. I'd just read the latest 'New Routes' email from Ryanair and discovered that, at long last, they were going to fly to Palermo in Sicily. A few clicks later and I'd booked our flights, destination Palermo.

We decided to explore the south and west of the island and soon we had an itinerary: we'd fly on the early morning flight to Palermo, head down the coast to Castellammare del Golfo for a night before cutting across to the south coast to our main destination, Sciacca, a name we couldn't even pronounce, for nine days and then another day in Castellammare del Golfo on the way back to Palermo.

Of course it's the western side of Sicily that has the bad reputation in relation to La Cosa Nostra. On some maps (including mine) the airport serving Palermo is still called Punta Raisi and while Punta Raisi remains its location, its name had been changed to Falcone e Borsellino in memory of the two magistrates who were murdered by the mafia in 1992.

At the time I was re-reading Peter Robb's *Midnight in Sicily* and thinking about these two men, Giovanni Falcone and Paolo Borsellino, who tried to bring the mafia to heel and ended up with their names on an airport.

In Italy their murders were a catalyst. Many Italians paused, came out into the streets and in so-doing signalled the beginning of the end of the 'heroic' mafia myth that some still adhered to. Battle was engaged and, if nothing else, nobody now could deny the existence of the mafia and its murderers.

Thanks to the drizzly weather we changed our plans and arrived in Castellammare del Golfo shortly before midday and headed for Via Guglielmo Marconi where we found a parking space about a few metres from our destination, the Residence Aziyz. We pulled in.

The street was deserted but for three people. One, a woman in her mid-50s, stood in the entrance to the hotel; another, a much younger man, stood on the pavement between us and the woman; the third, a man in his early-60s, was on the other side of the street opposite the woman. They were clearly looking for someone or something but, when we pulled up, their attention began to focus on us.

Slowly we exited the car. They were clearly watching us, albeit trying, and failing, to be nonchalant about it. We could 'do' nonchalant too and chatted casually as we walked to the boot of the car and raised it. Still no obvious reaction other than the straining of a neck or three. It wasn't till I took the first bag out of the boot and set it on the pavement that they struck.

Almost before we realised it, the two men had left their posts and had made a bee-line for us at the back of the car and, having confirmed that we were indeed heading for the Residence Aziyz, insisted on carrying our bags into the hotel where the woman was now waiting to greet us.

It wasn't till we settled into our room and had a chance to catch our breath that all was made clear. We were, it seems, their first ever guests and they'd been waiting for us all day. Little did they know that, but for the drizzle, they would have had several more hours to wait!

Residence Aziyz was an old renovated mansion and the whole family, mother, father and two sons, had worked hard to reach this point. Being their first guests, we were expected to inspect the works from top to bottom, and to register our approval. This we did in the interests of diplomatic relations between our two great nations (in my case that was Italy and Ireland) and we most definitely approved.

It was truly magnificent. What they hadn't spent on air-conditioning, they'd spent on marble and simple and stylish décor. On their website this was understated as 'utmost care and attention'.

In a nutshell, we were honoured to be their first guests and when we returned from an evening meal overlooking the harbour we sat with the family in their open-air courtyard surrounded by two dictionaries, one Italian-English, the other English-Italian, well into the wee small hours helping make their dream come true.

For the record, when we came back this way just over a week later, we were also their second guests ... and were honoured to be so; their third guest was an American woman, three days later.

The next morning we set off for Verdetecnica, an old Sicilian farmhouse converted to self-catering units on the western side of Monte Kronio, the mountain that oversees the coastal fishing port of Sciacca (pronounced *shaka*).

Verdetecnica was run by Salvatore, a Sicilian, and his French wife Pascale and, surprise, surprise, they both spoke near-perfect English. As well as offering accommodation, the site housed a small nursery run by Salvatore to supply his garden design business.

We seemed to have done it again, our 'unit' was just the right balance of exposed beams and mod cons and the whole setting was stunning. But Verdetechnica was the sum of its parts and the two most important 'parts' here were the jaunty Salvatore and the gentle Pascale. Always there, always helpful, always open.

It wasn't long before Salvatore and I realised we had something in common. I was eyeing up the library behind the reception area and spotted a copy of *Midnight in Sicily* in English and mentioned the book to Salvatore who immediately became animated.

"You've read it?" he asked as if he'd found a soul-mate.

"Yes, and I'm reading it again, I've got it with me. Did you read it in English?"

Salvatore shrugged his shoulders, {I had to ... it's not published in Italian."

"Why not?"

Another shrug, "Italians don't want to hear these things."

I understood what he was saying and it was a subject we returned to from time to time, particularly when he heard that we'd just come from Castellammare del Golfo.

He was surprised to hear that I already knew quite a lot about Castellammare del Golfo and its mafia connections, including the inter-family feuding of the early 1930s in Prohibition America which spilled over to their Castellammarese homeland

On our one afternoon in Castellammare del Golfo we'd wandered round the town and all seemed quite normal—castle, beach, restaurants, closed shops. Later, en route to the harbour, we discovered the old tuna fishery, all that was left of the industry once based here. The harbour itself was picturesque and we ate well in a restaurant overlooking the sea. No men in dark suits and dark glasses, no severed horse's head, no-one burning copies of *Midnight in Sicily*. Nothing untoward. Light years from mafia mythology.

And yet I was aware that, at the height of internecine feuding in Castellammare del Golfo itself in the 1950s, some 80 percent of the adult male population had been in prison while some 60 percent were said to have been involved in at least one killing. I could of course be guilty of repeating another myth for I'm not exactly sure how the latter statistic was arrived at. A door-to-door survey doesn't seem likely.

———

Back in Sciacca all was well with the world. We had found a place to eat, Santa Lucia, in the shadow of Monte Kronio, and we knew almost immediately that this was the place for us, not only because it was frequented almost exclusively by locals but also because of the quality of the food. Perhaps one is a prerequisite of the other.

It was run by a husband-and-wife team, Carlo the chef and Francesca the waitress, and it was while eating here that I first began to assess restaurants by the quality and variety of their antipasti. At Santa Lucia this an antipasti buffet of home-made dishes made with *melanzane, asparagi, zucchini, funghi, peperoni, carciofe, cavolfiore, cipolle, uova, pomodore* and *proscuitto*. All were mouth-watering masterpieces and you could choose what and how much you wanted.

The couple had three children, ten-year old Gino, nine-year old Tommaso and seven-year old Maria and the two boys were already doing their bit for the family business. Normally it was Francesca who would take our order but both Gino and Tommaso had been well trained and particularly liked to help out with waiting on us—as soon as we came in they'd have our usual jug of red wine and a couple of glasses on the table in seconds. I think they liked having us around because they could practise their few basic English words and phrases ... and when Maria tried to get in on the act she was very quickly shooed away by her brothers into the adjacent dining area.

On our last night here, a Monday, we were paying the bill and saying our final goodbyes—we were actually leaving on the Wednesday but Santa Lucia closed on Tuesdays—when Gino had an animated argument with his mother and father, the gist of which was that he didn't want them to close this particular Tuesday so that we could eat there. I think Francesca considered it but Carlo was clearly weary after a hectic weekend and needed his rest.

And so it was that on the Tuesday we ate at the more up-market, more fashionable, more tourist-orientated, more self-congratulatory with its name, Le Gourmet, restaurant. Well, if being up-market and fashionable requires that you watch the largest cockroach you've ever seen walk across your tablecloth, then I guess this place was top notch. Equally disturbing was the way in which the waiter whisked it onto the floor, in the vain hope that we'd not actually seen it, and hastily crunched it under foot as if we were deaf as well as blind.

Sciacca was different from Siracusa in that, for us, it was initially a base from which we could explore southern Sicily and less of an attraction in itself. But that changed and once we got to know the town we enjoyed exploring its narrow streets, the cafés and markets.

There are, in effect, two towns: there's the walled town sited on a

broad plateau overlooking the 'other' Sciacca, the port and its
attendant community below. And overseeing both is Monte Kronio.

The mafia notwithstanding, southern Sicily is a fascinating place.
Qw visited plaves like Eraclea Minoa, Gibellina, Marsala and Menfi
that are not always top of the average tourist's itinerary and the most
fascinating of all was the the tourist magnet of Agrigento.

Like everyone else, we were drawn to the Valle dei Templi and we
did indeed wander in and out and around the remains of the Temples
of Hercules, Concord and Hera as they basked in a hazy midday sun
surrounded by meadows of poppies swaying in the gentle breeze.

It was an extraordinary day, albeit one that the hundreds of other
visitors to the Valle dei Templi never experienced.

As we headed for the *templi*, it was the wrong turning I took before
we got there that turned out to be the highlight of our day.
Inadvertently we ended up in a livestock market, in the shadow of
Agrigento, in the middle of nowhere in particular, just there, a
seemingly impromptu Sunday get-together of the local agricultural
community, mainly men, by the side of the road.

We had to stop and, not surprisingly, we got some strange looks,
perhaps it was the shorts, more likely the white legs, from the many
ageing, weather-worn faces, eyes still curious, shoulders and hands
work-weary, *coppola* (Sicilian cap) firmly fixed at a jaunty angle,
teeth an optional extra. The younger generation was there too, more
animated, shouting the odds, doing the deals, drawing on cigarettes,
waiting for i*l telefonino* to ring.

Although there was some farm produce for sale alongside bits and
pieces of machinery and tools, this was basically a chance to barter
for and buy livestock, much of it sooner or later for the pot. Central
to the process was the sharpener of knives, his foot ever-treading the
trestle to spin the large grinding wheel that would sent everyone
home with tools fit for purpose ... killing, cutting up and carving.

This was the sort of haphazard gathering that would not happen
in the UK because of issues around the treatment of animals or

health and safety regulations. But we did not see any animals being maltreated, other than being the focus of attention as an 'item' for sale or to be bargained over. Back home we kept chickens, probably the most mollycoddled chickens in the universe, and we have seen how chickens are sometimes kept in Italy and, yes, it's not always up to our back-garden-in-rural-England standards but still infinitely better than the life inflicted on the average supermarket, non free-range, bird.

The basic difference here was that people were buying their *secondo piatto* while it was still alive and kicking, they were cutting out the middle man, the *supermercato*. In the case of the chickens, it meant that two or three defiantly squawking birds were put into a cardboard box peppered with air holes, the box not the chickens, taken home and despatched as required.

As well as *galline* (chickens) there were *cavalli* (horses), *puledri* (foals), *maiali* (pigs), *bestiame* (cattle) and *pecori* (sheep) and although the horses may well have had a few years work left in them, they were just as likely to have been for the pot. In some parts of Italy, particularly Apulia and Sardinia, *cavallo* is often on the menu, very occasionally the only meat on the menu.

We would have had liked to photograph this place and these people going about their Sunday business but had deliberately left our cameras in the car. In a sense we were intruders and it did not seem appropriate to turn the normality of the occasion into a curiosity.

The templi 'done', we headed back towards the sprawling, untidy hillside mass that was Agrigento itself. On the lower slopes we happened upon a busy *pasticceria* that sold the most wonderful pastries imaginable and indulged ourselves as we watched the world go by. But this was as far as we got for, unusually, we felt ill at ease here. There was no logic to it, perhaps it was the contrast with the 'other' Agrigento, the *templi*, even the market. Or maybe it was because I already knew too much having read Tobias Jones' *The Dark Heart of Italy*, which shed some light on the other side to

Agrigento, also known as the *zoccolo duro*, the mafia's 'hard hoof'.

Writing in 2002, Jones described the local phenomenon of *abusivismo*, illegal building, 'not chaotic lawlessness but precision profiteering', that was out of control in and around Agrigento and which the authorities were cracking down on. He was in Agrigento the week the bulldozing was supposed to begin but it never did for a new Prime Minister had just been elected, one Silvio Berlusconi, the first ever to have secured all 61 Sicilian parliamentary seats.

Back on the main road we looked up at the town and thought how lucky we were to be staying in Sciacca

We left Verdetecnica early in the morning for we wanted to revisit Marsala and continue on to Trápani, Erice and, if possible, the promontory of San Vito lo Capo before returning to Castellammare del Golfo in the late afternoon Salvatore called Residence Aziyz and told them when to expect us, the last thing we wanted was the whole family cluttering up the streets in fruitless, though understandable, anticipation.

Our last port of call, San Vito lo Capo, was dramatic, it was hot, the limpid aquamarine sea was stunning as was the attendant beach except that, being covered in bodies, you couldn't see it.

San Vito lo Capo was a holiday resort, a magnet that suits many people, particularly families with children, but that we instinctively avoid. Still, we'd made it this far so we did what we always do in such situations, we look for the best source of *gelati*, ice-cream. It wasn't difficult to find and we sat in the shade to enjoy our treat when we were joined by the English family-on-holiday from hell.

Unfortunately we had already run into this family. Our paths had crossed during and after the flight from Stansted to Palermo. When we landed at Palermo we were more than a little relieved to know that we'd never clap eyes on them again. But here they were, stalking us in a café in San Vito lo Capo. And, true to form, they were running round, shouting, knocking things over, swearing ... and the children were almost as bad. But worse was still to come; we overheard—it wasn't difficult—their plans for the next day. Yes, you've guessed it, they were catching the same flight as us back to London.

Time for us to get a head start. We shot out of San Vito lo Capo and headed south, despite its mafia past the tranquility of Castellammare del Golfo beckoned and we arrived on schedule to another effusive welcome.

We were, after all, the second ever guests at Residence Aziyz.

—

We returned to Verdetecnica at Christmas and once again became regulars at Santa Lucia where Christmas lunch was a curious affair, not because of the food but because of the company. There were two tables laid, one for us, the other for a party of 18. And that was it. At the time I suspected that the large group had persuaded Francesco to open on Christmas day and they in turn invited us as a diversion.

Our fellow guests comprised at least three generations of a large family: grandparents, their middle-aged children with their spouses and various grandchildren. Everyone was dressed very smartly and it was clear that the grandfather was in charge, very much *il padrone*. He wasn't the first to enter the dining room but when he did, he and his wife immediately acknowledged our presence and wished us *Buon Natale*. Thereafter each guest greeted us in the same fashion.

Since we first came to Italy we had eaten with or close to many family gatherings but this felt different. We weren't sure if it was a class thing, a status thing, a money thing, a shifty thing or any other 'thing'. They were simply different, *particolare*. At first we thought it curious too that they were eating here on this particular day but then, basic local fare it might have been, but it was cooked with skill and passion and it showed. Perhaps somewhere along the line this family was a part of either Francesca or Carlo's extended family, though if they were it wasn't obvious.

We had all just finished our antipasti when one of the women, tall, elegant, sophisticated and dressed in black, stood up, left the table and purposefully walked across to our table.

"Do you speak English?" she said with a clear American accent. When we said that we did, she seemed relieved and continued.

"I'm from Detroit", she said, "my husband over there ... we met in Detroit when he first came to the US but now he's decided to return to Sicily to live. So here we are, my first Christmas in Sicily."

And that was it. We had just time to explain that we were on holiday, we'd been here before and were staying down the road before she said goodbye and returned to her table and her new family. She looked apprehensive and from time to time would catch our eye and give a smile of recognition or an almost clandestine wave of the fingers. A brief but intriguing encounter with a woman not in her comfort zone, a woman encased in a group whose laughter was always muted, in a family who seemingly had never heard of the craic.

The meal progressed, we had all just finished our *primo piatto* when one of the younger sons or older grandsons, it was difficult to tell, took out a packet of cigarettes and was just about to light up when *il padrone* admonished him and nodded in our direction, clearly indicating that we might not approve.

As he stood up to leave the dining room to have his cigarette outside, the offending male apologised to *il padrone* and also to us as he passed our table. Thereafter the smokers in the group excused themselves and headed out into the crisp Christmas sun.

No sooner had they all eaten, than they left. One-by-one they filed out and, as they passed our table, they all said goodbye to us in Italian, including the enigmatic wife from Detroit. I had little doubt that she was not happy in this set up, nor was she overcome with joy at the prospect of spending the rest of her life in southern Sicily where she was out on a very lonely limb.

We stayed a little longer and had a chat with Francesca and Carlo who went on to share some breaking news with us. They asked us if we knew the other, larger restaurant, La Traviata, on the road between Santa Lucia and Verdetecnica. We confessed that we had eaten there on our first visit, the first Tuesday when their place was shut; we were quick to add that we didn't enjoy the food and that we were the only people there that evening. All of which happened to be true.

Francesca and Carlo were asking because they had acquired La Traviata and, early in the new year, they even had an exact date, they would transfer the food and the ambience of Santa Lucia 500 metres down the road. The four of us shared a celebratory drink and we wished then well with their n eew venture

It was our last night in Santa Lucia and we were eating at our usual table by the fire. It was a busy evening. A middle-aged Italian couple came in. We recognised them for, like us, they'd eaten here before. We nodded in recognition as Francesca showed them to the table next to ours. Francesca returned with the menus and there followed what can only be described as a heated discussion in fast, furious and animated Italian. And it was to do with us.

We didn't understand all of what was being said, but we got the gist of it. Basically the woman was complaining that we always had the table by the fire. As politely and firmly as possible, Francesca explained that this was because we always got there first, at eight o'clock on the dot. Rocket science it wasn't.

As evidenced by her use of the word *stranieri*, we were fairly certain that the displaced woman also brought the fact that we were not Italian into the debate. Tapping her watch it seemed that she even asked Francesca what time we would be leaving, presumably so that they could swap tables. Her husband knew his place and refused to become involved. All he wanted was to get on with things, he didn't care where he sat as long as he could eat and drink.

I suppose it's possible that we got it all wrong, and it was just that they supported rival football teams or were discussing Berlusconi's latest clamp-down on the freedom of the press. But I doubt it. From time to time Francesca gave us some knowing looks and, of course, she could never be quite sure how much of the conversation we actually understood. Of one thing we were fairly certain—

Francesca knew that this was our last night in Sciacca but, as far as I could discern, she omitted to mention it to them.

As a gesture of solidarity, I turned round my chair to warm my hands at the fire for the last time. Next time we came to Sciacca we would be eating down the road at La Traviata.

—

It was late spring when I came across this, an internet blog by an American woman who stayed at Verditecnica in April:

"That night we headed up the mountain to a restaurant that had just opened that day, La Traviata. That day was their grand opening, and they did not have a lot of what was listed on the menu as the deliveries were to come the next day. With the waitress's small knowledge of English combined with our small knowledge of Italian we were able to put a meal together. We ordered Pasta alla Emiliana, which to my happy surprise was berette (flat spaghetti), peas and ham in a pink sauce. I thought pink sauce may be an American thing, I was pleasantly surprised to have found it in Sicily. It was delicious. I then had swordfish and my boyfriend had the shrimp speciality of the house. Everything was really good."

We knew it was Francesca and Carlo's intention to re-open La Traviata on 15 January but we also knew that, in Italy, dates and time tend to have an elastic quality particularly when you are relying on third parties.

Thank goodness we decided not to see through our original intention to return to Sciacca for a few days just to be at the opening.

NEVER THE SAME AGAIN

A house swap was something we'd never tried before and, as we lived near Bath, we reckoned it wouldn't be too difficult to find people who wanted to spend time there. I registered with an online site and started browsing.

We had always been keen to visit New Orleans and when I found someone there interested in a house swap, I got in touch. When Barbara got back to me to say that she had no plans to go abroad in the immediate future and therefore wasn't interested in a house exchange at that time, I returned to the drawing board.

Out of the blue Barbara got back in touch with a quite different proposition. As she owned two properties, one in New Orleans and one 60 miles away at Pass Christian on the Gulf of Mexico (since 2025, the Gulf of America) she suggested we rent each one for a week, at a price which seemed unbelievably generous,

When I asked her about the price, she said that anyone who was prepared to let her stay in their home must be house-trained, respectful and open-minded and, that being the case, she was happy to let us stay at her properties and pay a token sum.

We accepted her proposal and spent the week up to Christmas Day at her beautiful home in Pass Christian (or The Pass as it is known locally), seconds from the sea, then moved to her apartment in the Faubourg St John area of New Orleans for the New Year. It was a house swap of a sort and we met Barbara briefly on the day we changed houses and exchanged keys. It was Christmas Day 2004.

Round the corner from Barbara's New Orleans apartment was a small Spanish restaurant, Lola's, the domain of restauranteur *extraordinaire*, Angel. This became our home from home and we ate there every evening. It was here we met a couple from Knoxville, Tennessee whom we visited the following year and, subsequently, met several times in various parts of the States and Europe to share a bit of international craic.

Lola's was extremely popular and, after a certain time each evening, it was impossible to get a table without queueing. Outside there was a lectern where people signed in and waited; those who signed in and weren't there when their names were called, forfeited their place.

As New Year approached Angel spoke with some of his favoured regulars and asked them to come and eat later than usual on New Year's Eve; these were the people who were invited to Lola's 'spontaneous' New Year's party. We had an invite and celebrated the dawning of 2005 with Angel and his friends on a mild evening outside the restaurant. Sadly, our Knoxville friends had already returned home.

At the time we did not know that was to be a new year like no other..

———

Before we left the UK, I had booked several 'special' things to do in and around New Orleans, one of which I left right to the end … it was to be a surprise for Kay. I suppose I did realise that a flight on a seaplane might not be her special event of choice. For 'surprise' read 'shock'. I would probably have felt the same if one of my grandchildren wanted me to go down one of those slide-tube things at a water park.

We drove to one of the city's southern suburbs, to the seaplane company's base next to a bayou that flowed into the Mississippi. Here the bayou was straight enough to be our runway. The seaplane itself looked like something out of an *Indiana Jones* movie, 'basic' is probably doing it more justice than it deserved. However, Dale, our pilot, seemed confident that he'd get us out to the Mississippi delta and back before taking us over New Orleans for one last look. I sat in the front with Dale, Kay was in the back.

For me, taking off from and landing on water was another ambition fulfilled. Yet another example of how, throughout my life, I have been drawn to water and yet, put me in it, and I flounder; on at least two occasions it has nearly claimed me.

We flew out to the delta and the swamplands which, at another time of year, would have been home to alligators. Even in winter it was still their home, it was just that they didn't come out much to play. Here there was more water than land so it was not difficult to find somewhere to touch down for a few minutes while Dale pointed out the wildlife, including those places the alligators would have been congregating had it been spring or summer.

Having marvelled at the invisible alligators, we skimmed across the water once more and were quickly airborne and heading back to New Orleans to fly over all the visible places we'd got to know so well in the previous week: the French Quarter, Canal Street, Jackson Square, Preservation Hall, City Park, the Superbowl and, round the corner from our apartment, the Fair Grounds Race Course.

My camera was clicking like a cicada. It was such an anticlimax when we turned south again and landed back on the bayou; Kay, on the other hand, was more than a little relieved to be back on dry land. That said, she perked up when she saw the state of the woman from another plane that had just landed ahead of us.

At the time we did not know that we were photographing a city that would never be the same again.

Just over seven months later Katrina, the mother of all hurricanes, changed New Orleans and the Mississippi Gulf Coast for ever.

Lola's was destroyed and Angel moved to Houston in Texas; New Year's Eve 2004 was to be the last such celebration for a some time. However, Angel was adamant that he would return to New Orleans, and he did. People are once again queueing to eat at Lola's.

Though the reporting around Katrina focussed on New Orleans where the protective levies gave way under the pressure of water, little was written about where Katrina actually made landfall on the Mississippi's Gulf Coast when it swept in with such force from the Gulf of Mexico.

That place, where the malevolent eye of Katrina first saw land, was a mere five miles east of a small town that nobody had ever heard of ... Pass Christian.

Most of the shops, bars, restaurants and homes in and around the town that we had come to know so well, including Barbara's beautiful home, were destroyed by the force of the 30-foot-high wall of water that strode into and through The Pass. Many buildings were just transformed into haphazard piles of unrecognisable rubble where they stood, while others were uprooted and deposited in another part of the town, almost intact.

The town's mayor, Billy McDonald, was told by a police officer: "Mayor, you're the mayor of nothing now."

Every day while we were staying there, we had gone for a brisk morning walk along the seafront before breakfast. On our route there was a memorial to all those who died in 1969 at the hands of Hurricane Camille, at the time one of the most powerful storms on record.

The Pass now has a newer memorial to remember the 28 locals who lost their lives at the hands of Hurricane Katrina.

ANOTHER LEAP OF FAITH

It was in the early noughties when Italy became our most frequent European destination. After Sardinia came Sicily and for two or three years this was our preferred destination, the only part of the island that we never really got to know was the south-east corner around Ragusa.

It was when I came across Charles Lister's book *From heel to toe:Encounters in the south of Italy* that I became interested in exploring Apuglia, the heel of Italy.

Although we made forays into other parts of the region, we always stayed in what is called the Salento, the actual heel, the part south and east of the two main airports, Bari and Brindisi. The story I retold on page 198 about trying to find our Brindisi hotel while tailgating a police car was the highlight of our first evening in Apuglia.

The next day we headed into the Salento and a *villetta* on the road connecting Cutrofiano and Corigliano d'Otranto where we were going to stay a couple of weeks. Our host Paola spoke no English but Francesca, her best friend, was close to fluent, having worked in London for a number of years.

At first we gravitated to Curtofiano where Francesca worked and were not over-impressed with its ambience. We soon shifted our attention to the nearby delights of Corigliano d'Otranro, a town that that had felt sleepy and devoid of restaurants when we went to the supermarket during the day but which, we discovered, took on a new persona after 8pm. Doors suddenly opened and tables, chairs, candles, napkins ,cutlery and glasses popped up in the narrowest of streets to transform the town into a smorgasbord of vibrant eateries.

Corigliano d'Otranro is one of nine towns in the Salento known collectively as the *Grecìa Salentina*, all of which have an historic connection to a language and culture known as *Griko*, some aspects of which have survived. What we did discover was that these towns had an ambience that was undefinably different from other towns in the area. And Corigliano d'Otranto had another unique attraction for here we found Il Bar del Arco and its irrepressible owner, Gino.

Gino's kingdom became our preferred watering-hole before and after eating at Corigliano (we usually dropped the 'd'Otranto' part). We soon discovered that Gino had a *villetta* in a rural setting close to the town and, when he took us to have a look at it, we decided there and then that would be our next base in the Salento.

In the meantime our friendship with Francesca was blossoming and she invited us to have lunch with her brother, Salvatore, and her parents, Attilio and Silvana, that introduced us to a less predictable Italian sub-culture.

We met up with Francesca outside the shop in Cutrofiano and she drove us into the neighbouring countryside to the small single-storey farm that was home. Attilio, robust and weathered from years of hard outdoor work and wearing shorts and a vest that looked like permanent fixtures, and Silvana, a comfortable, florid, no-nonsense housewife who knew how to keep her man in his place, welcomed us like long-lost children.

Introductions over, Silvana swung into action in the kitchen, while Attilio and Francesca showed us round the adjoining small plot of land that the family worked. Here they grew anything and everything that could be put on the table and also kept a few chickens and pigs in outhouses away from the house. Kay and Attilio were soon talking the same market gardening language aided and abetted by Francesca's translations. I was nodding and trying to remember all the Italian names for the vegetables.

The one local crop conspicuous by its absence here was tobacco. Nearby Galatina was an important centre of the Italian tobacco industry and, locally, we had come to recognise the plant's broad leaves. When I mentioned this to Attilio he shook his head, he didn't want to have anything to do with the tobacco industry. Francesca looked uncomfortable as she fiddled with her lighter.

Although this was a working environment, there were pockets of shade and corners of buildings where time had stood still; where an unused bucket, a length of pipe, a coil of wire or an antiquated tool lay abandoned, sometimes gathering foliage and a dusting of the rich red earth, perhaps awaiting a second chance. I spotted a makeshift canopy adjoining the side of the house and, curious, took a closer look; I thought as much, this was where Attilio kept his Ape.

I had always fancied having a go in an Ape (Italian for 'bee') one of those three-wheeled utilitarian farm vehicles, with handlebars rather than a steering wheel, that buzz about all over the southern Italian countryside, sometimes packed with people rather than produce, more often people and produce and always just in front of you on those winding mountainous roads. Surely 'How many people can you cram into an Ape?' must eventually become a challenge for the *Guinness Book of Records*.

I did toy with the idea of asking Attilio if I could take his Ape out for a spin until I noticed it was laden with vegetables that I assumed he would sell. Perhaps another time, I thought.

Salvatore still hadn't put in an appearance when Francesca summoned us to the table.

This was a working household; the kitchen and adjacent dining room were extensions of the garden and its produce. They were not showcases and had probably remained unchanged for decades, a place of old, dark, functional furniture. few airs and graces and, it has to be said, no obvious sense that there was a place for the craic at the table. As we sat ourselves round the table just, and as Francesca was subtly warning us that her father was about to say 'grace', Salvatore rushed in, made his apologies and fell into the waiting chair.

Formalities out of the way, we tucked in to *orecchietti*, a small ear-shaped pasta which is an Apulian speciality, in a tomato sauce followed by a rich meat stew accompanied by bread, vegetables, potatoes and red wine and rounded off with the regulation *torta* we had brought with us, the last being almost the only thing that was not home-grown or home-made.

Francesca was our interpreter as we extolled the virtues of this down-to-earth *cucina tipica* and made sure that both Attilio and Silvana knew how much we appreciated their hospitality, their kindness and their hard work. The eating over, Attilio went to the tall, glass-fronted sideboard and took out another bottle of red wine and offered it to us. We took this as a signal that we should be on our way. We were aware that we were encroaching on their time of rest, *il sonnellino*. Clutching our bottle of Attilio's best red, Francesca drove us back to our car in Cutrofiano.

This short journey was full of surprises as Francesca explained that her mother and father (and most of her family) were Jehovah's Witnesses which was, apparently, the second largest religion in Italy. Initially I found this assertion difficult to get my head round and felt compelled to check it out on the internet. It was correct. Though there are just over 250,000 Jehovah Witnesses in Italy, in numerical terms, it is indeed Italy's second religion.

Apart from the 'grace', this revelation seemed somehow out of step with our lunchtime experience so we had a few more questions for Francesca. What about the wine and the drinking? We thought that Jehovah Witnesses didn't imbibe? Francesca explained that, as she understood it, they could drink but not get drunk, a plausible, if unlikely, rationale. We pressed on. What about the door-to-door bit? Yes, they did that too and her father wore a suit on such occasions.

It was all rather bizarre, mostly because it didn't fit in with our experience. I suppose the answer was that these were Italian Jehovah Witnesses and our only encounters had been with the UK branch. The cultural and historic influences were different and so too was the end result: Italian Jehovah Witnesses who enjoyed their red wine and might even pinch your bottom if you'd convert.

Eight years of living and working in London had 'cleansed' Francesca of her parents' religious bent and, she confessed, there were often areas of conflict which could lead to periods of little or no communication.

We liked Francesca a lot and shared some of the anguish and frustration she experienced through a simple need to be allowed to think for herself. Attilio and Silvana had made us very welcome, over and above the call of duty and we wondered later how they might have coped had they known that they had had two heathens in their midst helping them not get drunk. I would like to think that, as friends of Francesca, they would have treated us no differently.

Paola and her family were also Jehovah Witnesses and it was through the local JW network that Paola knew that Francesca could speak English and, decadent or not, her language skills would prove useful in the holidays-for-heathens business.

Still trying to make sense of this cultural jigsaw, I came across some research that suggested that, of all religions, Catholicism was the most likely to supply a fertile pool of recruits to Jehovah Witnesses. The rationale being that 'both religions continue to blindly follow the organisation in spite of major doctrinal changes, reversals and flip-flops' and that 'both view every other church as heretical and false'.

But from Francesca there was yet another revelation to come. The meat Silvana had so lovingly prepared for us was *cavallo*, horse, though, of course, we didn't know it at the time. Back in Cutrofiano, we leapt out of the car, whinnied and waved ciao to Francesca.

We had already noticed that *cavallo* was a feature of many Apulian menus and we later ate in one place where, apart from *salsicce* (sausages), *cavallo* was the only meat on the menu; naturally we ordered the sausages. It was some months later that the penny dropped for, at the time, it had never occurred to us that the *salsicce* we chose were almost certainly left-over-pieces-of-horse sausages.

To a meat-eater, what is the difference between eating horse as opposed to, say, cow, pig or sheep? It must be simply cultural. In the UK and Ireland horses are on the 'domestic' side of the continuum along with cats and dogs and they generally have names. In parts of southern of Italy and in some other European countries they straddle the borderline between domestic and livestock. To expect Italians in such areas not to eat horse meat is like suggesting he or she should give up onions, olives or pasta; it is, they would argue, lean, protein-rich, finely textured, bright red and firm ... and completely BSE-free.

And, I can testify, it is very tasty though, truth be told, I don't think I could eat a whole one.

THE CRAIC AND THE CRACK

It was during our first stay at Gino's *villetta* in the Salento countryside outside Corigliano d'Otranto in the heel of Apulia when we met Giuseppe. Where, on most days, he worked his *orticello*, an allotment adjoining the *villetta*'s garden.

Giuseppe was of indeterminate age, somewhere between 75 and 85, and sported a single tooth. Older Italians, we discovered, rarely made any allowances for the fact that you might not understand them and pressed on regardless, teeth or no teeth, Nevertheless, we had many an interesting chat with Giuseppe, usually about the vegetables he was planting, watering or harvesting.

A few times the conversation ventured beyond horticultural considerations and on one occasion, out of the blue, Giuseppe started bad-mouthing someone whose car he recognised passing down the lane in front of the *ortocello*. We didn't really get the details of his distaste but as soon as he made a particular hand-gesture, we recognised it as shorthand for saying that this was a 'bad' person. In most cases 'bad' meant one word: mafia.

Although mafia-type groups are normally associated with three areas of southern Italy—Sicily, Calabria (the *'ndrangheta*) and the Naples area (the *camorra*)—Apulia clearly felt left out and in the late 1970s a similar criminal organisation evolved and duly gave itself an instantly forgettable name: *sacra corona unita* (united sacred crown).

Such emotion was uncharacteristic and it never came up again. Yet it brought us all a little closer and, before departing, we left him some bottles of his favourite beer and, in so doing, cemented a friendship that was, for me at least, to have unpredictable repercussions.

The next time we stayed at the *villetta* we saw much more of Giuseppe and his tooth; it was June, it was hot and there was more to do on the land and Giuseppe was happy to take a break every now and then for a chat and a bottle of beer … until, that is, he sensed that Gino might just be around the corner.

Almost every morning we found a little box of vegetables on the table in the sheltered front verandah; a lettuce, a couple of tomatoes, some beans, a green pepper, some zucchini. Gradually the boxes got bigger as did the amount of fresh fare that Giuseppe was leaving for us until one day, one fateful day, he left us a loaf of bread as well.

Every day when we thanked him for his kindness he would shrug his shoulders and say, *di niente*, it's nothing; but on this particular day he went on to tell us that his wife had made the bread specially for us. We were even more humbled that a woman whom we'd never met should have gone to such trouble.

We were both looking forward to lunch. The table on the verandah was set. We had fresh vegetables and fruit, some cheese, a glass of red wine and, pride of place, a loaf of Apulian bread, handmade for us. I remember thinking how hard it must be for Giuseppe to eat such fine fare with that solitary tooth, especially the bread.

It's funny how a single moment can change something in your life … over the course of the next decade that first slice of Giuseppe's wife's bread cost me almost £2500.

I distinctly heard the crack but wasn't sure what it was at first. I chewed a little more before my tongue found the gap and I realised that I'd lost a tooth but knew that it was in fact a crown close to the front. Slowly I swallowed the bread, my tongue all the time searching for the wayward tooth to make sure I didn't swallow it too. I found it, spat it out and went off in search of a mirror to survey the damage to that enigmatic smile.

The peg of the crown was still attached to the tooth so I was able to replace it and it seemed to fit snugly enough but dropped out again as soon as I loosened my hold. I called my dentist back home and made an appointment for the day after we returned.

That evening, before we ate, we called into Gino's bar for an *aperitivo* and I showed him the damage, without mentioning Giuseppe's bread, and asked about the local dentist. As ever Gino, or Mr Fixit as I sometimes called him, was on the case and within seconds I was pointed in the right direction holding one of Gino's business cards with the name of the dentist's nurse scribbled on the back.

Less than five minutes later I was sitting in the waiting room with about half a dozen others though I was the only one swotting up all the relevant words in the 'At the Dentist' section of my phrase-book. I already knew that the most important one was *dottore* as dentists in Italy are always referred to as doctors and it is deemed polite to use the title when addressing them.

I think that my fellow patients must have spilled the beans for when my turn came, *il dottore*, his nurse and another assistant had an expectant air about them as I was ushered into an ultra-modern surgery, complete with hi-tech chair. I tried to explain what had happened—*la mia capsula è rotta* (my crown has broken)—and showed them the damage. I also tried to make some sort of conversation by mentioning Gino and that we were staying in the countryside, *in compagna*.

I obviously got all that wrong as I heard the assistant whisper to the nurse that she thought I was actually from Campania, probably Naples … as if that was enough to explain my lack of language and the appalling accent; I corrected this misunderstanding and explained that I was Irish, English-speaking and staying in Corigliano. At least I think that's what I said.

It didn't take long for the crown to be glued back in place but I could see that *il dottore* wasn't sure that it would last. I got the distinct impression that there was another problem. It was only an impression, my Italian wasn't good enough to pick up on the finer details.

The deed done I thanked everyone and tried to pay but instead was ushered out with a firm *di niente*, its nothing. Two minutes later I was back at Gino's, where I once again showed off my enigmatic smile to Kay and anyone else who was interested while Gino was basking in the self-congratulatory glow of being, once again, Mr Fixit.

On our last morning in Corigliano, we popped in to see the dentist and took him and his colleagues a huge tray of mouth-watering pastries from the local *pasticceria*. Much to the amusement of those sitting in the waiting room and the puzzlement of the woman he abandoned in the chair, mid-treatment, *il dottore* came out to accept in person his payment in kind. It was the least we could do to repay such generosity.

On our way back to the airport we spent a few hours in Brindisi and were sitting quietly in the sun in Piazza Cairoli watching the world go by and wondering how to spend our last few hours in Apulia when the muted bustle of a hot day was interrupted by the loudest "Fuck off!" I had ever heard.

This English shrieker was a high-heeled 20-something blonde, dressed in pink from head to toe and trailing a matching pink suitcase-on-wheels. The object of her 'affection' was about ten metres nearer us, an older 20-something in jeans and tee-shirt, a small rucksack on his back and a clone-pink valise in one hand.

Suddenly he hurled the valise towards his erstwhile companion with an endearing, "Well, you can fuck off too and carry your own fucking luggage for a change."

As she stopped to reunite valise and suitcase, the guy did as he was bid and did indeed 'fuck off' in the general direction of the sea hotly pursued by a screaming and swearing pinkness fighting with her luggage and her heels to stay in an upright position.

A few Italian eyebrows were raised as they got the general flavour of what was going on; The local barber merged from his salon and leaned against a nearby lamppost to take stock of the *craic*. But, nosey to a fault, only Kay and I decided to do some follow-up work.

First of all, unlike the Pink Panter, who had momentarily suspended swearing to adjust her footwear, we noticed that the man in her life had made a left up a side street about 50 metres down the Corso Umberto. We followed the PP and watched as she sped past the turning, still spouting loud expletives at no-one in particular. We turned left and, unknown to him, joined the fucked-off fugitive for a cup of coffee in the sun while somewhere a few streets away the air was blue with pink.

He quickly downed his *espresso* and headed back towards Corso Umberto but went straight across and down another side street. We were about to follow when we became aware of the PP's dulcet tones approaching back up Corso Umberto and decided to wait and see what happened next. She trundled past us, blonde hair uncontrolled, arms and attached, recalcitrant baggage flailing.

For the first time, we were really not sure what to do. We knew where the erstwhile love of her life had gone but should we intercede and tell the PP? Would that be the right thing to do? Did we run the risk of her turning her pink wrath on us?

As we hesitated the moment had gone, she was heading back towards the Piazza Cairoli where it had all started; perhaps he would do the same and they'd reunite, arms outstretched in a gleeful slow-motion embrace and all would be well with the world. And if that was not to be the scenario then, we wondered, who had the tickets for the next stage of their journey?

A couple of hours later we were in Brindisi Airport queueing at the check-in on the last leg of our Apulian adventure. It was a sad time but we had already booked another week at Gino's *villetta* in September.

I was thinking back to the craic in Brindisi earlier when, in the corner of my eye, a flash of pink momentarily interrupted my thoughts. I turned round for a second or two and then whispered in Kay's ear.

"Don't look just yet ... but guess who's got their tongue down who's throat and is going to be on the same flight as us?"

———

Back home, as I moved *my* tongue to one side, my dentist was telling me that, as I'd heard a crack, it was likely that the root had split in which case no 'repair', such as *il dottore* had done, would last more than a few days. After a bit of jiggling and poking, he confirmed the worst: it was probably this that *il dottore* had been trying to explain to me.

I deliberately hadn't mentioned how I'd paid *il dottore* until the time came to settle up for my consultation and the subsequent plan of action. Tongue firmly in cheek, I asked him, "Cash or cakes?"

Not surprisingly he looked puzzled until I explained how I'd paid *il dottore* in Apulia; he thought for a moment and said that cakes would be fine, it would make a pleasant change.

Next day I dropped off a large tray of cakes at the surgery. Sadly, the subsequent treatment had to be paid for in the old-fashioned way.

GETTING THERE

We were off to Italy again but this time we didn't need to take the long, circuitous route across England and round London, from Bath to Stansted Airport. Instead we were heading for Bristol Airport and the new easyJet service to Ciampino, Rome's smaller airport on the southern outskirts of the city. Here we would stay one night in a nearby hotel before heading south the following day.

From our small cottage in Upper Swainswick, where we'd lived for 13 years, to the main road that led to the motorway was no more than 300 yards; we were less than halfway, still in the village, when we realised we had a puncture.

I pulled over at the widest part of the narrow road, opposite some houses that we passed every day, either on foot or in the car, and I changed the wheel. It took no more than ten minutes but I realised we'd have to return home for a few moments so that I could wash my hands. No problem, we had just enough time.

As we were replacing all our luggage into the car's boot, a woman emerged from the garden gate opposite and asked if we'd like to freshen up after our misfortune, maybe have a cup of tea before getting back on the road. A kind gesture but one that also said something about living in this village on the outskirts of Bath. Although we recognised her, she had absolutely no idea that we were locals, almost neighbours, and had assumed instead that we were tourists who had just pulled off the nearby main road to change the tyre.

I thanked her for her generosity before explaining that we lived just around the corner and were going to nip back home to tidy up a bit before setting off again. I promised to hoot as we passed for the second time that day.

Cleaned up and en route to the airport once more, we reflected on how different life was in our corner of the English countryside compared to our destination in southern Italy. We knew we would be welcomed there with open arms by, among others, bar owner Gino and his colleague Andrea, hairdresser Angela, her husband Nicola and gardener and odd-job man Giuseppe. And yet after 13 years in this small pub-less, shop-less community of fewer than 300 people, we felt like strangers.

In theory at least, it being the beginning of a new millennium, the remnants of the English class system should have been seen off, even in a small village on the outskirts of Bath. We were, we concluded, just the wrong sort of people for this village: tenants rather than owners, incomers rather than locals, emailers rather than letter writers, red blood rather than blue.

We realised that, after 13 years here, the only people we really knew, apart from the postman, were other incomers like ourselves. Perhaps if there had been a pub, things might have been different but even if there had been such a place with a roaring winter fire, perhaps it would have had a special, colder corner for incomers to chat among themselves.

While the village itself was pretty and compact in a very English sort of way, I think it's fair to say that, even in its heyday, it was not a place abundant with the laughter and bonhomie associated with the craic.

———

Despite the false start, we made our flight at Bristol and were soon on board and pulling away from the terminal.

But it wasn't to be as simple as that for we had only moved a short distance when we came to an abrupt halt. Moments later the pilot made an announcement to the effect that there was an unspecified problem at Rome Ciampino which would delay our take-off for about ten minutes.

Ten minutes came and went but he was almost as good as his word for it was not long before we were moving again and heading for the runway. Once again the pace slowed and we pulled over onto the apron and stopped.

The pilot announced a further problem at Ciampino and he would have to wait a little longer for further instructions before taking off. Agitated doom and gloom descended on his flock. It was late afternoon and the prospect of eating out in Rome seemed to bless and less likely.

Twenty minutes passed and once again the pilot's voice broke into the growing sense of despondency. He started with the bad news: we would not be going to Ciampino. He let that sink but, before the despondency became too audible, he chirped in with the good news: he had managed to get clearance to fly instead to Rome's other airport, the much larger, intercontinental airport, Fiumicino.

He then told us he'd remain on the apron for a further ten minutes so that passengers who needed to, could have time on their mobile phones to make or change arrangements at the Rome end.

Sometimes budget airlines get a bad press, but I think easyJet did us all proud that day; they got everyone to Rome, albeit to another airport, and they also made sure that we had the opportunity to make alternative arrangements if necessary. For us that meant one call, to our car rental desk at Ciampino to ask them to change our pick-up to Fiumicino. The only inconvenience we could foresee was that we'd get to our hotel near Ciampino a little later than planned. But at least we were going to get there.

And get there we did. We were about an hour and a half behind schedule and had already given up on the idea of an Italian meal in favour of a snack on the plane.

Having explained our lateness and checked in, we temporarily resisted the notion of sleep in favour of some restorative wine and, having thrown our luggage into the bedroom, headed straight back down to the bar and the receptionist-cum-barman.

I asked for two glasses of red wine … he took one look at our jaded jowls, reached for two tumblers from the shelf, opened a bottle of wine and poured half into each glass.

He could obviously read our minds; or perhaps he'd googled 'Upper Swainswick' and knew that we'd be just dying for a drink.

A DAY AND A HALF

We had been in Apulia for two weeks and, as we had done on our journey down from Rome, had arranged to stop off for another two nights at Sant'Agata sui Due Golfi with Carlo and his family at Villa Belvedere.

Experiencing the ruins of Herculaneum and Pompeii was to be the highlight so, as we'd done on our previous visit when we went to Mount Vesuvius, we drove down to the coastal community of Sant'Agnello to catch the train northwards alongside the Bay of Naples.

We knew the routine: first we stopped off at the tobacconist's to buy our scratch-card parking tickets for the whole day then on to where we'd parked the time before, just round the corner from the station. Except that nobody told us this was market day and all the parking spaces were covered with traders and their stalls.

We drove on a bit, round a few corners, down a few streets and all the time keeping a mental picture of our location in relation to the station; eventually we found a space, parked up, marked the scratch-cards, left them visible in the window, and made our way up and round to the station just as a train was pulling out.

We knew the trains were every half hour, plenty of time to go to the loo and queue for tickets until, that is, we found ourselves behind yet another British-holiday-family-from-hell. First of all they weren't sure where they were going and then they didn't seem to know how many there were in their group and whether or not they were adults or children and then all those foreign coins and notes were such a bother; and of course they expected the ticket office to be in the capable hands of a patient, fluent English-speaker.

As they blustered, fumbled and dithered, the next train came and went. The family of indeterminate size and mental faculties were in fact going just one station in the opposite direction to everyone else, to the terminus at Sorrento, and could have walked there in less time than they took to get their tickets. It was another half-hour later before we were finally under way and heading northwards towards the Bay of Naples.

—

Before we left home a friend had told us that, to get a flavour of the devastation caused by the eruption of Vesuvius in 79CE, Herculaneum was the site to visit rather than Pompeii. Not true.

If time is of the essence, then, yes, ruins of Herculanium are part of a smaller, more manageable site but otherwise there is no real comparison with Pompeii. Our various setbacks at Sant'Agnello shortened our time at both sites and the afternoon we spent at Pompeii was simply not enough.

That said, we did our best. We tried to be economical with the available time and squeezed in as much as possible in the certain knowledge that we would never see it all. What we did manage to see left us in awe at the scale of the disaster that hit this city—it is estimated that the then port of Pompeii had around 20,000 inhabitants when nearby Vesuvius erupted.

But it is the clarity with which the mind's eye is able to reconstruct this place that takes you by surprise; here there is no need for computer graphics to appreciate the size and scale of important structures such as the Forum and the Villa of the Mysteries; no need for a map to experience the broad thoroughfares, the side streets, the shops and the alleyways; no need for a guidebook to wonder at the beauty and diversity of the countless murals and mosaics. All you need is time and imagination and then, when you happen upon the plaster casts of the carbonised bodies unearthed at the time of the original excavations, all you need is compassion for those who lived, loved and died here almost 2000 years ago.

As our train headed back to Sant'Agnello, my mind was still wrestling with images of Pompeii, not just as we'd seen it that day but also as the setting for Robert Harris' remarkable novel, *Pompeii*, which I was reading at the time. Set just before and during the eruption, Harris paints a picture of a city oblivious to its fate, a city used to Vesuvius' frequent rumblings, a prosperous city, a vibrant port focused on the present rather than what was just around the corner. Sometimes fiction written with empathy and historical authority paints the best picture.

I also had fleeting visions of another Pompeii, the Pompeii of the comedian Frankie Howerd and his irreverent creation, the slave Lurcio. For half an hour every week in the early 1970s, the nation it seemed came to a standstill as colourful tongue-in-cheek characters, masters and mistresses of the *double entendre*, sent up the city of Pompeii. I had seen signs and sites around Pompeii that afternoon that triggered memories of the fictional *Up Pompeii!* and wondered whether its creator, Talbot Rothwell, had done a lot more research than may have been supposed. Who knows?

We arrived back at Sant'Agnello and retraced our steps to the car, a ten-minute walk from the station. Kay saw it first—they just look the same in all languages—a parking ticket tucked neatly behind a windscreen wiper. Sitting in the car we read the indictment, that we'd been parked there all day without a permit and now had to pay a fine of €20.

In case I'd scratched off the wrong date or times, I examined every box of the scratch-card permits we'd bought earlier but everything seemed fine. Then, out of the corner of my eye in the car's wing-mirror, I saw a parking attendant heading our way. Politely and with a touch of 'we're just simple-minded, illiterate foreigners', we confronted him with the evidence, the parking permits correctly completed and his parking ticket implying the opposite.

He looked at both and nodded, he could see that we'd completed them correctly and said as much but, he went on to explain, the permits we had used were for the *comune* of Sant'Agnello and we were now parked up in the adjacent *comune* of Piano di Sorrento which had, of course, its own customised parking permits. By having had to drive thatr little bit further to find a parking space earlier in the day, *after* we'd bought the scratch-cards, we had innocently strayed across an undefined border into a different *comune.*

The parking attendant was a sympathetic young man and could see how we'd come to make such a mistake but, having issued the ticket, there was nothing he could do—we'd have to pay the fine. I reached for my wallet but he shook his head … we couldn't pay him, we'd have to go the municipal offices for that. He wrote down the address and gave us directions round the complicated one-way system and suggested that it was worth trying to argue our case there.

On the third lap of Piano di Sorrento we found it, except that there was nowhere to park. I was rapidly losing the will to live so did what any Italian driver would have done in such circumstances: I parked up anyway and left Kay in the car to explain things should another parking attendant turn up.

I went into the office and managed to collar a genial-looking, bearded 50-something who listened to my story and, like his colleague, understood how such a thing could have happened and, clearly a lateral thinker, he thought it was unfair and that we should not have to pay the fine.

Confident that he could sort it, he took the paperwork into a back office where his superior was lording it over an empty desk and a cradled phone. I could see My Hero trying to explain the situation and the shrug-of-the-shoulders response that his boss gave which clearly meant, 'and what do you want me to do about it?'. More animated and audible but incomprehensible discussions ensued and it became increasingly clear there was some previous needle being reprised between these two and it was obvious who was going to come out on top. Once again I got a negative vibe from my craic-ometer.

My Hero returned to the front counter, shrugged his shoulders and apologised; he'd done his best but I'd have to pay the fine. As I took my debit card out of my wallet, he shook his head and waved his finger—cash only. I didn't have the cash, nor did Kay, so I asked him where the nearest Bancomat was and hoofed it about a half a kilometre down the road, quickly explaining to Kay where I was going as I passed the car.

When I returned and finally paid the fine, My Hero was nowhere to be seen so I crossed behind the counter—nobody seemed to mind or show any curiosity about my motive—and wandered up and down corridors, poking my head round every office door until I found him. I shook his hand and thanked him once again for doing his best; he shrugged his shoulders for the umpteenth time that day and said, "*La vita è così*". Yes, life *is* like that.

This day still not done with us. It was two weary travellers who eventually unlocked the pedestrian gate into the courtyard at Villa Belvedere; the household pet, a bouncy dalmatian, opened a solitary, disinterested eye in recognition. Inside the apartment we slumped into armchairs, separately mulling over a day to remember, unaware that worse was to come.

I took out my camera and began to flick through images of Herculanium and then Pompeii. I decided to delete one and instead deleted them all and, in frantic vein, I sought the 'undo' button that my camera didn't have.

This day was going from bad to worse. Crestfallen I took a shower.

It was gone eight when we left the apartment, descended the marble steps and crossed the courtyard towards the security gate; the dog was still dozing. I was a little ahead of Kay so that I could press the button that, from the inside only, automatically released the lock on the gate. We think it was the audible click of the gate that triggered what happened next.

Kay, being that little bit closer, heard it just before I did. It was the unmistakable pounding of paws, fast and aggressive. Next moment the hitherto placid and user-friendly family pet was barking excitedly while sinking its paws and claws into Kay's back. Pandemonium broke loose as the dog ran off and I helped a shaken Kay to her feet as Carlo rushed out to help and his father retrieved the dog and tied it to a tree.

Kay's top was ripped and there was clearly blood underneath. Amid all the apologies and offers of help, I explained that we had antiseptic and plasters with us and ushered Kay back to our apartment to assess the damage. It was not as bad as we feared but bad enough; the skin was broken and bleeding in several places, all of which our first-aid kit coped with. With Kay bandaged and both recovered we decided to try that once again; we needed to eat almost as much as we needed a large glass of red wine.

The dog remained tied up and Carlo and his father were still there waiting for us as, once again, we headed for the gate. They were clearly upset and genuinely perplexed about the whole incident; they were sure that the dog had never done this before and, anyway, he knew us, we'd been in and out many times. I tried to explain that I thought it was the sudden noise of the gate being unlocked that had broken his sleep. It had just come at the wrong moment and he had probably reacted instinctively.

A quarter of an hour later we were down in the town, the red wine on the table; we were just about to start our second glass.

It was gone eleven when we were returned to Villa Belvedere. We unlocked the gate a little more carefully and slowly than usual; all seemed quiet until, that is, we started to cross the courtyard. Out of the apartment below ours came Carlo, his father and his mother, *la mamma*, still adjusting a hastily thrown on dressing gown. They had clearly been waiting for us.

The apologies continued but they wanted us to talk to Carlo's sister on the phone. We'd met Anna on our previous visit and knew what they said was correct, her English *was* better. Anna told us the dog was 'clean', it had had all the right injections, at the right time. Nevertheless, as a precaution, Kay needed a tetanus jab and that it was important to have the injection as soon as possible and certainly within 24 hours.

She was right, of course, and she went on to explain that they would pay for the sterilised anti-tetanus 'kit' from the pharmacy and that *la mamma* would administer the injection the following morning. Her mother nodded profusely and smiled a knowing smile. In Italy, it's never quite what you expect.

Our initial negative reaction towards this suggestion was soon dispelled when Anna explained that her mother did all the injections in the family and always had *and* that she was very, very good, better than any doctor. It was this last bit that persuaded Kay and so an appointment was made for ten in the morning when the needle-wielding *mamma* would appear.

La mamma arrived bang on schedule. In the light of day and sporting her normal day attire and her teeth, she looked infinitely more the part than she had in her pastel-pink dressing gown the night before.

First of all, like some stage illusionist seeking her audience's approbation, she showed us that the packet had not been opened and that its contents were therefore sterile. She washed her hands and forcefully ushered me out of the apartment while Kay stood nervously awaiting her fate.

Outside I paced up and down and chatted to Carlo, clearly still perturbed by these strange and embarrassing events and perhaps worried too that we might have some future litigation in mind. I also kept an ear to the apartment door half expecting to hear a scream at any moment. None came and a few moments later a beaming *mamma* appeared, the deed done.

Behind her back Kay gave me a thumbs-up sign ... and later explained that it was the most painless injection she'd ever had.

Clutching our ten percent discount voucher for any future stay at Villa Belvedere, we were soon on the road, heading north towards Rome's Ciampino Airport and home.

Surprisingly we never did use that discount voucher. Once bitten, twice shy?

NEVER JUDGE A BOAT …

It was our third time in Corigliano d'Otranto in Apulia and finally we had agreed on the best place to eat. It was here on our first dinner, post-agreement, that we got talking to Marco and his 14-year-old daughter Gabriella. It was almost obligatory to strike up some sort of conversation for, on the restaurant's mezzanine floor, we were the only four people.

Marco hailed from Otranto on the Adriatic coast where he was a judge and Gabriella and her younger sister, who wasn't there that evening, appeared to live in both Otranto and Gallipoli where their mother worked. We never quite got to the bottom of the domestic situation; it could have been a separation or simply a work or schooling arrangement but, whichever, it seemed to suit everybody.

We talked mainly about Corigliano and Otranto: for us Corigliano was the place we like to stay and Otranto on the east coast the place we most liked to visit; for Marco it was the exact opposite. He lived in Otranto and liked to come to Corigliano of an evening to eat, particularly at this restaurant which he reckoned served the best food in this part of the Salento. At least we were in accord about the restaurant.

Both Marco and Gabriella spoke excellent English so our conversation was less riddled with infinitives and wild guesses. Marco was particularly intrigued about how it was that we discovered Corigliano d'Otranto in the first place. He explained how it was a little oasis hereabouts that tourists rarely picked up on and, in doing so, realised he'd answered his own question for he could see that we weren't tourists in the conventional sense. We agreed Corigliano had something 'different' but, like us, he couldn't pinpoint that difference, it was just a feeling that we all shared.

We went on to talk about Otranto and its turbulent past before Marco suggested that we visit him there that Saturday when, weather-permitting, we could go out on his boat and get a different perspective of the eastern coastline and visit parts of it inaccessible by land. Before we went our separate ways we exchanged telephone numbers and Marco said that he'd call on the Friday to finalise arrangements.

As we walked back to our apartment we talked about the evening and first of all tried to make a stab at guessing Marco's age. He seemed to be in his mid-40s but did they have judges that young in Italy? We didn't know. Then we speculated about whether or not he actually would get in touch again for the thought of sitting back, glass of wine in hand, on the iridescent *Mare Adriatico* was appealing. Perhaps less so to Kay who is not such a good sailor. Also, it crossed our minds that somehow, yet again, we had been taken on board (seemingly literally in this case) by a complete stranger. It was beginning to seem like some sort of affliction.

Marco did indeed call on the Friday and we agreed to meet outside Otranto's Aragonese castle at ten the next morning.

Saturday dawned. It was a beautiful summery day, scarcely a breeze, the temperature beginning its climb up into the low 30s; we headed to Otranto, parked up and got to the castle right on time. When, by ten past ten, there was no sign of Marco we began to wonder whether we were in the right place for there were seemingly two entrances to the castle. Experience had taught us that Italian meeting arrangements have a unique fluidity both in terms of time and place and are rarely what you expect. So Kay stayed by the more obvious meeting place while I flitted between her and the other one, all the time trying to recall exactly what Marco looked like.

On my third lap, heading back towards Kay around ten-thirty, I spotted him ambling along the footpath heading our way. Greetings over, he explained that we would go back to his apartment to get the food ready and meet up with some other people who were also going out on the boat. This boat was getting bigger and bigger.

At Marco's apartment we met his other daughter and a couple of her friends as well as another, slightly older, slightly greyer, but equally amiable, judge and Marco's housekeeper who was busy preparing a sort of late breakfast for everyone, including us, as well as getting together some baskets of goodies for a late lunch at sea. It was gone half eleven when our little group, minus the housekeeper, finally headed for the harbour.

As we approached the quayside, I had painted mental pictures of Marco's boat and was looking forward to sitting up on deck in the sun watching the world go by. We knew we were fortunate to be here at all with this generous group of people.

Everyone stopped for a break by a small row of rubber dinghies tied to the stone jetty; at least I assumed it was a break for all the larger craft were a bit further on and some were anchored a short distance out, mid-harbour. But no, Marco's boat was indeed this very rubber dinghy complete with a massive outboard motor and then I realised that we must be going out on the dinghy to one of the larger craft anchored in the harbour. I just wasn't sure which one.

With everyone aboard, we cast off and, weaving slowly around other boats, headed towards the harbour exit and the protective concrete arm of the pier. The girls were already in sunbathing mode but it wasn't until we crept past the end of the pier that the penny finally dropped This large rubber dinghy *was* Marco's boat. And, worse still, Marco was a boy racer at heart for, seconds after crossing that imaginary demarcation line between harbour and sea, Marco put his foot on the gas and the outboard responded dramatically as the bow of the boat shot up into the air. We were off.

This was not what either of us had imagined when we woke up that morning. Nevertheless, everyone else seemed to be loving it but Kay,

at sea not her location of choice, was hanging on for grim death as
was I, definitely a better sailor but not too hot on the swimming front.

At breakneck speed we headed north from Otranto, hugging the
coast and surging past lesser craft who clearly didn't have a madman
as a skipper. After about 15 terrifying minutes skimming across the
Mare Adriatico we stopped for a few blissful moments alongside a
much larger craft, the sort of boat we *thought* we were going out on
while Marco partook of some socialising with his friends.

As we pulled away Marco explained that he'd arranged to stop off
here for an *aperitivo* later in the afternoon on our way back to
Otranto. Kay and I couldn't wait … we weren't sure we'd last that
long without a stiff drink.

Like the proverbial bat out of hell, Marco was off again but after five
minutes he slowed down as we approached an exquisite, secluded
sandy cove, its offshore peppered with small boats like ours, most
of their occupants already in the sea or lying on the small arc of
golden sand. We dropped anchor 100 metres offshore.

Within seconds everyone aboard Marco's boat was ready to take
the plunge; everybody, that is, except for Kay and me. We had been
expecting a sightseeing trip, it had simply never occurred to us that
this outing was no more than an opportunity to sunbathe and cool
off in the water. It should have been obvious, I should have joined
the dots of what I already knew about the Italian psyche; and this,
their take on a bit of aquatic craic, was my idea of holiday hell.

Of course, as a non-swimmer, the urge to jump into the sea was
not something on my agenda and Kay, who does swim, hadn't
thought to bring her costume—it was safely tucked up in a drawer
back home.

As bad luck would have it, the genial Enzo, judge number two,
came to what he thought was my rescue when he announced that he
was pretty sure he had brought two costumes. *Bastard*, I thought to
myself. He proceeded to rummage away in the depths of his
rucksack with dedicated fervour before letting out a whoop of
delight as he proudly waved aloft his spare pair *and* he had a spare

towel too. He knew I could not be other than overcome with gratitude and would have none of my futile protestations. It was nothing, *di niente*, what are friends for?

There was no escape, I'd have to show my appreciation for this act of unsolicited kindness and plunge my pristine-white body into the *Mare Adriatico*.

As I was still slipping into Enzo's spare trunks, everyone else was already in the water doing their own thing: the girls had met up with some friends from other boats; Marco had already made it ashore and was chatting up a young female friend and Enzo was circling the boat like an expectant basking shark waiting for someone to play with … me.

I asked Enzo how deep it was so he stood up to show me that the water came up to his neck … I reckoned I was fractionally shorter than Enzo but that I would probably get away with it. Plunge I did not. Ever so slowly, a fake grin on my face disguising the fear in my eyes, I slipped over the side, one hand firmly holding on to the boat until I found the soft sandy bottom with the tips of my toes.

Letting go completely, I did my impersonation of swimming before walking ashore.

Truth be told, I had a great time in the water that day and really wished I could do more than walk and make half-hearted, and generally futile, attempts at getting my feet off the bottom for any length of time. Kay was the one who missed out and although she enjoyed sitting in the boat, the sun to herself, she made a mental note to pack her costume next time. I, on the other hand, would continue to 'forget' mine.

As I climbed back on board, the irony did not escape me that it was here in the same *Mare Adriatico,* 35 years earlier off the opposite coast on the Croatian island of Rab, that I had first propelled myself forwards in the sea. Sadly in that time my unique technique was still not an Olympic sport and I had already become resigned to the fact that, were it to become so, I was probably too old to participate.

It was soon time to eat and dry off back on the boat; simple fare it was—bread, cheese, ham, tomatoes, water and wine—exactly what we all needed. For the adults, an extra glass of wine was what was called for; for the girls a last plunge into the sea to say goodbye to their friends, and then, the anchor safely on board, we headed back, at a more sedate pace this time, to the boat we'd stopped at earlier.

Now this was a proper boat with tables and chairs and cabins and a fridge, a toilet and an engine hidden out of sight somewhere—the sort of boat we had thought that Marco was sure to have. We sat in the late afternoon sun, shared a few nibbles, a few stories, a few glasses until, that is, the girls got restless and threatened mutiny unless we headed back to dry land The 'big' boat finally evacuated, Kay and I clung on for dear life as Marco opened up the throttle for the grand finale as, once again, we shot across the water like a bullet from a gun, the entrance to Otranto's harbour our fast-approaching respite.

Back on *terra firma*, Marco invited us to have a pizza with him and his daughters that evening in Otranto but we had to decline as we had arranged to see another friend back in Corigliano.

As we returned to Corigliano we wished we could have stayed a little longer in Otranto with Marco, Enzo and the girls; it was a day that, for all sorts of reasons, we would never forget.

It was just one of so many other days which had not turned out as we expected but, in a strange sort of way, it was a typically Italian day. Italians enjoy playing hard and they love to share the things that give them the greatest pleasure and a brief encounter with two complete strangers in a restaurant is enough to trigger this openness and generosity.

The fact that we got it all wrong and hadn't anticipated a bare-knuckle ride with a genial madman at the helm was our problem and one that we, as non-Italians, would always have to get used to.

THE BOURBON FACTOR

My nephew Graham—or Neff as I prefer to call him—and I have done some travelling together down the years. I'm not sure how it started or what was the catalyst for our first such venture, a road trip through America's bourbon country, Kentucky and Tennessee. Might have been the lure of the bourbon.

At the time he was based in Seattle so we met in Chicago where we spent a few days before heading south to Indianapolis to take a bus trip round the famous Indianapolis 500 race track. Neff's idea, not mine.

We stayed in bed & breakfast accommodation and, each evening, with both of us lying across the same bed, browsing on our respective laptops, I would send him an email with a suggestion or two about the following night's possible resting place. Neff would email back with his thoughts and I would book it. Very occasionally we might discuss the choices by actually talking to each other; but not often.

We visited Louisville, the birthplace of Muhammad Ali who, a couple of years later, visited the town where I lived, Ennis in County Clare. Ennis was the home of his great-grandfather, Abe Grady, who emigrated to the United States in the 1860s and settled in Kentucky.

We stopped at Elizabethstown, Abraham Lincoln's birthplace and where I recall writing something disparaging in the Visitor's Book of the Lincoln Museum about the mishmash of so-called dioramas—models depicting a three-dimensional scene from his life—that didn't even seem to be in any obvious chronological order. Perhaps for the 150th anniversary of his assassination in

2015, they got their act together. If so, I'll be happy to take some of the credit.

Obviously 'birthplaces' was our theme of the moment so it would have seemed appropriate if, in between, we should witness the 'birth' of a bottle of bourbon at one of the many distilleries whose alluring billboards we passed. The temptation was almost too much but we decided to leave that experience until the next day when we'd check out the Jim Beam Distillery.

Bardstown and a different bourbon experience beckoned.

Downtown Bardstown has three distinctive buildings next to each other: on the left is the old Courthouse (now the centrepiece of a roundabout) in the middle is the Talbott Tavern with its famous Bourbon Bar and, on the right, is the old Jailhouse.

Historically the three had an obvious connection: you got drunk, uncooperative and obnoxious in the Talbott, were apprehended and escorted next door to the jail, then next morning frog-marched past the place of your alleged misdemeanour to the Courthouse and, in all probability, ended up back in the jail.

If the misdemeanour was of a more serious nature, then, up until 1894, it was possible to become the centre of attention at one of the public hangings which took place in the jail's back yard.

Neff and I were planning to spend time in two of these three buildings, the Bourbon Bar and the jailhouse for the last had embraced a new way of life and become a bed & breakfast. Indeed we had breakfast out the back where the gallows used to stand enclosed by a wall where people, including children, used to sit and watch.

The bedrooms are all spacious rooms on the first floor but there is one of the original cells downstairs which guests can stay though it has been upgraded somewhat since the last prisoner left. I'm pretty sure he or she didn't have an en suite and wi-fi.

The owner, Paul, told us the story of the woman who booked this as a birthday surprise for her husband; she thought he would see the funny side of it. Her husband, a police officer, was far from amused and insisted they have another room or he would leave. They left.

On our first evening there, we ate at the Talbott Tavern and then adjourned to its Bourbon Bar to sample the wares. Here Neff noticed a sign plugging the bar's bourbon menu by offering a choice of five at a fixed price. We perused the extensive menu which had about 40 to choose from. Should we have had difficulty making up our minds there was another 60-plus adorning the wall behind the bar.

Not being connoisseurs, we opted for the fixed menu and scrutinised it as if we actually knew what we were looking for. I was hopeful that I might recognise the name of that wonderful bourbon I'd had in Portland over a decade previously. I didn't.

In the end we chose five bourbons that neither of us had ever heard of and watched as each glass was poured; we had already asked for a pen and paper and were studiously writing down the name of each. Our five of choice were brought to our table, five each, ten in total. We lined up our five glasses on the table in the same order as the list for we had decided that, to become more bourbon-savvy, we should rate each out of ten and then maybe we'd find our favourite. We might be a little wiser but less sober.

Other customers only saw the ten bourbons sitting in two neat rows on the table and watched, while pretending not to, as we worked our way along our respective rows. Eventually a man at an adjacent table could stand it no longer and came over to enquire about what was going on.

"You guys got a problem?" he drawled, on the presumed assumption that we were locked in some sort of dispute that could only be solved by drinking lots of bourbon until one of us passed out.

"No," I said vaguely, "we … we just like bourbon."

He looked a little embarrassed, unconvinced even; clearly this, the most obvious scenario, was not one he'd thought of. Awkwardly he returned to his table where his friends were eagerly awaiting the disappointing outcome of his research.

Still the focus of attention, an elderly man from another table, en route to the bathroom, stopped by to explain how bourbon and this very bar had been his downfall and how, in his youth and long before he went to live in Florida, he'd spent a night 'next door' for his indiscretions. He was more than a little impressed that we were actually staying 'next door' by choice and later introduced us to his travelling companions, his daughter and grandson, for whom this was some sort trip down *his* memory lane and a possible lesson about the evils of drink. In that respect he was probably delighted to have two, ready-made, Irish visual aids to hand.

Finally left to our own devices, we evaluated our separate researches into the five bourbons we were comparing and contrasting and found them to be almost identical. Now that we were getting the hang of it, we decided to order a couple more just because we could.

We slept soundly on the first floor of our prison.

The next day we were a bit slow and decided to explore Bardstown itself before heading up to the aptly-named Happy Hollow Road and the Jim Beam Distillery.

Although I clearly enjoyed bourbon and was fast becoming an expert through increased intake, Jim Beam was not one I'd often sampled; at the time my favourites were Wild Turkey and that mysterious, wondrous, nameless nectar I'd sampled in Portland.

As one of us had to drive, we tossed a coin to see who would participate in the anticipated tasting at the end of the Jim Beam tour … I won. That said, the samples offered were in such tiny plastic glasses that the small amount of alcohol therein would have scarcely intoxicated a flea.

Nevertheless, it was at the Jim Beam Distillery that I had my 'eureka' moment, the moment when I knew I had finally found that mystery nectar from Portland. Everything about it, the name, the label, the taste of course, came flooding back. Until then, I had no idea that Jim Beam made other bourbons and not just those carrying the larger than life Jim Beam logo.

There was a whole range of others—some of which, like the oft ridiculed Knob Creek, I had heard of—and at the top of the Jim Beam tree there was Bakers; simply exquisite.

I insisted that Neff take the smallest of sips and retold the Portland story before we bought a bottle each to take home. Well, that was the unsophisticated plan. We hadn't reckoned on the Bardstown factor.

The Talbott Tavern restaurant was closed that second evening so we went in search of food elsewhere before returning to the Bourbon Bar for a bourbon or three. Back at the Bourbon Bar, more bad news; it was early-closing evening and, try as we might, we were unable to extend the hours.

But we came up with another, less costly, alternative: a plan evolved to relocate the Bourbon Bar, its staff and the only other customer there at the time, to our bedroom. It helped that the bar staff knew we had at least one bottle of Bakers in the prison. My fault, I had to open my big mouth.

Everyone was also curious about the prison itself for, although they all lived in or around the town, nobody had actually been inside. The evolving plan therefore satisfied their curiosity and, by bringing a selection of plastic cups and other paid-for beverages of people's choosing, everyone's drinking time was extended in a congenial, albeit custodial, setting.

Neither Neff nor I could remember whether or not Paul slept on the premises nor did we know if there might be other visitors staying there so the strategy for getting to our room was simple: turn all keys slowly and be as quiet as mice.

There were seven of us in the bedroom and, as far as we could tell, we had successfully got there without alerting anyone. As well as some nibbles from the kitchen of the Talbott, we had enough alcohol to keep us going for as long as people wanted to stay. We lacked just one chair so I went on a reccy and returned a few moments later; mission accomplished.

Inevitably, we opened my bottle of Bakers and closed it empty; neither Neff nor I mentioned that there was another bottle in the room; having acquired the taste, we were saving that for later, there was no way it would ever see home.

When all sources of refreshment were depleted, someone suggested that we should go to his (or her) apartment. Before we did so, I had to replace the chair I'd requisitioned and, as I had now no memory of where I'd found it, I left it in a space in the landing which looked as if it might be missing a chair.

I do recall it was much more difficult for we seven mice to leave the jail as quietly as we had arrived; there was a lot of giggling and people making more noise by telling others to be quieter. It was gone midnight when we all piled into a couple of cabs and headed somewhere out of town, I know not where, to resume the 'party' in an upstairs apartment. Somehow word got out and the numbers soon doubled.

For some reason I had become the star attraction. It wasn't just my good looks or my super powers, but rather, I imagine, because of my age (in relation to everyone else's), my propensity to indulge in a bit of the craic *and* my ability to stay upright and *compos mentis* was as good as, if not better than, many of those around me. Also, tales of our ability to hold our bourbon, as witnessed by a bar full of people the previous evening, had already become the stuff of folklore, soon to be legend, and of course our actual intake had been exaggerated to make it a much better story. We may have helped with that.

Somewhere among the haze of conversations that evening, I picked up that one of the reasons that so many of our new-found friends were interested in the erstwhile prison was that it was supposed to be haunted. Had I been more in charge of my faculties when I heard this, I would have explained to the assembled audience that there is no such thing as a room or a building that is haunted, only people's susceptibility to believing nonsense, particularly if it's marketed well. Maybe these 'ghosts' only 'appear' to those who have already heard the story or don't drink enough bourbon to sleep soundly.

Sometime around 3am we were ferried back to our jail and, for the third time that evening, pretended to be the quietest of mice.

The next morning we were slow, very slow. Even the crunch of breakfast muesli was headache inducing. Paul, on the other hand, was full of the joys of spring and didn't seem to notice our lack of enthusiasm or verve. Or perhaps he knew all about our late-night/ early-morning shenanigans and was just making us suffer.

As we left our room for the last time, I stopped to take a look at the chair I'd left in the landing, it seemed oddly out of place but I still couldn't remember from where I'd plucked it. Maybe, if it was meant to be somewhere else, Paul would automatically blame the resident ghost for having moved it and, in so doing, add another 'strange but true' story to its repertoire.

It was time to get back on the road for we had a rendezvous planned that day in Nashville with the Knoxville couple Kay and I had met in New Orleans. Well, almost the same couple … in the few years we'd known them Claire had kicked one husband into touch and got herself another one and a damn good choice she made.

Neff, whose turn it was to drive, still had that glazed, baleful look he'd brought to the breakfast table which suggested he was in no fit state to walk, let alone get behind the wheel. As Neff threw the last of our bags into the trunk, he confirmed my suspicions and threw me the car keys.

The following day, having stayed overnight in Nashville, we were on the road again, heading south to Lynchburg in Moore County, Tennessee. We knew Moore County to be a 'dry' county, a county where alcohol sales are proscribed; and no, we had not turned over a new leaf, we had not signed the pledge. On the contrary, we were visiting the Jack Daniels Distillery.

It is indeed a strange manifestation of the 'American way' that probably the country's most famous branded spirit, Jack Daniels, is produced in a county where it cannot be bought or sold. The nearest place to the distillery where you can actually buy a bottle of Jack Daniels is a dozen miles away in neighbouring Coffee County.

That said, outside the distillery, at an adjacent store, a loophole in the local laws allows people to buy a speciality bottle and even have it engraved; it is mere coincidence that the bottle happens to have Jack Daniels inside but the money that changes hands makes no allowance for this, the payment is for the bottle not the liquor therein.

After the tour, Neff remarked on how the tour guide seemed to be fixated on me, in a slightly agitated kind of way; I was also aware of it but was too modest to talk about it at the time. Everything of course pointed to my good looks and charm but I suspected the real reason was my new baseball cap—the one I bought at the Jim Beam Distillery.

When, three days later, we parted company at Atlanta Airport—Neff to Seattle, me to Chicago—the second bottle of Bakers had gone the same way as the first, except that we didn't share it with anyone.

I had intended to buy a replacement at Chicago O'Hare but, thanks to a massive accident on the freeway between Chicago Midway and O'Hare, I was lucky I even caught the flight.

Except for some wonderful memories—and some hazy ones too—I returned home empty-handed.

Little did I know that I would be back in America a fortnight later, reprising the bourbon factor ... the lengths people will go to to buy a bottle of Bakers bourbon.

VIRGIN ON THE RIDICULOUS

Two weeks after Neff and I wrestled free from our farewell embrace in Atlanta, Kay and I were preparing to do it all over again. As had happened before when I went to Sicily alone, Kay and I decided to reenact the journey and the craic that Neff and I had shared south from Chicago through bourbon country. But the intrigue and absurdity began before we even boarded the aircraft.

Unknown to Kay, on our first evening in Chicago we would be dining with Neff and his American girlfriend, Jo. What Neff and I had planned was that Kay and I would drop into an Irish bar where, astonishingly, we'd find him and Jo already sitting there or, as indeed as it eventually turned out, the other way round. Either way, the aim was to surprise, or even shock, Kay.

Just before we set off to the airport, Neff emailed me to ask me to pick up a particular book for him at the airport. Of course, as Kay didn't know we would be meeting him, his request put pressure on me to find the book without her being any the wiser.

We were air-side, relaxing in one of the hospitality lounges at Heathrow awaiting our Virgin Atlantic flight, when I left Kay, ostensibly to go for a wander, but with the real aim of buying Neff his book. When I returned I found Kay in a very agitated state; agitated to the point of being distraught.

Before continuing I need to explain some particular and relevant details pertinent to what happened after I returned to the lounge; these relate to where I was born for, uniquely, two countries lay claim to my body.

My place of birth, Belfast, is in the 'Northern Ireland' part of 'The United Kingdom of Great Britain and Northern Ireland'. It is also part of the island of Ireland. Though not administered by the government of the Republic of Ireland, that country's citizenship laws apply the island of Ireland and therefore allow me, and most others born in the six counties of Northern Ireland, to claim Irish citizenship and to carry an Irish passport.

In effect, this enables me to possess *two* passports, an Irish passport and a British passport. For a short period I had both concurrently, but normally I only travelled with one, my Irish passport. Born-in-London Kay, on the other hand, has a British passport.

For our outward flight to Chicago, I checked-in online having previously entered our separate passport information—Irish for me, British for Kay—into the Virgin Atlantic website.

As we had one bag to check-in, we joined the relevant queue at Heathrow Airport where our passports were checked and a dated security sticker affixed to the back of each by a Virgin Atlantic representative moving along the queue. When we got to the bag-drop counter itself, our passports and eTicket were once again checked.

The reason Kay was in such an agitated state when I returned to the lounge was that, while casually flicking through her passport, she discovered that it was in fact *my* British passport.

Somehow she had sauntered through all the security checks up to this point using a passport that did not belong to her, something that, it is reasonable to suppose, should have been picked up by at least one of the Virgin Atlantic staff who had checked it.

Even to a partially-sighted security officer, coping with a

hangover, a pending divorce and terminal cancer, there were some pretty obvious indications on the passport Kay presented, and which had been 'checked', that she was definitely not me. These are the obvious contenders:

Her name: she has always used her maiden name.

She is female.

Unlike me she did not have white hair.

Nor did she wear glasses.

Nor did she have a full beard.

Apart from the above, we were hard to tell apart, no more than a couple of unique male-female twins with the same name and exactly the same photo.

While it appeared that the security community at Heathrow, and Virgin Atlantic in particular, were sloppy, we were all too aware that were two additional hurdles down the line. And even if Kay were to 'pass' the final passport and security check before boarding the plane, there was no way, absolutely no way, that the eagle-eyed American Immigration officials would not pick up on most if not all of the five discrepancies listed above. And even if they did, there was the minor additional problem of what would happen when their electronic scrutiny of the passport number would not correspond with the one checked in online.

Risking it was not an option; the very thought of it conjured up images of handcuffs snapping shut as we were read our rights before being re-attired in orange jump-suits. The only upside of such a scenario was that we could probably sell the film rights.

Although I didn't normally carry both my passports when I travelled, I nevertheless spent the next five minutes frantically rummaging through my hand luggage on the off chance that I had. The alternative, cancelling our journey, didn't bear thinking about.

Finally, tucked away at the bottom of the front pocket of the case, I found Kay's passport, the one with her photo and all the other distinguishing characteristics that confirmed her identity as being different from mine. Her expression of incredulity turned to relief before settling for anger.

Following a brief inquest which confirmed that I was the guilty party and had got our two British passports mixed up when I checked-in online, there was one final hurdle to overcome before we could be assured of going to the ball. There was that sticker on the back of *my* British passport that said we had been cleared by security, albeit a security system with a penchant for slapping stickers on any old passport that's thrust in front of them.

This was the hard part: we had to peel off the security sticker from one passport and stick it onto the other without damaging it in any way. For obvious reasons, we didn't have any sharp-edged objects with us so had to improvise with finger nails and the edge of a bank card. It was a slow, painstaking and nerve-racking process but eventually Kay's passport, the one with her actual photograph inside, was now emblazoned with a security sticker and we were quietly confident that nobody would notice that it had been relocated.

We were now whole again. We were two different people with two different passports and two different nationalities.

Even so, that final, and much more thorough, passport check just before boarding the aircraft was an edgy affair. Both passports passed with flying colours. We would go to the ball and we wouldn't be wearing orange jump-suits … well, not unless they found the Kalashnikovs in our hand luggage.

I decided there and then that, when my British passport expired the following year, I would not renew it; one passport and one nationality was usually enough for most people.

———

Later that evening in Chicago, the subterfuge that Neff and I had concocted went according to plan and, for the second time that day, Kay was totally stunned when Neff and Jo casually sauntered into the bar, ambled over to our table in a casual way and asked an unsuspecting and speechless Kay what she was doing in Chicago. For Kay it was the end of a day she would rather forget.

A few days later we were back in Bardstown, back staying at the erstwhile jailhouse.

As we were being shown to our room, I was frantically scouring the wide communal landing, preoccupied with locating the chair I'd 'replaced' there three weeks previously. I was not totally surprised it wasn't where I'd left it and could see that it had been moved to another part of the landing That, at least, was a kind of relief for I couldn't be sure whether or not I'd found it in somebody else's bedroom.

I assumed it was likely that Paul would have made the link between Neff and me and the itinerant chair. Or, of course, he might well have blamed it on a sedentary ghost, tired of all that walking around, making 'oooOOOooo' noises and trying to frighten gullible clients.

Paul never said a word about the chair, nor the ghost, but I could see he wasn't as sure about what I might have told Kay about my previous visit to Bardstown with Neff or what, if anything, he should divulge. As with the chair, he settled for the diplomatic approach.

"Those guys sure knew how to drink. Here in Bardstown, they're still talking about them."

A proud moment that was.

Back in the UK, I wrote to Virgin Atlantic in which I questioned their security measures at Heathrow. I was able to give them an accurate description of the guy who was a little over-enthusiastic about doling out security stickers for any old passport. They promised to investigate and to keep me in the loop.

At first they appeared to be doing both and then, even though there were some outstanding matters, I was dropped from the loop. When, some weeks later, I sent a cryptic email to a national radio station in response to something I'd heard one of their so-called 'experts' say, I was contacted by the show's producer and persuaded to elaborate.

When I did so, I was interviewed anonymously and related the Heathrow experience as outlined above. I got several follow-up invitations to appear on national television outlets but declined all.

The radio station contacted Virgin Atlantic and were assured that their security regime at Heathrow had been tightened. They had also located their 'over-enthusiastic' employee with the dodgy eyesight and he had been retrained. They did not say whether or not this retraining included an eye test.

A WALK ON THE WILD SIDE

Unusually, we had forsaken our beloved south of Italy and opted for a short February break in Frascati, just south of Rome.

Early evening in Frascati was just like every other Italian town and city, it was time for the *frascatani* to partake of that uniquely Italian walking ritual, the *passeggiata*. Time to dress up and head towards the open spaces around Piazza Roma and Piazza Guglielmo Marconi to promenade and gossip with style and more than a mere hint of theatre and, as ever, with an eye to who's out and who's in, who's talking to whom and, ears sharp as radar, who or what they're talking about. A kind of Italian craic.

Although we had experienced the Italian *passeggiata* before, it was here in Frascati where it seemed to have become almost an art-form. Two things were different, the time of year and the number of women on parade; and these two were not unconnected. It being February it was cold and, for many of Frascati's womenfolk of a certain age, this was an opportunity to show off their fur. And show it off they most certainly did.

Usually in pairs, and with a panache that lacked any hint of embarrassment or concession to being, or not being, politically correct, they strolled gracefully up and down, down and up. Many of these fur-framed ladies trailed furry little pooches on leads, presumably leather rather than plastic, which in turn, bearing in mind the season, needed to be decked out in the right gear—nothing as indiscreet as fur on fur of course, that would be a little over the top, but tartan seemed to be both 'in' and appropriate.

Still further behind were the menfolk. They knew their place and kept their distance in the certain knowledge that this was not their show. But they had a function, their job was to carry the umbrella and be ready, at the merest hint of rain, to protect their good lady, and their investment, from the elements.

Although it was the fur-clad womenfolk that caught my eye, other *frascatani* were out and about: young and old, families with children, smouldering couples, doting grandparents, work colleagues, all lustily chattering, gesticulating extravagantly, wheeling and dealing, sending messages, making calls, exchanging glances.

Wherever you see it, the *passeggiata* has a rhythm that is dictated not just by the people, the season and the local culture but also by the space within and around which people are walking. There is a place to turn, an undefined, invisible mini-roundabout where people stop, turn and begin the process all over again; there is a subtle order to this apparently haphazard flow of humanity that somehow avoids collisions and last-minute changes of direction. It is an evening ritual that has no beginning, no end and involves no planning. It is uniquely Italian and, for the outsider, singularly compulsive viewing. And, should you decide to join in, there are no conditions, there is no impediment and no charge.

Later the same year I was visiting Santa Severina in Calabria where, because I was there for several weeks, observing the town's *passeggiata* became, for me, something of a ritual in itself. Every evening, between about six and seven-thirty I sat outside the Rosa dei Venti bar—or, as I preferred to call it, Carlo's—in the town square for a pre-prandial *aperitivo* and watched intently as Santa Severina's *passeggiata* unfolded.

In essence the *passeggiata* here was no different to those I had experienced at Frascati or elsewhere, though there was a noticeable absence of fur coats, even in the winter I would have guessed. Also the oval shape of the piazza made for a more ordered and predictable route from church to castle, from castle to church.

Every so often people sitting at the four bars on the fringes would get up and filter in; just as often some of those walking would slope off and bag an empty table. There were five points of entry and exit to the square where people joined in or took off home; few did as I did and headed straight across this line of traffic to get to my favourite bar and my favourite vantage point.

From the safety of Carlo's I watched this ritual every evening and, as is the way of routine, I couldn't help but notice the regulars, their characteristics and their foibles.

The 'regulars' in rural communities such as Santa Severina, were mainly men; generally any women were either one half of a young couple showing their togetherness to the world or perhaps part of a small group, most often in their 30s or 40s, who had probably grown up and gone to university in a world very different to that of their mothers. Of course there were the inevitable exceptions.

There was one more mature couple among the regulars but there was something else that made them different … their little dog. It was rarely 'with' them but always knew where they were, always seemed to know which four feet, in a forest of feet, belonged to those that fed it. It would weave in and out, this way and that, it would wander off to take a look at something interesting, have a sniff here or a sniff there, chase off a incautious cat or two, but it was never more than seven or eight metres away from those four familiar feet.

There was a young lad who always walked by himself, listening to his music, acknowledging no-one; a man who was never without a cigarette; two teenage girls who, arm in arm, walked faster than everyone else and talked to match; a man who never seemed to be without at least one *telefonino* held against an ear; small mixed groups of young adults at the pre-couple stage, the boys trying to impress, the girls trying to look cool under pressure.

There was a group of mature men who argued and gesticulated a lot but seemed to be the best of friends and always from their midst the distinctive aroma of pipe tobacco; a short, bespeckled boy on a bicycle who went from stabilisers to independence before my very eyes; a man who always smoked a cigar and carried a book and looked forgetful; there were small groups of older men with a life of toil written into their faces, their hands and their bodies but who always smiled and seemed to enjoy life and were always incredibly courteous.

With the clock approaching half-seven, the *passeggiata* would start to wind down. Slowly, almost imperceptibly at first, the square would begin to empty as, first, the 'independent' women headed home to prepare dinner, leaving the more senior, mostly male, citizens to do a few more circuits before they too wandered off home to see what delicacy their womenfolk had prepared.

By the time the church clock struck a quarter to eight, the square would be almost empty; time to head back to the *agriturismo* for dinner too.

UNDER A VENETIAN SKY

Neff finally did the deed and got himself hitched on a beautiful Venetian bridge over a canal in the busy Piazza San Marco on a bright, cloudless May day. After the brief ceremony he and his American wife (his 'first wife', as he would later introduce her) stepped onto a gondola, clinked their champagne-filled glasses and set off on a short, romantic glide along the still waters under that clear blue sky and its occasional flurry of wispy clouds. Their guests' cameras clicked to record the moment.

Alas …

The sky was false

The clouds were on a loop.

The gondola was electric.

And the Piazza San Marco and its bridge were in a shopping mall in the Venetian Hotel in Las Vegas.

The only things that were real were the champagne, the glasses, the guests and the water, the last a lot cleaner than you might expect to find in Venice.

Although in the previous decade I had become something of an Italophile, I had never been to the real Venice and I knew this was the closest I was likely to get for some time. The only problem was that, initially, we were not even meant to be there.

As a graphic designer, I had some commissions and commitments that came round once a month, once every quarter, once a year; one of the these was for an annual festival programme. Unfortunately it was always behind schedule, largely because its organiser was never able to keep to his own deadlines. For me this translated into frenetic efforts to meet his deadline and the occasional all-nighter. I had no reason to believe that 2008 would be any different and therefore had to decline Neff's invitation to his Las Vegas nuptials and the madness of the American way.

Then, miracle of miracles, after years of nagging, I finally managed to steer my client into getting his act together and the unimaginable was going to happen, the festival brochure would be going to print several days *ahead* of schedule. We could go to the ball after all.

Inexplicably, family and friends had been disappointed that we would not be making an appearance and Neff decided that we'd keep it that way. He had already set off for Las Vegas—he and his best man, Justin, were driving there from America's east coast—but en route he booked Kay and me in to the Flamingo Hotel and set about planning how to orchestrate a surprise for everyone.

Both families and their guests were staying in one of the Flamingo's 3600-plus rooms and, as we would arrive there very late in the evening, two days before the wedding, it was unlikely that we would be spotted as I was the only night-bird in the Allsop clan. The next evening there was to be a large gathering culminating in a meal with both sets of families and friends.

Assuming we could survive the next day without being rumbled, the plan for the Allsop side of the family and Joanne, the bride-to-be, was to meet in a bar at five where, surprise, surprise, they'd bump into us. Well, that's what Neff led us to believe.

That morning Kay and I had already planned to breakfast out of town, not for fear of being spotted in the Flamingo's gigantic breakfast room, but because it was something we wanted to do, something we always did when visiting cities such as Las Vegas.

Having already googled 'The 10 Best Breakfasts in Las Vegas' before leaving home, we knew exactly where to pick up the bus to the out-of-town Blueberry Hill Family Restaurant where we knew we could relax away from the madding crowd in the expectation that the food there was likely to be more real and less plastic. In that respect we were not disappointed.

It was on that first morning at Blueberry Hill that we ran briefly into Josie. She was sitting at the next table with all the assurance of a regular who knew the menu inside out and all the waitresses to boot. We guessed she was marching confidently towards 80, her jet black hair with its one strategically placed slash of white curling upwards just left of centre. If she had let it, the white would have been her natural colour but she had cleverly made it look the other way round, that she was just turning white. Before we even spoke, I knew I'd like her.

Our indecision about what to order caught her ear and she leaned over to offer her services and experience. She assured us we were about to eat in a gem of a place and that everything on the menu was better than the best. It was almost as if she had shares in the place for she was adamant that there was nothing to match it anywhere else in Vegas, possibly in the States.

Josie admitted that, for her, the Blueberry was almost an addiction and that she breakfasted there several mornings a week but rarely 'did' Sundays as it was sometimes difficult to get a table. Josie left before we did but not before we made a tentative arrangement to meet up again for breakfast the morning after the wedding, despite the fact that it was a Sunday.

———

Back in downtown Vegas we managed to avoid anyone we knew as we traipsed wearily round the various themed hotels that line Vegas' famous 'Strip'. Killing time was tiring so we indulged in a short afternoon siesta before our rendezvous at five with the rest of the Allsop contingent.

But Neff was up to his tricks for everyone else had been told to gather at five-thirty; the misinformation relating to five was for three people only: bride-to-be Joanne, Kay and me. Neff's cunning plan was that Joanne—whom we'd met before—should bump into us in the bar and get the shock of her life. And that's more or less what happened. First Joanne and then other family members, all of whom were convinced that we were still on the other side of the pond. One had even sent us a bringing-you-up-to-date text message which of course we had received from only a few yards away.

So began a long evening, at the end of which, five-thirty *in the morning*, the only two people still standing, best-man Justin and I, finally out of money and out of energy for any more craic, succumbed and headed back to our respective rooms.

Breakfast was a late-morning pint of Guinness en route to the Venetian Hotel.

By early afternoon everyone had gathered in the fake Piazza San Marco to witness the deed. The bridge itself had been closed temporarily and shoppers who weren't intrigued by what was going down, had to make short detours to cross the canal. It was all very surreal and I was already looking forward to the normality of breakfast the following morning at Blueberry Hill, with or without Josie.

As it happened it *was* with Josie as all three of us arrived at almost the same moment. Being a Sunday, tables were at a premium so it seemed sensible to sit together.

Even as Josie spoke, there was no hint of an accent other than American; no trace of the Sicilian accent she was born into. She and her family had left Sicily at the end of the war and headed for the States; she arrived as Giosepa and became Josie in America.

As a young adult she met and married a Pole, Malik, whose family had left Poland in the late-30s to come to England. In the Battle of Britain Malik's father had been a pilot in the RAF's 303 (Polish) Fighter Squadron; after the war the family moved on again and emigrated to America.

We breakfasted with Josie the following morning too, the morning of the day we flew home. The three of us shared many of our travel stories and she was surprised to discover we had been to Sicily several times; she was more surprised that we'd passed through her native Nicolosi, a small town nestling in the foothills, just south of mercurial Mount Etna. I was even able to share a bit of craic with her about an Austrian woman I encountered in the supermarket on the town's main street.

In those couple of days Josie seemed to have become almost as much family as those who were indeed family but preferred to breakfast downtown at the Flamingo. No amount of persuasion would ever get them on a bus.

Josie kept her best story to the end, until she knew us well enough to be confident that she'd get away with it; and to be certain we'd finished eating.

It was the mid-70s and, with travel restrictions to and from Poland having been relaxed, Josie and her late husband Marik grabbed the opportunity to visit family members still living there. They flew to West Germany where they hired a car and drove through what was then Czechoslovakia and into Poland.

It was their last day there and, with those final emotional farewells behind them, they were heading for the border; they both knew it was unlikely they would ever return.

It was lunchtime and they stopped to eat at a large first-floor restaurant by the main road. Off a short landing on the stairs, Josie noticed a bathroom door slightly ajar.

"Always a good idea to know where the bathroom is." She said with the merest hint that this observation might have some later relevance to her story.

"It being our last authentic Polish meal, we ordered *bigos*—pork, cabbage and sauerkraut. Mind you we'd eaten almost nothing but *bigos* with Marik's family; nevertheless there we were, tucking into yet another plate of *bigos*, with potatoes, of course, when it hit me.

"I can't be sure whether it was the food or the emotion of the day, or a combination, but I was suddenly overcome with a terrible feeling of nausea. I felt I was about to explode but at first I wasn't sure from which end."

At which point Josie threw in a few hand gestures just in case we hadn't got her meaning.

"I stood up, grabbed some napkins from the table and, hardly able to focus, headed for that bathroom I'd spotted on the way in.

"I slammed the door shut and plonked myself down on the toilet seat; by this time I knew which end was about to erupt. And erupt it did, Etna had nothing on me.

"I was sitting there, eyes watering, head in hands, groaning and moaning but happy that I had made it in time. Slowly I took my hands away from my face to take in my surroundings. For a few moments I sat there in stunned shock.

"This bathroom was not yet a bathroom, it was no more than a work in progress. It was a bathroom under construction and its floor was strewn with washbasins, toilet bowls, pipes, tubes and tools. Worse still, the toilet bowl I had utterly desecrated was not plumbed in, it was just sitting there in the middle of the room.

"I realised that the plumbers working here must have gone off for their lunch break and might be back at any moment. While I was wondering which would be worse—the shock of them seeing me sitting there with my knickers round my ankles or the pungent aroma now enveloping their place of work—I stood up quickly, tidied myself as best I could and, without daring to look in the bowl, beat a hasty retreat.

"Back in the restaurant, and without explanation, I told poor Marik, mid-mouthful, to abandon his lunch, put on his coat and pay up. We were leaving.

"In the car, I gave Marik a shortened version of what had happened, told him to put his foot down and not to stop until we'd crossed the border and were out of Poland."

Finally, Josie paused for breath, but not for long.

"You know, for a few weeks afterwards, I had nightmares about what happened, I couldn't stop thinking about those poor workers returning after their lunch break. Their noses would have been the first to suffer and then, well, God knows what they found in that toilet bowl and what they did with it. Maybe they chucked the whole thing, bowl and all, or got one of the skivvies from the kitchen to clean it up. Who knows?"

Momentarily she paused again to reflect and then, quite unexpectedly, she burst out laughing. She was still trying not to laugh as she recalled again their escape from Poland.

"Then there was that madcap drive to the border … with me tossing and turning in the passenger seat, still trying to adjust my clothing …" and in what appeared as an afterthought, she added what was clearly a rehearsed and oft-repeated conclusion to her story. "… all I wanted was not to be in Poland … there no way I wanted to get pulled over by those shitty Polish police."

Meeting Josie in Las Vegas was just one of those chance encounters that became special and memorable. Over those few days we had all probably exhausted our repertoire of tales, anecdotes and memories but why we chose to share with each other will remain a mystery.

Josie didn't do email. Nevertheless, were we to return to Las Vegas, we would know where to find her. By which time we would all have a lot more craic to share.

There's the one about Neff's divorce, for example …

EARLY DAYS IN SANTA SEVERINA, 2009.

EMIGRATING

It was following our return from our third stay in Calabria in 2008 that Kay and I decided to move there, to emigrate to the small, hilltop town of Santa Severina in the Province of Crotone.

The first step was to contact friends in Santa Severina in the hope that they might help us find temporary accommodation. When, five hours later, we had found a place to live, we decided to make the move sooner rather than later and gave ourselves eight weeks to sort out the paraphernalia of one life and prepare for another.

We met our deadline and, on a warm evening in mid-September, vacated the cottage in Upper Swainswick near Bath where we had lived for 14 years.

The short drive to the motorway in our new car, an ageing left-hand drive Clio, passed in silent contemplation as we reflected on the enormity of what we'd managed to achieve in just eight weeks. It was as if we'd completed the largest jigsaw in the world and, with our brief stop at the post-box to drop in one final bill, we had put the last piece in place.

Our heads were spinning with feelings of exhaustion, relief and exhilaration: exhausted after eight weeks of mental, emotional and physical mayhem; relieved that we'd accomplished what sometimes had seemed impossible in the time frame we'd set ourselves; exhilarated by the prospect of the journey and the new perspectives to come.

All such thoughts came to an abrupt end when, less than half an hour into our journey we got two snippets of news. The bad news was that today of all days someone had decided there would be a fire in the Channel Tunnel; the good news was our Tunnel tickets would be valid for the only other means of getting across to France, the ferry from Dover.

Our Folkstone hotel was no longer in the right place so, scarcely refreshed, we rose earlier than planned to a dank, drizzly morning, a typical English morning on the cusp of autumn. Just below our feet there was a tunnel; it all should have been so easy but here we were, driving in the opposite direction, following the road signs to Dover.

Hundreds of others were doing the same and we were the second last aboard the ferry when it cast off. A quarter of an hour later the whitish cliffs around Dover were no more than a greyish blur. France beckoned and with it my first chance to drive our little Clio on its correct side of the road.

France was dank and depressing and soon became Belgium.

Belgium was one long, frustrating traffic-jam and eventually became Holland.

Holland was brighter, less congested and short-lived and finally became Germany.

Germany was our destination. We were heading for Düsseldorf and the train that would take us and our Clio on a journey through the night to Verona in Italy.

———

The car safely strapped in and with passenger coaches and car wagons united, we boarded the train where we had a six-bed compartment to ourselves. This was to be our mobile home for the next 16 hours.

Bang on schedule at six, we stood by the window and watched as we crept out of the Düsseldorf station to head south into the German countryside.

I was on the look-out for one particular town south of Bonn, a little place close to the river Rhine called Bad Honnef where I lived and worked as a teenager for nearly three months. I was there to improve my German and found work in a small jam-making factory here called Dienel und Jakob Konservenfabrik (see earlier chapter, *Finding my Feet*, page 57). From internet maps of the area, I knew that the rail-side factory, just along from the station, didn't exist anymore but I was interested to see if there was anything of this little place that I might recognise after nearly 50 years.

There wasn't. We were travelling too fast and the light was fading. But it didn't stop me momentarily reflecting on a time that I recall as if it were yesterday.

I knew we had just flashed under the modern incarnation of the footbridge that spanned the railway and couldn't help but think back to the day I stood there with my Limerick friend Liam O'Brien. And how, standing there, we worked out how easy it would be to get a free lunch at the engineering works on the other side of the tracks.

Following the muted excitement at seeing a part of my indecorous youth flash by, we had a couple of hours in which to stretch out in our little overnight kingdom before dinner. This was the first opportunity we'd had to relax for weeks; we didn't have to do anything, see anyone, be anywhere, focus on a deadline, check emails or tend the bonfire that had consumed so much of the detritus of our previous lives.

This time, this space was our own and we relished the freedom just to sit back and do absolutely nothing and marvel at the fact we'd got this far in one piece, to wonder what these next days and weeks might bring.

By 8.30pm we had returned to the real world, albeit a long and narrow world, and walked along the corridor to the restaurant car where we had to wait almost half an hour to be seated. But it was worth it.

Eating on a moving train was not a novelty to either of us but this was an altogether different experience. This was no two- or three-hour jaunt, this was coursing through Europe in an olde-worlde, romantic setting that was the stuff of Agatha Christie whodunits. There was just the slightest hint of intrigue as we surveyed our fellow diners for that tell-tale mannerism that said there was more to him or to her or to them than met the eye.

Each table had its quota of suspects, their faces only partially given form by the brash, yellow glow from the stylish, semi-circular table-lamps. Which one, I wondered, would be the victim, who was the spy on the run, apart from me, who was the other internationally famous sleuth pretending to be interested in no-one, but missing nothing?

In reality I suppose we were the ones with the story to tell, we were the ones who had defied all the odds and got ourselves onto this train. We were not running away but, for me, this part of our journey created the inexplicable sensation of fleeing,. It was as if we were on the run, and tomorrow we would wake up safe and sound in Italy.

This feeling of being on the run was not new to me for, over a quarter of a century earlier, I came to face to face with myself on another moving train.

I had decided that the time was right for me to leave teaching and I had no inclination to work my notice which would have been five months at that time. I resigned; effective immediately. I knew I was leaving my school and its children in capable hands; in that sense the hand-over was orderly.

But the local press and then the nationals had other ideas for I was not your run-of-the-mill Head—I had a beard, an earring, was Irish and nobody knew where I was. The perfect trashy headline beckoned, something that was sure to grab the attention of all those low IQs. Something along the lines of 'Irish Headmaster with beard and earring vanishes'. The first I knew of it was when, sitting on a train . I found myself staring at the back of a newspaper being read by the only other occupant of the compartment. There I was, reduced to no more than a headline and a mug-shot, pride of place on a Sunday rag.

Inexplicably, my first instinct was to make a run for it for it did look remarkably like a wanted poster though, as far as I could tell, there was no reward being offered for information as to my whereabouts.

Then I wondered whether or not the guy reading the paper would recognise me and, if he did, what would he do with this information of such national importance? My final concession to my developing paranoia was to turn up my collar, put on a cap, pull it down over my eyes and to read a book, punctuated with frequent furtive glances towards my companion.

Finally, when another passenger came in carrying the same paper, I got up, left and sought out a newspaper-free zone.

While I was mulling over that earlier, more publicised, flight, we were joined at our table by a German couple who used this route to Italy regularly; it was so simple, they said in almost embarrassingly perfect English, it cut out most of the driving and, of course, the fuel, the tolls and the alpine tunnels.

Still in international, murder-mystery mode I made what I thought was a comical quip about already having solved the crime. Our German friends didn't understand my humour until I explained about *Murder on the Orient Express*. Even then I'm not sure they got it—their craic-ometer needed nurturing.

As it happened they were from the Bonn area and knew Bad Honnef well. They confirmed that Dienel und Jakob was indeed long gone and, they thought, the engineering works where I lunched every day, had also closed down or was about to do so. They enjoyed my story about the free lunches there and promised not to report me to the authorities.

We shared our story with them, the only part they found difficult to grasp was why we were going to Calabria. They had been to many parts of Italy but had clearly avoided the deep south; they had, I assumed, succumbed to the oft-broadcast notion that the south was the pits, the arse-hole of Italy, the unsophisticated and uninviting rump of an already fragile nation.

We were not unaware of this reputation, this stereotypical view of a part of southern Italy that has had such a chequered and uncompromising history, home to ruffians, kidnappers, bandits, brigands, and their modern incarnation the *'ndrangheta*, that even some Italians would think twice about setting foot in it.

The *'ndrangheta* is Calabria's equivalent of the Sicilian mafia or the *camorra* of Naples. Despite its lesser international status it has a reputation for aggressive criminality and violence equal to, if not worse than, the Sicilian mafia; its main organisational base is said to be in Reggio Calabria. Their main claim to international notoriety was when, in 1973, they kidnapped the 16-year old Paul Getty III and then sent one of his ears to his family in the post in an effort to focus his grandfather's attention to meeting their ransom demands. It worked.

I'm not sure we convinced our German friends that we wouldn't be on the same train as them in three weeks' time; they heading back home to Bonn, we scurrying post-haste back to Bath. Or perhaps they saw us as another couple of ruffians that would fit in just fine in Calabrian culture.

Back in our compartment, the train still rattling through the night, the body still undiscovered, the murderer still at large, we recalled the catalyst for our first visit to Italy less than a decade earlier—the moment we happened upon the Capetti's restaurant in Bath and, later, when Vic took that map of Italy off the wall and his jabbing finger told us where we should go to for our next vacation.

But our friendship with Ivano and Vic, born in England of Italian parents, could so easily have had a different outcome if they had been offended by my rush to smut when they told me the story of their grandfather and the family name. They could just as easily have thrown me out and perhaps none of this would ever have happened.

Capetti sounds Italian but is not a common Italian name; indeed, apart from close family, it is almost non-existent elsewhere in the country and Italian communities world-wide. According to the story, the brothers' grandfather was abandoned as an infant and brought up nameless in a nunnery.

This was not an uncommon scenario for, from mediæval times, women in Italy and other European countries often took advantage of the so-called 'wheel' to secure what they hoped would be a better life for their newborn infants that they felt unable to keep.

The wheel, its 'axle' fixed vertically in the centre of the convent wall, was a wooden turntable with several separate compartments or boxes where food and other contributions for the convent was left. All the nuns had to do was rotate the wheel from inside the wall. Any infant placed in the wheel would likewise find itself inside the convent where it would be brought up.

Whether or not grandfather Capetti found himself abandoned in this way is unknown, nevertheless, for whatever reasons, he ended up in a convent to be raised by its nuns. When the time came for him to make his way in the wider world, he needed a family name and, so the story goes, some of the nuns—Caterina, Angelina, Paola, Elena, Tazia, Teresa and Isabella—put their heads together and came up with an appropriate surname.

It was when Ivano and Vic told me this story that my smut-button kicked in and, almost without thinking, I suggested that it was fortunate that the nuns hadn't been called Francesca, Ursula, Camilla, Katerina, Emelia and Donetta. Our friendship could so easily have ended in tears there and then but, thank goodness, we were on the same wavelength and my smut triumphed. Who says Italians, even English-Italians, don't recognise a bit of the craic when they hear it?

And somehow our friendship had brought us to this point: lying in bed on a train on our way to a new home and a new life in southern Italy with most of our worldly goods in a van on some autobahn behind us and the rest rumbling along in the Clio at the back of the same train.

And, if we ever got any sleep, we knew that the next morning we would wake up in the country that was to be our new home. And, assuming our car was still clinging on behind us, we be in Calabria the day after.

And, no, we wouldn't be coming back in three weeks.

THE LAST OF THE LINE

Neff and I were on the road again but with a purpose. I wanted to retrace DH Lawrence's journey from Taormina in Sicily, where he and his German wife, Frieda, lived at the time, to Sardinia and back, a nine-day jaunt that he brought to life in *Sea and Sardinia*. Now that I lived in nearby Calabria and, with Kay visiting family in England, I saw my chance and took it.

To replicate this journey had become an ambition, some might say an obsession, from the moment I first read *Sea and Sardinia*. I planned to make my journey in the same time-frame as the Lawrences, use the same modes of transport and stay in the same places. I knew that the Lawrences travelled in January but decided my obsession didn't quite go that far.

When Lawrence lived in Taormina he rented a villa on the hill on the eastern extremity of the town called Villa Fontana Vecchia, as did the Truman Capote, author of *Breakfast at Tiffany's* in the 1950s. There was another aspiring American writer, Norman Harrison, who had also lived in the same house and Norman was its last tenant before Villa Fontana Vecchia was sold. Norman still lived in Taormina and, though we had never met, we had exchanged a number of emails. Norman didn't know I was planning to visit Taormina.

But first, Mount Etna, about which Lawrence frequently waxed lyrical, though I suspect he only ever saw it from a distance and never actually set foot on it.

I, on the other hand, had set foot on it several times and will for ever remember the first time for 'setting foot' soon became a painful process.

What should have been an amazing experience was marred by a poor choice of footwear. I was wearing sandals and, as everyone knows, it's not cool to wear socks with sandals so, ever the slave to fashion, I didn't.

Big mistake. Big, big mistake.

At the time Etna's summit was covered in a very fine, cinder-like ash and it got everywhere and in my case, the 'everywhere' I didn't want it to get was between my feet and my sandals. When it did— which was most of the time—it was like walking on broken glass. I loved and hated every minute of it: I loved being there in a place that had both raw beauty and such lethal potential in equal measure; I hated having to stop every few minutes to sort out my feet and as a result missed so much of the guide's patter and his occasional statistics. Not that I would necessarily have understood a lot but I wanted to be part of it and not constantly standing on one leg like some sort of incontinent dog.

By the time I returned to the car, the pain had almost worn off, never was a pair of socks more welcome. I sat there and looked back up at where I'd just been. I knew I had experienced something very special, somewhere totally unique, almost primeval. There and then, I determined that I would return some day with appropriate, and fashionable, footwear.

This, my fifth time on Etna, the first for Neff, was also memorable for it was the first time that Etna didn't play ball.

That day it was the weather. It had closed in and the slow, unnerving ride up in the little orange cubicles of the chair-lift to the lower base was as far as we could go; the jeeps that snaked their way up the precipitous tracks to the summit were all grounded.

The Dalmatian-like landscape, its patches of discoloured snow hanging on to cold, brittle-black lava trails was all that we saw; the essence of Etna, its cone, its gaping mouth, was shrouded in swirling, flighty mists and low, flimsy clouds that pranced up and down the mountainside, there one minute, moving on the next.

I put away my descriptive gene and studied instead the restless jeep-drivers, like us marooned in the small café-cum-souvenir shop. They wandered round aimlessly wishing these mists away, wistfully looking out for a break in the weather, eager to get back up on track with their payload of tourists and their bounteous tips. I almost felt sorry for them.

It was early evening when we arrived in Taormina, still as much a popular tourist attraction as it was in Lawrence's day. Then it was more of a tourist retreat, a place for the wealthy, the fashionable, the literati and even royalty to be seen and heard and to revel in the warm Mediterranean sun. Popular but scarcely populist; today all you need is a low-cost flight to Catania Airport and the price of a bus-ride.

We settled into B&B Fontana Vecchia which was indeed on Via Fontana Vecchia and about 100 metres closer to the town than Lawrence's home here, Villa Fontana Vecchia.

But that evening our priorities were basic: we had been travelling since eight in the morning and all we wanted was food, a glass or three of red wine and a good night's sleep. Taormina, Villa Fontana Vecchia, Norman Harrison and even DH Lawrence could wait until we were ready.

The next day our first port of call was the villa where the Lawrences used to live. Villa Fontana Vecchia was just up the road from our B&B of almost the same name.

I have always found that looking at houses where famous people lived to be an unrewarding pastime. Even being inside can be a bit of an anti-climax, given the propensity for curators to sanitise everything even to the extent of installing dioramas that, however they dress it up, still look like tailors' dummies.

Thus it was with mixed feelings—probably indifference and apathy—and that Neff and I stood and looked up at the small wall-plaque that recognised Lawrence as an erstwhile occupant; the house itself was no more than an unpretentious, on-the-road frontage that gave little away. I was tempted to ring the bell but thought better of it.

We back-tracked to seek out a better view of the walls behind which the Lawrences lived and loved and which they adored so much.

"I feel at last we are settled down and can breathe." Lawrence wrote to a friend. But did he know, I wonder, about the heavy breathing that Frieda apparently indulged in here?

In her book *DH Lawrence: The Story of a Marriage*, Brenda Maddox suggests that Frieda had more than a few local lovers and in 1990 in Pittsburg, Pennsylvania, one actually turned up and owned up.

In the early 1920s, Peppino D'Allura claimed he was a young and impressionable mule driver and wine merchant in Taormina when, one day as he was passing Fontana Vecchia, Frieda appeared naked in the doorway. The assumption is that no money changed hands for the wine.

As we walked into town, images of the seductive Frieda soon faded and we were seduced instead by spectacular views and the sparkle of the distant sea and, just beyond, the shimmering coastline of Calabria.

Close to the fountain on the wall that gave this road its name, I saw an elderly man standing by the kerb-side. He was the first person I'd seen here with a life of toil written into his face, the first person who did not seem to be serving the needs of the tourist industry that was now king here.

At first I thought he was trying to cross the road, then I realised he was watching the world go by from his kerb-side vantage point; he was taking pleasure from what Taormina had become, these people from every corner of the world and this place were his playground. There must have been other men and women in

Taormina just like him but probably they stayed indoors and watched television.

He wasn't going to win the Best-dressed-Man-of-the-Year Award but then he didn't care about such trivia, he was a proud man. When he left home that morning and took one last look in the mirror before donning his camouflage baseball cap, he felt and looked just right for this day.

His checked shirt was tucked in, his fawn jacket a tidy fit, as were the black trousers and matching suede shoes. His glasses were straight, his moustache trimmed; he probably just forgot to check on the burgeoning ear-hair. He carried a cane, had a penchant for recycling his own phlegm and checked the small change in his trouser pocket as regularly as he hitched them up. Proud Man was the first real person I had seen that morning.

I crossed over, said, *"Buon giorno,"* and shook his work-ravaged hand.

He touched his cap with hand and cane, smiled and said *"Buon giorno"* in return with toothless clarity.

I asked how life was, *"Tutt'a posto?"*

"Sì, tutt'a post'," he nodded.

I said what a lovely day it was, *"Che bella giornata, sì?"*

He agreed. I told him I must be on my way and he waved with his stick as I crossed the road to find Neff, lost behind a couple of parked delivery vans and still trying to work out which shop I'd gone into.

We spent the rest of the morning working out the best way to get from the town to the old track down to the railway station on the coast that the Lawrences had used. After a few false starts we found it and celebrated our resourcefulness with a late, wine-accompanied lunch before heading back to B&B Fontana Vecchia for a well-deserved *sonnellino*.

It was gone 9:30pm when we walked into the bar I knew to be Norman Harrison's home from home. I recognised him immediately as he sat nursing a glass of white wine, clearly neither his first, nor his last. He was just like his photo, silver-haired with beard to match, his face already ingrained with Mediterranean colour, his features still saying North American. I went up to him, proffered my hand and introduced myself.

After his initial shock and with the pleasantries out of the way, we sat together, ordered some wine and I explained to Norman, or Norm as he preferred, why I was interested in Lawrence and Villa Fontana Vecchia.

We talked about his erstwhile home and how Neff and I didn't get beyond the views from the road. I told him how a friend had helped me write a grovelling letter in the most formal and obsequious Italian to the current occupants. The lack of a response did not surprise him.

Norman had an melancholic streak. Like the Lawrences, he adored Villa Fontana Vecchia and rued the day that, when ownership changed and the new owner put it up for sale, that he did not make an offer sooner. His hesitation cost him the home he loved and it is clear that he still missed it very much. He did not like how the new owners had altered things and called himself 'the last pre-renovation tenant'.

Norm was keen to share his memories of living there and recalled again how that door-window on the lower verandah that wouldn't fasten for Lawrence hadn't changed over the years. I quickly found the page in *Sea and Sardinia* and together we read Lawrence's words as he prepared to leave:

"Fasten the door-windows of the lower verandah. One won't fasten at all. The summer heat warped it one way, the masses of autumn rain warped it another. Put a chair against it."

"That's exactly how it was for me," he confirmed as he jabbed his finger at the book, "I couldn't get the bugger to fasten either."

"You really know this book inside out, don't you?" he went on.

He was probably right, I had lived it for months.

"Tell Neff the Hemingway story." I said, changing the subject.

Norm was in good form as he related a story he had heard 'somewhere' about how Ernest Hemingway had also stayed at Villa Fontana Vecchia some time before the Lawrences moved in and how he was supposed to have slept the night in the Roman tomb in the garden there.

All thoughts of Hemingway napping in a Roman tomb were interrupted as we were all taken by surprise when a guitarist-cum-singer sitting on a little dais behind our table, suddenly burst into voice with a medley of Italian love songs.

A Stan Laurel look-alike accompanies the guitarist, clapping, tapping and dancing like a human percussionist and within minutes the bar became a focus for those with foot-tapping tendencies and soon there was scarcely an empty table. People were standing in the street listening and clapping.

Between songs I asked the guitarist if he could play the *tarantella*, a traditional, haunting, frenetic melody, seemingly without end, and usually played on the *fisarmonica* and the *tamburello* (accordion and tambourine). The *tarantella* can last two minutes, two hours or two days, as it generally did in the days when dancing to this hypnotic rhythm was said to alleviate the bite of a venomous spider.

The guitarist obliged and soon everyone within earshot was foot-tapping and clapping to the fast, rhythmic beat. The Stan Laurel type had clearly been bitten by something and his frenetic feet were just a blur. The music reached a crescendo and then was gone; those who heard the *tarantella* for the first time that evening would never forget it.

When the excitement had died down, Neff and I picked up an Irish accent or two from another table and when the word 'craic' wafted its way towards us, it was not long before we were five. Teresa and Ken were from Dublin and visited Taormina regularly; they also happened to be Lawrence *aficionados*.

It was already tomorrow. The music had finished, the musician and the musician's mate had gone and Norm had learned a new word.

People drifted off until there were only five stalwarts still nursing their glasses. Neff and I were all too aware that we should have been in bed hours ago but the craic outflanked the logic. Two northern Irish, two southern Irish and an American, some would say a heady mix … just as well it wasn't St Patrick's Day.

It had been an evening to always remember and now came the hardest part when we all had to go our separate ways with our separate memories. There was much kissing and hugging and finally Norm and I embraced as old friends, parting but not leaving.

Back in our bedroom, the evening's craic still buzzing round my head, and before sleep caught up with me, I felt almost duty-bound to refresh my memory on the simplistic nature of Lawrence's reasoning for going to Sardinia in the first place:

"Where then? Spain or Sardinia. Spain or Sardinia. Sardinia, which is like nowhere. Sardinia, which has no history, no race, no offering. Let it be Sardinia."

In 2012 I helped Norman Harrison to finally publish his book, *The Entity*, a project that had been his passion since the first day he moved into his beloved Villa Fontana Vecchia.

After my *Keeping up with DH Lawrence* was published, I had, from time to time, tried to find out more about the Ernest Hemingway story to see if he had indeed been in Taormina around the same time as the Lawrences and if he had even lived in Villa Fontana Vecchia before the Lawrences moved in.

Of course the story about him having spent a night in the Roman tomb in the garden, while certainly Hemingway-esque, did not necessarily mean he was living in the house at the time.

By 2012 I had unearthed some new information but only shared this with Norm after we had finished work on *The Entity*. We met in Sicily and I began to feed him what I'd learnt in dribs and drabs, teasing him till I got to the grand finale.

I began with the fact that I'd found evidence that Hemingway did stay in Taormina over Christmas 1918 seemingly in a villa 'owned' by one James Gamble but there was no specific mention of Fontana Vecchia.

"It must have been Fontana Vecchia," Norm interjected without a hint of doubt in his voice. "can only have have been Fontana Vecchia."

I continued, "According to a Sicilian writer—whose name I can't pronounce—it was at a villa in Taormina, owned by an elderly remnant of the British aristocracy, Alexander Nelson-Hood, where both Hemingway *and* Gamble stayed as guests that Christmas. It was not Gamble's property at all."

From the description of its isolated location, I too was sure it had to be Villa Fontana Vecchia for that fitted in with everything I knew about the location of the Lawrences' home. I carried on:

"It seems that Nelson-Hood was keen that his Taormina villa should become a sort of 'retreat' for artists and writers and that, apart from Hemingway, others benefited from this eccentric, philanthropic landlord, notably TS Eliot, Somerset Maugham and …" I paused momentarily, " … David Herbert Lawrence …"

"So," I said to a gobsmacked Norm, "I think we can safely assume that Hemingway, and several other *literati*, did indeed stay at Villa Fontana Vecchia. It seems you were the last of a long line."

I went on to suggest that we pop round to Villa Fontana Vecchia right now and ask the owners to have its 'Lawrence-lived-here' plaque updated to include a few more names.

Also, and aware of Norm's military background, I added that the 'Nelson' part of Alexander Nelson-Hood's name was indeed Admiral Horatio Nelson, the victor at Trafalgar, who originally bought the property in the 1780s.

In 2015, however, I dug a little deeper and came across some additional information about the *literati* listed above who hovered around Taormina after the Great War and specifically in the early 1920s. This called into question my earlier conclusions which I had shared with Norm.

The villa that they all stayed in, by which I mean those who, *unlike* the Lawrences, were short-term residents of Taormina, was *not* Villa Fontana Vecchia but rather Villa Falconara. The villa was not only the one owned by Alexander Nelson-Hood in Taormina but also clearly fitted better with its grander Nelson-esque provinence.

La Falconara is situated on the main road up to the town from the coast, on the eastern promontory that overlooks the sea. Both properties could have been described as 'isolated' back in the early 1920s and the Lawrences may well have visited La Falconara before, or while, living at Fontana Vecchia. Indeed it could have been because of a visit there that Lawrence and Frieda decided to settle in the town.

As well as artists and writers, British royalty, most notably King George V and Queen Mary in 1925, also stayed at Villa Falconara. A royal visit is harder to imagine at Fontana Vecchia.

I never got the opportunity to share this new information with Norman Harrison before his death in 2015.

... AND WORLD PEACE

It was a warm, pleasant spring morning when my dear friend Vincenzo called to ask a favour. In his capacity of past-suzerain of the local Rotary Club and present-suzerain of Le Puzelle, the *agriturismo* that had first endeared me to Calabria, Vincenzo was hosting four young American Rotarians for a few days and needed some help.

His charges would be taken on various excursions during their stay but they had one full day in Santa Severina under Vincenzo's wing, a wing which spoke no English, in the same way as his charges spoke little Italian. It being a Wednesday, Vincenzo saw the potential in conveying them to the town square to absorb the delights of market day with the town's only English speakers as their guides.

Santa Severina's Rotary Club was, and still is, a thriving organisation and, directly and indirectly, there had already been unsuccessful attempts at securing its only English-speaking members. I should add that Vincenzo himself had never made such an approach.

Nor were those who did, privy to my thoughts on such a scenario for they could not have known that I had already dipped a toe into similar waters before moving to Calabria. As a Headteacher in the west of England I had been invited to attend a meeting of a similar group, the Lions, as an observer and, they hoped and probably expected, a willing disciple.

I went and I observed but, after an excruciatingly boring evening listening to a monotonous guest speaker followed by the sights and sounds of deferential back-slapping, I declined the offer though promised to reconsider my position as and when such organisations could demonstrate that roadsweepers, bricklayers and plasterers could be found among the rank and file.

In Calabria I felt the same way but my respect for my friend Vincenzo went beyond his social calendar and, though we never discussed it, I was pretty sure he respected my position. Thus I saw no conflict in repaying his many kindnesses to me by helping him out that particular market day with his American Rotary friends.

We met Vincenzo and his charges in the car park and, as Vincenzo drove off on some other errand, we walked up to and into the square where the market was already in full swing.

In general, most Americans I had met previously had been outgoing, on the louder side of the spectrum, craic-seekers rather than brooders. These four, however, were unusually introspective and not at all what I was expecting and, naturally enough, I saw it as part of my mission to liven things up a little.

Initially I had little success. Truth be told, Santa Severina's market day is not always a colourful and unmissable occasion. Rarely are there more than ten stalls and, once you've done the rounds, all you can do is do it all again in case you missed something or retreat to one of the bars and people-watch from a distance.

I was on the cusp of suggesting just that when I espied a unique opportunity to spice things up as, momentarily, my mind flashed back to the 2000 film, *Miss Congeniality,* wherein all the hopefuls in a beauty contest, when asked about their main goal in life, sought only 'world peace'. All, that is, except FBI 'plant', Sandra Bullock, who only added "… and world peace" as an afterthought in response to the pained expression on her interviewer's face.

My once-in-a-lifetime opportunity to make a contribution to world peace had just entered the square, my friends and near-neighbours, the Majid family, Sajjad and Laila and three of their five children.

The year was 2009, several years after the start of the Iraq War and less than three years after the capture and death of Saddam Hussein.

As I understood it, the Majid family had been living under duress within Hussein's palace where Sajjid, an accomplished artist and sculptor, was employed as a teacher to his leader's offspring. Even in the relative safety of Italy, Sajjid forbade his children to use the interned (through which his whereabouts might be traced) and on several occasions I had to deny the entreaties of one of his older sons, desperate to gain access via my connection.

Thus, it occurred to me, how many Americans have ever met a real Iraqi family in exile? Not many, I thought, as I gently ushered my charges across the square and towards the Majid family.

It was only after the formal introductions that I dropped my bombshell relating to the respective nationalities of the two groups as, with the goal of world peace still at the forefront of my mind, I looked for a positive reaction.

The Majid family carried on as before, affable, chatty, curious, open and in no way taken aback my being face to face with a group of Americans. They had, no doubt, met many Americans in their home country, albeit ones wearing uniforms and carrying guns.

It was the reaction of this sample of American youth that was not as I had expected. From at least two there was an audible intake of breath when I casually disclosed the origins of the Majid family. This could have been for one of two reasons: they could have viewed all Iraqis as the horn-headed enemy or they might have been surprised at the lack of horns and long knives and been shocked by the normality of their so-called 'enemy'.

It was clear that they had been shaken up by this turn of events. The last thing they expected to happen in sleepy Santa Severina was to bump into an Iraqi family who exuded the air of being established residents of the town. The fact that, until relatively recently, the family had been residents of Baghdad, was also a surprise. Perhaps it was just as well that I omitted to mention where they actually lived and worked.

I would be doing the group an injustice if I did not mention that one in particular showed no fleeting moment of wariness and embraced the occasion with the warmth and openness that I was expecting while another seemed both unfazed and curious. Maybe these two were the only ones who had also seen *Miss Congeniality*?

My flirtation with being an ambassador for world peace had not quite gone as I anticipated. Although ostensibly there were smiles on all the faces surrounding me, I could tell that two were forced.

Before this brief encounter I had met many young Americans both on their home turf and elsewhere, mostly in Europe, which was why I was indeed perplexed for I could think of none who would not have been both excited and curious about running into a normal Iraqi family in an unthreatening setting.

In my mind's eye I tried to visualise how they might have retold the experience back home. Did those, I wondered, whose smiles didn't reach their eyes have had time to rethink the experience and perhaps rue their missed opportunity to join me and their friends in the promotion of world peace?

This is, after all, what chasing the craic is all about.

SEEING RED

Still keeping up with the Lawrences, Neff and I were aboard the overnight ferry from Sicily to Cagliari, the capital of Sardinia.

As Neff was unpacking, I noticed how he sniffed each item of clothing with a real sense of purpose. He glanced my way and, sensing the question in my expression, explained that he was just doing the sniff test; he said it in a way that suggested I should know what he was talking about.

He then anticipated my next question.

"Just categorising my shirts," he explained, holding them up in turn, "this one, a full day, this one half a day … I'll get another half day out of this, maybe even a day."

He carried on with his single-minded sniffing and arranged his shirts into three piles. I was just hoping I wasn't in the room when he got round to his underpants.

There being two bunk-style beds in the cabin, Neff was not entirely convinced that we are not going to be sharing it with two others. I tried to explain the system and how I definitely booked a cabin for just two rather than two berths in a four-berth cabin.

Scanning the cabin's four bunks, he remained unconvinced and conjured up a scenario whereby we would be joined by two hairy truck-drivers before the night was out; wishful thinking on his part, I suggested, just before a pair of unclassified underpants shot past my head. Luckily I held my breath.

The sniff test completed, Neff changed into a shirt with a zero rating before we set off on a reccy of our floating home, and its glitzy, orange-yellow-clad saloon, to sample their red nectar.

It was a strange place: a central bar surrounded by seating arranged in arcs and semi-circles, all occupied, mainly couples taking up have a dozen seats. Few had actually bought a drink.

Along from the bar, facing a mirrored wall, there was a row of bar stools where, clutching our glasses and our little quarter-litre bottles of red wine, we sat down a few stools from the lone, 30-something guy in the red baseball cap and red shirt.

Red nodded a brief hello as Neff and I filled our glasses, clinked them and wished ourselves *buon viaggio*. We were still taking in our surroundings when several things happened at once. We noticed that one of the semi-circles near the door was being vacated and were just about to go for it when a middle-aged couple, she little, he lofty, came in and sat there. Then we were momentarily distracted by a noise to our right followed by what seemed to be our neighbour, he with the passion for red, crumbling to the floor. Red appeared to be tying a shoelace that didn't need tying; he returned, slowly, guardedly, to the upright position while rubbing a reddish mark on his forehead and looking warily towards the door. Most strange.

Our puzzlement became his embarrassment. Seeing his empty glass I offered a top-up from our little bottles in the hope that it might simultaneously loosen his tongue and soothe his forehead. He accepted but wanted to move to one of the arcs with its back to the door where a young couple were already sitting, holding hands and staring into each other's eyes. As Neff went back to the bar to fetch another three bottles of red wine, the young, interrupted couple thought of something better to do and left.

The noise we heard was our new friend's head hitting the edge of the bar as he descended rapidly to the floor in a successful effort to avoid being seen by the same middle-aged couple who, from the point of view of Neff and me, had just 'stolen' our seats. Or, as Red called them, the Germans.

Red was French, a wine *aficionado* who worked in southern Germany; he had been taking a break in Sicily and had had just about enough of this particular German couple. They had inadvertently spent almost a week together at an *agriturismo* in south-west Sicily where Red had come to indulge his passion for red wine while the Germans, more the little Frau than the lofty Herr it seemed, were just making a nuisance of themselves.

Red paused long enough to allow his politically-correct gene to kick in and to assure us that he had nothing against Germans; his girlfriend, whom he was meeting up with in Cagliari, was German. It was, he assured us, just this particular couple, or rather this particular Frau.

He then explained how, on his first night at the *agriturismo*, he unwittingly sat at the table where the Germans had sat the night before and the little Frau just came and stood by the table staring at him, trying to intimidate him into moving until the waiter shooed her away and told her straight that you couldn't lay claim to a table.

Red spoke in the most beautifully simple and clear Italian, right down to the hand gestures, he was a pleasure to listen to and to watch; even Neff was managing to keep up with some of it. Nevertheless our constant requests for clarification led to the inevitable and he switched to English which was, of course, far superior to my Italian.

I was more than a little envious of Red's linguistic prowess for, like DH Lawrence's wife Frieda, I spoke 'sledgehammer Italian'. When I first read Lawrence's unflattering description of his wife's Italian accent, I knew exactly what he meant, I recognised it as our guttural inheritance, common to both Frieda's German heritage and mine from the north of Ireland. I lived for well over 40 years in the UK, most of my life, and still my accent never left me. Sledgehammer Italian was, I fear, with me to stay.

Working in the kitchen of the *agriturismo* was Anastasia, a local 30-something who had lived and worked for more than a decade in Germany and who was delighted to have three German-speakers to chat to. Her father, who was well into his 60s, had just started to make his own wine—remarkable enough in itself, even more remarkable the fact that he didn't drink.

Just before their last evening meal at the *agriturismo*, Anastasia presented both Red and the Germans with a litre of her father's first vintage, a brave act in itself given Red's known interest in the stuff.

Red left his gift in his room along with some other bottles of wine that he had 'unofficially' bought at another *agriturismo* in the foothills of Etna. 'Unofficially' because *agriturismi* normally make wine for residents and clients to consume on the premises, they are not for sale as such. Somehow Red had persuaded his erstwhile hosts to part with a few bottles.

Red was well into his first course before the Germans sat down at their own table, the forbidden zone, on the other side of the restaurant. He acknowledged their arrival and, in an impulsive act of reconciliation, went over and suggested that, as it was such a bright, warm, summery evening and their last together, that they should all partake of a glass of wine outside after dinner; he would open the bottle Anastasia had given him.

What started as three soon became half a dozen as Red then invited the owner, the chef and the waiter to his impromptu soirée; Anastasia heard what was happening and invited herself to watch the 'tasting' but, being heavily pregnant, she wouldn't be partaking.

When Red had finished his meal, he borrowed a few glasses from the waiter and went outside to set things up at one of the garden tables. He fetched the wine from his room, opened it, arranged a few chairs and the glasses and waited for the others. When the waiter popped his head round the door and said everybody would be out in a couple of minutes, Red poured himself a glass of wine.

Of course these were a couple of Italian minutes, which gave Red time to swirl his glass of wine, poke his nose into it, take a slurp, run it round his taste buds and spit it out into the nearest flower pot. Put simply, it tasted like rat poison. Just to be sure, he stuck his nose to the bottle. Definitely not red wine as he knew it.

Red paused to assure us that he was not being elitist about the wine, it was truly awful and had more in common with rat poison.

Almost without thinking, he was back in his room pouring the rat poison down the sink and washing out the bottle. He quickly—and reluctantly—opened one of the prize bottles he had bought earlier and poured the contents into the rat poison bottle, then raced back to the table just as the others started to exit the restaurant.

Those who were acquainted with Anastasia's father asked for small glasses, the Germans were less cautious and Anastasia herself of course declined. Red was the only one who knew that the wine that everyone was about to drink was absolutely exquisite.

Following the toast and everyone's first sip, the owner, the chef and the waiter asked for a top-up while the Germans gave each other a knowing look in the certain knowledge that they had their very own bottle of this wondrous nectar packed away for the folks back home. The very thought of which gave Red immense pleasure.

Anastasia couldn't wait to get home herself to tell her father that everyone thought his wine was *buonissimo*, *ottimo*, *squisito* and that clearly he had missed his vocation.

By the time he got to the end of the story Red was almost crying with muffled laughter and, between sobs, he managed to explain that he's been dying to tell someone since an attempt to tell his girlfriend on the phone ended in disaster when he couldn't stop laughing long enough to finish it. Neff and I were his sole confidants.

It still wasn't clear why Red was avoiding the Germans—if they were taking the wine home, what was the problem, I wondered? Red explained about the recurring picture in his head: he could see them back home hosting a dinner party for some special friends, the highlight of which would be the bottle of wine they believed to be superb. They'd open it, let it breathe and build up expectations.They'd fill the glasses and watch dumbfounded as their friends writhed in agony. Red just started to laugh every time he thought about it.

Pre-empting my next question Red explained that he had dressed deliberately in this rather loud manner as it was the very opposite of how the Germans had seen him the rest of the week. And then there's this he said, furtively raising his baseball cap a little to reveal his close-cropped red hair—he seemed blissfully unaware that it was his extraordinarily long nose that dominated all else.

Red went on to explain that the German couple knew they were all going to be on this same ferry to Cagliari but he had reasoned that he stood a good chance of avoiding them as he'd assumed they'd go straight to their cabin and stay there … that is until he caught sight of little Frau and lofty Herr and made his reflex dive to the floor. He knew it would be almost impossible to engage in meaningful conversation with them without starting to laugh.

I needed to visit the bathroom and took a circuitous route out of the bar so as to avoid any sort of contact with Red's German friends. But on my way back I paused at their table and exchanged a few pleasantries with them. When I rejoined Red and Neff, I casually mentioned that they seemed a nice enough couple, very courteous.

"You spoke to them?" asked Red with undisguised agitation.

"Just a few words. I checked that they were German and told them I had just shared a urinal with a young man who was looking for some German friends who matched their description. They asked me where you were and I said you were in the lounge on the next deck wearing a blue baseball cap and shirt.

"They obviously think you're a special friend," I say to Red as I turned round, "I think they've already gone."

A little later Neff retraced my steps to the bathroom and returned with a broad grin on his face.

"Very funny," he said as I feigned innocence, "you knew that nearly everyone in that other lounge was wearing blue, didn't you? It must be some sort of team or club outing."

My innocent smile broadened.

"What about another three bottles?" mooted Red who, it seemed, was beginning to get the hang of the craic.

TOILET TALK

We'd had a hard couple of days; this travelling with a purpose and keeping up with the Lawrences was taking its toll.

The Great Mandas Kidnapping never made the headlines but, for Neff and me, prisoners of the Mayor of Mandas for eight hours, it had been exhausting, Freed at last just after midnight, we'd had less than five hours sleep before catching the unofficial 5:50am train to Sòrgono and then four hours standing in the driver's cab.

It was two wearisome travellers who were deposited at Sòrgono; all we wanted to do was find our hotel and recuperate, even if it was only ten in the morning.

We crossed into the town's main street and there, right before our very eyes was the Bar Risveglio. But this was no ordinary bar, this was part of the same building that Lawrence stayed in when it was the RISTOR*AV* TE Risveglio, with its capital N back to front. At the time it was the only accommodation in town and the Lawrences had no option but to sleep and eat here.

Lawrence arrived in better shape than we did and was contemplating a stay of a day or two. All this enthusiasm dissipated within minutes of entering the Risveglio and seeing their room for the night. Back out in the street for a walk, he described Sòrgono as a 'dreary hole!'.

Despite the lure of a bed, we went in for a coffee and a bite to eat and were greeted by an ebullient, white-haired, paunchy man, the spitting image of ageing American actor of Italian extraction, Ernest

Borgnine, who turned being a 'baddie' into an art-form and even won an Oscar for it. His clone, alive and well in Sòrgono, welcomed us with an infectious smile and an inquisitive nature; he was clearly a man for whom the glass was always half-full rather than half-empty.

The reception the Lawrences received in this very same building was a tad different:

" … and at length appears mine host … I instantly hated him for the filthy appearance he made. He wore a battered hat and his face was long unwashed … And he led the way down the passage, just as dirty as the road outside, up the hollow, wooded stairs also just as clean as the passage …"

For David and Frieda it was to get worse, a lot worse.

Back in today's Risveglio, almost every square inch of wall space behind where we sat was covered with a haphazard array of photos, some quite old. Mostly they were related in some way to the railway but one, a mixture of photos and some text, caught my eye because Lawrence's name featured in the first line. I translated for Neff:

The English writer DH Lawrence stayed the night here on his trip to Sardinia in January 1921.

At this time this building was a boarding house called the Risveglio and was host to Lawrence and his wife Frieda for an afternoon and a night.

The writer wrote about his impressions of Sòrgono and the Barbagia-Mandrolisai in his book Sea and Sardinia published in May 1988 by Newton Compton/Della Torre.

I explained to Borgnine about our interest in Lawrence and, as if it was all in a day's work, he walked me over to the wall, took a photograph out of its sleeve and pointed to a man.

"This is the guy who owned the bar when Lawrence stayed here," he explained matter-of-factly.

There he was, a short, shambolic man sporting a grey, almost white, beard a dark suit and a flat cap, name of Trabadore Mereu and definitely *not* ebullient. Although he owned the Risveglia, which means 'awakening' or 'revival', Mereu didn't run the establishment; there was a man and a woman who did his dirty work for him.

As we got up to leave Borgnine was explaining how he was only one of many locals interested in Lawrence. I reminded him that Lawrence hated Sòrgono and directed much of his antagonism at his predecessors, the couple who ran the bar; he called them *ignoranti*, with the emphasis on the uneducated meaning of the word.

None of that mattered to Borgnine, what was important was that a man of the stature of Lawrence came to Sòrgono in the first place and then wrote about the experience. What he wrote was irrelevant.

I was pretty sure that Neff and I would probably have to run naked up and down the main street to have any chance of competing in the long-term memory stakes in the way that Lawrence clearly had.

I knew we had lots more to talk about but, having brought Borgnine up to speed with our recent misadventures, we made our excuses but assured him we'd be back—and in much better form—later in the afternoon.

It felt strange turning down an opportunity to indulge in a bit more of the craic but our craic-ometers needed recharging, big time.

A voice woke me some time in the afternoon, a plaintive little cry but, then again, perhaps I was just dreaming. Fighting off my need to sleep, I forced myself to focus on Neff's bed and convinced myself that he must be under that blurred and crumpled heap of bedding.

There it was again but this time with more clarity:

"How do I get out of here?"

With the bed coming into sharper focus, I could see that it was indeed Neff-less and guessed he must be in the bathroom. The voice was getting more agitated, half pleading, half talking to himself:

"How do I get out of here? How do you open this fucking door?"

Fortunately I had already been to the bathroom and was able to share some technical advice with him.

"Push it in the middle … it's a concertina door," I suggested.

His dishevelled form reappeared and, still swearing at the door and his inability to see how it worked, fell onto the bed and within seconds was fast asleep. We both were.

Later, I confessed to having had the same experience a bit earlier when I'd got up for a pee myself. Worse still, in the middle of the act, I noticed that the toilet roll seemed more than an arm's length away from the toilet-bowl. In my half-sleep state, I was still puzzling over this little conundrum when I realised it wasn't far away at all, it was just that I was using the bidet.

An easy mistake to make at that time of day.

By late-afternoon we were back in the Risveglio to renew our acquaintance with Borgnine.

No sooner were we in the door than Borgnine made a call and a few minutes later a local Lawrence 'expert' arrived which, after the politeness of the introductions, initiated a heated discussion about whether or not it was possible to follow the same bus route as Lawrence between Sòrgono and Nuoro and then on to Olbia.

First of all, the Expert told us that the bus no longer went via Tonara unlike the bus Lawrence took. I produced a copy of the timetable which said that it did go to Tonara and our genial friend came up with a typical Italian 'get-out-of-jail-free card':

"Oh, that bus, yes, that bus does go to Tonara. I meant the other bus," he said without the slightest hint of embarrassment or awareness that he might just have contradicted his previous assertion.

Still pursuing a win on the 'it's-not-possible-to-follow-the-same-route-as-Lawrence' theme, he now insisted that the bus from Nuoro to Olbia didn't go via Orosei any more. I hadn't got that particular timetable with me but knew that it did—and two days later proved it. In the meantime we agreed to differ, it was a scoreless draw but a game played in a spirit of fun.

Others were summoned to the bar and some just dropped in. One, short, grey-haired good-natured man in a light suit was introduced as il prete, the priest. For some reason that completely passed me by, his theological status was elevated and he became il papa, the pope, which initiated a lot of laughter. There was something going here that I didn't get, a private joke that just went over our non-Sardinian heads. I just hoped he wasn't expecting us to kiss his ring.

Voices were raised as, increasingly, everyone was a Lawrence expert and out-drinking and out-talking each other in a good-natured way was the order of the day.

Another, less excitable, Lawrence-savvy, senior citizen popped in and again there was no way of knowing whether he had been invited by Borgnine or had been just passing by and wondered what all the fuss was about. I showed him the part of the Italian edition of Mare e Sardegna where Lawrence described Sòrgono's open-air, public toilet which totally freaked out Frieda:

"We went up a little side-turning past a bunch of poor houses towards a steep little lane between banks. And before we knew where we were, we were in the thick of the public lavatory. In these villages, as I knew, there were no sanitary arrangements of any sort whatever. Every villager and villageress just betook himself at need to one of the side roads. It is the immemorial Italian custom."

He laughed as he read it, the more so when I asked if he knew where this place was. He explained that there used to be three such places in Sòrgono, one at each extremity of the town but he didn't know which one Lawrence was referring to and anyway it was long gone.

Tapping a glass with a spoon, Borgnine called for a modicum of order so that he could make an important announcement: hitherto we'd been drinking the locally bottled Mandrolisai wine but, from now on, he would be serving his own version, 15% proof and totally biological … and exquisite.

The bar was now full of raised glasses and friendly, raised voices. Three brave teenagers came in and pushed their way round and between bodies en route to a secluded corner at the back; they clearly were not sure what to make of this rowdy group of oldies and the two foreigners who had temporarily requisitioned their favourite bar.

I drew Neff aside for a moment to observe what we had unwittingly started by asking a few questions about a traveller who had passed this way almost a century earlier and had written about his experience. To these people, it mattered not whether that experience was good or bad; what was important was that he had come in the first place.

The craic was reaching a crescendo and slowly began to wind down towards the reality of early evening. People began to drift off, but not before shaking hands and wishing us well with a final *buon viaggio*.

Apart from the three bemused teenagers in the corner, there was only Borgnine, the Expert, Neff and I left.

The Expert and I talked some more about Lawrence and, for the first time, we talked about his personality, rather than what he wrote, though of course one was the precursor of the other. We agreed that he was irksome, often angry, frequently opinionated, generally impatient and sometimes rude and aloof in a way that some might attribute to his Englishness ... it was at times like this that I liked to remind people of my Irishness.

The Italian word *simpatico* came into the conversation and we agreed that this was something Lawrence was not. We may have agreed to differ about bus routes but pretty much saw eye to eye on the Lawrence psyche.

It was time for the Sòrgono branch of the Lawrence Appreciation Society to break up for the day amid the usual round of handshakes, kisses and exchange of email addresses.

We finished as we started, just Borgnine, Neff and I. Somehow the three teenagers had escaped unnoticed. Earlier I had indicated to Borgnine that we would like to pay for everything but found that we have been out-manoeuvred, there was no bill.

s

Back at the hotel we decided to eat in; we were still tired and were happy for our host to make us a bowl of hot pasta and open a bottle of red. But here too we could not escape Lawrence for, when he sat down for a chat, he turned out to be yet another person who had clearly taken an interest is Lawrence's one-day sojourn at Sòrgono.

He too was particularly interested in the Lawrence temperament and suggested that Lawrence did not cover over as simpatico because Frieda Lawrence was the opposite; she was *simpatica*.

Certainly Frieda came across as the more easy-going of the two, more inclined to accept people as she found them, less inclined to be judgmental and irascible; more likely to indulge in a bit of the craic like she is reputed to have done with the obliging, young wine merchant in Taormina.

Of course most of the information on Frieda was via the words of Lawrence himself for it was he who incorporated these emotions and reactions into his portrait of her; they were his account of her character. If she was *simpatica*, it's because he made her *simpatica*.

Since we arrived in Sardinia, Neff has been keeping up with the Lawrences by reading Sea and Sardinia on the move and following our day-to-day itinerary. Back in our room that evening he was a day ahead of himself and reading about the couple's early morning hygiene shenanigans in Sòrgono. While Lawrence 'gingerly' washed himself in the broken basin, Frieda was contenting herself with a 'dry wipe'.

This latter concept engaged Neff so much that he texted several female friends worldwide seeking advice on this novel morning hygiene routine. He drew a blank ... though he did come up with a few alternative suggestions.

After breakfast we headed back to the Risveglio for the last time. Borgnine must have seen us coming for, within minutes, another Lawrence aficionado arrived and apologised for not being able to make the high-powered, inaugural conference the day before.

In his late 50s, this latecomer was short, quietly spoken, dapper and sporting a flat cap; his eyes suggested he should have been wearing spectacles but couldn't find them that morning. Quietly and generously, Latecomer explained that he heard we were in town and wanted to know if there is anything else he might be able to help us with.

I asked about my one remaining obsession, the public toilet on the edge of town that freaked out Frieda.

"Oh that," he said, "that's was on the road out by the cemetery, you can't miss it, it's right by the bus-stop. You'll see the sign to the cemetery there."

Before we all parted company, he led us out onto the main road from where we could take in the whole extent of the building that was once the Risveglio. He then took us on a virtual tour of how the Ristorante Risveglio looked 90 years earlier: where the bar was, where they roasted the kid, where the Lawrences ate and where they slept … even where Frieda had her 'dry wipe'.

Half an hour before our bus was due in, we said our final goodbyes to Borgnine and the Latecomer and, walking past the bus-stop, followed the sign to the cemetery as directed.

We got to the designated area and put our noses to work, this way and that. Not a thing, not even a hint of dog pee. Then I catch a whiff of something, definitely human … no, false alarm, it was just something emanating from the zero-rated pocket of Neff's rucksack.

As the bus to Nuoro, via Tonara, was winding up the hill out of Sòrgono, I looked back at the town and realised that Neff and I wouldn't have had to run naked up and down the main street to leave our mark. We had already done so by introducing some of its citizens to a slice of Irish craic … including three bemused teenagers who probably had no idea what was going on.

SOMETHING FOR MY 'TO DO' LIST

There was a time when those of us from Belfast, or indeed any part of the island of Ireland, could only escape via a ferry and, apart from the Larne–Stranraer route, generally at that time, an overnight ferry.

Travelling between Belfast and England or between Holyhead and Dun Laoghaire, I used to wonder about the itinerant lifestyle of those who worked the ferries and the relationship between the ports that relied on their services for a living. Holyhead and Dun Laoghaire were very different, but developed an affinity that grew from the ferry services. Perhaps it was aboard such craft that I first became an irrepressible people-watcher with a masters in where people came from based on honed earwigging skills married to a propensity for deciphering accents, languages and other non-verbal idiosyncrasies.

It is this ability—or this affliction—that is at the core of this book for many of my travelling encounters have come about through listening in to people's conversations before inflicting myself upon them. Of course the 'picking-up-an-accent' game works both ways and from time to time, as happened with the Great Flood, I have been the focus of that first exploratory question:

"Is that a northern Irish accent, I'm picking up?"

Occasionally people get it wrong and brand me as Scottish; given the history of the north of Ireland it's a fair mistake to make. I have of course nothing against the Scots; my mother's family was Scottish.

It was years since I'd been on a ferry, a proper overnight ferry as opposed to those that make short cross-channel hops like Dover to Calais or Reggio Calabria to Messina.

The persistent rain enveloping Olbia's port terminal reminded me of Belfast in the 60s; inside it was more akin to a modern airport where those waiting to board the overnight ferry from Sardinia to the Italian mainland, could wine and dine in style.

It was in the restaurant that I picked up on an unusual intonation from the elderly gentleman seated at the next table. Even though he was speaking Italian with what looked like a family gathering, he was unable to disguise that hint of a Scottish accent. And, later, when I caught his eye and bid him 'good evening' his response in English had even more than a mere trace of his Scottish roots.

And yet he was clearly of Mediterranean descent, from how he dressed to his naturally tanned features with their topping of strong, wavy, white hair. His mannerisms, how he used his hands to the rhythm of his own voice, as if he were conducting himself, all said Italian. Yet there was something else, that out-of-place Scottish intonation that he couldn't disguise.

Briefly, just before we were given the go-ahead to board the ferry, we exchanged backgrounds and nationalities. He, it turned out, had been just as confused by my accent and had decided I had a linguistic Scottish connection which was why he was as eager as I was to set the record straight. But his story was infinitely more interesting than mine.

Bruno was born in Scotland, the second generation of a Glaswegian family of Neapolitan immigrants who had left Naples in the first decade of the 20th century to introduce the Scots to the wonders of Italian ice-cream. That was all I got before we shook hands and headed for the ferry with a hasty, "Maybe catch up on board."

It was as if we had sought each other out for, no sooner had Neff and I tossed our luggage into our cabin, and Neff had confirmed that it was a hairy-driver-free zone, than we bumped into Bruno as we all made our way to share some red wine and a few stories in one of the ferry's many bars.

I was already armed with a question that I had been going to ask earlier for, having once worked with a publisher on a book that covered some related issues, I knew something about this particular wave of immigration and how the Second World War adversely affected even second and third generation Scots, and others, of Italian and German descent.

I went straight to the point and asked Bruno about what it was like for his family in Scotland at the beginning of the Second World War.

"*Not good, not good,*" he repeated.

Momentarily I felt a sense of guilt for I could see that I'd broached a difficult subject. I watched his eyes glisten as he tried to control the intense melancholy that had suddenly overtaken him. He calmed himself, took a deep breath and launched into a painful, though not unique, story.

At the beginning of the war he happened to be visiting family near Naples when the then British government decided to intern all Italian and German residents, even second and third generation, on the Isle of Man.

"My family felt let down, betrayed, angry even. Many of us had been born and bred in Scotland; our families paid their taxes, we spoke English, Scottish English, and considered ourselves loyal subjects of the King. Never heard of anyone interested in the politics of that Mussolini fellow in Italy.

"But we were of Italian descent and there were no exceptions. We were given two choices. We could accept internment on the Isle of Man for as long as the war lasted or we could opt for deportation to Canada. My parents eventually opted for internment, but *all'inizio* planned to accompany my mother's brother and his family to Canada."

The more emotional he became, the more faltering his English became; occasionally he would throw in the odd Italian word, one of which, *purtroppo*, unfortunately, he used when he spoke of his uncle.

From what I already knew about this period I guessed where his story was going. I felt a sense of inevitability about what happened next.

"You're talking about the Andorra Star," I ventured in the vain hope that it might ease his burden.

He corrected me, "No, it's the Arandora Star."

In putting me straight, he was acknowledging that I was on the right track and somehow this seemed to make the denouement of the story easier for him.

"You know what happened then?" he asked.

"I think so."

"Do you know how many?"

I shook my head.

"Over 700," he said, "over 700," he repeated, "and most, nearly 500 of them, were Italians. And there were Germans too."

He paused and wiped away a tear as I placed my hand on his forearm in a show of solidarity. For a moment there was an almost unbearable silence as we both took solace in a sip of wine and our private thoughts.

Momentarily I saw those helpless faces aboard the Arandora Star when the torpedo from U-47 struck just off the north-west coast of Ireland. There was a cruel irony in the fact that people whose families sought a better life in Scotland perished that night en route to another place of refuge. Many bodies were later washed up on the Irish coast.

As if reading my thoughts, Bruno continued.

"The worst thing was that most of the Italians were in third-class at the back of the ship and didn't stand a chance. My parents had changed their minds at the last minute, and only decided to stay in Britain to be closer to Italy because I was there with my older brother.

Another moment of near silence, was punctuated by deep, calming intakes of air as we both tried to come to terms with our own personal picture of what happened that morning out in the cold depths of the Atlantic.

I wondered why he was telling me this and could think of only three reasons.

From my experience in Calabria I was aware that the elderly Italian male generally found me *simpatico*, perhaps because I was of a certain age.

I wondered too if these events were fresh in his mind because he'd been visiting family and it was something they'd been talking about.

I also wondered if the fact that I was not English made it easier to share these tragic events. I knew that the internment policy of the early 1940s was attributed to that most English of Englishmen, Winston Churchill, who, according to the Cabinet Minutes at the time, is reputed to have said 'collar the lot' in respect of German and Italian aliens. Furthermore, and in he same vein, many of those who survived the Arandora Star were returned to England and then deported again.

t was probably a mixture of all three.

Changing the subject I asked about his father and the Isle of Man.

"*Bene, bene*, better than the bottom of the Atlantic. You can't play football at the bottom of the Atlantic."

"Did they play a lot of football?" I asked in a scarcely disguised attempt to steer things away from the bottom of the Atlantic.

"*Si, Si*, they had their own little European league in the camps: Scottish Italians, Welsh Italians, even from your country, from Northern Ireland as well as Germans, Poles, the guards, the prisoners-of-war, the soldiers. Everyone had their own team."

I assumed the omission of English Italians was an oversight.

"But only the Scottish Italians had Gino," he added, but in a way that guaranteed that I would ask about Gino.

"Gino was a natural. Had it not been for the war my father reckoned he would have been an international … for Scotland, of course. A brilliant player and a natural goal-scorer, the pride of the Italian-Scottish squad."

Bruno said this with such assured conviction that it was almost as if he himself had seen Gino dribble that ball round a stunned defence.

"He was so good that the soldiers' team, who played against other local civilian and forces' teams outside the camp, used to dress him up as one of their own and take him with them and pretend he was a British soldier. Only problem was, he wasn't allowed to speak or drink; just play and score."

"The 'not drinking' and 'not talking' would have been difficult for a Scottish-Italian," I said, "particularly the talking bit."

The mood lightened and for the first time Bruno allowed himself a smile.

"*Infatti*," he said, as he nodded in agreement.

Bruno was in a happier place than he had been five or ten minutes earlier and immediately launched into another football story about life as an internee on the Isle of Man. Despite the heavy start, we were now sharing a bit of the craic.

"Like most other teams, the Italian team's strip was a bit of a hotchpotch. They wore anything they could find, as long as it was some shade of blue, of course until someone came up with the idea of writing to every team they could think of to ask if they would donate them a strip.

"Only one team responded and sent them an old strip which they played in till the end of the war."

Neff immediately said 'Manchester United' which was his answer to all footballing questions. It was my turn to guess and arrived at the right one quickly enough by assuming that it was likely to have been one that played in blue. My second guess, Manchester City, was indeed the club that sent them their strip; blue was the colour of the Italy, Scotland and Manchester City.

I came up with another war story featuring Manchester City but Bruno already knew about the German prisoner-of-war, Bert

Trautmann, who stayed on in England after the war and became Manchester City's goalkeeper.

I made one last attempt at telling him something he didn't know about Manchester City but he also knew how Trautmann played for most of a Cup Final with a broken neck—and e was on the winning team.

There was one last-ditch story I had about Manchester City but, uncharacteristically, decided that Bruno should have the last word.

Simultaneously we were aware of being on the move and heading out to sea. For Bruno this was like some prearranged signal for he stood up and said it was time to head back to his cabin.

One warmly-shared hug later, we parted company to go our separate ways; to return to our separate cabins and back into lives that cherished different memories.

As I wound my way down into the bowels of the ferry, I could not shake off the memory of Bruno's family and the tragic death of so many innocent people, Italians and non-Italians alike, aboard the Arandora Star.

I turned round and went back up to the bar where we'd sat and stepped out onto the deck. The rain had almost withered away and, as I looked back at the fading lights of Sardinia, I couldn't help bring to mind all those disparate and desperate families back in 1942, going through this same symbolic ritual as the place they called home, Britain, slipped out of sight.

Why was it, I wondered, that, for me, travelling by ferry had always been a more emotional experience? In the past, as I watched Ireland disappear into the dusk or saw it again for the first time across the dawning mist of a new day, I would well up and fight to control shedding a tear or two. Travelling by air did not have the same effect.

I realised I had not crossed the Irish Sea the traditional way for nearly three decades. Not listened in on that mix of Irish and Welsh accents as the crew went about their duties; not speculated on which of her colleagues that feisty, female steward was keen on; not wondered why the American couple were travelling by ferry and not by air; not theorised on the clandestine relationships between the middle-aged foursome; not imagined what the lone Arab woman was making of it all.

As I welled up, I determined that sometime soon I needed to stand on a deck such as this and see somewhere special come into focus and beckon.

Something else for my 'to do' list.

THE GREAT FLOODS

I have alluded a few times to my occasional sorties into the world of cycling: the planned ride to Dublin that never happened, the incident with the sunglasses and my uncle and the brief flirtation with two smaller wheels.

Also, I have demonstrated an occasional passion for reprising trips with Kay that I had originally made without her; like the time we travelled to Sicily and later to America's Bourbon belt, in both cases a fortnight after I had returned from an almost identical trip,

These two predilections came together on a short break from Calabria when we drove to the Marsala-Trápani area of south-east Sicily. True, we had been to Marsala before when, lured by the town's famous sherry-like wines of the same name, we were caught out by the scourge of the Italian propensity for shutting down everything to facilitate the afternoon *sonnellino*. Not for the first time, I had underestimated the time it would take to get there and we arrived just 15 minutes before the beginning of the end ... of shopping that is.

Nevertheless, undaunted, we lengthened our stride and found what we thought was somewhere we could buy Marsala; sadly it was the Marsala Museum where we could find out all about the renowned liquor but not actually leave with a bottle; this became apparent when I tried to extract one from its glass case. The museum's curator was adamant but helpful and pointed us in the direction of Morsi & Sorsi, about 200 metres down the road but scheduled to close in less than five minutes. We decided to make a dash for it while the kindly curator gave Morsi or Sorsi a call to say that there were two hardened drinkers on their way and that they were loaded with cash.

We made it. It felt good to have outflanked the *sonnellino*, The shop was now shut but we were on the inside. Before we got to sample anything, we were given the grand tour, including the history of Marsala and its strong British connections. When our guide was sure we understood the differences between the *Fine*, the *Superiore* and the *Vergine*, we were finally allowed to partake. An hour later, clutching our purchases, we fell out of Morsi & Sorsi and into the sunlight and what was left of the *siesta*.

While Marsala was a place we subsequently got to know well, the nearest we ever got to neighbouring Trápani was when we visited the Ettore e Infersa salt flats in between it and Marsala.

I, on the other hand, being committed to religiously follow in the footsteps of DH Lawrence's *Sea and Sardinia*, had spent half a day in Trápani with Neff and it was my experiences there that I was hoping to reprise with Kay; and in particular the boat trip that Neff and I had undertaken to and from the Egadi Islands.

To experience the same vista as Lawrence, I needed to view the approach to Trápani from the sea, and in particular to see lofty Erice in the background, about which Lawrence had waxed lyrical. Unfortunately such a vista was possible thanks to modern ferry schedules which no longer included the journey he made round the coast from Palermo. With Plan A, to persuade someone to ferry us from Palermo to Trápani, an ignominious failure, Neff and I travelled to Trápani by train where I hoped that Plan B might bear fruit.

Although I was aware that there were regular boat excursions to and from the three main Egadi Islands of Favignana, Lévanzo and Maréttimo, I had little interest in the islands as a destination in themselves. I had a passing interest in Lévanzo but only because Lawrence mentioned his own passing of it on his approach to Trápani.

With a trip out to the islands no more than a means to an end, I fomented confusion at the ticket kiosk when, instead of asking for a return ticket to one or more of the islands, I asked for a return to Trápani; Neff and I just wanted to return to Trápani, from Trápani, out and back.

The ticket-clerk, thinking I, an obvious foreigner, had made a linguistic error, asked me in monosyllabic English at which of the islands we wanted to disembark.

"None of them. We're not going to get off. We just want to come back here, to Trápani," was my simplistic response in non-monosyllabic Italian. I even drew it for him on the counter-top.

With his face still in questioning mode, I wondered whether the honest answer, 'I want to take a look at Erice from the sea … maybe take a few photographs', might only invite further confusion, disbelief even. I opted therefore for what I hoped would be a less esoteric, alternative explanation.

"We haven't time to get off."

From the shrug of his shoulders, the head-scratching and even a phone-call to the Confused-Ticket-Clerk Helpline, it became clear that he didn't know how to charge us for a ride on his boat without an island as a destination. Still scratching his head, he tried something on his computer but wasn't happy with the outcome. Further, more intense, head-scratching clearly generated inspiration and he had another go, but checked once more that he hadn't lost something in translation.

"Are you sure you don't want to get off?"

"Absolutely certain," I said, "only when we get back here, to Trápani."

With a well-fingered flourish he pressed the 'return' key and out popped two returns to Trápani, from Trápani.

"That'll be 31 Euro," he said with the pride of the problem solver.

Neff and I threw the money at him lest he change his mind; we would have willingly paid double for two hours without having to carry our rucksacks.

Having seen the islands up close and personal, and without having actually set foot on any of them, I was looking forward to remedying this with Kay but, alas, it was not to be. Weather-wise we had chosen our Sicilian break badly. The island ferries were not running. We made do instead with wandering round a wind-soaked and wet Trápani, killing time in anticipation of our last Siciilian meal before returning to Calabria. The restaurant was church-quiet until, that is, the other couple came in, nodded to us, and sat at an adjacent table.

It was our practice, whenever we spotted non-Italians, to indulge in a bit of ear-wigging and lip-reading in search of a nationality. On this occasion, to my surprise, I found myself tuning in to what I thought might be a northern Irish accent from the loftier male; his more discreet and quietly-spoken, diminutive companion was more difficult to pin down from a distance. I shared my suspicions with Kay who had already picked up that they were almost certainly English-speaking.

Unknown to us at the time, the couple in question were themselves participating in their version of the same game and he had passed on to her his suspicions that I might be from their very own neck of the woods.

When we had all made subtle eye-contact to the cusp of being unsubtle and, to save us all any further embarrassment, I decided to go for the jugular. But I was pipped at the post …

"Is that a northern Irish accent, I'm picking up?" Was the half question, half statement thrown across the room to me.

"It is indeed. And you sound like northerners yourselves?" was all I could salvage from being outflanked.

My apparent question was in reality a statement and didn't warrant a response other than a hasty rearrangement of tables and chairs. It seemed logical that, rather than continue grasping at each others' origins across tables, we should amalgamate our resources and share our stories in convivial harmony.

We already knew a lot about each other. The fact that I had said 'north of Ireland' instead of 'Northern Ireland' told him something about me. The fact that he hadn't queried it, told me something about him. When two people from the north of Ireland, or even Northern Ireland, meet, there is invariably a political and social subtext that only they understand.

On reflection, 'convivial harmony' is not something that immediately springs to mind when I think of Barry Flood. His wife Catherine, yes, but not Barry. 'Funny to the point of pain' best describes Barry; perhaps it was all those years as a Tax Inspector in Ballymena that allowed his original sense of humour to blossom to the point of fermentation.

Barry and Catherine were, we discovered, extreme cyclists; they would not use the word 'extreme', but I would. Both well past the age of retirement, they were on a cycling tour of Sicily with the simple aim of circumnavigating the coastline on two wheels; that's about 600 miles.

As I listened to stories of their cycling exploits, in literally every corner of the known universe, all my past two-wheeled endeavours and aspirations paled into insignificance and I thought it best to keep them to myself.

———

Being Belfast-born and bred, I did not know a lot about their home town of Ballymena. For me it was just one of the places we used to crawl through en route to and from our annual holiday at Ballycastle on the north coast of County Antrim. But there was one Ballymena event, or rather non-event, about which I was able to share my strongly-held views with Barry and Catherine.

I recalled how the episode in question had often helped me illustrate, to those not familiar with the northern Irish mentality, the endemic ridiculous and sectarian outlook of many of Northern Ireland's citizens.

Actor Liam Neeson was born in Ballymena and, in 2000, it was proposed that he should be awarded the Freedom of the Borough of his home town in recognition of his achievements. A not unreasonable proposition many, if not most, might assume.

Step forward the 'enlightened' voices of Ian Paisley's Democratic Unionist Party councillors, the type of person already pissed off by what they saw as Liam Neeson's sympathetic portrayal of republican leader Michael Collins in the film of the same name, who objected to the proposal on the grounds of alleged unflattering comments he had made about his experiences growing up in the town.

He was quoted in the, now defunct, American magazine *George* as saying that he felt 'second class' as a Catholic in the mainly Protestant town and felt he had to stay indoors during the 'loyalist' 12 July commemoration of the Battle of the Boyne in 1690.

Such observations were just too much for some, too close to the truth, too near the knuckle in daring to highlight the arrogance and parochialism used to excuse the 'celebration' of what was no more than rabid sectarianism given dubious justification by one flimsy moment in history.

Having been brought up on the Protestant side of the divide, I knew all the historical, hysterical and ethnic rationale but felt exactly the same as Liam Neeson; as did fellow Protestants with a brain, a conscience or burgeoning historical and political awareness. I too felt I had to stay indoors on 12 July though, even indoors, I could still hear the triumphalist musical rants of those I was supposed to see as my co-religionists. Above all, I could not understand why they felt no embarrassment, no shame, no sense of foolishness.

I realise I may have just blown any chance there might have been of being enticed back to the city of my birth with promise of the Freedom of Belfast. It's a cross I'll have to bear.

Neeson, not wanting to be divisive himself, felt he would have to decline the honour as it did not have the full support of the Council, to whom he later wrote the following:

"I will always remain very proud of my upbringing in, and association with, the town and my country of birth, which I will continue to promote at every opportunity.

"Indeed I regard the enduring support over the years from all sections of the community in Ballymena as being more than sufficient recognition for any success which I may have achieved as an actor."

Through talking about the absurdity of the Liam Neeson episode we established that, despite being from different backgrounds, Barry, Catherine and I, spoke the same language; though Barry did so with more natural wit than I could ever muster.

Our post-meal chit-chat did not endear us to the restaurant staff who were clearly getting edgy about the four foreigners still hogging the only occupied table in the restaurant. We were clearly thwarting their inclination to shut up shop for the evening. When, finally, we did get the message, we adjourned to a nearby bar to continue bonding.

The bar we chose was, like most others in the area, full of young people; but at least there was a free table for four, albeit cheek by jowl with others. We four oldies got some strange looks at first but we were all used to that … ageism generally only worked in one direction.

It appeared that our table was home to the only serious drinkers in the place, something we could not help but notice. I explained this phenomenon by telling Barry and Catherine about the summer evening when we were part of a group of about a dozen people, all way younger than us, at a bar in the square of a small Calabrian town. Apart from Kay and I, there were two other foreigners in the group, both women, one American, one French. When the waiter took the order there were only four who ordered something alcoholic … no prizes for guessing which four. It's a cultural thing, I explained, as we ordered another round.

I had already noticed that some of those sitting at neighbouring tables were beginning to give us more than passing glances and surmised they were trying to do what we do in reverse and pinpoint which branch of 'English-speaking' we belonged to; I guessed that Irish, was probably not on their list.

It was when some of the glances started to become more akin to consternation that the waiter came over and asked us to take things down a decibel or two, other customers were complaining about the racket the four elderly 'English' were making. I didn't know whether to be proud or contrite. Although neither Barry nor Catherine understood the detail of what the waiter was saying, they got the gist of it and all four of us—though there were clearly only two real offenders—did our best to show a bit of decorum more in keeping with our age.

It was, of course, our age that eventually caught up with us and dictated that it was time to call it a day, to exchange contact details and bear hugs, and head to our respective hotel rooms.

The next morning, nursing slight hangovers, Kay and I set off on our return journey to Calabria. As we drove out of town and passed Marsala's Archæological Museum, I noticed two small-wheeled bicycles strapped to a railing by the entrance and couldn't resist stopping if only to see what Barry and Catherine looked like in daylight and in their working clothes. We were certain the bicycles belonged to them, the 'Ireland' stickers were proof enough and, besides, who else would be mad enough to cycle round Sicily at this time in the morning?

Despite confirming with museum staff that such a couple were indeed somewhere inside, we never did find them. The only logical explanation seemed to be that they'd seen us coming and hidden in the toilets.

A little over a year later, Kay and I were returning to Santa Severina from separate trips; I had been visiting some of the remoter parts of Calabria, Kay had been in the UK. I collected her at our local airport and we were soon on the lower slopes of the approach road that disguised the severity of the forthcoming climb to hilltop Santa Severina.

Up ahead we spied—as we expected we might—two gyrating posteriors astride two small-wheeled bicycles festooned with panniers, straining their way onwards and upwards, determined to pedal through the pain barrier and reach the top of the hill.

We drove past and stopped about 25 metres in front of Barry and Catherine, on a short jaunt from Sicily to Rome, via Santa Severina; we offered their panniers and rucksacks a lift to the top. Even though we also offered to return for them and their folding cycles, they stoically insisted on making it up to Santa Severina's famous castle the hard way.

In the few days they stayed with us, Barry and Catherine became local celebrities; the fact that they'd cycled from Palermo in Sicily and were heading for Rome soon paled into insignificance when their Irishness gathered momentum and, with it, the suggestion that they might have actually cycled from Ireland to import a bit of the craic.

Catherine it was who brought the Liam Neeson saga up to date. In January that year he was finally given the Freedom of his home town. On her phone she showed us a photograph taken at the reception afterwards when, among other things, he was presented with an original painting by a respected local artist. Her name was Catherine Flood.

Catherine was glad of the few days' pause at Santa Severina; it was an opportunity to get inspiration for some future paintings. The Great Flood, on the other hand, was soon itching to be back in the saddle and, all too soon, with their panniers packed, their rucksacks adjusted and their cycles unfolded, they set off on the next stage of their journey to Rome in the certain knowledge that, the first part at least, was downhill.

Two years later, as guests of Barry and Catherine in their native

Ballymena, the Great Flood introduced me to parts of the north of Ireland that had hitherto escaped me … and not once did I have to get on a bicycle.

That said, I think I could have managed it for it couldn't have been any more difficult than having to choose one of Catherine's paintings to take home with me.

AS GOOD AS IT GETS

In the autumn of 2012 I was in America for almost a month visiting the descendants of Calabrian families who had emigrated to the United States, some as far back as the early 20th century. This venture took me to various cities and states, including Albuquerque in New Mexico. On my return from Albuquerque to my Airbnb 'base', a brownstone house in Wayne Street, Jersey City, I changed planes at Dallas-Fort Worth.

I fastened my seat-belt ready for take-off on the second leg of my journey back to Newark. I opened my bag to take out my iPad and went white … it wasn't there. The iPad was not only my link with the outside world, but also contained all my contacts for the rest of my time in the States. Everything relating to my trip was on that iPad.

People were still filing on to the plane as I was trying not to panic but to focus on where I might conceivably have lost it and what I should do next. There were two possibilities: I could have left it on the in-coming flight from Albuquerque or I could have taken it out of my bag while I was in an electronics shop in the terminal where I was considering buying a stylus for it. I decided that if it was on another aircraft there was little I could do about it at that time; if it was in a shop little more than 100 yards away, then the least I could do was to return there to check before the flight left.

Passengers were still boarding and blocking the aisle as they sought their seats; among them there was a flight attendant going with the flow. I stood up, looked him in the eye, and matter-of-factly brought him up to speed.

"I need to go back to a shop in the terminal where I've left my iPad".

I expected an argument but instead he shrugged his shoulders, indicated that there were still people coming down the aisle and that, not only would I have to hurry but that I'd have to 'swim against the tide' for much of the way, by which he meant push past everyone coming in the opposite direction, looking for their seat and somewhere for their hand-luggage.

Aware that he was probably breaking all the rules, I went for it and pushed and shoved my way back up the aisle.

"Sorry." "Excuse me." "Sorry, excuse me." "Excuse me, sorry."

I reached the door just as the last passenger stepped aboard and quickly told the attendant hovering by the cockpit that I'd be back in a minute, my iPad was in the terminal. I didn't give him a chance to answer. I just ran.

I shot back up the tube, round and up, up and round, till I arrived back at the gate inside the terminal; I ducked under the blue-tape barrier beside the desk and ran round the curve of the terminal, all the time looking for the store I'd been in, all the time hoping I was going in the right direction.

I spotted it, Airport Wireless. I ran in and breathlessly threw a question at the assistant serving another customer. I didn't have time for the niceties.

"I was in here half an hour ago and left my iPad behind." It was a statement rather than a question.

Without taking his eye off his customer, he slowly and deliberately reached out with his right hand to an adjacent shelf, lifted an iPad off it and handed it to me. He never said a word nor doubted that the iPad was mine.

I snatched the iPad, shot out of the shop, tore back round the terminal looking for my gate, ducked under the tape once again as I waved my iPad at two surprised employees, then down the tube I ran and launched myself back onto the plane and almost into the arms of the same attendant I'd dashed past no more than 90 seconds earlier.

"Got it!" I said as, once more, I brandished my iPad like a hard-won trophy. Nonchalantly, sporting an it's-all-in-a-day's-work smile, I returned to my seat as if nothing had happened.

Apart from which the flight was uneventful.

Uneventful it may have been but, when I'd finished lovingly caressing the iPad and promising it that I'd never let it out of my sight again, and I was once again online somewhere over Texas, I made a momentous decision.

I had been studying a map of Newark and located where I was staying overnight in relation to the airport and realised that, without my any trusty navigator, it was not going to be easy to find. It was all my own fault, I had inadvertently forgotten to book accommodation with Sherrie in Wayne Street for this one night and had had to find a last-minute alternative. Fortunately she'd let me leave my bags there until I returned.

And now, against all my instincts I was going to have to bite the bullet and ask that the rental I was picking up be fitted with GPS.

For years I had successfully traversed America and Europe with my own built-in GPS, my brain—I simply called it the being-able-to-read-maps part of my brain—but, five miles up and approaching Tennessee, I knew that I would need some additional assistance on this trip.

Still not sure if I should, or could, give in to such thoughts, I back-tracked for a few moments and tested myself to see if I could remember the route to 8th Street from the airport. I failed miserably and finally conceded that there was nothing else for it but a car with GPS. What's more I'd have to learn how to use it pretty damn quick, a veritable baptism by fire.

At Newark I took the shuttle bus to the off-airport rental base. The young woman behind the counter was clearly new to the job but, after a few false starts, we seemed to be doing just fine; she had my print-out confirmation, my bank card and my driving licence, my Italian driving licence.

She was busy punching in numbers when the door behind her

burst open and a fresh-faced, well-dressed, upwardly-mobile, young man emerged; he strode purposefully in my direction.

"Are you Italian?" he asked.

I didn't respond immediately.

"I saw your Italian license on the monitor in the back." he continued.

"I live in Italy," I said, "but …"

"So you're Italian then?"

He was on a roll and didn't give me a chance to respond

"I'm Italian too, my family's from Spezzano … I was born there … you've probably never heard of it, it's only a small place, it's in the south, it's …"

" … in Calabria?" I ventured.

"Yes," he said, "yes, it's in Calabria. How do you know Calabria?"

"I live in Calabria," I said, "in Santa Severina in the province of Crotone. Spezzano's in Cosenza, at the other end of the main road from Crotone, isn't it?"

My new best friend, Carlo, or Charlie as he preferred, went on to give me a potted history of his family and how they 'had to' leave Spezzano and come to America. He didn't explain the 'had to' part but I was fairly certain that somewhere along the line 'had to' generally spelled 'trouble', the sort of trouble some Calabrians don't like to talk about.

I told him why I was in the States and that I would love to meet his 'had to' parents and find out some of the family's history in Spezzano and how they came to settle in New Jersey. He seemed interested though I suspected his 'had to' parents might not be. If I was right about the 'had to' element of his family's emigration motive, then they would almost certainly assume I was an undercover agent of some anti-mafia police agency; after all, I undoubtedly looked the part.

While this was going on in one ear, in the other the woman

processing my rental was, as always happens, trying to persuade me to upgrade to a larger car. After years of renting cars in the States I knew that if you book the 'economy' model, rental companies invariably try to persuade you to upgrade, mainly because they rarely, if ever, actually have the smaller 'economy' models. If you stick to your guns and insist that your mind is set on an 'economy' car, they have no option but to give you a car from the next range up for the same price. An old trick but it works every time.

As Charlie was writing out his email address and telephone number for me, I asked if I could have GPS as well and was told what the extra charge would be for my eight-day rental.

Charlie abruptly took command of the transaction and told his colleague that I was to have the Chrysler, the one with the built-in GPS.

"But," she protested, "he only wants an economy car."

But Charlie would have none of it … I was to have the Chrysler for the same price. After all, we were both from Calabria; we were almost family.

We shook hands, I said I would email him later and was looking forward to perhaps meeting his 'had to' parents. I thanked him for what I guessed was some sort of modest upgrade, which I would have probably had anyway. He wished me well, said he would call his 'had to' parents and disappeared into the back office to monitor some other transaction.

The paperwork finished, I was handed my keys and the young woman took me outside to the car.

It was black, it looked like a car but in reality was the size of a small house. It was clearly the largest and most expensive car in the place which was why the young woman, now effortlessly demonstrating the car's features, balked at such an upgrade *and* for the same price.

Initially the only feature that I was interested in was how the GPS worked. I gave her the address where I was going, she showed me how to enter it into the system and I was ready to go. She had wanted to programme my iPhone to sync with the GPS (or something along those lines) but at the time that was a technological step too far. If I'd been thinking more clearly I might have asked how to fill it up, an omission I later regretted.

Alone at last, and finally in the driver's seat, I was ready to go. Two minutes later I was back in the office in search of someone to show me, a shorty, how to move the seat forward. I was also shown how to lift it, tilt it and heat it.

I tried again. I switched on and put the car's joy-stick into what I thought was driving mode. It wouldn't move. I tried again. Nothing. I returned to the office in search of someone to show me how to make it go.

You'd think that I'd never driven in the States before but I had, many times. I was very tired and I just didn't remember that D was for drive and N was for neutral. I was trying to drive with the joy-stick in the N position. I have no idea what I thought it stood for.

Third time lucky. Finally, and slowly, I moved out of the parking lot though every time I braked the car shook and stopped abruptly. This one I worked out for myself: being used to driving with my 'stick' change, I was still using both feet, my 'heavy' clutch foot for the brake and my right foot for the accelerator instead of my right foot for everything.

I wondered if Charlie, whom I could see was surreptitiously watching my antics, was already regretting his extravagance?

As well as the initial erratic braking, I was trying to get used to the GPS and that other voice in the car, an American woman who kept telling me what to do next or what to do in 300 yards, or that the next turn would be to the left but not for ages yet.

When she said 'turn right in 50 yards and then left', I discovered she was actually telling me that the next turn *after* the right hand one would be to the left and not, as seemed logical to me, that I should turn left immediately after turning right. I lost count of the number of times I did that before another penny dropped and the invisible woman stopped saying 'recalculating, recalculating'.

Eventually I found myself outside the correct house in the correct street in Newark. The short street seemed pleasant enough as did the house when, finally, after a call to my host, I found out where he'd hidden the key and actually got in. He also told me that I would have the place to myself and could choose whichever bedroom I liked.

I was weary and all I wanted to do was shower the tiredness away and eat. I also thought it best to email Charlie, to say that the car was still in one piece and that I was still keen to meet his 'had to' folks. As I suspected, I never heard another word.

Re-energised, I stepped out again into the world that was Newark expecting to find a good restaurant and an even better bottle of red wine. All too soon my enthusiasm abated when I discovered that this 'pleasant' street was a little oasis of normality in what was otherwise an area that did indeed resemble the dark side of the moon. Those wise words of Sherrie, my Wayne Street host, about some parts of Newark were ringing in my ears.

Still, I found two places to eat. One was a small and not very inviting pizzeria tucked away near some shops; all had that rundown look that suggested pending redevelopment. The other one was a desolate-looking Burger King on the other side of the main road. Neither jumped out as the answer to my hunger but the Burger King seemed the lesser of two evils.

Perhaps I could get a cab to take me somewhere that might be a bit more stimulating but there wasn't much traffic about and certainly I never saw a single cab. Perhaps they don't come this way except by invitation, I thought. I gave in to my hunger pangs and crossed the road heading for the Burger King but couldn't quite bring myself to go in; I hovered a while outside still keeping an eye out for a cab that had lost its way.

I heard a car pull up in the car park at the back of Burger King and, ever hopeful that it might be a cab, I wandered over to take a look. Around the corner came a huge, seven-foot tall Hightower-look-alike cop. Hightower walked with a rolling, don't-mess-with-me swagger, just as if he'd stepped off a movie set. For a moment I wondered whether or not he was a real policeman. Don't-mess-with-me swagger or not, he looked friendly enough and didn't immediately go for his gun when I approached him.

"Excuse me, officer," I said in true I've-watched-thousands-of-American-movies style, "but where can I get a cab around here."

"No problem, sir," he'd obviously watched the same movies,"I'll call you one," was the reply I was not expecting.

I thanked him profusely as he took out his cellphone and continued on his way into the Burger King. A few moments later he reemerged and said that my cab was on its way and that I was to wait round the corner in the parking lot. I followed him there and discovered that he was indeed a real policeman ... unless, that is, he'd stolen the large black and white patrol car from the movie set along with a uniformed buddy.

At last, I thought, this day is taking a turn for the better ... I must learn never to think such thoughts.

When my cab arrived, I asked the driver to take me somewhere to eat, not too far away, that was neither a pizzeria nor a Burger King. He pondered momentarily and said he could think of two: a Japanese or Chinese joint. The clue should have been in the word 'joint' but at the time my expectant stomach and tired brain didn't pick up on it. I opted for the Chinese.

En route, I noticed that perhaps the area around where I was staying wasn't so bad after all. We seemed to be heading into more gloom and doom, the sort of place they make movies about where people get lost in a terrifying no-mans-land and have to rely on their baser instincts to survive. I'd watched all those movies and was ahead of the game.

Survival-in-Newark Tip Number One, I thought, get the cabdriver's phone number so that you can call him when you need to get back to base.

He dropped me outside the Chinese 'restaurant' and I promised to call him ten minutes before I was ready to leave. Actually, I would have fared better if I'd called him immediately and gone back to the Burger King.

The word 'restaurant' didn't apply to this 'joint'. It was more of a Chinese takeaway with a few tables and chairs and no alcohol. I wondered … how come, bearing in mind all the programmes they make about Health Inspectors visiting and closing down restaurants, cafés and takeaways worldwide, how come they'd missed this place? And that was before I'd even tasted the food.

I ordered sweet and sour chicken but instead got a huge plate of boiled-for-ever rice and a bowl of chicken-like meat drowning in a vile-looking and—I soon discovered—vile-tasting, sticky, fluorescent-orange sea.

I ate enough of the chicken to satisfy my hunger and left most of the rice and the orange liquid for another unsuspecting customer, though I couldn't imagine that anyone else would actually eat here by choice. There was in fact another customer; well, a customer of sorts. He sat alone at his table and played with his phone, he never spoke to anyone or ordered anything. Perhaps he had already eaten and was digesting, perhaps he was a friend of the family … perhaps, my increasingly vivid imagination mooted, he was 'casing' the only other customer.

When that thought crossed my mind I decided it was time to call my cab-driving friend who, clearly impressed by the speed with which I ate, said he'd be there in no more than ten minutes.

I paid and went out to survey my surroundings. Across the road there was a liquor store and parked outside was a cab from the same company that had brought me here. As I crossed the road, I was pretty sure it wasn't the same driver so carried on and into the liquor store.

Survival-in-Newark Tip Number Two. I thought, always buy a bottle of wine with a screw-top just in case there's no corkscrew where you're staying.

Back outside, the other cab was still there. I wondered whether they'd sent someone else and that he'd got there early and *was* actually waiting for me. So I asked him and, between bites into his burger, he asserted he was indeed waiting for me. Even though his car's livery said he worked for the same company, I didn't believe him.

Survival-in-Newark Tip Number Three. I thought, never get into a cab when the driver is eating, is clearly lying and protests vociferously when you walk away.

With my fare-stealing cab-driver still protesting his innocence, I started to cross the street with the intention of taking up my post outside the Chinese joint but never got that far as another cab drew up and I could see a friendly face poking out the window.

On the way back I told him about his burger-munching, so-called colleague who had tried to steal his fare. To say he was not best pleased would be an understatement.

Back in what was clearly a better part of Newark I toyed with the idea of getting some takeaway fries from Burger King to go with the fine wine I'd bought but I just didn't have the energy to cross the road. That bottle of red wine and a good night's sleep beckoned and I succumbed.

That night I dreamt about the wonderful Saigon Café in Jersey City, my adopted home from home, where I knew I would eat the next evening and enjoy a bit of craic. I couldn't wait.

———

I woke up to a drizzly morning, packed and headed out to the small-house-mobile. It was still where I left it and all four wheels seemed to be in place. I keyed my Jersey City destination into the GPS and renewed my acquaintance with 'the voice'.

After several wrong turnings and 'recalculatings', I finally found myself going in roughly the right direction and eventually arrived back in what I recognised as the Wayne Street area where I began the search for somewhere to park the small-house-mobile that wouldn't result in it being towed away. All I wanted was a parking lot, normally no big deal in America.

I went up and down and across street after street for almost an hour before I stumbled upon my first parking lot … only to be told that I couldn't leave the small-house-mobile there overnight. But the guy was helpful and said he thought there was one lot where I might be able to leave it overnight; he gave me directions to a street not far from where I was staying, indeed much closer than his lot would have been.

Here I met young Mitch who said I could come and go with the small-house-mobile any time of day or night, at $9 a day. He had one space left and, as it didn't look big enough, he said he would park the small-house-mobile for me. I knew he just wanted to drive it, he probably had never been behind the wheel of something like this and clearly enjoyed the experience. And so began a great working relationship with Mitch over the next couple of weeks—I had no-hassle parking day and night and Mitch sometimes got to park or move the small-house-mobile.

I returned to Sherrie's apartment and, as I had a free afternoon and didn't want to lose my parking space, I decided to walk to the large mall, the Newport Center, she'd told me about. It was only a few blocks out of town,

En route, I happened to pass the Saigon Café and noticed it was open and, in an effort to expunge all memories of that awful meal the night before *and* make up for the fact that I hadn't had any breakfast, I decided that a bowl of Vietnamese soup would be the perfect antidote. And it was.

By the time I got to the mall, via a few other interesting retail outlets, I was tired and decided I'd come back the following morning in the small-house-mobile and do some serious shopping; among other things I had to buy presents for three Calabrian children.

I returned to the Saigon Café that evening and took up residence at what had now become 'my' table. I got to know all the family members by their Americanised names, mother and father, Kim and Danny, and daughter and son, Karen and Steve.

It was also that evening when I first vacated my table and headed, glass in hand, for the small bar to finish my wine, possibly partake of another and chat to Steve. Just as I was leaving, Kim came over to me with a small package containing a 'takeaway' bowl of the soup she knew I liked and said it was for my lunch tomorrow. When she suggested I microwave it, I wasn't even sure if Sherrie's apartment *had* a microwave. It had.

Next morning, after a late breakfast of wonderful Vietnamese soup, I was heading back to the Newport Center in the small-house-mobile and, for the first time, I didn't need any help from 'the voice' … or thought I didn't.

I turned right off the main road onto a two-lane highway; the next left I knew would take me into the area between the mall and its multi-storey parking. Unfortunately I found myself in the wrong lane to make a left-hand turn; the traffic coming up behind meant I couldn't change lanes.I spotted a bank to the right and pulled into its car park, turned round and headed back to the exit where I would be able to drive straight across all four lanes of the dual carriageway and on to the mall's parking lot.

I crossed the first two lanes (with traffic coming from the left), the two-lanes I had just vacated, and went on to cross the next two (with traffic coming from the right). Only problem was that, for some reason, I just didn't check whether anything was approaching from that direction.

With all the force I could muster I stamped both feet onto the brake pedal as the other driver, hand on horn, swerved round the front of the small-house-mobile and got clear unscathed before I, shaking, continued across the road as quickly as I could, turned left into the car park, snatched the ticket from the machine as the barrier lifted, raced up several stories, and hid inconspicuously—if indeed it were possible to hide the small-house-mobile inconspicuously.

I sat there for several minutes, still shaking, pondering the enormity of what I had almost done … the car I had almost broadsided was a New Jersey Police patrol car.

I did my shopping with little enthusiasm, ever-watchful for two burly policemen scouring the mall for a diminutive, white-haired fugitive. When I got back to the small-house-mobile I half expected it to be the focus of a stakeout ... at the very least I anticipated some sort of note behind a wiper telling me to report to the nearest precinct headquarters.

The small-house-mobile was such a difficult car to conceal that I was more than a little relieved that I would be heading out of Jersey City for the rest of the day and wouldn't return until late.

——

I was heading up-state, to Fairview, to meet a Calabrian family, Gino and Sina Sculco, but first I had to make a slight detour to find an Italian *pasticceria* in Hoboken that I'd located on the internet. I thought I should take Gino and Sina some traditional Italian pastries.

Thanks to 'the voice' I quickly found the *pasticceria* ... but it was not quite what I was anticipating.

For a start it was rather gloomy, nothing like the brightly-lit, brash emporia that I was used to in Calabria. The display cabinets were a bit sparse, not crammed with the wonderful Italian delicacies I was hoping for; and, worst of all, there were no cream pastries, just tray after tray of almond-based cookies. Still, they were Italian almond-based cookies.

At the sound of the door-bell a man's head emerged from below the counter at the far end of the shop. Slowly, shakily even, he made his way round to where I was standing. His features did not seem as old as his demeanour and gait suggested. Just a little world-weary, I thought.

Pointing to the display cabinet and his shelf of trays behind, I asked for a large tray of mixed cookies. He seemed a little taken aback.

"That's a lot," he said. "Perhaps this size would be better," he continued as he slowly turned and selected a smaller tray from the shelf and held it up.

"No, I'll have the larger tray," I said pointing.

"Are you sure?" he persisted still brandishing the smaller one.

"Yes," I said, "the larger one please."

He shrugged his shoulders in silent recognition that the customer is always right and set about selecting a range of cookies for me.

A door opened and a young woman dressed in white overalls and matching hair-net popped out as if to see that things were going smoothly in the shop.

"Checking up on me," he said as if reading my mind.

As he continued with his selection, I asked him where he was from and he told me he was born in Naples but had lived in the States for over 40 years. I told him that I had been in Naples a couple of times and we exchanged a few anecdotes about that frenetic city. I told him I lived in Calabria and how I was on my way to visit a Calabrian family and that I was sure they'd love his cookies. His demeanour was lightening and I could see he was warming to our brief conversation.

I asked him how much Hoboken had changed and he made a typical Italian gesture to an accompanying, barely audible, aspiration which I understood to mean 'more than I could possibly ever describe'. I asked him about Hurricane Sandy which, from all accounts, had wreaked havoc with parts of Hoboken a couple of weeks earlier and his shop was only a short distance from the Hudson River. His reply left me momentarily speechless.

"We didn't really take much notice … my wife died that week."

Clutching my gift-wrapped cookies, I shook his hand, thanked him for his two-dollar discount, reiterated my condolences and returned to the sun.

DIVERSIONARY TACTICS

That I returned later than anticipated to my Wayne Street base from upstate New Jersey was my own fault.

On the edge of Jersey City, I got caught up in the confusion of roadworks at an already complex junction. With 'the voice' telling me one thing and the diversion signs indicating something completely different, I found myself almost the only vehicle on a bleak highway, fenced in by stark iron-bridge girders spanning fathomless, brackish water.

It was all too clear that I had make a monumental mistake and that this road was taking me away from Jersey City and into some uncharted netherworld.

Instinctively I took the first exit off the highway on the reasonable assumption that it would not be difficult to get back up in the opposite direction and head back towards Jersey City. But instead I found myself following the one-way signs around all four sides of a massive block, a seemingly deserted block in semi-darkness, its hotchpotch of eerily lifeless buildings and the struggling street lights casting sinister, flickering, intimidating shadows.

The whole feel of the place reminded me of the opening credits to the wonderful *The Sopranos*. It was the monotony of those iron-girder bridges which, for me, were gaunt, repetitive icons of this down-at-heel, unappealing, slightly threatening corner of New Jersey and were the essence of those first few erratic frames of *The Sopranos* and the accompanying sound-track. All that was missing was Tony Soprano himself sitting beside me, eyeing me up and down, engulfing me in a fug of cigar smoke.

I knew I was in the wrong place but hopefully not at the wrong time. I had seen the movies; this was exactly the sort of place where innocent, straying bystanders like me got caught up in the seedy underbelly of urbanity, in a craic-less netherworld.

The sort of place where strangers are not welcome; the sort of place where an under-class of unsavoury characters feels at home

The sort of place not to be driving a flashy car such as the small-house-mobile.

The sort of place that the police department was not inclined to voluntarily patrol.

All I could hope for was that the picture the movies painted was bursting with extravagant poetic licence and shamefaced hyperbole. It usually is.

For a nanosecond my natural curiosity struggled with my inclination for survival; the latter triumphed and I decided it would be best not to appear too inquisitive about my surroundings lest I make eye contact with anybody or anything. Head down, I obediently followed the one-way signs even if at first they appeared to be taking me further away from the highway I craved.

One side, two sides, three … four … the end was in sight … at long last I could see the ramp back up onto the main highway, the road back to civilisation.

By the time I reached the sanctuary of adequate street lighting and people going about their normal, late-evening business, my heart-rate had got back to normal.

Somehow I had been in the wrong place at the right time.

—

Three days later I was once again returning to Wayne Street from another late evening trip to northern New Jersey.

And yet again I got caught up in the same diversion and could scarcely credit that I found myself heading for a second time between the same bridge girders along that self-same highway to who knows where. On the plus side, having spent a few days in the

Chicago area, I was now driving a different rental car, a less ostentatious vehicle, albeit one with the same 'voice' and her out-of-date information.

As I was getting over the shock of my stupidity, I toyed with the idea of driving on to the second exit rather than the one I knew led down to darkness and possible danger.

In those few moments of indecision, as I repetitively assaulted the steering wheel and pointlessly swore at 'the voice', I suddenly came up with Plan B and, just in time, I swerved off at that same first exit and drove down once again into the depths of the no-mans-land that I knew so well.

But this time, I thought to myself, screw the one-way signs, I'm not going through all that again. I slowed down as I neared the end of the slip road ramp while all the time looking round to assure myself there were no police cars lurking by the shadowy concrete pillars supporting the highway above. When I was as sure as I could be that the coast was clear, I speeded up and performed a tyre-screeching U-turn, to turn against the nonexistent traffic and screech up the opposite ramp that fed me back onto the other side of the highway I'd just left.

Watching all those American movies and television series hadn't been such a waste of time after all.

A quarter of an hour later, and still smiling the contented smile of someone who had beaten the system, I turned into Mitch's car park, left the car there and walked back to Wayne Street.

There was a spring in my step as, unconsciously at first, I found myself silently singing along to the theme song of *The Sopranos* …

Woke up this morning …

PUTTING A BRAVE FACE ON TOOTHLESS PAIN, 2013.

TEETHING TROUBLES

Despite the fact that my father was a dentist, and a good one, I was a poor patient and in later life paid the price for my sins.

One of these prices I have already alluded to, the cost of that free loaf of bread in Apulia. Included in that cost was the bridge, the sophisticated repair my dentist had made to my enigmatic smile when we returned from Apulia, the cost of having it stuck back on again after it came off a few days before we moved to Italy and the cost of having a partial denture in its place when it came off for a third time in Calabria. I finally ended up with two partial dentures, one lower, one upper.

I loathed these and eventually decided, after a chance encounter in Santa Severina's square, to throw in the towel and investigate a new mouth.

The catalyst was Vincenzo, a local man who had done well for himself and had an Optician business in Rome. Unfortunately he was of an age where he had inherited the then Calabrian propensity for shunning dental care and hygiene; a gappy, discoloured toothscape is not exactly an encouraging vision when you're having an eye test.

Vincenzo returned to his home town for a month every year but on this occasion he had an added incentive: he wanted to show off his new teeth. Generally most people were not enthused by his bright, new pearly-whites; some voiced a sceptical tone, convinced that, whatever he said about them being fixed, they still came out at night.

Ironically many of these agnostics were Vincenzo's peers from his school-days and their scepticism came pouring out of mouths that were missing many teeth and those still hanging on in there appeared none too healthy.

It became clear that I was the only one at the grand opening that day who was remotely interested in Vincenzo's new mouth and I soon became his most fervent admirer by bombarding him with questions. He was delighted to have finally found a genuinely receptive audience and was more than happy to spend time going through the outs and ins of the whole process.

I thought perhaps he was embellishing his story just a little for it all seemed too straightforward. In a nutshell: he went to Serbia, paid €5000, came back a week later with a mouthful of implants and a new smile. His wife went with him and she came back with a new mouth too and, lest I doubted it, he insisted on taking me home with him so that I could see for myself that they had a matching set. He also gave me the name of the clinic in Serbia though, as all the actual documentation was back in Rome, he threw in a disclaimer to the effect that he might not have spelt it correctly and that perhaps they got a good deal because there were two of them.

My only reservations I had regarding Vincenzo's Serbian teeth was that they still had all the false charisma of dentures; worse still I couldn't help but see in them a caricature of Italy's then leader, Silvio Berlusconi; definitely not a good look.

It was another month before I began my research by trying to source the €5000 deal Vincenzo had snapped up in Serbia. I never did, nor did I find a clinic there with the unpronounceable name he gave me. So I went back to the drawing board and scoured the dozens of clinics offering so-called dental tourism in eastern Europe. Via email I travelled to Bulgaria, Croatia, Hungary, Romania and Serbia in search of something approaching a €5000 bargain until, that is, I realised that not only were there teeth and teeth, but also different processes, different time-scales, different standards, different outcomes.

I was looking for teeth made from zirconia, at the time the top of the range regarding both looks and durability, but there were other options, notably acrylic, which was cheaper and generally did not last as long nor look as natural.

After countless email enquiries and questions and a few calls, I finally settled on Željko and Ivan, father and son, in the coastal town of Rovinj in the part of northern Croatia known as Istria, an area I'd passed through both by coach and in our makeshift motor caravan over 40 years previously when I saw it as the gateway to Yugoslavia.

———

Everything was organised with the precision of the seasoned tour operator: a car to pick us up at Italy's Trieste Airport just north of the Slovenian border, an apartment 200 metres from the clinic and brochures of what to do in and around Rovinj when you're not in pain. Unlike the conventional tourist, the morning after our late evening arrival, instead of a walk into to town or down to the harbour, this particular 'tourist' had a dental appointment at nine. It turned out to be a long day.

Before they saw me that morning in person, all Ivan and Željko had to go on was a four-year old Calabrian X-ray with my partial dentures, which I had scanned and emailed to them. The first thing they did when they met me was to remove the partial dentures, explain how they had done more harm than good and ceremoniously chucked them to the bin. These were my kind of people.

They then took another X-ray and made plaster impressions of what was left of my upper and lower crags; these became the focus of a long discussion between father and son about how to proceed. Finally, they conveyed their decisions to me, in English of course.

Since I had last been in Croatia, when it was part of Yugoslavia, English had replaced German as the second language of choice. Here in Istria, Italian was also spoken widely for, between the wars Rijeka, then known as Fiume, was an Italian city.

When it came to communicating with Ivan and Željko there was therefore no problem, both spoke Italian and Ivan's English was almost word perfect.

They planned to extract one tooth, prepare what was left to accept bridges that would be linked to implants, lift my sinuses, give me a bone graft, fit and cap seven implant fixtures and stitch the lot up in preparation for my next visit to Croatia in May. They would begin the work at midday.

In the meantime I had details of some drugs to buy, one to relax me before they started and others to help control any later pain.

I had been in the chair for almost four hours when Ivan, having decided not to do the extraction at that time, tidied everything up with 40-plus stitches.

Before sending me home to suck my evening meal, Ivan flagged up two activities I was not to indulge in for as long as possible, up to six months was ideal, but it was more crucial that I desisted over the next few weeks: because they had raised my sinuses, I was neither to blow my nose nor to sneeze.

The former was easy enough, I had two good shirt cuffs that were still occasional substitutes but, as for the sneezing … well, as soon as he mentioned it, I could feel one coming on. Ivan explained that sticking my finger under my nose wasn't going to hack it, I needed to open my mouth as wide as possible and breathe quickly and deeply. He taught me well and to this day, I rarely sneeze, a technique that, unknown to me at the time, would prove more than a little useful a few months later.

Back at the apartment I saw myself in the mirror for the first time. It looked as if that bouncer-type that Magda and I had successfully evaded in Spain had finally caught up with me and slapped me once for every year he'd been looking for me. Apart from which I was fine.

And, besides, there was work to be done. Depending where we were going and the time of year, Kay and I often travelled with a Scart cable and a small DVD player (and of course a few DVDs). Experience had taught us that, on the few occasions when we might want a tele-visual diversion, most local programmes were barely watchable, generally because of the language. As initially I wasn't likely to be going out too much of an evening, out came the Scart cable and the DVD player.

And, just in case I hadn't seen and tasted enough blood for one day, we settled down to an episode of Dexter before I fell into a drug-induced asleep.

The next morning I looked like a lopsided hamster that had just filled one of his cheek pouches more than the other. A quick midday visit to the clinic confirmed that all was well and that I was supposed to look like a hamster and in all likelihood would retain my rodent-like looks for a day or two. I sensed there might have been a 'but …' in there somewhere and the next morning I discovered what it was.

While still retaining the hamster-like aspect, I now looked like a hamster that had been repeatedly punched on the side of its face by its mate; not so much black and blue, more yellow and purple. In painting a picture of how I looked, it has to be said that I really did not experience much pain that I couldn't control by the occasional paracetamol or two.

Despite having temporarily lost my boyish good looks, I had no problem in hiring a car two days later; nor in driving it.

I was keen to see some of northern Croatia and in particular revisit Rijeka which I'd passed through several times on my visits to Yugoslavia back in the late 60s. I remembered absolutely nothing. We walked the broad boulevards standing back from the sea, gazed up at the grand apartment buildings and walked the fashionable streets. Only the sea was as blue as I remembered it.

Back in Rovinj my treatment took its course throughout the week: all the stitches were finally removed and I left Croatia sporting some temporary teeth at the front, made from acrylic. These would do me until my next appointment in May. They looked and felt infinitely better than the two partial dentures that I arrived with.

On that first Monday, I had asked Ivan if he could retrieve those partial dentures from his waste bin; I wanted to take them home with me as a sort of grotesque reminder of bad times. As he carefully put them in a plastic bag and sealed it, he made it clear that they were never again to enter my mouth.

Later in the week, I asked him if I could have the two plaster impressions he had made when I first arrived. He thought my request odd until I explained that, back home, impressions and dentures would be reunited as an avant-garde installation, a three dimensional interpretation of the craic.It would also serve as a constant reminder of what my mouth looked like before I met him.

In May, I returned to Croatia for some additional work to prepare me for my final appointment in the autumn when I would leave Croatia with a new mouth.

On that final visit, the implants buried in my gums were exposed and became the pillars that, with the pointed remains of my remaining real teeth, supported an almost full set. I left Croatia with 24 new teeth and one original still hanging on in there at the back.

On the flight back to Calabria, I reflected on my many dental mishaps in search of one defining moment that brought me on this journey to Croatia and to finally get my mouth back to where it had started … well almost.

Vincenzo showing off his new teeth in the square that day certainly had been a spur to action but the more immediate catalyst was biting into that piece of bread in Apuglia which set off a new chain of oral events that led here.

The more I thought about my dental history, the more I realised the important part dentistry and teeth, my teeth, had played in my life. Is there a book in it, I wondered?

Tooth be told or *The whole tooth* or *Before the crack* … the scope for catchy titles was endless, I thought to myself, as I flashed my new, permanent, enigmatic smile at an unsuspecting, and unimpressed, flight attendant.

OTHER PURPOSES

People have assumed that, because I lived in Italy for eight and a half years, that I might be well acquainted with the capital, Rome.

Apart from passing through the city's two airports, Fiumicino and Ciampino, from time to time, I have been there six times but only the first of these was as a curious visitor; the other five had other purposes. One day I will have to return to experience the Roman craic.

The first visit was the first time we travelled to Italy and stayed at Monterchi; it was no more than a day-trip on the train, the highlight of which was a visit to the Coliseum. We were on the train longer than we were in Rome.

The second visit was when Neff and I literally passed through Rome Termini station following in the footsteps of DH Lawrence. We had just enough time for a cup of coffee before making our way to the platform that hosts Italy's impressive, high-speed train to Naples, *la Frecciarossa*, the Red Arrow.

The third visit was another day trip, the main purpose of which was to visit the American Embassy there to finalise some paperwork that would allow me to receive book royalties in America.

I left Crotone on the early morning flight and returned the same evening. Inside my shoulder-bag I carried another bag, large enough for my secondary mission—a visit to Rome's Asian quarter which I knew was close to the Termini station, in and around Piazza Vittorio Emanuele II.

Calabrians are very conservative when it comes to trying anything else other than Calabrian or Italian dishes and this is reflected in foods available in local shops and supermarkets and, at the time, in the virtual non-existence of restaurants that serve anything other than local Calabrian cuisine.

I recall having a pre-lunch *aperitivo* in Santa Severina's square with my friend Toto, a man in his mid-60s, and I asked him what he was having for lunch. His answer, tinged with the merest hint of resignation, was both illuminating and, for me, depressing.

"I don't know exactly what it will be but it will definitely include pasta." was Toto's half-hearted reply.

For at least 23,000 consecutive days, man and boy, Toto had eaten pasta for lunch; no wonder I picked up that hint of resignation in his voice.

I had a self-imposed criterion for eating out when I was not in Italy—I ate neither pasta nor pizza. On one occasion I rented an apartment for a week near Belfast and the well-meaning proprietor, aware of where I lived, sent me a list of all the Italian restaurants in the area. I thanked him for the kind thought and said I would prefer to see the other list, the one of all the non-Italian restaurants in the locality. He apologised and, by way clarification, explained that all his previous Italian guests had only ever eaten at Italian restaurants.

Being in Rome for a few hours was therefore a great opportunity to buy all the ingredients to cook Asian dishes that I couldn't get in Calabria.

I was like a kid in a sweet shop and soon my extra bag was bursting. I bought everything I needed in the same small supermarket and chatted to the Chinese owner about the problem, as I saw it, we had in Calabria.

She asked me if I wanted some Marmite and said that all her British (by which I assume she also meant Irish) clients always bought Marmite.

"What do you do with it?" she asked

—

My fourth visit to Rome was altogether different. The good news was that I planned to be there for longer than all my previous visits lumped together; the bad news was that I was attending a clinic to have a prostate biopsy.

We arrived in Rome on Friday, the day before the biopsy, and the next morning walked to the clinic, Villa Salaria.

The plan was that, post-biopsy, we would return to the bed & breakfast by bus—there was a stop just outside the clinic—have a light lunch and just rest all afternoon. I only mention this because that's not what happened.

Having been given a local anaesthetic my urologist, Dottore Manlio Cappa, a Calabrian himself, began to take small samples from my prostate; he explained to me that I wouldn't feel a thing.

He was right … but he omitted to tell me about the sound. As each sample was taken it sounded a bit like a staple-gun firing, not at all what I was expecting and at the time a little disconcerting. I felt nothing, just noise pollution

I started to count … one … two … three … four … I knew that twelve was the norm.

Then I noticed that he was watching a monitor, the back of which faced me. I asked if he was looking at my prostate and he said he was and asked if I'd like to watch too. I nodded and so he repositioned the monitor so that we could both see it; as he was guiding the needle-like sample-snatchers, I was watching its progress and trying to marry up what I was seeing with the sound I was hearing.

The action on the monitor seemed just like the scan we are all used to seeing of the unborn child in the womb. I thought I'd lighten the proceedings by asking if he could tell whether it was a boy or a girl. Somehow my attempt at a joke in Italian got lost in translation. Or perhaps he thought I was just hallucinating.

Twelve came and went; he took 18 samples.

Cappa—I started to use just his surname, though not directly to him, which I knew flew in the face of the Italian convention of calling everyone by their professional title, even a best friend—Cappa knew about my dental treatment in Croatia and asked me how what he was doing compared to the four non-stop hours, seven implants, two sinus lifts, bone grafts and 40-plus stitches that he knew I'd had there.

I genuinely had to think about it and found it difficult to equate the two experiences, particularly as one was self-inflicted, a choice, while the other was a medical imperative. In addition, the latter was a work-in-progress and, depending on the result, could lead to a more live-threatening scenario. Nevertheless, I said the dental work was worse for I knew it would make him feel better about what he was doing to my poor prostate.

The biopsy over, I felt none the worse for my experience, apart from a little stiffness from having been stuck in the 'giving-birth' position for nearly half an hour.

I returned to the waiting area for a coffee with Kay. Cappa said he'd see me again in an hour or so to check that I was fit enough to leave.

It was approaching lunchtime when I returned to Cappa's consulting room to be told I was good to go. He confirmed too that I was fit enough to travel to Croatia two days later for another round of dental treatment.

Before leaving, I made an appointment to see him again in Crotone in three weeks time—by which time he would have the biopsy results and I would be less dentally challenged—shook his hand, thanked him and rejoined Kay in the reception area.

Kay suggested we pop in to the clinic café-bar to have lunch but I was keen to get back 'home' and we decided to pick something up on the way. We left the clinic and walked to the nearby bus-stop to wait.

Almost a quarter of an hour into the waiting I realised I'd left some papers relating to my treatment on Cappa's desk and Kay volunteered to return to the clinic to fetch them. While she was away the inevitable happened, the bus came and went. It's called Sod's Law.

Almost a quarter of an hour into the second period of waiting, I was leaning against the pole of the bus-stop, my arm wrapped round it, when I slowly started to descend ground-wards—Kay said afterwards that it was as if I was rehearsing a new, slow-motion, pole-dancing routine.

Kay ran behind me to try and support me before I became a crumpled heap but, fortunately, a passer-by caught me and supported my weight while I gradually regained my focus on the world around me. Slowly he started raising me upright, pausing several times to check that I was ready to proceed a little further towards the adult world.

At this point another, younger, man appeared who just happened to be a physiotherapist from the clinic and, when he heard I'd just had a biopsy there, suggested I return to be checked over. Then a car drew up, a Jaguar no less, and the driver and his wife offered to drive us back to the clinic even though it was no more than 100 metres away.

Forty minutes after leaving Villa Salaria, I was back there. Cappa had left for the day and I was now up on the second floor having my blood pressure taken. It was, as I had already surmised, very low.

The problem was simple; it was five hours since I'd eaten and in the meantime I'd had an invasive medical procedure and, instead of eating at the clinic or getting a taxi back to our bed & breakfast, I'd opted to wait for a bus; twice. My blood-sugar had dropped like a stone and, barely holding on to the bus-stop, I had followed suit.

Basically I should have known better, I should have listened to Kay when she said we should eat something in the café-bar before leaving. The duty-doctor suggested I go downstairs and rectify that situation immediately and then he'd check my blood pressure again after an hour or so.

It was nearly four in the afternoon when the taxi dropped us off. I went straight to bed for a nap, not because of any after-effects from the biopsy as such, I was just very, very tired.

Post-nap, I decided to check out something I'd read on the

internet, that font of contradictory, untested misinformation when it comes to medical issues. It was an extract from a book, *The Decision: Your prostate biopsy shows cancer. Now what?*, a description of the prostate biopsy, apparently written by an urologist. It read as follows:

"You've just experienced the anxiety, humiliation and pain of having your prostate biopsied. Since the biopsy you have endured the sight of blood in your urine and bowel movements, blood in your semen, and burning when you void."

Having just had my prostate 'biopsied' I could truthfully confirm that I felt a little anxiety beforehand (who wouldn't?), absolutely no humiliation and no pain that merited a stronger word than 'discomfort'. In retrospect, I recall a minuscule amount of blood in my urine for no more than a day.

I think such remarks are not only crass but also unhelpful to people who are considering having such a procedure, particularly as they are clearly describing only one biopsy technique. Worse still, they pour out of the mouth of someone who is supposed to be authoritative and yet all they demonstrate is disrespect to the many doctors, like Cappa, who try so hard to limit anxiety, humiliation and pain. Little wonder I am so wary of so-called internet experts, peddling dubious medical procedures and alternative hocus-pocus.

With Monday's dental trip to Croatia (the May appointment from the previous chapter), we would have successfully negotiated another of our planned summer excursions. Our next visit to Cappa at Crotone for the biopsy results would settle the fate of the third, Neff's upcoming June wedding in London.

———

My fifth visit to Rome was almost a week after Neff's wedding. Alas, the biopsy results threw an unexpected spanner in the works and I couldn't attend; my Rome visit was for surgery. Although I got to stay there for ten days, I saw only the inside of the same clinic where I'd had the biopsy and a hotel about 600 metres away.

The highlight of my time there, apart from knowing that I was now going to live a bit longer, was meeting Dan Chebac. When Cappa booked me in for my prostatectomy he quipped that he would be having an international day of surgery: first Dan Chebac a Romanian living near Rome and then me, an Irishman from Calabria.

Dan and I first met two days after our respective surgery when I finally got out of bed and felt revitalised and more like a human being. I thought it was time to stick my head out the door and take a look at what was going on in the wider world. It was at this moment that a large man wearing shorts, complete with protruding tubes, was walking past. He hesitated for a moment and held out his hand.

"You must be Cappa's other patient," he said in near perfect English, "I was hoping we'd meet. I'm Dan."

"Must go, my wife will be here in a minute."

And off he went, round the corner and presumably back to his bedroom. Not only did Dan, the Romanian, speak English, but he also called Cappa by his surname only.

I was trying to work out how it was that Dan seemed to be so much more active than me. I could see that he was definitely a physically stronger specimen and, I guessed, he was probably eight or nine years younger … *and* (I was now clutching at straws) he did have a head start, his operation was a good six hours earlier than mine and mine included a complication which meant it lasted longer.

It was good to have met him and I hoped we'd meet up again and swap stories about drugs, drains and catheters, about how we met Cappa and which nurse was the most *simpatica*.

Later, while Kay was headed down to the café-bar for some breakfast before going off to do some shopping, I thought I'd clean myself up and wash my hair before taking my tubes and their mobile pillar for a walk in the corridor. That slow shuffle proved to be a major turning point for, no sooner had I stepped outside than I bumped into Dan again and we walked and talked together for over an hour. It was in that hour that my shuffle became a more confident, albeit short, stride.

We swapped notes about all sorts of things and found that our prostate experiences, pre-Cappa, were not dissimilar in that we'd both seen other urologists and we'd even had our biopsies on the same day. We found too that we'd had the same experience the day before when we'd kept asking to get out of bed but nothing happened.

One thing I was able to help Dan with was his sneezing; Cappa had told us both that, for a few days, sneezing was something to be avoided. And, of course, following my dental work in Croatia, I was the expert in keeping a sneeze at bay. Sneezeless in Salaria, we continued to extol the virtues of Dottore Manlio Cappa.

We were in agreement that we had been incredibly fortunate to have met Cappa when we did; we knew he was an extraordinary individual. I placed him on top of an even higher pedestal by telling Dan how, despite being Rome's top urologist, he was in fact Calabrian and how, every four weeks, he drove down from Rome to Crotone to hold a surgery and to give something back to the community that had raised and educated him. There are, I suspect, not many eminent doctors or consultants who would regularly make a 13-hour round trip for such altruistic motives.

Dan was an extraordinary man too, a giant of a man in every sense. Born and educated in Romania, he spent his formative years living under the harsh communist regime of Nicholai Ceausescu. Dan became a respected folk singer and, through his music, a dissident of sorts. He was not a political activist, rather someone who used his words and music to inspire others.

In April 1981 he finally slipped out of Romania and found work in Düsseldorf in Germany. Six years later, he moved to Italy and settled in Ostia, near Rome, where he met married his Italian wife, Stefania.

More recently, Dan had found unexpected fame through YouTube where one of his most famous songs—protesting about how the Ceausescu regime got rid of all Romania's horses and replaced them with tractors—has been given a new lease of life with some clever graphics. We watched it together on my iPad.

We talked a little about his home country pre- and post-1989 when the Ceausescu regime was finally overthrown and he was surprised to hear that I had several Romanian friends and had travelled there the previous year.

As we walked and talked, we knew we'd both undergone a unique, defining experience. We were aware that this experience and this hour together had established a bond between us that would help us both through whatever these next days and weeks would bring. Independently we knew these things, but it was all unspoken.

Cappa gave us both our discharge papers on the Wednesday and we prepared for an early evening return to civvy street. Free at last.

Well, almost free; there followed many emotional farewells which started, and finished, with Dan. Together, like veterans of some long-remembered wartime campaign, we did the rounds of the second floor of Villa Salaria and thanked everyone for their many kindnesses to both of us. Back at the nurses' station we embraced the sister and her team of nurses and orderlies. In the background there appeared a face I didn't initially recognise until his hand shot out from the group to shake mine. It was the duty doctor who had looked after me that Saturday afternoon when I had to return to the clinic following my post-biopsy dizzy spell.

Down at reception Kay called a cab and ten minutes later we were settling in to our temporary 'home' in the York Hotel.

I felt both elated and a little nervous.

I couldn't wait to return to Calabria to recuperate but it was another five days, punctuated by several check-ups at Villa Salaria, before we finally set foot back on Calabrian soil and I felt that the worst was finally over. Yet again the Eternal City itself had alluded me.

My sixth, and most recent, visit was the nearest I ever got to being in Rome by choice and with time to observe.

There is one chapter of *Thank you Uncle Sam* which I called the 'virtual' chapter, for I never actually met the main protagonist, Carolina Ventrelli, when I visited her home city of Chicago in 2012. I had two other people in the area to visit and a plane to catch. It was simply not possible to meet. Nevertheless through the wonders of email and the internet, I was able to research and write the extraordinary story of her family and how they came to emigrate to the United States in the 1960s and, unknown to her at the time, even further back to the early 1900s.

Despite the fact that we had never actually met, Lina and I became close friends so, when I heard she was going to be stopping overnight in Rome as part of a whistle-stop tour of Italy with a friend, I booked a flight.

In preparation for our meeting I was charged with finding somewhere to eat on a Sunday evening. As I have already indicated, it has been my practice when outside Italy to eat everything except pasta and pizza and, unlike Calabria, Rome offers a much wider choice. My research led me to a Korean restaurant and initially everyone agreed with that choice.

What also intrigued me was that, when I read the reviews of most of Rome's non-Italian restaurants on TripAdvisor—be they Korean, Thai, Chinese or Indian—many started with a variation of the same sentence:

"This was a welcome change after having eaten nothing but pasta since we arrived."

"My group got tired of pasta during our two-week trip to Italy …"

That others felt the same after only a few days, made me feel less guilty about my inclination to eat non-Italian cuisine when the opportunity arose.

In the end, when we did meet Lina and her friend, the rules had changed. Lina was wonderful, everything I expected and more, but her 'open-minded' friend had just read on the internet that Korean restaurants serve dog and though 'fake news' hadn't been invented at the time, she was obviously part of the initial study into people's gullibility and lack of an enquiring mind. In the end we ate Italian, nor was it the best Italian

Only after we'd eaten did I impart to Lina's friend my own fake news about the Italian restaurants that served local rats from the Tiber.

She, the friend, went on to demonstrate a propensity to indulge in historical amnesia. Like Lina, she had the right to call herself American because her grandparents had emigrated to America and, like millions of others, were once new immigrants in a strange land.

She had been in Rome a few hours when the first manifestation of her amnesia went from brain to mouth and she noted that the city was 'full of immigrants'. Other than this, she offered no other insights into being in the Eternal City.

Furthermore, it was clear from her tone that she didn't remotely see these immigrants as a good thing. She had, for example, no way of knowing whether they were legal or illegal immigrants. Nor, from the perspective of her white, middle-class American background, would it have made any difference if she had known for she had no empathy with all such people. They were all lumped together, except unseen Caucasian immigrants with a right to be there. Like I was, for example.

I remember casting my mind back to how an elderly descendent of another Calabrian immigrant, mindful of the contradiction in being seen to be anti-immigration, later espoused a new rationale to explain away his distaste for the new wave of immigrants in his cosy corner of America:

"It's the fact that they're not European … that's the problem."

What he was really saying was that they were not Caucasian; they were in fact from Honduras which made me wonder whether or not he would consider the Italian-born Guatamalan wife of my Calabrian friend to be an acceptable immigrant? After all, despite being Italian, she does not look European.

The issue should be, I would suggest, whether or not, as with those who emigrated to America from Calabria in the early 1900s and after the war, they are *legal* immigrants. America is a nation of immigrants but those earlier immigrants came to the country legally. There were hurdles to jump, conditions to be met before entry was approved. And those who did not meet the statutory requirements were returned whence they came.

Post-Brexit Britons, Caucasian to a fault, now find they too have to jump through bureaucratic hoops in order to settle in what were previously seen as immigrant-friendly European Union countries.

On the other side of that coin, many young Argentinians of Italian lineage who seek European citizenship, arrive legally and spend up to three months legally acquiring their Italian identity and a passport. Some return home, others go on to contribute to the Italian and European economy.

Visit six was, above all, about meeting Lina, and we have met since in Calabria, but it was also about wrapping up visit five.

It was like a breath of fresh air when, the following day, I met up with another legal immigrant, the European, Dan Chebac.

In Rome's coastal community of Ostia, with his wife Stefania and his two sons, we celebrated having survived Cappa's knife. One Romanian, one Italian, one English and one Irish toasted their diversity; Stefania coped well with being the only non-immigrant at the table.

A DAY-OUT IN BANDIT COUNTRY

Living in Calabria it was difficult not to be aware of the influence of the *'ndrangheta*, the Calabrian mafia. Mention the name of any town or village to a Calabrian and they would know to what extent, if any, there was a mafia presence. Their way of communicating this was generally non-verbal, no more than running the back of the thumb diagonally down a cheek.

The Calabrian mafia, the *'ndrangheta*, is now more influential world-wide than its counterparts in Sicily and Naples. Almost every superlative, except those relating to the 'good' side of the spectrum, can be cast at it. In mafia terms it is the worst of the worst.

The deep south of Calabria is the area most tainted with the scourge of the *'ndrangheta*. Located here, in the foothills of the Aspromonte mountains, are two towns that stand out as both hard-core *'ndrangheta* and generally off the grid to outsiders: Platì and San Luca.

Unlike my fellow Calabrians, I was more than a little curious and decided to ignore their advice and visit both towns to see for myself. A day-out in bandit country beckoned.

I had decided to approach Platì via the longer route from the west coast, traversing the Aspromonte mountains where, in the early 1970s, the *'ndrangheta* had held captive young John Paul Getty Jnr; initially with two ears, then with one. I wasn't anticipating a craic-filled day.

From Delianuova on the western foothills, I intended to turn east into the unknown and cross the mountains, via Platì, to Bovalino on the Ionian coast. But Delianuova was not an untypical Calabrian town in that someone had decided to dispense with the convention of directional road signs, or at least the one that I would have found useful. And, because I had been so sure it would be straightforward to find my way onto the right road, I had not set up the car's GPS which I tended to only use in cities.

When I realised that the choices I had already made—at two junctions where there were no signs—were clearly wrong, I drove back into the town, stopped and asked a couple of local men for a bit of guidance.

I explained that I wanted to go to Bovalino via the Platì road, a route they just discounted immediately and, as if they'd misheard me, started to give me alternatives. I repeated that I wanted to go via Platì and they told me in no uncertain terms that I couldn't go that way, their suggested routes were much better. They didn't say 'safer' but I knew what they meant; or I thought I did. I persisted with my chosen route and told them I had to go via Platì and, not unreasonably, they wanted to know why. They clearly had never met anyone, especially a foreigner, who was adamant about wanting to pass through Platì.

Finally they gave in and told me to turn right at the next junction and to keep climbing on the same road. Thus began a road trip I shall never forget.

Even as I left Delianuovo, I was constantly on the lookout for at least one road-sign that might, albeit belatedly, confirm that I was on the right track. There was nothing. I continued to climb as instructed.

At first the route was not unlike other tree-lined, little-used roads on the fringes of the Aspromonte: mostly gloomy, sometimes downright dark, always wet, often misty and partially covered with heaped clusters of fallen, russet pine-needles swept to the verges by the wind and the occasional passing car. Enchanting it was not.

The weather was closing in and gradually the morning mist became a fog and a road, already difficult to define, became adept at disguising its boundaries. I saw no other vehicle on the move for perhaps six or seven miles and then, just ahead, I picked up the tail-lights of a car going in the same direction as me. Abruptly it pulled over on the left and stopped on the verge; I slowed down and pulled alongside, still eager to have some confirmation that I was indeed on the right road.

I asked the woman passenger if we were on the road to Platì. She looked at me vaguely, shrugged her shoulders and said she didn't know. Her male companion, who had now got out of the car, looked just as vague and offered no further insight into where exactly we were.

As I pulled away, still none the wiser, I was trying to work out why this couple were here in the first place, parked up on a road to nowhere in particular. If it was to indulge in a bit of hanky-panky, then why on earth didn't they pull off the road miles back? It would have been just as private, just as dark and just as inclement, wouldn't it? And weren't they at all curious about this road? After all there were many places where it was decidedly hard-going, where the surface had been eroded or butchered and never repaired. It was an obstacle course of weaving around or over huge potholes; sometimes there were so many they were impossible to avoid as were the large expanses of black surface water which, it occurred to me, might easily have been fathomless sinkholes. And, that being the case, what the hell was I doing here?

That may have been the only car on the move but there were lots of goats on the go, taking their morning constitutional, it seemed, along a road where they clearly did not expect to see moving vehicles. Once, after sneaking past about 20 of them in a rare, mist-less moment, I stopped and got out to take a photo … camera-shy, they all turned and ran off.

On the other hand, overall I did pass maybe a dozen cars parked up by the side of the road, but never a driver in sight. To keep me sane I started to mentally list the possible reasons for this phenomenon. Had the cars simply been abandoned? Had the driver gone for a walk in the woods never to be seen again? Assuming the season was right, was someone hunting for mushrooms, collecting asparagus, gathering chestnuts? Maybe they were all goatherds looking for their wayward goats? Was it possible that so many people could be having a very long, secret, off-road pee? Perhaps a couple had abandoned their vehicle to indulge themselves on a a moist and misty forest floor? Was someone digging a shallow grave, body or bodies temporarily propped up against a nearby tree? Who knows?

My speculation took me straight back to the couple in the car I'd passed earlier and the only rational explanation. It was obvious now, they were in the middle of nowhere to get rid of the body in the boot, his wife or her husband, it didn't matter which, perhaps both. It was the only logical explanation. They weren't going anywhere, they had arrived.

To assuage that niggling doubt about where I might be, I pulled over where there were no parked cars and no wandering goats and set up the GPS. I entered the address of the bed & breakfast I was staying at in Bovalino that evening, knowing that, if this were indeed the road to Platì, then the GPS would pick it up as being the shortest route there. It did occur to me that there might be no satellite signal in these woods as it was already clear that my cellphone was not picking up anything. Thankfully the screen sprung into life and that soft, purposeful voice I knew so well gave me hope as, with the merest trace of emotion, she confirmed that I was to keep going in the same direction along the same road. I wanted to give her a hug but made do with blowing her a kiss. I pressed on.

The mist and the drizzle were lifting as the trees stepped back a little from the road to let the odd shaft of sunlight penetrate. The mist had become a haze and I could see some light at the end of the tunnel when, suddenly, something truly extraordinary appeared on the horizon. I did a double-take. It was nothing short of miraculous for when I was least expecting it, I could actually see a road sign, the first since before passing through Delianuova. It was like discovering water in a desert.

I was approaching a sort of staggered crossroads and 'the voice' was giving me precise directions but, despite her reassuring ways, on this occasion I doubted her. The built-in GPS in my head was saying something different. Unquestioning, I had already started to follow her instructions but after only 200 metres decided to pull over and check it out on a real map. I soon found the configuration of roads that I was seeing on the GPS monitor. It was a revelation.

First of all I was right to have had doubts about 'the voice's' chosen route to Bovalino … it certainly seemed likely to be a better road but was longer and did not pass through Platì. Also, I discovered that I had reached this point from Delianuova via a different road completely and not the one I thought I was on. Indeed, according to my trusty Touring Club Italiano road atlas, my travelling-in-Calabria bible, this secondary road was defined as 'passable with difficulty' and therefore not a recommended route at all. I was sure the worst was over for the next part of the journey to Platì was, according to the atlas, nine miles on a 'narrow, asphalt regional connecting road', the designated SS112 and a level above what I had just experience.

The juxtaposition of roads finally implanted in my mind, I turned round and headed back to that junction and turned left to take the more direct route to Platì.

Almost immediately I passed a sign that I recognised advising me that the route was *interrota*, a familiar sign on Calabrian roads and one generally ignored by Calabrians. It means that the normal flow of traffic has been interrupted, usually by some sort of natural disruption, a landslide onto the road or part of the road itself having fallen away. Sometimes both.

At that time there had been an *interrota* sign between my home-town, Santa Severina, and neighbouring San Mauro Marchesato, for nearly four years but, as far as locals were concerned, the road was never closed. The rationale is simple: if there is just enough room for a car to sneak past officialdom's half-hearted attempt at closing a road, then it's not a serious obstacle. Almost as a matter of principle, Calabrians ignore such signs and carry on. Which is exactly what I did.

There were many times in the next 45 minutes when I was to regret that decision. Unknown to me at the time I was setting off along a road that resembled a war-zone. My natural instinct for survival continually did battle with my curiosity and my ever-expanding Calabrian gene. I wondered what Norman Douglas, the English writer who famously wrote about Calabria in *Old Calabria*, would have done?

I didn't have to think too hard. I had no doubt that Douglas and his stiff upper lip would have carried on.

As far as the eye could see, the profile of the road was consistent. To the right a high, mountain-wall faced with ragged, restless rock. Then came the road itself, originally wide enough for two cars to pass comfortably. And, on the left, the edge, perhaps once fenced off but no longer so. Beyond this there was the drop down into the valley below. This 'as far as the eye could see' profile was inevitably short-loved on a road that was essentially serpentine. A road unwilling to share its crumbling secrets until you turned around the next bend.

Huge boulders had tumbled down the mountainside onto the road. Where there weren't boulders, what asphalt there was left was terminally scarred and strewn with rocks, rubble and earth of all shapes, sizes and hues. It resembled a man-made set for some apocalyptic movie that the crew forgot to clear up afterwards. But these were real boulders, not painted polystyrene; and the drop into the valley was both real and unprotected.

It was difficult to decide which part or stretch of the road was particularly *interrota*. Depending on your definition it was either all or none. For me, pressing onwards, it was clearly he latter, but only just.

There were frequent stretches where parts of the road itself had fallen away leaving a ragged asphalt edge and a potential plunge into the abyss. But, with care, even these were passable and soon weaving round the endless rockfalls and other debris became almost second nature, as did trying to avoid the occasional groups of small pigs foraging in the debris and clearly not used to seeing a car in their backyard.

Perhaps it was all of this that the two guys back in Delianuova had been trying to warn me about, and not the prevalence of the local mafia. Most likely both. What they probably didn't factor in was the sheer mental effort in negotiating this road, on avoiding the larger boulders while keeping an eye on the edge, or what was left of it.

The sad irony was that this was not some back-road but the SS112, a highway that dissects a designated National Park. When I had occasion to take my eye off the road and take in the view, I was privy to a glorious, breathtaking landscape, the Aspromonte in full spate. I also realised that I was one of the few people, in recent times, to have ever seen it so.

As I passed another three wandering pigs, all black this time, I could see, tucked away in the valley below what I knew must be Platì, I stopped a couple of times to take photographs, much as I had done on other roads; only this time I was pretty sure I wasn't going to encounter any other vehicles; the odd pig perhaps, but no traffic. I was definitely the only person travelling to Platì that day from the west; probably that week, maybe that month, possibly that year.

From my vantage point in the hills, Platì looked just like any other tidy, compact, inviting, Calabrian town nestling in the folds of the valley. There was no large finger pointing from above warning the unwary that this was a mafia stronghold. Nor would the innocent observer have known that, until recently, underneath the town there was a tunnel network, once kept in good order by the local mafia bosses to facilitate their hasty exit should the long arm of the law come a-knocking.

When the *Carabinieri* did drop by, the tunnels became national, even international, news for a while. But, it seemed to me, the media focussed not on why some people in Platì needed to escape in the first place, but instead on the ingenious nature of the tunnels, particularly the one that had its entrance from the back of a pizza oven which was a great photo opportunity for the young *Carabinieri* who showed it off.

Any sense of anxiety I may have had before setting out that morning had long dissipated, the rigours of the drive had already seen to that and, instead, I was now being seduced by the splendour of the Aspromonte landscape, even by my bird's eye view of Platì.

In the last mile or so the serpentine road began to return to some sense of normality as it slowly descended to merge with the random housing that defined the outskirts of Platì.

I drove through the town slowly, through streets that were dowdy, featureless and monochromatic, though less so than as I had expected. It was the views from above on the approach to the town, the multifarious terracotta hues of the roof tiles, that gave this town colour and character and an illusory sense of normality.

There were more cars than I expected and I even got snarled up in one of those short-lived, Calabrian traffic jams when two cars travelling in opposite directions stop so that their drivers can have a natter. The few people on the streets were mostly young men chatting in groups, their womenfolk—mothers, sisters, wives, girlfriends—were surely attending to the midday pasta.

My pale-green Stilo turned a few curious heads, and I could clearly see that people knew there was a stranger in their midst. Once or twice I nodded and grinned in confident salutation, probably more of a grimace than a grin. Given the direction from which I had come, they probably thought I was lost or having a senior moment. I passed what looked like a new road project on the outskirts of the town where a concrete viaduct took a more direct route towards the town centre than the road I was on. Something was not quite right about it. How can a road look both new and derelict at the same time?

I didn't know what to expect as I left the eastern outskirts of the town to descend to the Ionian coast and a late lunch at Bovalino. But this half of the road was just as surprising for being unexpectedly and boringly ordinary. It was a different world, a good road with what looked like a new section midway. This was Platì's only real link to the outside world now that the way west, my chosen route, had been all but abandoned.

Before continuing my journey to San Luca, I ate at a small restaurant in Bovalino run, as it happened, by two young men who had escaped from Platì. One helped fill me in on some of the details about that viaduct to nowhere; the rest I gleaned from the internet.

The viaduct was (and, in theory, still is) part of a grand project, a new east-west artery linking the A3 autostrada near Delianuova to the west with the eastern Ionian coast road. For some inexplicable reason, the road was started in the middle, on the outskirts of Platì. That in itself was a bad idea for it is likely that the funding somehow found alternative coffers to fill and the project withered on the mafia vine. Apart, that is, from the few hundred yards of pointless viaduct, with neither beginning nor end on the outskirts of Platì.

That said, there was a grand opening of sorts in 2012 of a little less than a kilometre halfway between Platì and the coast.

I wondered if this project could explain the apparent abandonment of the road west of Platì for the new road would have replaced this, albeit with fewer views of the National Park unless they were to be painted on the walls of the proposed six-kilometre tunnel through the mountains.

After lunch I headed south on the old coast road before joining the main highway that runs north-south the length of the eastern seaboard

On the outskirts of Bovalino, sandwiched between road and railway, I passed an apartment block known locally, though not in any official way, as the Paul Getty Apartments, apparently so-called in recognition of the Getty family's involuntary contribution to financing their construction. Still reflecting on the fate of young Paul Getty and his treatment at the hands of the *'ndrangheta*, I turned inland towards their second notorious stronghold in the area, San Luca.

As I approached the town, which I could see nestling in the comforting arms of the Aspromonte foothills, I was trying to recall conversations with Calabrian friends about which town had the worse reputation, Platì or San Luca. The consensus seemed to be San Luca.

San Luca was not as I expected. It was early afternoon and therefore I was not surprised that streets were all but empty. Nevertheless, as in Platì, the few heads that were out and about turned noticeably when they saw a car that was not local. Perhaps they thought I was an under cover member of the Flying Squad?

What did surprise me was that many of the apartments, drab and devoid of character as most were, had balconies festooned in all sorts of greenery, Whatever else transpired here, people seemed fond of their plants and appeared to take a pride in their upkeep, even if the apartment itself was clearly a work-in-progress— unrendered, unpainted, unfinished and, some would say, unlikely ever to be.

Beyond San Luca to the west, tucked away in the lower folds of the Aspromonte's highest peak, Montalto, lies the sanctuary of Santa Maria di Polsi, for centuries a place well-known for its annual festival.

But these days the festival has come under the aegis of the *'ndrangheta* and is yet another example of lines between church and mafia becoming blurred, entangled even, with the former seemingly unable or unwilling to disentangle itself with much determination, still less success.

On my way into San Luca I passed a somewhat battered road sign telling me I was now entering the European Community town of San Luca. I stopped to take a photo for I was more intrigued by the sign underneath which proudly displayed details of San Luca's twinning with the towns of Vallerano in Latium and Cascia in Umbria. This struck me as odd for I could not imagine any other town to knowingly want a twinning arrangement with San Luca. Other than Platì, of course.

Later I checked it all out on the internet. On the official websites of both Vallerano and Cascia I could find no reference to San Luca. On the San Luca website the twinning was mentioned in one short sentence but there is no other information. Curious.

———

As I retraced my steps to the coast and my overnight stopover at Bovalino, I reflected on my madcap drive that day and particularly on Platì and San Luca. I knew that when I returned to Santa Severina and told people where I had been, they would look at me with the sort of disbelief associated with a holiday in Baghdad or Mosul.

Calabrians have grown accustomed to labelling these towns—and others—with the stigma of the *'ndrangheta* and, by default, they gradually evolve into no-go areas and their segregated existence becomes self-perpetuating.

Both Platì and San Luca are in glorious settings, they are in an ancient and magnificent mountain range that is now a National Park. Without the 'mafia' tag both would be bursting at the seams with visitors, bed & breakfasts would be overflowing and that great little restaurant run by Ciccio and Franco in Bovalino, would be chuck-full of happy eaters, laughing and over-indulging … and sharing a bit of the craic in their home-town of Platì.

Without mentioning the mafia directly, Leslie Gardiner, in his 1966 travelogue, *South to Calabria*, reflected on what renowned Calabrian writer, Corrado Alvaro (1918–1956), had to say about the 'permanently sick face' of his native San Luca when he called it a face 'on which sorrow finds no place, because sorrow is its natural expression'.

Alvaro also wrote the following:

"The blackest despair that can take hold of society is the fear that living honesty is futile."

One day, in Platì and San Luca and other mafia strongholds, that fear will pass, but only Calabrians can make this happen.

BRIEF ENCOUNTERS

I was in the habit of visiting places like Platì and San Luca when Kay was visiting family in England but generally my on-the-road encounters were in less extreme and extremist corners of the region.

Also, more often than not, I (and occasionally 'we') encountered some interesting characters and sometimes I got to share a bit of the craic with them in Italian.

———

Lamezia Terme, on the edge of the Tyrrhenian Sea and the western extremity of Calabria's narrow waist, is the custodian of the region's only international airport and a major station on the west-coast line between Rome and Sicily. For many travellers it is the gateway to the toe of Italy.

What most travellers don't realise is that historically there is no such place as Lamezia Terme for it is a toponym, formed in 1968 by the amalgamation of three towns: Nicastro, Sambiase and Sant'Eufémia Lamezia.

I visited Sambiase for the first time by taking a wrong turning so decided I might as well satisfy my curiosity about its name for I knew from reading accounts of some 19th century travellers to Calabria that it used to be called San Biaggio.

The town's narrow streets and alleyways, its *centro storico,* were a cheek-by-jowl hotchpotch of what is, what was and what might have been. I imagined that some of these very houses, still relying on each other to keep upright, were part of the San Biaggio that those earlier travellers experienced. Perhaps the very building where Craufurd Tait Ramage caused such a fuss by just being a foreigner was still hanging on in there:

"Here I wished to dine, but there was no locanda. The shopkeeper, however, of the village undertook to furnish me with dinner, and I tried to get some rest by stretching myself on a hard bench. Meanwhile the inhabitants collected round the door, and jostled each other to get a peep at me. To think of sleep was useless unless I could eject a large body of the inhabitants, who showed much anxiety to question me on many points respecting England. The Thames Tunnel they had heard of, and that seemed to give them a higher idea of the power and riches of England than any fact in her history with which they were acquainted."

(From *The Nooks and by-ways of Italy: Wanderings in search of its ancient remains and modern superstitions*, 1828.)

My imagination was still searching for Ramage's shop-cum-inn, when I happened upon an elderly man sitting outside a featureless house on a rickety, old chair which seemed much older than he was. His tanned and wrinkled face was taking the air, watching the same old, monotonous world go by until, that is, he spotted a new face crossing his domain.

I stopped to greet him, to shake hands and satisfy the unmistakable curiosity in his expression. But I was curious too and asked about the name of the town; I wanted to know when its name had changed from San Biaggio to Sambiase.

Still holding on to my outstretched hand like a lifelong friend, he shook his head as he asserted defiantly that it had always been Sambiase, never been anything else, never heard of it ever being called anything else. When I asked if he'd lived here all his life, he confessed he was, like me, a relative newcomer to the town where he'd lived for more than 50 years but, nevertheless, he repeated his assertion that it had always been Sambiase.

Finally we disengaged and, as it was close to that time of day, I wished him *buon pranzo,* have a good lunch, before continuing uphill where I espied another elderly resident as if expecting me.

This 70-something had falteringly turned the corner out of a narrow alleyway and, using his stick to steady him on one side and the wall of a house on the other, slowly began to descend the uneven surface towards me. His shuffling progress was not helped by backless slippers that seemed determined to assert their independence from his feet.

I guessed he was probably en route to lunch at the home of one of his children, grandchildren even, and would be, I surmised, glad of the respite when I stopped to have a chat. As our eyes met, he straightened up as if to deny any lack of mobility I might have witnessed seconds earlier while blaming it on a new hip that wasn't working properly yet.

"*Piano, piano*," he said, trying to convince himself that there was no need to rush or perhaps entreating me to slow down. Maybe both.

Before I could get a word in edgeways he had already gleaned from my colouring and demeanour that I was indeed a foreigner. No, not German as he thought, but Irish and living in Calabria in Santa Severina (of which he had heard) and, like others before him with a hearing problem, he flirted temporarily with the notion I might be *olandese* rather than *irlandese*. With my pedigree and nationality sorted, it was finally my turn to speak.

I started by confirming that he was indeed a local and had lived in Sambiase *all* his long life. He was and he had. He added, lest I might deem it relevant, that he had once been to Catanzaro. Again, I tried San Biaggio on him as a possible name he may have heard his parents or grandparents use and once again I drew a blank. He was adamant, Sambiase it had always been. Not in fact true, but any latent memory to the effect had long since evaporated.

He continued his faltering descent while I went onwards and upwards, reflecting on the vagaries of life and what my own life might have been had a been born here. I hoped I might have got further than the 40 kilometres to Catanzaro.

On my return ten minutes later, both men were gone, only the chair remained. It was time for lunch; the aromas wafting through the narrow streets told me that, behind closed doors, mothers, daughters, wives and sisters—and even grandmothers—were bringing the pasta to the boil for their menfolk.

—

Undoubtedly the perceived hero of Italy's unification story in the mid-19th century, though many southerners today might be inclined to use the word 'scoundrel' instead, was Giuseppe Garibaldi.

Following the initial flush of success with the unification project, Garibaldi retired to the island of Caprera off the north coast of Sardinia. Two years later, in 1862, frustrated that the Papal States and Rome itself were still not part of a unified Italy, he decided to reprise his previous successes and take matters into his own hands. Assuredly he believed this venture would be a walk in the park compared with 1860.

Once again he landed with a small army of 2000 men in Sicily and then crossed to Mélito in Calabria from where he proceeded north through the Aspromonte mountains, deliberately avoiding towns and villages where he might have come into conflict with the Italian army. What happened next is a cross between an anti-climax and a farce.

In the skirmish that inevitably transpired, Garibaldi was hit three times but only one of these was considered to be serious. The wound—he was shot in the foot—healed eventually but only after several doctors, from several countries, prodded, poked and postured in search of the elusive bullet.

Early one summer I visited the spot in the foothills of the Aspromonte where this unfortunate skirmish put an end to Garibaldi's second foray into Calabria in pursuance of his unification dream, to the place where he was shot in the foot both literally and figuratively, the *Cippo di Garibaldi*.

The *Cippo* (meaning memorial) lies on the western foothills of the Aspromonte mountains and consists of a dead-end clearing in the forest with one fenced-off tree and a small mausoleum nearby which commemorates his exploits. The tree itself, with its large central recess, is where Garibaldi was apparently taken to rest after being shot.

At first it was not easy to picture the events here in August 1862, particularly when the only other people there were a family with three disinterested kids and a young, starry-eyed couple who clearly had other things on their mind. They, it seemed to my warped mind, were more interested in finding the right tree against which to cement their union. In the short time I was there they had tried, and seemingly rejected, two or three. Not that I was watching, you understand.

Of course they might well have been looking for the sunniest spot as the shafts of light penetrating the clearing were indeed spectacular. Then again perhaps they had their sights on that special tree, the one behind the low circular fence, and were just waiting for everyone else to leave them to it. Perhaps they were thinking that being conceived in such an iconic spot would give their firstborn, little Giuseppe or Giuseppina, the perfect start in life.

With difficulty I tried to refocus on my reason for being here, to picture instead in my mind's eye this charismatic, popular and usually victorious Italian hero propped up against that same tree, smoking a cigar, having just been shot in the foot by the army he helped create. Then having to surrender to a detachment of the same army with hundreds of bewildered and red-shirted volunteers swarming over the hillside and jostling for the best view of this historic moment from beside, behind and up trees. And all this following a skirmish that lasted no more than ten minutes with a total of 15 casualties on both sides.

It was then I became aware that the young man waiting his turn by the tree was sporting a red tee-shirt himself which set me wondering whether he had a greater sense for the drama and irony of history than I imagined. Perhaps I had got it all wrong and in their own way they were trying to bond with events here in 1862. ~And who could blame them?

When, to everyone's relief, the family of five finally departed, the couple looked unashamedly happy so I decided to make them suffer a little longer and made a couple of nonchalant visits to and from the car for nothing in particular before finally leaving them to their tree and their unusual sense of history. I knew enough about Garibaldi's private life to feel sure that whatever they got up to in my absence, he would undoubtedly have approved.

When I finally turned the key in the ignition and headed back down into the present, a backward glance told me that I was making two young people very happy. I suspected that, like me, they were not unaware that it was lunchtime and that few Italians would be out and about at this time.

———

Few realise, or care, that the largest and most important sites of ancient Magna Græcia—Greek settlements in southern Italy and Sicily, dating from the 8th and 7th centuries BCE—are concentrated on the eastern seaboard of Calabria, the Ionian Sea: Sybaris, Kroton, Scyllacium, Caulónia and Locri.

On a warm Saturday in February, Kay and I set off from Crotone with our friend Denise for a weekend excursion south along the Ionian coast and a planned walk round the excavations at Locri. After Sybaris, Locri is arguably Magna Græcia's most important archæological site, though these days the town's claim to fame is generally more related to its undignified mafia connections. I should have known things would not go exactly as planned. This was Calabria, after all.

Denise was at the wheel when, unexpectedly, she took an off-road detour just south of Lido di Catanzaro.

"Thought you might like to see this place," she offered by way of explanation, "it's called Roccelletta. I'll call Eugenio, he doesn't live too far away, so he might turn up if he's not still in his pyjamas."

Knowing Eugenio, an ex-colleague of Denise and occasional acquaintance of ours, I knew that the pyjama scenario was a distinct possibility. With Eugenio part of the equation and only an hour into our journey south, I was even more certain that this day was not going to turn out as expected.

Dishevelled, but otherwise fully dressed, Eugenio did indeed turn up just as we finished our walk round the ruins of Roman Scolacium (which sits on top of the, as yet unexcavated, Greek Scyllacium) at Roccelletta. Eugenio convinced us that it would be impertinent to be so close to Squillace and not visit the place where the great Roman statesman, writer and inventor, Cassiodorus was born and to gaze upon the town's impressive Norman castle. He offered to accompany us.

To cut to the denouement: shielding our eyes from the light, we all eventually staggered out of the restaurant next to the closed Squillace Castle a little before 5pm. Everyone, except driver Denise, very much the worse for wear. Some more so than others.

Somehow, somewhere, between Roccelletta and Squillace Castle, our group had swollen in number to eight, all male friends of Eugenio. Essentially this band of genial Calabrian brigands had hijacked us, seduced us with unsolicited hospitality and for almost four hours they oversaw our eating and drinking while offering themselves as the entertainment, in the only restaurant they could find that was open.

I already knew, but at the time it had slipped my mind, that Calabrian gatherings of friends, impromptu or otherwise, are always about the lunch, particularly so at the weekend. My lapse of memory was unforgivable for, a few weeks earlier, I had been to a Calabrian wedding where I thought that the huge buffet in the garden was all there was and tucked in with relish. It was in fact the pre-starter, starter; there were another 18 courses to come at the sit-down event inside. I left, scarcely able to walk, after course nine and went home to bed.

I have no idea who paid for our indulgences at Squillace or, specifically, what we ate other than fish, or how many courses we worked through. I do recall that the extraneous males spent half their time sweet-talking the waitress, and seeking her advice on what we should eat and drink next, there being no menu and no limit to the number of courses we might want to have. The other half the spent trying to outbid each other in how best to woo Denise.

They clearly knew, as did we, that Eugenio's recent advances towards Denise had been rebuked, partly because he was engaged to someone else at the time while still technically married to a third party in another country. With their friend Eugenio's rebuttal to spur them on, each saw it as a personal challenge to do better. Part of their strategy involved ingratiating themselves with Kay and me by speaking in English, praising our Italian and generally setting us up on a pedestal, presumably in the hope that, as Denise's best friends, we would have some role in helping her choose which one was to be her new beau.

When, finally, everyone conceded defeat, vis-a-vis wooing Denise, and our hijacking had run its course, we were let loose to continue our journey.

As we got under way once more, I realised that, after more than six hours on the road, we were still closer to our point of departure, Crotone, than we were to our destination, Locri. That afternoon's planned visit to the Magna Græcia remains of Locri and its new museum was not going to happen.

It was already dark when, exhausted from our indulgences, we finally pulled up outside our bed & breakfast at Locri.

Dinner that evening was a light affair.

Castrovillari lies in the foothills of Calabria's largest mountain range, the Pollino, which straddles the border with neighbouring Basilicata in the north and spans the region almost coast to coast, Tyrrhenian Sea to Ionian Sea. It is the largest town in the area and for centuries was an important staging post for those entering or leaving Calabria across the mountains by way of the only pass at nearby Campo Tenese.

On my first visit there I only planned to stay long enough to get a feel for the place and particularly the older town. I felt especially pleased with myself for having found the only space in a small car-park close to the centre. However, my euphoria was short-lived for, having studied the signs indicating the hourly parking rates, I was unable to locate the ticket-machine. Brandishing my ingrained north-European scruples, I could not possibly leave the car park without paying. In desperation, I accosted a replete shopper returning to her car and asked her what I should do.

She shrugged her shoulders.

"They tried that," she said with a nod towards the hourly price information, "but nobody paid so now they've taken away the ticket-machines. It's free again, like it was before."

Then, as an afterthought, and with a reprised shrug of the shoulders, added: "This is Calabria, you know."

This was not the first time I'd come across a similar story. Generally Calabrians have an aversion to the notion of having to pay to park and sometimes will go to extremes just to save a Euro, or less.

Cheaply parked, I went in search of my mid-morning coffee fix and, no sooner had my bottom hit the seat, shaded from the heat of the late-morning sun by a kerb-side tree, than I was joined by a well-meaning local, sporting his loud, 'I'm-a-lumberjack', checked shirt.

As he proffered me an outstretched hand, he uttered just two words, "Barack Obama.".

I couldn't quite be certain whether or not there was a question mark at the end. Was he introducing himself as Barack Obama or was he wondering if I was called Barack Obama? Or perhaps it was just something he liked saying to people? I finally opted for the last as the name was never mentioned again.

My new best friend was one of Castrovillari's finest 50-somethings and seemed like a man who might be described as not being 'the sharpest pencil in the box'. This often happens to me; I'm not sure how it works exactly but sometimes I feel as if there is a large neon sign hovering above my head which invites those of questionable mental agility to come and talk to me.

He asked me if I might be able to help with lighting his hand-rolled cigarette. I couldn't. Undeterred, he left the table momentarily, found a light elsewhere, and then returned to engage me in meaningless conversation.

He told me how, the minute he saw me, he knew that I was German and, before I could put him straight, dug an even deeper hole for himself by explaining how he used to live in America, in Brooklyn to be specific, and therefore spoke some English but, sadly, not German. When I was finally allowed to explain that I was Irish (and therefore English-speaking) and went through that whole rigmarole that always plagues me of explaining the difference been irlandese (Irish) and olandese (Dutch), his ability to speak English somehow seemed to have evaporated. Except, that is, for the name of the (then) president of the United States.

He went on to explain, in Italian of course, how he'd had to return to Calabria because of a mysterious illness contracted in Brooklyn which had affected his memory which was why he was having difficulty with his English on this particular occasion. He also confessed to feeling homesick for 'la bella Castrovillari'.

Until he spoke, his unshaven look could conceivably have been taken for the latest in designer stubble but the dentally-challenged open mouth, the smoke-haze and the stubble together soon put paid to such a charitable notion. I glanced at my watch and explained that I needed to go to the post office and that there had been a queue there 'earlier' and it was important I get there before it shut. This, I knew, was the perfect Calabrian excuse to get out of such situations for, wherever you might be, it will always be true.

Despite having implied that I had already been there once, he offered to accompany me, to show me where it was. A generous gesture which generated a modicum of guilt even as I said I was fine and knew where it was—which was actually true as I'd spotted the sign to it earlier. I allowed my conscience this small concession having reasoned that my little white lie cancelled out his bigger one about his ability to speak some English. We were well matched.

I walked past the post office not only to confirm that the queue was indeed lengthy and to feel a little less guilty, but also because I knew it was on the way to one of the older parts of town, one which I wanted to explore.

Six months later I was back in Castrovillari, not 'passing through' this time but staying instead at a very pleasant bed & breakfast. Clearly things have changed somewhat since the Irish cleric, Richard Pococke, and his companion found themselves in Castrovillari at the end of their six-day race through Calabria in 1733:

"[We] ascended the hills to a poor town called Castra Villari, where we had no accommodations but an old empty house …"
(From *A description of the East and some other Countries*, 1745)

Settled into my infinitely more salubrious quarters, I went for a walk in the early evening drizzle, to get my bearings and take in the Christmas lights. Imagine my surprise therefore when, passing a small bar, I was unexpectedly pounced on and unceremoniously embraced with a bear hug of joyous recognition and the two words I was least expecting, 'Barack Obama'?

Yes, my new, old friend not only recognised me but he even remembered the password.

Later I did some discrete local research and discovered that 'Carlo' was a man to whom not being 'the sharpest pencil in the box' was not an appropriate epithet. Apparently he had two university degrees which belied his apparent mindless behaviour, itself seemingly the result of being thwarted by the one and only love of his life whom he never got over.

From what I could glean, the 'Barack Obama' part of his repertoire was unique to me.

Long before I moved to Calabria, I read *Stolen Figs: and other Adventures in Calabria*, the story of American Mark Rotello's travels when he revisited his Calabrian roots; since then I had always wanted to visit Tiriolo near Catanzaro.

The appeal of the town was not just its elevated position but that, from the castle-topped hill behind the town, you can see the Ionian Sea in one direction and the Tyrrhenian Sea in the other. It was also a town known for the extravagance of the local peasants' traditional costume, a tradition still important to Tiriolo.

It was a beautiful June morning when I scaled the heights of the castle to take in the views east and west; to gaze down, with no more than a slight twist of the head, at the Ionian and the Tyrrhenian Seas, both of which had, over the years, become a part of my life in different ways.

Having satisfied my curiosity, I descended to the *centro storico* in the hope that I might fulfil the secondary part of my mission that day. It wasn't long before I saw what I was seeking.

I espied two ladies of a certain age sitting and chatting side by side in a wide, sun-facing doorway and made a beeline for them. I was sure these two were from the right generation. They were just who I was looking for and I had something to show them.

Their ageing faces belied the curiosity still in their eyes and I knew they would be completely unfazed by a stranger clutching a sheet of paper intent on interrupting their sunny, Sunday morning routine.

The sheet of paper was a photocopy of a photograph from Eric Whelpton's *Calabria and the Aeolian Island*s; a photo of three young women, taken by Whelpton's wife Barbara, all of whom were wearing the same traditional costume, albeit in black and white, that had clearly enthralled so many travellers to the town.

We exchanged a few pleasantries about the weather before I explained that I was writing a book about Calabria and was interested to know if they knew any of the women in the photograph and, if so, did any still live locally. They told me to hold on, *aspetta*, as, in synchronised unison, they reached down for their handbags and began rummaging around until they located their respective spectacles.

Properly equipped for the task on hand, they scrutinised the photograph. Slowly they studied, pointed, nodded and muttered in the local dialect before looking up to confirm that they could name all three. They were more than a little pleased with themselves; it was as if I had asked them to participate in a game show and they had successfully completed the first round.

This was more than I could have hoped for but, before I could extract any further details, one volunteered some additional information:

"Of course, they're all dead now," she said, matter-of-factly before her friend chipped in.

"All three died very young, just a year or two apart. Such a shame, we were all such good friends. We went to school together."

They rattled off the names of all three as if they'd only been speaking with them the day before yesterday, then paused for breath and looked suitably contrite as if they'd let me down in some way.

For a moment or two they were lost in thoughts and memories that waded back across half a century or more until one refocused on the here and now and became unexpectedly animated; she started waving her hands in recognition.

"I know who you are," she exclaimed with absolute certainly, "you're that writer, the one from America … the one who was born in … in …"

Still getting over the shock that they should have thought I actually had Calabrian roots, I helped out.

"… in Gimigliano?" I suggested.

"That's the place, Gimigliano … up there in the mountains." Lest I might be disorientated, she flicked her head a little to the left to convey the general whereabouts of Gimigliano.

"Mark Rotella." My response was more of a statement than a question.

"Yes, yes, Rotella … of course, I remember now … the Rotella family from Gimigliano … you're the one from America who writes the books, aren't you?"

I hated to disappoint two of Mark Rotella's devoted fans but I had to admit that I was not he … but that I knew who they meant and had read and enjoyed his book about Calabria. Indeed I also had to confess that I might never have come here to this town had it not been for his *Stolen Figs*.

It was Mark Rotella's description of Tiriolo that, ten years earlier, had put this small hilltop town, not far from Catanzaro, at the top of my must-visit places in Calabria.

I was disappointed that I had not been able to talk to one of those three women in the photo for I had hoped to find out a little about Eric Whelpton. Still, I think I gave two ladies of a certain age something to talk about that day.

—

On the evening of the day when I had visited both Platì and San Luca, I ate at a small restaurant in Bovalino, the domain of two young men from Platì, Franco and Ciccio, who could not possibly have created the same ambience in their home, *'ndrangheta*-infested, town. My words, not theirs.

That evening, a Friday, it was packed to the gunwales and so I thought it prudent to book for the following evening. When I arrived promptly at eight, I had the whole place to myself: when I left at two in the morning, I was still the only paying customer in the building.

I really did try to leave several times before Saturday became Sunday/ I was feeling guilty that I was taking up a table for two on a busy evening when groups who hadn't booked were being turned away.

I got up several times and indicated that there were people

waiting to be seated but each time I was told to sit and not to worry.

"*Non ti preoccupare*," my genial hosts, Franco and Ciccio, would tell me as they kept me topped up with another glass of their gorgeous house red wine and explained that those waiting for tables were all groups of four or more and that my table in the corner only seated one comfortably and two at a pinch. I decided finally to do as I was bid, to focus on the wine and nothing else.

Then, somehow, I found myself sharing a bit of the craic with my neighbours, a large eccentric, birthday-celebrating family which seemed to possess a degree of fluidity; not only did they keep changing places but even the people changed, some disappeared, others occupied the vacant chair. They were amused to have an English-speaking, token Calabrian from Ireland, at the next table and made sure my glass was always full as all the inter-familial relationships were explained to me … they clearly thought I still had the capacity to remember them.

As they got up to leave, I tagged along behind and almost got as far as the cash-desk but, being the last in the line, I got chatting to a family of latecomers just finishing their meal at a table close to the door.

This foursome, two adults—he Calabrian, she Brazilian and living in Rome—and their super-intelligent children, one girl, one boy, were all keen to practise their English and invited me to join them for a last *liquore*, or two, or maybe it was three. After all, we were all emigrants and immigrants of one kind or another and had lots of stories to share.

It was now well past midnight and when my international friends got up to leave, I followed suit. Out of the corner of my eye I could see that the staff, glad finally to see the back of us, had already started to prepare a long table for their own after-work feast.

This time I did actually manage to get as far as the cash-desk and settled my account. The hard and dangerous sorted, I was denied those final few steps into the outside world by Ciccio (or maybe it was Franco) and escorted instead back into the restaurant where a place had been laid for me at the staff's table where, within minutes, a piping hot seafood spaghetti and a carafe or two of red wine appeared. I didn't have the mental capacity to argue and, besides, it was getting on for five hours since I had eaten. And I was hungry.

Somehow, with faltering steps, I managed to locate my bed & breakfast. It was gone 2:30am when I eventually crawled into bed, desperately trying to cling on to fond flashbacks of my several memorable meals while anticipating the reality of a 175-kilometre drive back to Santa Severina later that morning.

VISITORS

On our first visit to Italy back in 1999, Kay and I passed through the town of Cortona in Tuscany. This was an intentional visit to the town near which was the home of Frances Mayes, author of *Under the Tuscan Sun* which we had both recently read. We were not planning to pop in to share a bit of the Tuscan craic, just being in the area was sufficient to put the book in some sort of perspective. And, in any case, the ambience of the book and 'popping in' did not immediately seem mutually inclusive.

Over a decade later, and having myself penned a few words about travelling in Italy and living in Calabria, there did not appear to be the same constraints on my readership and many not only came to Santa Severina but also felt they could indeed pop in. And they were right to do so for we met many interesting people that way—some of whom just literally turned up at the door, some of whom introduced themselves first in an exploratory email- and many lasting friendships ensued.

It was mostly Americans who did the popping in, but there were also British, Irish, Romanians and Poles who dropped by and we shared many good times together. Two couples—one American, one Irish—went above and beyond the call of duty and each stayed a week or more at Le Puzelle, the *agriturismo* where our own Calabrian adventures began.

———

In 2014 a feisty American couple, Deane and Mary Logan who

hailed from Salem in northern Oregon and who, having read about what an hospitable place Santa Severina was, decided that a stopover at Le Puzelle in late October was the perfect way to spend part of their two-month vacation in Europe. Perhaps there would be a bonus and someone at Le Puzelle might reveal the whereabouts of whoever was responsible for the seductive words that brought them this far south in the first place. Or they could have just wanted their money back.

At Le Puzelle it was Giuliano, who spoke enough English to spill the beans and reveal my location. I arranged to meet Deane and Mary at Sant'Antonio's, then a small restaurant-cum-pizzeria in the lower town.

So began a friendship between Deane and me in particular based on a shared sense of humour, liberally peppered with mutual verbal abuse, that lasted beyond the ten days they stayed in Santa Severina. Later he described our first meeting with characteristic, good-natured, acerbity:

"I don't know why, but I pictured in my mind that you probably looked like a Darragh McKeon or Daniel Seery," he mused as he threw the names of two more worthy Irish wordsmiths into the mix.

"But, hey, leprechaun-ish is okay too," he added.

Despite their advanced years, Deane and Mary were in good shape; we shared a passion for travelling, discovering and experiencing new places and taking risks.

In the risk-taking department they had opted to spend ten days in a small town that was scarcely a preeminent destination for travellers in the summer. They were Le Puzelle's only clients at the time. They had no Italian other than of the basic meet, greet and eat variety. They were, however, aware that Santa Severina had at least two English-speaking residents but had no idea whether or not they might be 'in residence'.

In other words they had done the sort of thing I might well have done myself but which, at the time, I wrongly surmised that I would not be doing at their age. Yet here I am.

I admired their attitude immensely and spent several evenings with them, usually at Carlo's bar and Sant'Antonio's, at the time owned by the multi-talented Enzo Gerardi.

Deane and Mary had inadvertently arranged their Calabrian vacation at the cusp of the olive harvest. Le Puzelle's acreage included several hundred olive trees and Deane who; like me, had an interest in such things, offered to lend a hand. As the crates of olives were being loaded onto a trailer attached to a pick-up, Vincenzo, asked Deane if he would like to come to the nearby olive-press to see the next part of the process, the pressing of the olives. The linguistic intermediary in this conversation was Le Puzelle's Giuliano who suggested that Deane follow the pick-up in his car.

Enthused by the prospect, Deane took a moment to explain to Mary where he was going, got into his car and then realised that Vincenzo and Giuliano had already turned onto the main road, though he couldn't be sure whether they had turned left or right. It seems that nobody had thought to share this piece of vital information or, if they did, Deane had not understood. When he got to the main road himself he decided to turn right for no other reason than it was the way he knew best and involved passing through the lower town which might have slowed up the pick-up and its trailer.

By the time he reached Sant'Antonio's, Deane realised that he had lost them and had absolutely no idea where the olive pressing plant might be, apart from out of town. But all was not lost, for he did recognise Sant'Antonio's and decided to pull into the car park and see if anybody had enough English to point him in the right direction. As luck would have it Enzo Gerardi was just getting out of his car and stopped to shake Deane's hand in recognition.

Later that evening, as the four of us ate at Sant'Antonio's, between bouts of hysterical laughter from all sides, we were privy to two versions of what happened next: one in English from Deane and one in Italian from Enzo. Their stories were remarkably similar given that neither had a clue what the other was talking about until Enzo thought he understood what Deane wanted and Deane thought that Enzo was on the case. What follows is the abbreviated version.

Though pronounced slightly differently, there are two words common enough to both languages: olive and olio. It was the latter that Deane kept repeating as he pressed his hands together to simulate the crushing of an imaginary olive in an effort to get over to Enzo that he wanted to find where the olives were pressed to become oil. Finally Enzo raised a knowing finger, an indication that he finally understood what Deane wanted. Or thought he did.

"Aspetta," he said, finger still in penny-having-dropped mode, "aspetta," he repeated on the assumption that Deane knew that this meant 'hold on a minute, wait here'.

Now tapping his cranium with the same finger, Enzo got into his car and with a final, "*Due minuti*," drove out of the car park.

Deane waited, unaware that the likelihood of hell freezing over was a surer bet than to expect the return of Enzo in two minutes.

A man on a mission, Enzo shot past the the local *supermercato*, did a U-turn and parked outside. He rushed in and scoured the shelves looking for the olives he was sure Deane wanted. He was not used to shopping for groceries and even when he found them, he didn't realise there were so many types: black and green, stones in and stones out, stuffed and not stuffed, normal-sized Italian and giant-sized Greek, freshly-bagged from the deli or in a jar or even a tin.

He opted for a large tray of green olives, stones in, from the deli counter, queued at the only check-out, paid and returned to the car park, to where Deane was eagerly awaiting the directions to the oil-press he was expecting Enzo would have for him.

Enzo screeched to a halt and, beaming the beam of someone who has helped his new American friend with the passion for olives, presented Deane with his purchase. And, lest Deane offered to pay, he immediately made it clear that the tray of olives was a gift.

Deane tried to rise above the realisation that Enzo had not understood a single word and, despite being touched by the kindness and resolve of someone whom he'd met only once before, couldn't stop himself from laughing. Enzo, realising he'd not got the right end of the stick after all, joined in with the laughter. He had done his utmost to help and Deane who, thanking him profusely for his trouble and still clutching his olives, got back in his car and headed up the hill back towards Le Puzelle.

But Deane was not one for quitting and, passing another small pizzeria-cum-bar overflowing with elderly beer-drinking locals, decided to try one more time. Even with a tray of the real things as a visual aid, mashing another imaginary olive between his hands had even less effect on Deane's new friends and, when they'd finished laughing at his antics, somehow persuaded him to take a seat and join them for a beer instead.

When, finally, Enzo heard Deane's side of the story and Deane heard Enzo's, and the laughter abated, Calabrian and American embraced in mutual respect and genuine affection.

But Deane had one final revelation. He found out later that the pick-up and its trailer had turned left out of Le Puzelle, and not right as Deane had thought. When Deane didn't follow immediately, they had parked up around the corner to wait for him to catch up. In the end they gave up and pressed on; by which time Deane and Enzo were already bonding and exchanging hand-gestures in the car park.

———

Paddy and Yvonne Fay were the first, and last, Irish visitors to descend on Calabria in search of their favourite author; such a shame they found me instead.

They too were staying at Le Puzelle and once again Giuliano acted as go-between and we arranged to meet for an aperitivo in the square, just the three of us as Kay was in England. Three litres of wine and three pizzas later, our bonding for the day having run its course, we parted company though not without making arrangements to do it all again the next night … and maybe even the next …

A couple of days into our bonding programme, I received an agitated call from Paddy. He had been negotiating a roundabout in Crotone when another car ran into the back of their hire-car. From experience, I knew that Calabrians generally did not really 'get' roundabouts; at the time they were a relatively new concept and mishaps were all too frequent on or near them. Ironically, Paddy had earlier shared with me how, after only a few hours in Calabria, he had already abandoned his preconceived notions about the Italian driving psyche.

"Nothing prepares you for Calabria," he said shaking his head, "whatever you think about Italian driving, it's nothing like the Calabrian experience. It's madness and mayhem on wheels."

I remember gently challenging Paddy's perception, but then I did so in the knowledge that I was now part of the problem; behind the wheel I had gone native and now drove like a Calabrian … except on roundabouts of course where my northern-European discipline automatically kicked in.

Stuck on his roundabout, and knowing that it was not his fault, Paddy was nonetheless worried that he would be 'shafted', particularly as the woman involved had immediately called her husband who arrived within minutes in his own car. If there was a bright side, it was that the husband spoke a little English.

"Where are you?" I asked. Paddy didn't know for certain but from his description I guessed he was at the large roundabout on the outskirts of town.

"It would take me at least 25 minutes to get there. Better if I give my friend Denise a call, she doesn't live far away and, if she can get to you, she'll help with the language. Her English is excellent."

I called Denise and left a message on her mobile; it was just as well she was busy teaching for I later discovered that I would have directed her to the wrong roundabout.

While I was debating whether or not I should head for Crotone myself, Paddy was busy assuaging his 'being shafted' fears by taking photos of the damage to his car's bumper as well as the number-plate (the targa, in Italian) of the car that had hit him. Aware that he was probably getting the linguistic runaround, he called me again.

"I'm sure I'm being shafted, there's a lot of talking, pointing and arm waving that I just don't understand. Can you talk to the husband and see if you can make sense of it all?"

I agreed, but first I asked Paddy if the husband knew what he did for a living. Paddy sounded puzzled but nevertheless humoured me and confirmed that telling his nemesis that he was an electrician from Drogheda wasn't the first thing he'd thought of mentioning.

I spoke to the husband for a few moments and will take up the story from Paddy's perspective at the scene of the accident.

Paddy was aware that, following our brief conversation, everything at his end changed. Voices were lowered, hand gestures were more conciliatory. The husband made a call and, in broken English, asked Paddy to follow him.

"Everything okay," he said, "No problem, the car is repaired for you. But you not to keep photo of targa, okay?" he said, pointing at the number-plate and Paddy's phone, "you must delete photo."

Paddy nodded in suspicious agreement as he and Yvonne got into their car and followed their new best friend to a street in Crotone bursting at the seams with panel-beaters. They pulled up outside one and Paddy, after confirming that he would not be expected to pay for any work, watched in awe as the car's rear bumper was transformed to how it had looked when he picked up the car at the airport.

During the couple of hours that the work took, Paddy called me to explain that things were now looking much brighter and that they would soon be back in Santa Severina at no extra cost.

"What exactly did you say to the guy? he asked, "whatever it was, it certainly changed things here. He not only started to smile at me, he even slapped me on the shoulder like an old friend."

"Well," I explained, "you have to understand that Italians are completely obsessed with titles, even when you meet a doctor or dentist socially, you are still expected to call him or her Dottore this or Dottoressa that. I just invented a new official title for you and called you Avvocato Fay which, from the husband's point of view, meant you were a lawyer. I never said you were a lawyer, I just kept saying the word Avvocato before your surname, as any Italian would, and left the rest to his imagination. That's why I asked you if he knew you were an electrician; Elettricista Fay doesn't have the same resonance.

"Basically I expected him to be shit-scared in case you were a razor-sharp Irish lawyer and would take him to the cleaners if he tried any funny business. Seems to have worked.

"And, by the way, he's preoccupied with that photo you took of his number-plate and wants you to delete it. Keep him on his toes and don't do it just yet."

That evening, back at Sant'Antonio's, the pizzas and the red wine were on Paddy Fay, the born-again Avvocato and the most unlikely looking lawyer—long hair, long beard and tattoo-covered legs—in the known universe. I imagined how his nemesis in Crotone took one look at Paddy and thought, *if this guy's a lawyer and looks like this, he must be a bloody good lawyer*.

The craic cost nothing.

THE TALE OF THE TAIL

It was in preparation for that first visit to Apulia, Italy's heel, that I read a book by Charles Lister, the retired BBC radio announcer who was once famously reprimanded by his superior for wearing yellow socks on air.

Lister's *Heel to Toe: Encounters in the South of Italy* was also about his travels in Calabria but, at that time, that part of his journey interested me less. It was some years later before I reread the description of his visit to what was now my home town of Santa Severina.

Charles Lister's adventure began on a bicycle in Apulia and ended in Calabria by which time he had been gifted a moped which he called AB; the capricious AB was long past its sell-by date when he approached lofty Santa Severina.

Lister and AB were at the point where the already gentle climb becomes more seriously steep before, through four hairpin bends, it ascends to the town's *centro storico*, over 1000 feet above sea level. Eventually he made it to the top; sadly AB didn't. These are the bare bones of what happened.

Clearly AB didn't like the look of the climb up to Santa Severina and gave up the ghost on the lower slopes. There was nothing else for it but to get off and push which Charles found hard and agonising; only possible in short bursts interspersed with long, panting rests. He considered abandoning AB but was concerned it might get 'nicked'.

Finally he passed a house where a woman came out to watch. He asked her for directions to the castle and was given the meaningless Italian distance of *due passi,* literally two paces, which he knew could mean anything between 500 yards and a mile.

When he asked if he could leave AB with her, the woman nodded and gave him a glass of wine 'as black as squid's ink'. He sat on her wall, drank the wine, and gradually felt more able to face the trek up to the castle.

A sinuous kilometre later, Lister had reached the top and was more than a little impressed with the Norman castle; equally appealing was the 'little village' atmosphere he experienced in the town's square, between the castle and the church.

When I first read his account, before I came to know Santa Severina, I tried to imagine the scene and wondered whether the story about the temporary demise of AB was perhaps a little exaggerated. One of the problems was that I could find no date to hang it on.

There is the publication date of the book—2002—but no indication within the text as to when Lister actually was in Calabria. I got the impression that it was quite some time before the book was published, perhaps a decade or more. I knew most of the houses up the hill to the town as I had often walked it and I also suspected that the woman involved may well have passed away and that most of the houses were now probably occupied by younger families.

Eventually I caught up with Charles Lister himself and at first he too was vague about exactly when he travelled and at the time his notes were in out-of-the-way places. His recollections of the trip were no more precise than 'the early '90s' and I felt it would be ungallant to push him.

From the things he did remember and his description of arriving at Santa Severina, I began to piece together the story from my knowledge of the town. I realised, for example that he had approached it from Crotone on the old road, now a long-abandoned route, though just about negotiable by those with masochistic tendencies and good posterior suspension.

Then, out of the blue, he sent me a detailed extract from his craic- and expletive-ridden notes which not only confirmed my instincts about when he actually was here, but was even more precise than I could have expected. Charles Lister, in his own words 'a panting paralytic', climbed the hill to Santa Severina's Norman castle on 27 April, 1992, the same day on which he managed to exert grievous bodily harm on one of the town's artefacts.

In the square, Charles encountered some children who acknowledged his 'Englishness' by barracking him with the only two words in English they knew: 'Manchester United'. Charles was not to know that, at the time, French taught in local schools.

As he crossed the square to enter the cathedral he was sure that the 'lady of the wine', the woman guarding AB, had come up to the square and followed him into the church. Just inside the door there was what Lister called a 'large wooden model of a dragon' over which he ran a curious hand; a heavier hand than he thought for its long serpentine tail broke off at the bottom in a shower of woodworm dust.

Thinking out of the box, Charles looked round, found some notices about forthcoming services which he rolled up and used to stuff into the tail's open fundament, and the other end into the tail itself. To all intents and purposes, the 'dragon' was almost as good as new.

When Charles retold me the story he assumed it was the woman supposedly looking after AB who was the none-too-pleased witness to his mutilation of one of the church's prize artefacts. Nevertheless, her sense of conviviality appeared to have got the better of her and, when he returned to the lower town to retrieve AB, she invited him in and he was shown typical Calabrian hospitality. Fed, watered and revitalised and clutching a bottle of the family's blood-red wine, a happier Charles Lister returned to Crotone.

I knew I couldn't leave it there. Charles' exploits in Santa Severina left me with at least two loose ends: I wanted to find the woman and the family who helped him, to hear their side of the same story and to locate the 'dragon' he had inadvertently mutilated in the church.

I knew that what he described as the dragon 'model' was no longer in the church and assumed it was one of the artefacts, along with others from the several now-defunct, local churches, that had found a new home in the adjacent Diocesan Museum. Was it, I wondered, initially moved for repair?

In the Diocesan Museum, with curator Raffaela as my guide, it didn't take me long to find the statue of the Archangel Michael slaying Satan. Though Charles Lister refers to it as a dragon in his book, his notes use the phrase 'serpent Devil' and, in some depictions of the same myth, Satan is represented by a dragon or a dragon-cum-devil. And here it was, before my very eyes and, it appeared, with its lengthy, serpentine tail in one piece.

Starting at the tail's forked extremity I started running my hand down its smooth, black form until I reached the point where it might have appeared to the innocent bystander that I was taking an unhealthy interest in Satan's anatomy. And it was at that point I felt something, a definite break in the hitherto smooth surface.

I bent down to take a closer look and there was no mistaking it, there had been some sort of breakage and, though everything appeared to have been put back together again and—possibly because it was in a place not generally seen by only the most curious of visitors—the break had never been 'tidied up'. Not even a lick of paint to disguise where there were definite, rough, white edges and a slight, uneven gap that clearly defined some previous mishap.

I could not be sure whether or not Charles' makeshift repair was still in situ, whether or not the two halves of Satan's tail were still held together by 1992's 'notices about forthcoming services'. Difficult though it was, I somehow resisted the temptation to investigate further.

On the other hand, I couldn't resist sharing the tale of the tail—if only to explain my uncharacteristic interest in devil-slaying folk— to Raffaela. She was unaware that the tail had ever been damaged, even when I pointed it out to her, nor did she know when or why the artefact had been moved.

Assuming that Raffaela had understood my rudimentary Italian, it seemed that only we two—and perhaps an, as yet unknown, local family—knew the full, sordid story of the tail-breaking English traveller. Naturally, the first person with whom I shared this hands-on evidence was Charles Lister himself by sending him photographic evidence of his vandalism.

———

There remained one final quest, the mystery of that family, and in particular the woman, who helped him that day. Charles, initially perplexed as to why I should even be interested in his tale of the tail, had been seduced by the thrill of the chase and was now as keen as I was that I should find the family. And besides, he wanted to pass on his heartfelt thanks once again.

Soon several of my friends were on the case but every lead drew a blank until Charles himself dredged up another clue from the recesses of his memory.

He recalled that the family had a daughter, 'a 17 year-old flame-haired beauty' who spoke to him about performing in the Greek tragedy, *Andromeda,* the following month in the castle. I was now looking for a family who, in 1992, had a daughter finishing off her education at the Liceo, Santa Severina's high school which also served other local towns and villages.

When I shared this new information with my teacher friend and neighbour, Silvana, she spoke with a colleague at the Liceo and together they found a copy of the poster for the 1992 performance of *Andromeda*. Her accompanying note was brief and to the point:

"*Sicuramente era Elisa Tigano.*" (It was definitely Elisa Tigano.)

In *Andromeda* Elisa Tigano played Corifea, the leader of the chorus and was, it seemed, the sole member of the named cast on the poster who came from Santa Severina.

Meanwhile, Charles was still doing his bit and, clearly inspired by what I was up to in Santa Severina, told me he had now come across some 'slides' of his visit but added that, due to his lack of technological know-how, getting them to me might prove problematic or, as he put it, 'If I know how to get two or three to S. Sev attached to a pigeon you might be amused.'

The pigeon was not required for shortly afterwards I received another email with four colour photos attached: three were of the castle and, posing outside their home, one the family who helped him: father, mother and daughter.

I printed off a copy to show Silvana fully expecting her to confirm it was Eliza Tigano and her parents. It wasn't but Silvana recognised them nonetheless.

"That's the Verzino family; they live down the bottom, the last house out of town on the old road" she said with certainty, "… I wonder why her name wasn't on the poster?"

The next morning I rang the bell of the last house as you exit Santa Severina on the old road to Crotone. A woman appeared on a first floor balcony; I asked her if this is where the Verzino family lived. She nodded and with that same nod asked me what I wanted—I was clearly getting better at deciphering Calabrian hand and head gestures.

I held up the photo like some hopeful Romeo and asked my Juliet if this was her family. She leaned down to take a closer look but I could see she wasn't sure though clearly my gestures were saying 'trust me' for she told me to wait a moment and she'd come down.

Maria Salerno—whom I had already recognised as an older incarnation of the woman in the photo—was scrutinising the photo as I told her how I'd come by it. I told her the story of the weary English traveller who came this way almost a quarter of a century earlier, the man who took the photo, the man who left his moped at her house, the man who drank her wine.

"Yes, yes," she said, her gaze still riveted on the photo as the memories flowed back across the years, "I remember him, his scooter had broken down. He left it here and went up to the town, he wanted to see the castle."

She handed me back the photo though I could see its image was still clearly fixed in her mind's eye.

"My daughter is thinner now," she said as if I were some itinerant suitor.

I returned the photo to her and told her it was hers to keep.

As we were talking, a pick-up truck pulled into the driveway and the man who got out, Maria's husband, was clearly the same man in Charles' photo. Apart from the loss of a few teeth, he had scarcely changed.

Upstairs in the kitchen, Maria, Vincenzo and I went over the story again. I listened as they elaborated on the detail and I knew I had finally found the 'lady of the wine'.

Within minutes I was downing a refreshing beer, experiencing first-hand the kind of hospitality Charles had encountered in the same house all those years ago.

Both Maria and Vincenzo beamed when I told them how Charles had described their wine, 'as black as squid's ink'; better still Vincenzo sprang into action and produced a five-litre demijohn as if he'd been waiting for just such an occasion to show it off. As he poured me a small glass, he explained that he wasn't being mean but that this brew was just as potent as the one back in 1992. But, he explained as he filled a plastic two-litre bottle, if I liked, I could take some home with me.

Vincenzo and Maria had three children, two were married and lived away, only the girl in the photo, their daughter Anna Maria, still lived at home though that day she was at work as a teacher in a nearby town.

As it was nearing lunchtime, and I could see that Maria's gaze was increasingly focussing on whatever was bubbling away on the stove, I suggested we reconvene early one evening when Anna Maria was at home. I said I would bring Charles' book with me and try to translate the relevant pages. I had yet to tell Maria that he called her the 'lady of the wine'.

Clutching my bottle of as-black-as-squid's-ink wine and a bag of fresh eggs, I headed home satisfied that I'd been able to find the family who helped Charles Lister. In my mind there remained just a couple of loose ends but I was sure that, when we met again, Anna Maria would help resolve those.

Meeting Anna Maria was a revelation; a sharp, erudite and engaging young woman who recalled the details of Charles Lister's visit as if it were yesterday. Together we cleared up the question of the poster for *Andromeda*.

Anna Maria was part of *Andromeda*'s chorus and she had the photos to prove it. At first she wasn't sure how her name came to be omitted from the poster until, that is, I put on my graphic designer's hat.

In 1992, when the poster was created, I was a graphic designer and I imagine that the technology for adjusting type to fit into a given space was probably in its infancy in Italy, given that it was only a few years older in the UK and America. Thus, whoever created the Andromeda poster was using the basic typographic technology of the time and decided it was easier to omit the name of the last member of the chorus—Verzino—as it would have created an extra, and very short, line of text.

When we talked about the woman who apparently witnessed Charles' act of vandalism on the devil in the church, neither Anna Maria nor her mother remembered seeing him do the deed though it was Anna Maria who followed him up to the square, not her mother.

Before we left, I revealed to Maria that Charles had called her 'the lady of the wine', a nickname she clearly relished. Mention of the red nectar prompted Vincenzo to spring into action and he disappeared momentarily and returned clutching yet another bottle of the very same, yet another bag of eggs and a bag of fresh broad beans. All bounty from the land around the Verzino home and, just as in 1992, shared with a traveller.

ARRIVEDERCI CALABRIA ...

One evening during our first summer living in Santa Severina, I was walking with my friend Guiliano by the open-air theatre behind the castle. We were sharing of bit of Irish-Romanian-Italian craic.

We wandered over to the railing that looked down on the lights of the lower town and I started to pick out landmarks, places I knew by day but had never seen at night. Giuliano lit up a cigarette and I watched the smoke drift down into the blackness below and the lights beyond. In melancholy mood I broke our few moments of silence.

I don't recall whether I was speaking to Giuliano or talking to myself when I said, "I have just realised that this is where I will die."

Not a particularly profound statement, nearer to stating the obvious as, at the time, I knew of no reason why I would ever move away from this place. It was no more than something which had just occurred to me and, as such, indicated a distinct shift in my life ... and, I suppose, my death.

It threw Giuliano; he didn't know what, if anything, he should say. In silence he rested his hand on my shoulder and probably put my melancholy down to a surfeit of red wine; of course he could have been right.

On reflection, as neither of us was speaking in our native tongue, perhaps something got lost in translation and he wondered whether I was about to throw myself off the edge.

As I said, not a particularly profound statement and, as it turned out, also erroneous.

Until early 2017 I had no reason to doubt those impromptu musings from eight years earlier as I marvelled at the beauty of my surroundings and how fortunate I was to live there.

Ironically, just a few months earlier, Kay and I had been to visit Italy's latest—and Calabria's first—crematorium near Cosenza. For eight years I had mapped the progress of Italy's crematoria as they gradually filtered south until, finally, Calabria had its very own. Following our visit we were planning to make sure that our local, part-time undertaker, and full-time grocer, was aware of our intentions in this respect.

Never had I felt as at home as I did living in Santa Severina. That November, thanks to my friend Denise Milone, my *Thank you Uncle Sam* was given an Italian voice as *La Calabria in America* and was launched in that same castle; for me a memorable occasion and an event that many of my fellow Santa Severinese were as proud of and moved by as I was.

At the time I could not have imagined that, in less than four months, Kay and I would be guests of honour at another such function when, in the Comune, the Town Hall, the same people would gather to wish us *buon viaggio* and *buona fortuna* as we prepared to leave for a new life in Ireland.

———

In early December, just a few days after the launch of *La Calabria in America*, we were eating with four friends in Crotone. Both couples—Calabrians Denise and Massimo and Romanians Laura and Stefan—were essentially our friends and, though everyone had met each other before, this was the first time we had all eaten together.

Kay and I had some news to share for it was earlier that same day that we finalised arrangements to house-sit for two months, January and February, for Caroline and Mick in Galway; we had already booked our flights out for New Year's Day.

Unknown to all of us, as we placed our orders, everyone had some news to share.

Denise and Massimo set the ball rolling: in early January Massimo was to take up a new job with Vodafone in Dublin and Denise would be joining him there but not until the end of the school year in June. Being alone for nearly six months, she was looking forward to seeing more of Kay and me.

Our news unintentionally put a damper on that. For Denise, our plans were more akin to a bombshell as we had just arranged to be in Ireland for the first two months of the new year while she was alone in Crotone.

Laura and Stefan had two bits of news: the possibility of a move to Milan some time the following year because of Laura's work; and they had just booked a holiday in August ... in Dublin.

At that time, none of us could have foreseen that the next time we six would all be sitting around the same table, would be almost nine months later when Laura and Stefan came to Dublin on holiday.

I have already described the bare bones of what happened when we stayed in Galway for two months and how the idea of a permanent move to Ireland slowly germinated; how we discounted Galway (though we both were very fond of it); and how, after a few false starts, looking at possible homes in Wexford and Roscrea, we stumbled upon Ennis.

While we were staying in Galway I had a short email conversation with a friend from Santa Severina, now living in England, who was curious about Ireland and my relationship with it. Until recently, Klizia, like many Europeans, classified people like me under the heading 'English'; and even if I insisted I was Irish, in their next breath, chances were that I would have become 'English' again. Perhaps if I hadn't lived in England for such a long time, or didn't speak English, albeit with a trace of a northern Irish accent, people might have got there quicker.

In Santa Severina we were known as *gli inglesi*, the English; visitors to the town who wanted to find us could do so in moments as we were its sole 'English' residents. It took eight years for some people to correct themselves in my company and acknowledge my

Irishness. Of course, it was all very light-hearted, nobody was ever seriously admonished for getting it wrong; it wasn't a hanging offence.

Nevertheless, my conversation with Klizia set me thinking about this relationship with Ireland that was so special to me.

Increasingly, as we prepared to make the move to Ireland, there was, for me, this one other defining emotion that began to take precedence for, though I considered myself Irish, I had never lived in Ireland, the country as opposed to the island.

I had lived in Northern Ireland for over 20 years.

I had lived in Germany for nearly three months.

I had lived in various parts of England for 42 years.

I had lived in Calabria for eight and a half years.

I had never lived in Ireland, the Republic of Ireland, the country which issued my passport; the place, above all others, with which I felt and voiced an affinity.

Apart from summer holidays in Dun Laoghaire, Dalkey and Brittas Bay as a teenager, I had waited until my early 70s to experience life in Ireland—by looking after someone else's house in Galway.

I can truly say that the fictional Jack Taylor and his Galway exploits changed my life, as did having Caroline and Mick as my Airbnb hosts when I went to stay there.

Having made the decision to move from Santa Severina to Ennis, from the toe of Italy's boot to the west of Ireland, one of the longest journey you can make in Europe, there were several hurdles to overcome, the most difficult of which was how we would explain to our fellow Santa Severinese, and in particular our dear friend, Silvana Gerardi, whose house we rented, why we were leaving.

Still in Galway, this was constantly on our minds, but we had to focus on what had to be done in the three weeks from when we found the house in Ennis and the day Caroline and Mick returned from their Australian adventure.

We signed a two-year tenancy agreement.

We opened an Irish bank account.

We arranged an internet connection for when we returned.

We arranged to have the electricity registered in our names.

We booked flights back to Calabria and return flights to Ireland.

We made an appointment for the day after we returned to Ennis to obtain our Irish PPS Number—Personal Public Service Number and the gateway to other services.

We received tenders from the few removal companies who were prepared to move our worldly goods in a van over 3300 kilometres. We chose one.

We arranged for some items, like Irish three-pin plugs, rolls of reinforced tape and an electric kettle, to be delivered to Belfast and my son Kieron delivered them to us in Galway.

We bought and delivered bedding, some cutlery, two plates and two wine glasses and a bottle of red wine to the house in Ennis. We would be arriving there a couple of days before our belongings so we needed some basics in the house to tide us over.

We ordered cardboard packing cases online for delivery to Santa Severina when we got back there.

The day after Caroline and Mick returned from Australia, we flew to London and then on to Calabria the next morning; it was 3 March.

We gave ourselves 16 days to pack and vacate; the removal van would arrive on Sunday 19 March; we would spend one night at the *agriturismo* where we stayed when we first came to Santa Severina in 2006; we would fly to London the next day and then on to Shannon where we would catch the bus to Ennis.

We would walk to our new home and open that bottle of red wine we'd left on the kitchen table at the end of February.

Tired from an early start to catch the dawn flight to Lamezia Terme in Calabria, we arrived back in Santa Severina at lunchtime Friday. As it happened our friend Laura was departing from Lamezia around the same time as we were arriving and, after a quick flurry of hugs and kisses in Arrivals, we hopped into her taxi to take us home. The next time we saw Laura was six months later in Dublin.

Back in Santa Severina, our priority was seeing Silvana, first to soften her up with her present of Irish fudge which she had become addicted to over the years, and then to break the news to her.

She was stunned, speechless; there was much hugging and many tears. She said she knew it might happen one day, she just wasn't expecting it then.

We asked Silvana to keep things under her hat overnight for there were some others we wanted to tell personally rather than let them hear via the razor-sharp Santa Severina grapevine.

Before we left, it never occurred to us to ask her if she had a hair appointment that afternoon, that well-trodden path for the dissemination of 'don't-tell-anyone-else' information and gossip; unfortunately she had.

We ate with Denise that evening and discussed her part in our plans. Her crucial role would be to come to Santa Severina on her day off and, with the relevant account details to hand, call all the services—gas, electricity, internet, phone—to find out how and when to cancel our contracts; much easier for a native Italian speaker to organise.

Also, if our experience with cancelling our Sky contract a year earlier was anything to go by, we suspected none of it would be straightforward.

On our way home that evening, we popped in to say goodbye to Silvana's sister Anna-Maria and her husband Attilio; we knew they were going to Rome the following day and would not be back in Santa Severina before we departed. In melancholy mood, Attilio insisted that we run our palettes across his latest flavouring experimentation with his home-made grappa, a distant cousin of *poitín*. It was a longer night than we planned for.

Thanks to Silvana's hairdressing appointment, by the time we got round to seeing all the people we wanted to tell personally, they already knew. One of these wasn't Carlo, who ran one of the town square's four bars and was our longest-standing friend there, a friendship that went right back to that first evening in 2006 when, as visitors, we stepped into the square for a pre-prandial *aperitivo*.

Every time I went to the bar to see Carlo that weekend, he was never there; his stand-in, Roberto, told me that Carlo and his brother Mario were working on the family land. It was another two days before I finally caught up with him.

I walked into the bar and, relieved at last to have found my dear friend there, gave him a very emotional hug. He was taken aback and looked slightly confused by my display of emotion which, momentarily, I thought might indicate that he was miffed that I had not told him our news in person sooner.

"I'm sorry I didn't catch up with you before now, Carlo, but you were never here when I came. I wanted to tell you myself." With my reconciling tone I was trying to undo any pique he might have felt.

"Tell me what?" he said with a worried expression on his face.

"About Kay and I leaving …"

"You're off again, you've just got back … where to this time and how long will you be away?"

"No, Carlo, we're leaving Santa Severina, we're moving to Ireland … permanently, *armi e bagagli*."

I could not be sure whether the shock on his face was because we were leaving or because I had rattled off the Italian for 'lock, stock and barrel' almost as if I hadn't looked it up that very morning.

It was clear then that somehow Carlo had not picked up on our news at all. Everyone else in the town seemed to know and I imagine most assumed that Carlo would have been one of the first to be told. The only explanation was that people, aware of our friendship, might have deliberately avoided talking to him about it. The grapevine works in reverse too.

Whatever the reason, Carlo, who always had his finger on the pulse of what was happening in the town—after all he ran a bar— inexplicably had remained blissfully in the dark; somehow the news of the moment had passed him by. It reminded me of the Japanese soldier abandoned on a deserted island and unaware that the war had finished 40 years earlier.

We embraced again; and this time we both knew why.

———

We had already started the daily grind of sorting out, packing and making choices about what to take and what to abandon. While we waited for our new boxes to arrive, we made use of some of those that we had kept following our move to Calabria over eight years earlier.

Soon we were surrounded by boxes and bags in almost every corner of every room; we didn't have time to sell things as we had done in England; there was no such thing as the car-boot sale in Calabria. We had to reconcile ourselves to leaving behind things like the fridge-freezer we had bought a couple of months earlier.

The timing of when we should sell the car was important as we would need it for the first ten days or so but didn't want to be left with it unsold … any cash from its sale was already earmarked for part of the removal costs. I finally advertised it on the local Santa Severina blog the following Friday and it was gone by Monday.

For the umpteenth time, it seemed, I confirmed that the man with the van would arrive on the Sunday morning to whisk all our worldly goods across Europe to Ennis. The planning of this had been crucial for there was no vehicular access to our front door; the nearest a car could get was the top of a steep slope 50 metres away and the nearest a Luton-style van could get was another 150 metres away in the car park by the Middle School.

It was these considerations that made the Sunday important. First of all the Middle School would be closed so there was likely to be a space for the van, hopefully on the flat. Secondly, being a Sunday, the route to and from the van would not be intermittently blocked by the small vans and three-wheeled Ape that normally sold their wares— from pots and pans to fruit and vegetables—from their rear doors.

Sunday was the only day that our friends and their Ape would have a free run between our apartment and the van. Raffaele and Aurelio said they would appear with the Ape at eight, assuming the van had arrived by then.

The most complicated situation we had to deal with was reconciling the various groups of friends who wanted to organise some sort of farewell function or get-together. Two were already 'booked'.

Silvana wanted us to eat with her family and friends on the Saturday, our last evening in our home there; of course we wouldn't have wanted it otherwise. Also the town's mayor had already arranged an official send-off from the town and its dignitaries in the Council Chamber on the Thursday.

Inexplicably there were other individuals and groups who wanted to wine and dine us in that last week and, had we gone along with them all, we would have been in no fit state to focus on getting everything done in time. It was very flattering but clearly not practical.

The compromise was a call to one of those already planning something, our American friend Vicki, and she was duly appointed as official Organiser-in-Chief of one single evening of craic on the Friday at Le Puzelle, the *agriturismo* where our Calabrian adventure had begun. I sent Vicki a list which started with about 20 names. In the end over 60 people turned up.

The official and unofficial festivities over, it was Saturday, our last full day in Via Grecia 77. We had everything packed save the coffee machine, a bottle of wine and our bedding. Empty boxes and parcel tape were ready for these few last-minute essentials.

We did our final round of emotional goodbyes before it was time to go for our last supper with Silvana, her family and friends.

As usual, Silvana produced a printed menu of the culinary delights and innumerable courses she had prepared for the occasion; we were just over half way through when my phone rang. It was part-time taxi-driver and part-time barman, Emiliano; he was calling from the Jolly Bar in the square.

"There's a guy here in the square, I think he's looking for you. I think he might be Polish."

"What's he driving?" I asked this because I could think of only one explanation.

"He's in a van. He doesn't speak Italian but I think he said your name."

"Tell him I'll be there in five minutes."

It was clear that all my double-checking had paid off; our man with the van, the most important piece of the jigsaw, had arrived on time, Well, almost on time, eleven hours early was fine with me.

I explained to everyone that I needed to go up to the square, and why; Enzo offered to drive me there. As we were leaving the house, I quietly asked Silvana if there was room for another at the table. She understood what I meant and said she'd take care of it.

Up in the square, the van was easy to find as it was basked in the curiosity of most of those out and about that evening, walking off their pasta. I shook hands with Yarik, the driver, as he confirmed that he was indeed our man with the van and, in case he was expecting to start loading there and then, made it clear we wouldn't be ready until the following morning. He said he had a bed in the cab but didn't argue when I suggested he stay with us.

Yarik followed Enzo's car down to the Middle School, grabbed a few things from his cab and came back to Silvana's with us where a place at the table had already been set and another chair found.

The evening progressed as usual; lots to eat and lots to drink, albeit with an extra mouth to feed. An hour later Kay excused herself and went back home to find some bedding for Yarik.

When he and I came home I managed to recall where I'd packed the spirits and I was able to introduce him to the delights of Irish whiskey.

By ten on Sunday all our possessions were already in Yarik's van. He keyed our Ennis address into his GPS and showed me the result: 3311 kilometres. He shook my hand, thanked us for our hospitality and said he'd see us in Ennis on Wednesday morning; about half-ten, he reckoned.

It was with an overwhelming sense of sadness that I walked back to Via Grecia 77 for the last time. After lunch, a more subdued affair than usual, Raffaele drove us to Le Puzelle where we had our last meal in Calabria with the family and staff there; fitting that we should be with those who were our very first Calabrian friends.

Next morning Giuliano took us to Crotone where we joined friends Denise and Massimo who, coincidentally, were driving to Lamezia Airport that morning; Massimo was taking the same flight as us to London, en route to Dublin.

It was a contemplative drive. As we passed through the small coastal communities that had been a normal part of our everyday lives for so long, it was hard to imagine that it would be many months before we passed this way again. And I suspected even then that I might be the only one to do so.

In silence we were lost in our own memories and reflections. I knew that for me Calabria would always have a strong pull, an intimate connection; I also knew that, for Kay, this drive to the airport was likely to be her final memory of Calabria. I also hoped I was wrong.

At Stansted we caught the last flight to Shannon and then the last bus from Shannon to Ennis. We had travelled with only hand luggage in which were the remaining essentials we needed to see us through until Yarik arrived.

We stepped into our new Ennis home about 10.30pm. Kay quickly put a sheet on the bed while I saw to the more important task of opening that bottle of red wine. I filled our glasses ready to toast our safe arrival and the beginning of a new adventure.

But first I switched on the central heating.

And the pump blew up.

At 10.20am on the Wednesday, ten minutes ahead of schedule, Yarik pulled up outside the house. A little over an hour later he was on his way again; I asked him where to next.

"Poland," he said as he turned the key.

THINKING ABOUT THE NEXT CHAPTER, 2017

KEEPING A PROMISE

On the last Sunday in September 2016 I was in Calabria alone. Kay was in England and I was still looking forward to my pending trip to Galway. I was, of course, unaware that my visit to Galway would be a life-changing experience.

That Sunday was, as it frequently was, the day of the Gerardi family's annual *vendemmia*, the grape harvest, the day when all the family, myself included, rallied to the call and headed for the Gerardi land just below the town; gloves and strong scissors at the ready. It was always a family gathering, a time when even pharmacist Sergio, the only family member to live away from Santa Severina, would return home to do his bit.

As usual, everything was done and dusted by late morning when Silvana and her two older sisters arrived bearing all manner of wondrous Calabrian dishes. As chairs and benches were dusted off, the table was laid outside and the prepared dishes, released from their tin-foil covers, arranged among bottles of the previous year's harvest.

By mid-afternoon, as things were winding down, I pointed to my tee-shirt which bore a number. I'd had it for 15 years or more and it was well past its sell-by date but I'd hung on to it just to wear that day, the first and only day when the number it bore corresponded to my age. It was my birthday.

It took a few moments for what I was saying to sink in. Silvana was the first to get it and wasted no time in giving me a hug and a kiss and wishing me *buon compleanno*. More kisses, hugs and greetings followed and corked liqueur bottles re-opened, Within a quarter of an hour, I know not how, a cake appeared on the table as, imperceptibly, the post-*vendemmia* party morphed into an impromptu birthday party.

———

At that time, I had no idea that, when the next *vendemmia* came round, I would be living over 3000 kilometres away in Ireland. That did not stop me planning to arrive on *vendemmia* day with my scissors, to keep the promises I made to return, to show that I meant it when I said that Santa Severina was a place to which I could never not return.

The problem with dropping in for the *vendemmia* is that it has no fixed date. Every family chooses a day, generally a Saturday or Sunday, that suits them best. It's normally around the end of September but then it all depends on how wet or dry it was in the spring or how hot in the summer and other local factors that tell people when their grapes are ready to harvest.

In early September I decided to take my chances and booked flights to arrive in Calabria late on a Friday with the intention of just turning up in Santa Severina on the Sunday morning at the Gerardi land to lend a hand. I knew they would like that.

Then several things happened in quick succession.

My Romanian friend Laura told me that husband Stefan and I would be on the same flight from Rome to Lamezia and wouldn't it be fun not to tell him and for me to book the seat next to him. I did. Also, as Laura was picking up Stefan, she would pick me up too and I could stay that night with then in Crotone.

Then, a week before I was to fly, I received a video from Silvana in Calabria in which many of our local friends sent a message to us. But, unusually, one of these was Silvana's brother Sergio who lived in Abruzzo and only ever came home for the *vendemmia*. This told me that the *vendemmia* was that weekend, a week before I had planned for, a week before I was travelling there. There was nothing I could do.

Then, two days before I was to fly, I received an email from Paddy Fay in Drogheda who clearly had not received the message I'd sent some months before about our move to Ennis:

"Hope all is good with you, long time no hear, speak and see. Myself and Yvonne are heading back to Santa Severina and Le Puzelle this Friday 22nd September, it would be great to meet up if you are about … ciao for now."

He and Yvonne were due to arrive in Calabria on the same day as I was but, unfortunately, I couldn't risk telling them for I knew the Santa Severina grapevine would soon have spoiled the surprise for Silvana and her family.

I didn't say I wouldn't be in Calabria though I did mention the move to Ennis. Paddy's disappointment was tempered with the knowledge that he could still meet up with other people he already knew and particularly our mutual friend Carlo. He and Yvonne would drink a toast to 'absent friends' with him at his bar.

I didn't have the heart to tell him that Carlo had sold up in the spring and that their whole Santa Severina world had changed for ever. Nor did I tell him that, almost certainly, we would meet up there on the Saturday.

My journey to Calabria was uneventful, except when, in the queue to board the flight in Rome, I tapped the shoulder of the man in front who swung round as I snapped a photo and sent it to his wife Laura. Until that moment the bewildered Stefan had no idea we would be on the same flight. He had no idea that we would be sitting next to each other and no idea that I would be sleeping in their spare room that night.

The next day, Laura and Stefan drove me to Santa Severina where, from the Middle School to Silvana's house, I ran the gauntlet of friends at windows and on balconies wanting to embrace, to talk, to ask questions but, as I literally shot past, all I would say was *"Prima di tutto, Silvana, Prima di tutto, Silvana."* It would have been inappropriate to speak to anyone before seeing Silvana first.

Seconds after all the hugs and kisses in Silvana's back garden, the news was out via photos she took on her phone and instantly despatched far and wide, to everyone in her address book.

In the afternoon, I walked up to the square and saw Paddy and Yvonne at a table outside what had once been Carlo's bar.

"*Avvocato* Fay, *Avoccato* Fay," I called as I walked across to them.

The only long-haired, bearded, tattooed, Irish lawyer in Calabria, nearly fell off his chair.

On Monday it was my birthday again though, this time, there was no post-*vendemmia* party and no numbered tee-shirt to match. Instead I had a memorable evening in a local restaurant with the Gerardi family and some special Santa Severinese friends; Stefan, Laura, Paddy and Yvonne were also there.

It nearly included two complete strangers for Silvana's husband Raffaele, not having ever met Paddy and Yvonne, recalled my description of them and, when a couple entered the restaurant who seemed to match that description, he commandeered them and frog-marched them to our table and almost pushed them into their chairs. At first Franco and Anastasia, on holiday from Ferrara in Emilia-Romagna, thought it was some crazy Calabrian ritual but, fortunately, when the real Paddy and Yvonne arrived a few moments later, they saw the funny side.

The only person missing that evening was Carlo, now an auxiliary nurse in the hospital at Lamezia Terme. But all was not lost for, en route back to Ireland a few days later, we met for a short, emotional reunion outside Lamezia's airport.

I returned to Ireland satisfied that I had kept all my promises, but also in reflective mood.

I knew I would return to Calabria again and again but, above all else, I fervently hoped that some of my Calabrian friends would want to understand what it was that brought me back to Ireland, would want to come here to experience and share, at first-hand, a bit of the Irish craic. It never happened.

AFTERWORD

There is one place to which I travelled five times and about which I have written nothing. It is a place about which I have waxed lyrical to others, it's a place that used to always excite me. It is also a place which, when I replay my times there, I can scarcely recall a single memorable experience or interaction with local people. Something which, as evidenced by this book, is, to say the least, unusual for me.

This craic wasteland is called Berlin.

But, on reflection, when I look back on my several visits to New York and Chicago and other American cities—Seattle, Boston, San Francisco, New Orleans. Las Vegas, San Diego—I have fewer stories and anecdotes to relate. Of course the obvious rationale for this, the one thing they have in common, is that they are all large cities. It is no coincidence that the chapters herein that refer to events in two of the above, take place largely outside the city (Las Vegas) or relate more to external factors (New Orleans).

That said, I couldn't quite see how Berlin fitted in for, as I have said, my initial impression was of a vibrant, yet down-to-earth city emerging from an extraordinary divisive past.

I first went to Berlin a decade or more after the toppling of the wall and reunification. I stayed in the 'old East' that first time and, indeed, on every visit thereafter. At first it was a part of the city that seemed unsure of itself, an erstwhile sector becoming accustomed to having to embrace, and be embraced by, an alien culture.

Everything felt positive until it wasn't.

On my most recent visit I found that the old East had become a place which had its head in the clouds, a place that had seemingly embraced everything that was trendy and unsubstantial. A place where the likelihood of meeting someone who was not trying to convert you, to 'sell' you the latest holistic route to nirvana or map out your future by examining your feet, was virtually nil.

Berlin's East had become the psycho-babble centre of Europe. It seemed to me that the ordinary people who once walked these streets had somehow been colonised. They had been overrun by a race of people who only speak in cliches and use these cliches to peddle lifestyle- and health-related absurdities to a science-deaf clientele. They speak of things that 20 years ago would never have found a place on nearby Museum Island. Perhaps, in some future time, there will be a space there dedicated to 'The time mankind lost its marbles'.

Now I realise that, in general, people who visit Berlin are there to drink in its past, revel in its architecture, seek out the remains of the wall, marvel at how the trains are on time, enjoy the view from Alexanderplatz Tower, wander around the Christmas markets, indulge in retail therapy at *KaDeWe* (*Kaufhaus des Westens*), eat a different cuisine every night or experience the vibrant night-life and might only ever see the other side of Berlin culture, particularly in the old East, by accident.

I, on the other hand, just yearn to meet ordinary people in their natural habitat and I find that, even off the beaten track in the old East, there is an increasing and constant barrage of incoherent, questionable, incongruous and transient noise trying to pass itself off as culture.

Now, before you raise your hands and your voice in horror, I know that my description is saturated with generalisations and loaded imagery and that there are indeed parts of Berlin—and again I am largely referring to the old East—where people lead lives untainted by this new and seemingly harmless form of *Stepford Wives* Syndrome. Sadly, and despite many weeks of dedicated research, they seem to go into hiding as soon as they see me. Can you blame them?

I have had a mere smattering of memorable encounters in the city one of which seemed arresting at the time but which, on reflection, was probably no more that a means to get me to spend more money. This was when a bar-owner, who saw me as a regular because I had frequented his bar every evening for almost a week, confided in me that he used to work for the Stasi, the East German state security service—in 007 terms, the Secret Police, the baddies—and that he, like many of his ex-comrades, was now hiding in plain sight.

It only occurred to me later that had he really been Stasi, it was unlikely that he would have shared such an inglorious past with anyone, let alone the likes of me. After all I could have been a shorter-than-usual, CIA operative with an Irish accent. Oh dear, I've already said too much.

The point of this little aside is about the reality behind it. It is a story that encapsulates much of what I increasingly started to observe in Berlin and why I have not returned there for a decade or more.

It is a story that is grounded in a sub-culture of imported, insidious, baseless psycho-babble, it's about accosting the listener with what the speaker thinks they want to hear. Had I complained of a persistent haemorrhoid problem, I have little doubt my 'Stasi' comrade would have been a regime doctor with an exclusive miracle cure at his fingertips or would have known someone who had.

Because I showed myself to be knowledgeable about Berlin's past and intrigued about the nuts and bolts of how exactly unification affected ordinary lives, I was given the Stasi story. Had this not been my last night in Berlin, he might well have tried to sell me his old Stasi cap, complete with badge, both fresh from the local Stasi replica shop.

For me one of the self-confident highlights of the new millennium was the iconic film *Good Bye Lenin!* set in East Berlin before and after both the fall of the wall and the German Democratic Republic. The film was a masterpiece, both entertaining and thought-provoking. And, for me, still is.

It painted a picture of a city in political turmoil but one that seemed to have a degree of social cohesion and optimism, albeit tinged with naivety and too many smiling faces.

And there's another positive. Although I suspect it has become a bit of a tourist attraction, there is a bar, tucked away in Mittelstrasse, close to Friederickstrasse station, called Treffpunkt.

During the day it's more likely to be peopled by tourists who, weighed down by bags, find this safe place to wind down by accident. At night it's the locals who get there first as tables are at a premium. The food is superb and the staff as authentic as the food.

I suspect that many of the tourist clientele may not realise they are in what was East Berlin and, for me, Treffpunkt is the only place that gave me hope for it was here that I met and interacted with more real Berliners than anywhere else. The staff were local too and it was here that I picked up my first whiff of dissent in how things were panning out. Don't get me wrong, nobody wanted to go back to the old ways but then not everyone was enamoured with the new ways either.

Back in 2016, in an article for *Slate*, American journalist and writer, and recurrent Berlin resident, Lucian Kim, wrote the following:

"Berlin is a victim of its own success. The eternal backwater now thinks it's the navel of the world. If the city's uncoolness was what once made it cool, its new coolness threatens to make it uncool again. Newcomers wanting to turn Berlin into something it is not are taking over the city. Some changes are undoubtedly positive, but too many of them are not.."

I feel better now that I found someone else who has picked up on some of the same things that I, as a more infrequent visitor, have observed about the new Berlin.

Should I ever return, I will look him up and perhaps we can share some real, transatlantic craic, and less pseudo-craic, at Treffpunkt.

NIALL ALLSOP …

… was born and educated in Belfast but began his working life as a primary school teacher in London and in 1971 took up his first headship.

He left teaching in 1981 to pursue a career as a freelance photo-journalist specialising in the UK's inland waterways and wrote extensively in this field both as a contributor to national magazines and later as author of several related books.

By the early '90s he was a graphic designer and in-house designer for a UK-based international photographic publishing house. Later he settled in the south-west of England as a freelance graphic designer, specialising in the design of exhibition catalogues for artists and photographers and other arts- and media-related projects.

In the late '90s, Niall and his wife Kay made the first of many visits to Italy and soon became captivated by the country's historical and cultural heritage. He read extensively about Italy and Italians and soon developed a close affinity with the country—particularly the deep south and the islands of Sicily and Sardinia.

It was during their first visit to the small hilltop town of Santa Severina in Calabria in 2006 that Niall started to chronicle his Italian travels and in particular the many remarkable and colourful people he met there. By the time *Stumbling through Italy* was published, Niall and Kay had already given in to the inevitable …

In September 2008 they left the UK and moved Santa Severina where they enjoyed a sort of retirement while continuing to struggle daily with the language in a town where they were the only English-speaking people.

Following a two-month stint of house-sitting in Galway in early 2017, Niall and Kay decided relocated to Ennis in Ireland.

In late 2022 Niall moved to Sardinia, remaining there for a year before returning to Santa Severina in December 2023. This time ie the main focus of his *Under a Calabrian sky*, published in both Italian and English in May 2025.

BOOKS BY NIALL ALLSOP

BOOKS WITH ITALIAN THEMES

Keeping up with DH Lawrence: On the trail of David and Frieda Lawrence in Sicily, Sea and Sardinia.

Sulle orme di DH Lawrence: Viaggiando con Davide e Frieda Lawrence in Sicilia e Sardegna. Italian edition of *Keeping up with DH Lawrence* translated by Sabrina Zumpano (2025).

Stumbling through Italy: Tales of Tuscany, Sicily, Sardinia, Apulia, Calabria and places in-between (2011).

Scratching the toe of Italy: Expecting the unexpected in Calabria (2012)

Thank you Uncle Sam: From Calabria to America; Family stories of Emigration (2013).

La Calabria in America: Racconti di Famiglie Calabresi Emigrate. Italian edition of *Thank you Uncle Sam* translated by Denise Milone (2016) and revised by Sabrina Zumpano (2025).

Calabria: Travels in the toe of Italy (2016).

Under a Calabria sky: Reconnecting with Santa Severina (2025).

Under a Calabria sky: Riconnettersi con Santa Severina. Italian edition translated by Sabrina Zumpano (2025).

Calabrian Tales: A skeptic's alternative interpretation of five Calabrian tales alongside other stories that most Calabrians have forgotten or never knew (2025).

MEMOIRS

Heads will roll: The true story of corruption, conspiracy and confrontation in an English Primary School (2013).

Experiencing prostate cancer: The fickle finger of fate (2014).

OTHER BOOKS

Fact & Fiction: Two authors | 20 titles | 40 stories. With Elizabeth Starr (2018).

Chasing the craic: Itchy Irish feet through smiling Irish eyes (2018 and 2025).

www.ingramcontent.com/pod-product-compliance
Lightning Source LLC
Chambersburg PA
CBHW030817090426
42737CB00009B/756